"Wine as a gift of God's love, wine as a witness to the in-breaking of God's kingdom of life and joy, wine as the drink that draws us more closely into the fellowship of Christ, and wine-making as our participation in the care and celebration of God's good creation — these themes and many more besides are lovingly developed in this beautifully conceived book. Gisela Kreglinger opens up the gift and the mystery of wine in these pages so that we can taste God's invitation to us to share in the divine love that heals the world and the deep joy that celebrates our life together."

— NORMAN WIRZBA
Duke Divinity School

"I wept upon reading *The Spirituality of Wine* by Gisela Kreglinger. Our restaurant has received *Wine Spectator*'s Grand Award for twenty years, so how is it that I had only tasted the tip of this reality, only touched the knowledge of its gifts? Profound and potent, intertwined with practical and tangible application, this book has completely astonished me. Like an exquisite wine in a bottle, I've been transformed from within."

— ALICE CANLIS
Canlis Restaurant, Seattle

The Kreglinger Chalice was commissioned by Gisela Kreglinger's
ancestors for a Franciscan church in Rothenburg, Germany.
(Photograph by Karlheinz Gisbertz)

THE SPIRITUALITY OF WINE

Gisela H. Kreglinger

Dear Jess,

I wish you a very happy birthday!

Thank you so much for your friendship over the last three (+ especially last two years)!

I thought this book, exploring the intersection of intoxicants and religion might capture the "spirit" of our relationship particularly well :)

WILLIAM B. EERDMANS PUBLISHING COMPANY
GRAND RAPIDS, MICHIGAN

Love, Niklas xxx

Published 2016 by

Wm. B. Eerdmans Publishing Co.

2140 Oak Industrial Drive N.E., Grand Rapids, Michigan 49505

Printed in the United States of America

22 21 20 19 18 17 16   7 6 5 4 3 2 1

Library of Congress Cataloging-in-Publication Data

Names: Kreglinger, Gisela H., 1967- author.
Title: The spirituality of wine / Gisela H. Kreglinger.
Description: Grand Rapids, Michigan : William B. Eerdmans Publishing Company,
[2016] | Includes bibliographical references and index.
Identifiers: LCCN 2015045473 | ISBN 9780802867896 (pbk. : alk. paper)
Subjects: LCSH: Wine — Religious aspects — Christianity.
Classification: LCC BR115.N87 K74 2016 | DDC 261.5/6 — dc23
LC record available at http://lccn.loc.gov/2015045473

www.eerdmans.com

For
Gertrud Kreglinger-Müller and Herbert Müller
and all those vintners
whose faith finds expression
in their fidelity toward the land

Contents

Foreword, *by Eugene H. Peterson*   ix

Preface   xi

Acknowledgments   xvi

Introduction   1

Part I: Sustenance

1. Wine in the Bible: God's Gift and Blessing   11

2. Wine in the History of the Church: Its Rise and Fall   37

3. Wine in the Lord's Supper: Christ Present in Wine   65

4. Wine and Communal Feasting:
   The Joy of the Lord Is Our Strength   83

5. Wine and Attentiveness: Tasting God, Tasting Wine   100

Part II: Sustainability

6. The Vintner as (Practicing) Theologian: Finder or Maker?   121

7. Technology, Spirituality, and Wine   143

8. Wine and Its Health Benefits   164

9. Wine and the Abuse of Alcohol:
   Rescuing Wine from the Gluttons for the Contemplatives   180

10. Wine, Viticulture, and Soul Care   199

    Conclusion   217

Contents

Appendix 1: Hebrew and Greek Wine Terminology
   in Scripture   221

Appendix 2: Crafting a Church Service for the
   Blessing of the Grapes   229

Notes   232

Bibliography   258

Index of Names   270

Index of Subjects   273

Index of Scripture References   279

Foreword

Dr. Gisela Kreglinger writes of growing up on a small family winery in Bavaria that has been in her family since the seventeenth century. It is a fascinating account of the craft of wine-making and the implications of how it affects our lives. It is a very personal story and prompts us to think about our place in the great community of God's creation.

Kreglinger talks with vintners in Italy, France, Bavaria, California, and Oregon. Her father, Peter, has a place in the story. And the Bible, of course, in which wine plays a major role.

It interests me that weddings (and, of course, the wine that goes with them) play a prominent role in the biblical narratives. In the story that John writes near the beginning of his Gospel, it is a wedding and wine that get the story moving. John has carefully organized his Gospel on a framework of seven signs that give witness to the nature of Jesus' presence among us. Then, in the final four chapters of Revelation, also written by John, he picks up this celebratory beginning in Cana and brings it to a celebratory conclusion: "for the marriage of the Lamb has come, and his bride has made herself ready" (19:7).

I have always delighted in the parallel wedding stories that John uses near the beginning of his Gospel and near the end of Revelation as the angel instructs him: "Write this: Blessed are those who are invited to the marriage supper of the Lamb. . . . Then I fell down at his feet to worship . . ." (19:9-10). St. John loves weddings. Weddings play a significant part in his recapitulation of the life of joy.

This invitation is followed by the bride herself: "And I saw the holy city, new Jerusalem, coming down out of heaven as a bride adorned for her husband; and I heard a great voice from the throne say, 'Behold, the dwelling of God is with men'" (21:2-3). A final mention of the wedding is generously welcoming: "The Spirit and the Bride say, 'Come.' And let him who hears say, 'Come.' And him who desires take the water of life without price" (22:17).

As Christ's salvation work among us is completed and as the New Jerusalem is established, there is this confirming but unadorned comment: "And its gates will never be shut" (21:25).

Never? Really? That is what the text says. Jesus doesn't want any of us to miss the joy.

EUGENE H. PETERSON
Professor Emeritus of Spiritual Theology
Regent College, Vancouver, BC

Preface

Two fields of experience and learning converge in the pages of this book: the field of Christian spirituality and the world of wine. I grew up on a small family winery in Franconia, Germany, a region that became part of Bavaria about two hundred years ago, during the Napoleonic Wars. Franconia had a long and independent history before then, and though the Romans seem to have brought vines to the area first, it was Benedictine nuns who first developed viticulture in our region, in about AD 600.

The winery was in bad shape after World War II, and my grandparents, together with my parents, worked very hard to rebuild it out of the ruins and plant vineyards. My mother and a wonderful group of women from the village were the workers in the vineyard. I spent the first three years of my life in a playpen at the bottom of the vineyard because my mother could not stay home to take care of us children. From our vineyards the views of the Main Valley are stunning. Friederike, an orphaned child, shared the playpen with me. One of our workers had taken her in and raised her. My father and the apprentices he trained performed the most physically strenuous work on the wine estate.

On rainy days I had to stay with my grandfather in the office. He was a gentle soul, and he did all the administrative work for the winery. I don't think that he enjoyed the distraction of small children crying and whining, but on a small family winery everyone had to chip in to make it work. There were four of us children, all girls, and my father must have worried about who would take over the winery one day. When I was born, my grandmother could not resist pointing out that my mother had given birth to yet another girl (number three); on top of that, I had red hair.

Life on the winery was very unusual for us girls. When we were in school, my mother often felt sorry for us because, as soon as we would come home, my grandmother had a long list of chores that needed to be done at the winery. Even as fairly small children, we worked a lot. Our friends did not like to play on the family estate. Sooner or later we would all get sucked into the never-ending hustle and bustle that makes up life on a family vineyard. I remember vividly having to crawl into the small opening of our wine vats and scrub them clean from the inside. It was dark, wet, and cold inside, and I could not wait to get out again. It was one of my least favorite chores.

The aroma of fermenting grape juice and other fruits such as pears, plums, and apples are some of the most powerful memories of my childhood. Dad not only made wine but also distilled spirits from the fruit of our orchards. I vividly remember my father shoveling the pressed and dried grape skins from a large pan onto a wagon that was then taken to a large compost heap. Sometimes we children were allowed to hold a small tasting glass under the winepress and sample the freshly pressed juice. The sweetest and most delicious grape juice danced on our taste buds and made us feel more alive. When the grape juice began fermenting, it had a lovely buzz to it. I had always marveled at how such intense and concentrated sweetness could come to be in such tiny grapes. It was a delight to be involved in something so beautiful, and while tasting the juice of those grapes, we could forget all the hard work for a moment.

The other vivid memory I have of growing up in a winery is the regular wine-tastings we had in our rustic tasting room. Crowds of people would come to the winery and spend an evening tasting wine and listening to my father talk about our wines, the soil, the weather, and other things that I did not quite understand. What struck me most is the transformation that took place during the wine-tasting. At the beginning of the evening the group would be quiet, reserved, and quite serious. As the tasting went on, however, the group would get livelier, faces would open up, and smiles would come more easily. The conversations became more engaging, and there was lots of laughter. There seemed to be a lot of joy when people tasted wine together. It was lovely to watch, and I was always amazed that this transformation would happen over and over again with each group that came. I felt that our wine-tastings did something important: they gave people a joyful evening, and those people seemed more alive by the end of it.

Bavaria is mostly Catholic, but Franconia had an important role to play in the Reformation, and our village embraced the teachings of Martin Luther in the early seventeenth century. To this day, my family is deeply rooted in the Lutheran faith and the rich traditions that come with it. Though we all worked hard and had very little time to ourselves as a family, we knew how to celebrate. Eating and drinking around the table was and still is the ritual that keeps us bonded not only to one another but also to the family winery and the land that we cultivate. Life on the winery estate is very special, and I still consider it home — though I left many years ago.

I learned early that somehow our lives — the work that we do at the winery and our lives of faith — belong together. In the autumn my mother would always cut the most beautiful branches with thick ripe grape clusters from the vines and decorate the church altar for our annual harvest thanksgiving service. But it was only at my confirmation, when I was fourteen years old, that I began to glimpse something about the life of faith that haunts me to this day. Like baptisms and weddings, confirmations are very important in our family, and we celebrate them in grand style. My family invited all of our relatives to witness me affirm my faith and celebrate with us as a family. I had spent two years in confirmation classes, during which I memorized the Ten Commandments, the Lord's Prayer, and Psalm 23, and I received my very own Bible verse to accompany me through life. Pastor Walz taught us about the Lord's Supper, the sacrament that we would receive for the first time. I was nervous because I had to speak in front of the whole church, then endure a question-and-answer session, and finally partake of the Lord's Supper for the first time in my life.

Pastor Walz taught that when we take the Lord's Supper, we remember and receive the benefits of Christ's death and resurrection for the forgiveness of our sins. I concluded from what I had learned that this was between God and me. But when the chalice came and I took a sip of the wine, it suddenly struck me that what I was drinking was the wine my family had made. The smell of the wine was so familiar, the taste so fresh and crisp, that it smelled and tasted like home. I remembered how much had gone into crafting this wine. I thought about all the people who worked for us: their lives and sorrows and our lives and sorrows. I thought about the fields and vineyards, the sun and the rain, and our daily listening to the weather forecast. During mealtimes my parents would always talk about the weather and how it would affect our lives on the winery. Would there be late spring frost that would freeze the buds on the vines? Would there be enough sun and rain? What if it hailed in the autumn and destroyed the grape clusters? When should we begin the harvest?

I thought about all the family fights and generational tensions between my grandmother and my parents and between my parents and us children. Life is so full and complex, so beautiful and yet so difficult.

I had a little epiphany as I took my first sip from that chalice. Could it be that God wanted to redeem not only my life but also all the hustle and bustle that life on the winery brings? We work so hard to make a living from growing vines and crafting wine. Could it be that God cared about it and perhaps was even involved in it? This idea is not quite what I had learned in my confirmation classes over those past two years — but was it not true? Had Jesus not made wine as well? My questions about who God is and how he might or might not be involved in our lives is something that never left me. When I told my father that I wanted to study theology, he was not pleased. He called it "breadless art" (German: *brotlose Kunst*) and was concerned about my future. I did pursue theology, became a theologian, and in this book I explore the spirituality of wine from a Christian perspective.

Let the reader beware, however, that this is not an exhaustive exploration of Christian spirituality. The focus of the book is on wine, a theme that will take us into the heart of Christian spirituality and the importance of it for our everyday lives. Wine features prominently in the Bible, in the history of church, and has been of immense cultural value. In light of this I shall explore the theological and spiritual significance of wine for the life of the church and for our lives, and I shall seek a meaningful dialogue between the world of wine and the Christian faith.

As part of this project, and in my effort to create a thoughtful and informed dialogue, I interviewed thirty vintners from the Old Wine world and the New Wine world. I interviewed vintners from the Rheingau and Franconia in Germany and from Burgundy in France, representatives of the Old Wine world. The vintners I interviewed from the Napa and Sonoma valleys in California and the Willamette Valley in Oregon are representatives of the New Wine world.[1] Most of the vintners I interviewed have small wineries and oversee the whole process — from growing vines and the work in the cellar to engaging customers in their search for a wine worth drinking. I use the term "vintner" to speak of those who seek to craft wines that reflect a particular place and particular vintages; I use the term "wine-makers" for companies whose primary goal is to mass-produce wine without concern for particular places and vintages. The primary aim of the latter is to produce a stable and predictable product at an affordable price, and their use of modern technology is often highly invasive.

My hope is that this book will be read not only by pastors, priests, theologians, and lay Christians, but also by those outside the church who are interested in a spirituality of wine, including vintners and wine-lovers. For this reason I have tried to stay away from Christian jargon and explain even basic theological terminology. This book — and each chapter in it — should not be understood as a definitive or final statement on the importance of wine for Christian faith and practice. Rather, it is introductory in nature. Given the relative neglect of this important subject matter, I hope that this book will open up a conversation that will enrich our understanding of Christian spirituality and the world of wine for many vintages to come.

Acknowledgments

The first seeds for this book were sown during my experience being raised on a family winery. It is my family and all our vintner friends with whom I grew up that I want to thank first for teaching me to love and respect our land, to appreciate the gift of wine and the blessedness of conviviality around the table.

Despite the enormous amount of information found on the Internet and the apps one can download in order to learn about wine, I still have found that the well-read and experienced owners of small wine shops are the best people to expand my knowledge about wine. Thank you to Tony Meyers, of Classic Wine Company in Birmingham, Alabama, for his patience in teaching me about wines around the world — and Bordeaux wines in particular. Thank you to Peter Wood, of St. Andrews Wine Company in Scotland, for exposing me to so many different small wine producers. Jack Evans's knowledge of wine and his ability to capture in words the exquisite beauty found in one small glass of wine has been a profound gift to me, and I thank him for sharing his wealth of knowledge and deepening my sense of wonder at the beauty of well-crafted wines.

The Institute for Theology, Imagination and the Arts, St. Mary's College at the University of St. Andrews, Scotland, welcomed me as a research fellow and generously provided me with an academic home. I was able to write most of this book in the tranquility of a medieval tower overlooking the ruins of St. Andrews Cathedral. It is a truly inspiring and blessed place. I am grateful to the faculty and staff of St. Mary's College for their support and convivial conversations. I would like to thank especially Michael Partridge, Bill Hyland, Mark Elliott, Gavin Hopps, and David Brown, whose comments on the text and conversations with me were insightful, encouraging, and full of wisdom.

Acknowledgments

A generous research grant from the Selah Foundation made it possible for me to stay in St. Andrews to research and write this book. It was the opportunity of a lifetime. I am very grateful to Eugene and Jan Peterson for their generous support.

I wish to thank friends whose comments on earlier versions of individual chapters have been invaluable: Jack Evans, Allen Ross, Piotr Malysz, Steve Innes, and Matt Jenson. Michael Summerfield, with his expertise in the geology and geography of wine, Phil Winn, with his expertise in neuroscience, David Sterns, with his expertise in the philosophy of technology, and Nicola Kreglinger, with her expertise in cardiovascular diseases — all were enlightening interdisciplinary conversation partners. To all of the above, and to many more whom I cannot name here, I am deeply indebted. I am also very grateful to my research assistant, Joshua Hays, who carefully worked over the whole manuscript and has patiently stayed with me throughout the writing of this book.

About thirty vintners took time out of their busy schedules to grant me an interview concerning the spirituality of wine. I am indebted to them for their willingness to share their wealth of knowledge and experience in crafting wine. I would like to thank especially Kurt Beitler and Paul Wasserman for helping me find and set up interviews with vintners in Sonoma Valley, Napa Valley, and Burgundy.

Finally, I would like to thank Ian Barnett and Tim Carlisle for allowing me to stay in their apartments right by the medieval harbor overlooking the North Sea during my time in St. Andrews. What view could be more inspiring for writing than sunrise over the North Sea? I am deeply grateful to both of them for their hospitality. And Jim Buttercase regularly supplied me with fish he had just caught off his boat. Thanks to Jim. The world is indeed charged with the grandeur of God.

Introduction

The term "spirituality" is in wide use today, meaning different things to different people. When I first began to interview vintners in California and Oregon about the spirituality of wine, several commented that the Christianity with which they had grown up was by far too small and narrow to account for what they experienced working with the land in their vineyards. This observation surprised me. I had grown up in a region where the world of wine and Christian faith had converged for centuries. Something seems to have gone missing along the way, with the result that Christians and those who grew up in the Christian faith are no longer able to see the rich connections between the life of faith, the work of the vintner, and the gift of wine.

In the pages of this book, I seek to contribute to the recovery of a vision of the Christian life that sees God at work in all things, even in the work of vintners and in the enjoyment of a well-crafted glass of wine. Christian spirituality is a strain of Christian theology that pays attention to the way we live life in light of our Christian beliefs and our understanding of God. Its emphasis is on the lived experience of the Christian faith. It seeks to avoid the abstract; instead, it seeks to stay grounded in the everyday and the personal as much as possible. The Christian spirituality I espouse in the pages of this book is rooted in Christian Scripture and nourished by the wisdom of the rich Christian tradition of our ancestors, those who have gone before us in the faith. My inspiration and emphasis is a creation spirituality that sees human life in profound relationship to and engagement with the earth. As such, this book will touch on many theological themes. Questions related to areas such as anthropology, ethics, and practical theology will emerge quite naturally from the following discussion. A relational anthropology — who we are, how we relate to God, one another, and the rest of creation — will be an especially important issue. We need to reconsider our place in God's creation and what it means to belong to it.

Talking about spirituality has its risks. The renewed interest in spirituality more generally speaking, and Christian spirituality in particular, has ushered in a time of fruitful and life-giving conversations. Yet, talk about "spirituality" has been fraught with dangerous misunderstandings. There has been and still is the temptation to ally "spirituality" with various kinds of dualisms. While some versions of dualism still acknowledge the importance of matter to some extent, the tendency is to devalue matter and emphasize the "spiritual" to the detriment of the "material." Another form of dualism divides life into "sacred" and "secular." Here the tendency is to isolate and separate out certain times (such as a church service or morning prayer) and places (church buildings) as "sacred," while ordinary times and places seem "secular" — and thus with little spiritual meaning. A decidedly Christian understanding of the spiritual life seeks to integrate faith into all spheres of life, including the material and the everyday.

This book presents an understanding of Christian spirituality that sees all spiritual dimensions of our lives and our world as deeply and thoroughly embedded and engaged in material things. But the spiritual is not solely material; all things have spiritual meaning in the Christian faith precisely because of our belief that God created the world in such a way that the spiritual and the material are profoundly intertwined. This fundamental character of Christian spirituality finds its climax in the incarnation of Jesus Christ, when God took on human flesh and lived among his people. The Lord's Supper further challenges dualistic understandings of spirituality. In the Lord's Supper we embrace, cherish, and practice the God-given interconnectedness between spiritual and material realities; we learn to see the extraordinary in the ordinary. The use of seemingly ordinary things, such as bread and wine, in the Lord's Supper challenges us to see that everyday aspects of our lives are imbued with spiritual meaning. The vintner's life and work with the land and its fruit is no longer a "secular" affair but has spiritual significance. What attitude do vintners have toward their vineyards, and how do they cultivate the land? Creation is a gift from God, and the way a vintner handles it is of spiritual significance. When we read Scripture with this in mind, we will receive new understanding.

Introduction

Wine is an important food and theme both in Scripture and in the history of the Christian church. The lack of attention to this important subject matter indicates a greater confusion within the church: the belief that matter is of little significance for Christian spirituality. The recovery of a spirituality of wine is thus an excellent way to overcome a dualistic spirituality that seeks to divorce the physical from the spiritual, to divide between secular and sacred.

How has this lack of attention to wine and what is material in Scripture come about? Christian spirituality has traditionally tended to focus on the introspective turn to the spiritual within, a very important — albeit limited — perspective. Richard Bauckham points out another important factor: he argues that the prevalent ideology of the modern West has influenced modern New Testament scholarship, an ideology that has understood human history as emancipation from nature. It no longer understands humans as embedded in nature, and it eclipses the profound interdependent relationship between human history and the rest of nature. Instead, it favors an assumed independence from and supremacy over nature. The way this perspective has influenced biblical theology is in its strong tendency to set history against nature and salvation against creation.[1]

This ideology, whether consciously or unconsciously adopted, has profoundly influenced the way modern interpreters have read the Bible. Bauckham says:

> References to nature in the New Testament, especially the Gospels, have been persistently understood from the perspective of modern urban people, themselves alienated from nature, for whom literary references to nature can only be symbols or picturesque illustrations of a human world unrelated to nature.[2]

Perhaps this, too, helps explain why the theme of wine in Scripture has received so little attention in the modern period. As we become more aware of these modern ideologies, we can take a step back and read the New Testament with fresh eyes, much more in continuity with the Old Testament. I hope that the following pages will reveal that a decidedly Christian understanding of the spirituality of wine does not lift us out of the natural world. Rather, it calls us to trust that God wants to heal our relationship with creation and the profound gifts that we receive from it, including wine.

* * *

The first part of this book explores and draws out the scriptural and theological foundations of a spirituality of wine. From Genesis to the book of Revelation, the theme of wine features rather prominently in Scripture. What is the role of wine in the Bible? Does it have a particular place in God's creative and redemptive purposes? Exploring this theme opens up a vision of the Christian life that is far more encompassing and encourages us to reconsider our own place in the great community of God's creation.

Wine has had an important role in the life of the church, including the early North American church. It is a history that is often forgotten and needs to be rediscovered, remembered, and celebrated. From the early church in the Ancient Near East to its growth in medieval western Europe and its expansion in Central and North America, the history of wine in the church is long and rich. Exploring how theologians throughout the history of the church have reflected on wine further enriches our understanding of the spirituality of wine. A whole tradition of Christian art emerged when artists began to depict Christ in the divine winepress. Exploring the role of wine in the history of the church also sheds some light on the historical roots of the rejection of alcohol by certain pockets of Protestant Christianity.

The use of wine in the celebration of the Lord's Supper offers rich insights into the importance of wine for Christian life and practice. What do we celebrate in the sacrament of the Lord's Supper, and what is the role of wine in it? Does the background of the Hebrew Passover meal help us understand its role? Understanding the spiritual significance of wine in the Lord's Supper brings us to the heart of a decidedly Christian understanding of the spirituality of wine. It is an embodied and communal ritual and anchors our experience of the Christian faith in creation. The mark of a decidedly Christian spirituality is not a flight from creation but a faith-filled embrace of it: thus wine used in the Lord's Supper becomes a defense against lingering dualistic tendencies that tend to devalue the importance of creation for Christian spirituality. All Christian denominations regard the Lord's Supper as a particularly sacred celebration. I will show how this sacred celebration can and should imbue celebrations — and feasting more generally — with added spiritual meaning.

Gratitude and joyful celebration are two important ways for Christians to respond to God's exuberant gifts of creation and salvation. In the Hebrew world that Jesus and his disciples inhabited, feasts and celebrations were important ways for believers to cultivate their spiritual lives. In them they remembered God's deeds of the past, embraced God's faithfulness in the present, and fostered expectant hope for God's redeeming intervention in the future. Rather than using feasts to escape the pain, suffering, and boredom of our lives, Christian feasting should become a place where we open up our lives to God's love and forgiveness. It is a place where the generosity of God's abundant love and grace forms — and transforms — us. From here we can go forth into the world with gratitude and joy, affirming life as a gift to embrace, treasure, and share. Joy as an expression of our gratitude to God should stand at the heart of a decidedly Christian understanding of the spiritual life. If this is the case, why is there so little joy in the world and especially in the life of the church? Joyful feasting has traditionally been an important way through which Christians have lived into and nourished a life of gratitude and joy. We need to recover a decidedly Christian understanding of festive play before God, and wine can play an important role in that. The film *Babette's Feast* informs our search for a decidedly Christian understanding of feasting.

A spirituality of wine and the recovery of a decidedly Christian understanding of festive play before God invite us to ponder the importance of the five human senses. We humans experience the world, including the spiritual, through the five human senses and not apart from them. The church has traditionally had a rather ambivalent posture toward the senses of taste and smell in particular. Is this attitude justified? How important are the senses of taste and smell for human cognition and for our pursuit of the knowledge of God? Insights from neuroscience suggest a more positive role for the senses of smell and taste. Can we reclaim them as gifts from our Creator for Christian living? If we understand our spiritual lives as fully embodied and physical, can the senses of taste and smell not also become vessels for prayer and contemplation?

The second part of the book builds on the first part and seeks a mutually enriching dialogue between Christian spirituality and the world of wine. Can a spirituality of wine add meaning and purpose to vintners and their vocation of crafting wines? Can the experience and wisdom of the vintner shed light on and deepen our understanding of the spirituality of wine and help us grasp more fully the potent scriptural metaphors from the realm of wine for the Christian life?

As a gift from God, and in its place in the Lord's Supper, wine teaches us that it is not secular matter without sacred meaning. If the vintner participates in crafting wine that is both a gift from God and the work of human hands, then his/her vocation has profound spiritual meaning. Is the vintner a finder or a maker? What do vintners do with what they find in the vineyard, and how much are they willing to work with such particulars as place, soil, and climate? Do they matter, and if so, why?

The role of technology in crafting wine is another important question today. The advances in modern technology have impacted all aspects of our lives, and we have to learn to make discerning choices as we use them. In reality, what is technology? When is it helpful, and when does the use of certain modern technology transform wine from a relatively natural good into a highly manipulated industrial product? The use of technology raises ethical, aesthetic, and economic questions. How can we approach them from a decidedly theological perspective?

The apostle Paul was neither the first nor the last to understand that wine has significant health benefits if enjoyed in moderation. The health benefits of wine have been known since antiquity, and wine remained a prime medical agent throughout the Middle Ages — and up until the nineteenth century. A historical survey reveals a rich medical tradition that has always appreciated and affirmed the medicinal value of wine. This tradition was forgotten for many years, though contemporary medical research once again affirms the health benefits of wine.

An exploration of the spirituality of wine must also consider the possibility as well as the dangers of the abuse of wine, and of alcohol more generally. Psychologists and sociologists are concerned about the rapid increase of addictive behaviors and disorders not only with regard to substance-focused addictions but also behavioral addictions. What does Scripture say about alcohol abuse — and other forms of substance abuse? How does contemporary research into the nature and cause of addictive behaviors and disorders understand them and their possible underlying social causes? How can the church engage with these contemporary perspectives from a theological perspective?

While there are no easy or quick answers to how Christians can respond to these challenges of contemporary life, the Christian tradition has always upheld the importance of soul care. The church must find ways to embrace those souls that are like untended gardens and bring them to the only true gardener, in whom we can find life in abundance — but not without the pruning of our addictions. The figurative language of viticulture in Scripture offers a rich and organic vision of the Christian life. It can baptize anew our Christian imagination as we seek to understand what it means to be the church in contemporary society and as we learn to consume in ways that are life-giving and honor God and his creation.

PART I

SUSTENANCE

1

Wine in the Bible:
God's Gift and Blessing

"For everything created by God is good, and nothing is to be rejected, provided it is received with thanksgiving; for it is sanctified by God's word and by prayer."

1 Timothy 4:4-5[1]

ine is a great mystery and a profound gift. Poets and kings, philosophers and politicians, priests and theologians have marveled throughout the ages at this beautiful and complex liquid called wine. And yet, when people think of the enjoyment and the bliss of drinking a well-crafted wine and reflecting on it, they do not usually think first of turning for information and ideas to the Bible or prayer. After all, some might think, the Christian faith is about living a holy life and keeping the body in check against temptations. Joy, delight, and the pleasure of drinking a "beautiful wine" (as Saint John puts it in John 2:10) are not often considered spiritual exercises. On the contrary, some might suggest, once you start on such a path, you have taken the first step toward addiction and a wayward life.

In light of such understandings of the dangers of worldly pleasures, it comes as a complete surprise to many that the motifs of wine, viticulture (the cultivation of grapes and grape vines), and viniculture (the making of wine) are frequent subjects in the Bible. Almost everyone is familiar with wine stories in the New Testament, of course, such as Jesus' first miracle of turning water into wine at the wedding in Cana (John 2) and the analogy portraying Jesus and his disciples as a vine and its branches (John 15). But there is little awareness of how frequent this theme actually is and how much these New Testament texts on wine and viticulture build on Old Testament themes. Just as the apostle Paul cautioned Timothy against a false and unbiblical asceticism (1 Tim. 4:1-5), so must we pay attention to the witness of Scripture regarding the nature and value of wine, and take it seriously. After all, it was Paul who recommended a little wine for various physical ailments (1 Tim. 5:23). Moreover, a healthy spirituality embraces all of creation as a gift from God, and trusts that God continues to sanctify his creation and causes humans to grow in gratitude toward the giver of these amazing gifts (1 Tim. 4:4).

Lothar Becker, a German vintner and theologian, has written a groundbreaking and thorough study on the cultural history of wine and wine-related themes in the Bible.[2] He has shown that of all the terms relating to plants and agriculture in the Bible, the cultivated vine (Latin: *Vitis vinifera*) and the technical terms related to the subject of wine are the most prominent ones. The wild vine (Latin: *Vitis silvestris*) also occurs. According to Becker, there are eighty-eight Hebrew terms, with 810 occurrences in the Old Testament, and thirty-six terms with 169 occurrences in the New Testament.[3] Considering that the New Testament teaching is rooted in and builds on the theology of Hebrew Scripture, the amount of theological material on this subject matter is impressive. We can only offer a short overview here. To contextualize this study, we need to look at the historical-cultural background of the theme of wine in the Ancient Near East, and Palestine (Canaan, Israel) in particular. It is from these cultures that the Judeo-Christian world emerged.

The Ancient Near Eastern Context

Wine, bread, and olive oil were the three main food groups of the Ancient Near Eastern and Mediterranean world. Grapes were primarily used to produce wine, but they were also consumed as raisins and used to make both honey and vinegar.[4]

It is difficult to reconstruct how and where the deliberate cultivation of vines for wine-making began, since there is almost no archaeological evidence. The earliest archaeological evidence dates back to the sixth millennium BC and comes from what is now western Iran.[5] Clear documentation in archaeology and literature shows that wine production and consumption have had an important cultural, social, religious, economic, and political role in certain parts of the world throughout recorded history. The Middle East is certainly an important and central place in this regard. The Neolithic period of the Middle East (about 8000-3300 BC) was a time marked by settlements and the beginnings of agriculture, including wine-growing.[6] The plains deposited over time by the Tigris and Euphrates rivers and the coastlands of the Mediterranean, such as Palestine, Phoenicia, and North Syria, provided excellent conditions for vine-growing.[7]

The great empires and advanced cultures of Egypt and the Ancient Near East all cultivated vineyards and considered wine of high cultural, religious, and economic value. Egypt, in particular, developed an impressive wine culture despite its less than ideal conditions for vine-growing. Through its extensive trade, Egypt was able to import highly prized wines from Palestine (then called Canaan) in exchange for other foods.[8] Archaeologists excavated 700 wine jars from the Dynasty 0 Royal Tomb (ca. 3150 BC), and chemical analysis of these jars indicates that they came originally from Palestine.[9] Egyptians offered wine to their gods, drank it regularly themselves (only the upper class), and used it for medicinal purposes.[10] The story of Joseph and his interpretation of the cupbearer's dream in Genesis 40 hints at this rich culture, which is so well documented in Egyptian art.[11]

Sumeria, Babylonia, Assyria, Greece, and the Roman Empire continued to develop this tradition. In Greco-Roman times wine was no longer a prerogative of the elite but had become a basic food item. Greeks, in particular, believed that the moderate consumption of wine (often diluted with water) set them apart from barbarians.[12] High Greek culture prided itself in the virtue of temperance, and its wine-drinking habits cannot be compared to, for example, the excesses of the Greek Dionysian rites or later imperial Rome.

All cultures that embraced the enjoyment of wine had to deal with the problem of abuse and drunkenness. Pittacus, one of the Seven Wise Men of Greece (sixth century BC), called wine a mirror of the soul and discouraged drunkenness.[13] The Jewish wisdom teacher Jesus Ben Sira (second century BC) also saw wine as probing into the inner workings of the human soul. Just as the work of a swordsmith is tested in the fire, he says, so does wine test the undisciplined.[14] Pliny the Elder (first century AD), a natural historian of the

Roman Empire, mentions and laments the abuses of wine, but at the same time upholds it as a gift to be treasured and celebrated.[15]

It is remarkable that Pliny devotes a whole book (Book Fourteen) of his famous collection *The Natural History* to the vine, grapes, wine production, and wine-drinking. He lists nearly two hundred grape varieties, mentioning the names and virtues of over one hundred wines. He discusses how wines age and develop their particular flavors. He also describes what kind of wines could be used in sacred rites. Greek wines, for example, were excluded because they contained a portion of water.[16] (Economically speaking, this was obviously considered a cheapening of wine, as it still is today, and thus not appropriate for sacred rituals.) Pliny was aware that the quality of soil affects the quality of the wine and wrote that "vines . . . drink up the juice of the soil with their grapes."[17] Contemporary research is only now beginning to explore how vegetal root systems interact with soils and how it affects the quality of the crops.

By the time of Jesus, the Greco-Roman world had developed an incredibly sophisticated understanding of viticulture, viniculture, and wine-aging, and Pliny's account gives ample witness to this sophistication. Wine had become an important cultural and economic force and a common drink in the Jewish diet. It was used widely for medicinal purposes and in religious ceremonies both inside and outside the Jewish context.[18]

What Is Wine?

In light of the developments of modern industrial food technology and how it can alter agricultural products, it seems appropriate to ask how wine has been defined historically. A traditional definition of wine is this: a beverage produced through alcoholic fermentation of juice from grapes only.[19] The vine variety (almost always a hybrid of the *Vitis vinifera*), soil, land slope, climate, the yeasts and bacteria (microbial populations) active in fermentation, and the culturally conditioned choices of the vintner — all these are important factors for crafting a wine of quality. The process of growing grapes and turning them into a well-crafted wine is rather intricate, and wine gains its meaning not only from what it tastes like but also from the region where it originates, and from the method used in making it.

The popular French term *terroir* seeks to hint at this complexity. *Terroir* is a disputed term because it is not only a wine term but also a term that is profoundly linked to the social construction of a very particular French identity tied to the land, the vigneron (wine-grower), and the wine. The term has become an important marketing tool for the French. Not surprisingly, the international wine market has also adopted it for their marketing purposes.[20] Nevertheless, it is a well-known descriptor to capture wines that seek to reflect a particular place and wine culture, and I shall use the term in this way only.[21]

Wine is "alive" in the sense that it continues to evolve even after it has been bottled, and thus it is not a static object. When vintners speak about wine having a "soul," they are hinting at this capacity of wine to evolve and mature over time. They speak about a wine with "soul" when it has at least some complexity and nuance, a wine that might even have an "imperfection" or "variance" and hence does not fit into a fixed idea of what it is supposed to taste like. Wine is subject to changing weather conditions and the human touch of a vintner. It is a great mystery, and to this day it cannot be fully figured out by scientific investigation.

Many learned women and men have marveled at this lavish gift of God and have put their delight and gratitude into poetry, song, and reflections. It should not surprise Christians that wine features so prominently in the Bible, but it often does surprise people, especially those in religious communities that view alcohol in negative terms only. The situation in Western Europe, for example, is a wholly different one from that of North America because the rise of Christianity in Europe and the expansion of viticulture overlapped. There are many examples of missionary monks establishing monasteries and planting vineyards at the same time, since they needed wine for the celebration of the Eucharist. We shall explore this history in more detail in the next chapter.

Wine in the Bible

The Bible begins with the narrative of God creating the heavens and the earth. This account envisions the created world with all its living beings as a deeply interconnected community and affirms it as something fundamentally good. Creation is an extravagant gift, and the psalmist leaves us in no doubt about it. Psalm 104, particularly, exhorts us to be grateful for creation and rejoice in it. Despite this reminder, some Christian traditions, especially Protestant ones, have developed rather ambivalent feelings toward wine and possibly the wider realm of God's creation. But the Bible affirms the created world as a gift from God and sees wine in particular as a special gift that gladdens the human heart (Ps. 104:15). We need to learn to see and understand wine in this larger context of God's good creation.

It is also important to realize that Scripture consistently portrays God's redemptive purposes as between God and a people living and working on the land God has provided for them, in order that all the nations might be blessed. God's plan of salvation embraces all things in heaven and on earth (Eph. 1:10), and the more we understand ourselves within this great community of God's good creation, the better we understand God's purposes for us as they are revealed in Scripture.[22] Wendell Berry rightly argues in this regard:

> I don't think it is enough appreciated how much an outdoor book the Bible is. It is a "hypaethral book," such as Thoreau talked about — a book open to the sky. It is best read and understood outdoors, and the farther out of doors the better. . . . Passages that within walls seem improbable or incredible, outdoors seem merely natural. This is because outdoors we are confronted everywhere with wonders; we see that the miraculous is not extraordinary but the common mode of existence. It is our daily bread. . . . [Consider] the turning of water into wine — which was, after all, a very small miracle. We forget the greater and still continuing miracle by which water (with soil and sunlight) is turned into grapes.[23]

As we begin to explore the theme of wine in the Bible, we need to keep this great community of God's good creation in mind. We need to realize that creation itself is a miracle filled with wonderful gifts and surprises and that they, too, have a part in God's purposes. Our identity as God's people is not developed apart from the rest of creation but precisely by being embedded within it. It will become clear that the theme of wine and viticulture is an important one that helps us recover our understanding of God as Creator and Redeemer. As we shall see, the two are deeply intertwined in Scripture. A biblical understanding of redemption encompasses all of creation, including the vine and wine. We will understand God's redeeming purposes in much broader ways when we re-envision ourselves within this larger community and realize that wine is first of all a lavish gift of an incredibly generous, loving, and forgiving giver.

Wine in the Old Testament

The attention given to wine and viticulture in the Old Testament is substantial, so in what follows we can only touch on some of the central aspects. We shall begin by considering wine and the vine as part of God's rich blessing of his people. As a gift, wine is used as a food, for medicinal purposes, and in cultic practices and religious celebrations. The abuse of God's gift of wine is another important theme; I will also consider abstinence from wine. The metaphorical use of the language of wine is yet another important aspect: wine and viticulture were such prevalent realities for the Israelites that they provided metaphors to describe God's relationship with his people. A final theme to be discussed is the role of wine and viticulture in framing speech about the messianic age.

Wine as Part of God's Good Creation: A Gift and a Blessing

In order to grasp the significance of wine in the Bible, one has to consider it within the larger theme of God's creation and humans' relationship with creation. In Genesis 2 we are told that God planted a cultivated garden, the Garden of Eden (from the Hebrew *ʿēden*: enjoyment, delight). It is in this garden of bliss and delight, later called "paradise" (Rev. 2:7), that God places his creatures and invites them to eat and enjoy its fruit (Gen. 2). It is a garden of great splendor with many bountiful and beautiful fruit trees (Gen. 2:9); in it God and humans live in harmony with one another.[24] This sense of paradisiacal splendor is remembered and recalled at later times in the Old Testament. The prophet Isaiah, for example, speaks of God's bringing comfort to his people in the form of transforming the land. He writes: "He will comfort all her waste places, and will make her wilderness like Eden, her desert like the garden of the Lord" (Isa. 51:3; see also Ezek. 28:13; 36:35; Joel 2:3).

Adam and Eve are depicted neither as owners nor as rulers of this garden. Rather, they are placed in it to work and keep the garden and to enjoy its fruit and live in harmony with God and their beautiful surroundings. Adam (from the Hebrew *'ādām:* man, human, humanity) was created from the dust of earth (from the Hebrew *'ădāmâ:* ground, land, earth) to till the earth (Gen. 2:5, 7, 15). This Hebrew wordplay between *'ādām* and *'ădāmâ* emphasizes the close kinship between the land and the humans God created to glorify God. Adam is referred to completely in terms of the earth and is dependent for his existence on the earth to sustain him.[25]

Within this fundamental sense of common creatureliness and interdependence between humans and nonhumans, humans are given a special role in taking care of the nonhuman creation. They are to "rule" over the other living creatures (Gen. 1:26) and to "fill" and "subdue" the earth (Gen. 1:28). What this actually means has been widely discussed.[26] Richard Bauckham suggests that the idea of "fill" and "subdue" the earth found in Genesis 1:28 seems likely to refer to agriculture. He argues that "fill" and "subdue" are closely connected. In order for humans to fill the land, they need to cultivate the earth to supply enough food.[27] In Genesis 2 we learn that Adam is placed in the Garden of Eden "to till it and keep it" (Gen. 2:15).

After the Fall, this harmonious relationship in Eden is broken down. The temptation to be like God results in the expulsion of Adam and Eve from the Garden of Eden. But even after the Fall, Adam's vocation continues to be defined in relationship to the earth and in terms of agriculture. Adam is to till the ground from which he was first taken, affirming once more this close kinship with the earth (Gen. 3:23).

The biblical narrative continues into bleakness when human sin then turns into violence against one another. Cruelty and wickedness become so rampant that God decides to bring judgment on the earth. He sends a great flood (chaotic waters) and brings to an end his once good creation (Gen. 4 and 6). Only Noah receives grace and is found righteous, and only his family is allowed to survive — together with representatives of each living creature (Gen. 6:8; 8:17).[28] Scripture continues to portray humans within the larger community of creation. After the flood God makes a covenant not only with Noah but with all living creatures. He promises to sustain creation and its fruitfulness and remain faithful to his covenant (Gen. 8:22; 9:9-10, 12, 15-17). The great community of creation is restored, though it is still marred by the consequences of the Fall (Gen. 9:1-5).

It is at this point that the story of viticulture in the Bible begins. It is rather striking that Noah's identity and vocation are once again defined in relationship to the land. Earlier in the narrative we are told that his father, Lamech, names him Noah because he is to bring comfort to those who work the land and are burdened by it: "This one shall bring us relief from our work and from the toil of our hands" (Gen. 5:29). In this passage the word "Noah" (Hebrew *nōaḥ:* most likely meaning "rest") is associated — probably because of phonetic similarities — with the Hebrew verb for bringing relief or comfort *(nāḥam).*[29] This promise of relief and comfort seems to come to fruition in Lamech's son's future vocation as a vintner.[30]

After the Flood, God reiterates his earlier command — this time to Noah — to be fruitful, multiply, and fill the earth. Noah is called a "man of the earth." He is the new Adam: like Adam, his name refers to the earth. This suggests that he is profoundly tied to the earth and utterly dependent on the soil to sustain him and his family. It is striking that Noah does not begin by planting grains, as his ancestors did (Gen. 3:18-19). Rather, he plants a vineyard and produces wine, which, we are later told, gladdens the human heart and brings comfort in times of distress and worry (Gen. 9:1, 20; Ps. 104:15; Jer. 16:7; Prov. 31:6-7).[31] Claus Westermann sees in Noah's vineyard-planting a development of the theme of agriculture in Scripture. The cultivation of soil now advances from farming to viticulture. Viticulture is traditionally seen as a higher form of agriculture: while the farmer produces grain, a necessity for life, the vintner produces wine, a culturally highly esteemed beverage that can bring joy, delight, and comfort. Though Noah is also the first person in the Bible to get drunk, the production of wine opens the way to celebration and festal drinking later in the biblical account. It should not surprise readers that the vine and its fruit also becomes a sign of the blessed life in the messianic age (Mic. 4:4).[32]

From the time of Noah, vineyards, vines, and wine become regular features in the biblical narrative. Abram (Abraham) samples wine in Canaan, where he enjoys King Melchizedek's hospitality: "And King Melchizedek of Salem brought out bread and wine; he was a priest of God Most High" (Gen. 14:18). When Jacob (deceptively) seeks a blessing from his father, Isaac, he serves him game and wine (Gen. 27:25). Isaac in turn blesses his son Jacob (thinking him to be Esau). This blessing includes fruitfulness of the land in the form of grain and wine: "May God give you of the dew of heaven, and of the fatness of the earth, and plenty of grain and wine" (Gen. 27:28, 37).[33] Here the elderly Isaac introduces wine and the vineyard as a blessing from God. This is a crucial theme for understanding the role of wine in the Bible.

A blessing in the Old Testament is intrinsically linked to God and comes from God. Only in God's name can others confer a blessing. It is closely interwoven with God's personal and redemptive presence that humans experience in covenant relationship with him.[34] When Jacob gives his blessings on his sons and the times to come in Genesis 49, he speaks of bountiful vineyards and an abundance of wine. Of Judah he speaks prophetically: "The scepter will not depart from Judah. . . . He will tether his donkey to a vine, his colt to the choicest branch; he will wash his garments in wine, his robes in the blood of grapes" (Gen. 49:10-12). This prophetic announcement, with its vividly colorful imagery, invites the hearer to envision a great abundance of vines and wine.[35] The vines of Judah's future life will be of such stoutness that one can even tie animals to them! And the harvest will be so abundant that wine will flow in great excess. This blessing evokes images of paradisiacal splendor.[36] The Garden of Eden, with its beautiful and bountiful fruit trees, is now re-envisioned prophetically as a lush and fruit-laden vineyard that produces wine in abundance. Jacob's prophecy instills a longing for a future age when paradise will be restored as a lush and fruitful vineyard.

At a climactic moment in the life of Israel, the bountiful vineyard once more takes a central place. For forty years the Israelites had wandered in the wilderness after their exodus from Egypt. Now they finally arrive at the borders of the Promised Land. Moses sends out men to explore this land of promise and they come upon "the valley of grape clusters," which now become a primary motif and symbol for the agriculturally rich and bountiful nature of the Promised Land. The scouts bring back on a pole a single cluster of grapes and report to Moses that this land is surely a land flowing with milk and honey (Num. 13:21-27), which is in stark contrast to the dust and the barrenness of the desert they have been wandering in (Num. 20:5). The valley itself is called Eshkol (Hebrew for "cluster"), named after the cluster of grapes the Israelite scouts found and brought back to their people (Num. 13:24). God's blessing on his people is envisioned agriculturally: he provides a place called the "Promised Land," a land renowned for its lush and fruitful vineyards. In it grow wheat and barley, vines and fig trees, pomegranates and olives (Deut. 8:8). God's love and blessing find expression in giving descendants to his people and providing an extraordinarily fruitful land, including an abundance of wine (Deut. 7:13).[37] When Moses declares God's blessing on the Israelites just before they are to enter into the Promised Land, this blessing includes the fruitfulness of the land once again, especially grain, wine, and olive oil (Deut. 6:11; 7:12-13; 8:8; 33:28).

The book of Judges (9:13) praises wine as a gift and blessing: it makes the hearts of God and men joyful.[38] Psalm 104:15 further affirms this positive and life-giving effect of wine. In 1 Kings 4:25, Israel and Judah, under the rule of Solomon, live in peace and safety, each under his own vine and fig tree. It is a beautiful yet humble reality, not of grand landowners but of small farmers with just enough land to provide for their daily needs and a little extra with which to make their hearts glad and rejoice in God, their Redeemer.[39]

The theme of wine also features prominently in the Song of Songs. This book celebrates the sexual dimension of human life as God's gift that is to be treasured. The rich garden imagery of this lavish love poetry reminds one of the paradisiacal splendor of the Garden of Eden and the agricultural richness of the Promised Land. Erotic love is often compared in the Song of Songs to entering a garden, and enjoying wine and other fruits of God's good creation. Wine, like erotic love, is fundamentally celebrated as God's gift that is to be received with joy and gratitude (Song of Sol. 1:2, 4; 4:10; 5:1; 7:2, 9; 8:2).

The idealist vision of 1 Kings and the Song of Songs is a reality that did not last. The Israelites' unfaithfulness, their stubborn disobedience, and their oppression of the poor, vulnerable, and marginalized (including orphans and widows) culminate in God's judgment. He removes his protection of them, and the Assyrians invade their land and deport them into exile, away from their own lush olive groves and bountiful vines of the Promised Land. When the Assyrian king seeks to lure Judah away from trusting God, he uses the vision of 1 Kings 4:25 to entice them to follow him (2 Kings 18:28-33; Isa. 36:16-18). This tactic is particularly striking because Jacob's blessing on Judah focused on the vine and an abundance of wine (Gen. 49:10-12).

The latter prophets look into the future and speak of a time when God will once more remember his people and redeem them. This vision is, of course, closely tied to a return to the Promised Land and its rich bounty, where they shall live in peace once more, each one under his own vine and fig tree (Mic. 4:4; Zech. 3:10; 8:12).

Wine as Foodstuff

Canaan had always been considered a place where viticulture flourished exceptionally well. Its wines had been exported at least since the Egyptians discovered it and imported it.[40] It was the vision of lush vineyards that impressed the Hebrew spies as they explored the Promised Land and brought back the grape clusters to Moses and Aaron (Num. 13:21-27). The primary goal of viticulture was the production and enjoyment of wine.[41] In a place where water was at times scarce and the risk of contamination real, wine was an important source of liquid that could be stored and consumed over long periods of time. Pliny mentions wines that had been kept for nearly two hundred years. Though this was unusual, it gives us an idea of how valuable wine must have been simply because of its ability to be stored.[42] To cultivate a vineyard and to press the grapes, but not to be able to enjoy the wine, was considered a misfortune (Deut. 28:39; Amos 5:11; Zeph. 1:13; Hos. 9:2).[43]

Wine seems to have been made all over Canaan, which is attested by the thousands of winepresses that have been found in this part of the world.[44] Though bread, wine, and olive oil seem to have been the staples of the Mediterranean diet, Deuteronomy lists a few more foods (Deut. 8:7-10).[45] Grain and wine are often listed together in the Old Testament, underscoring their fundamental significance in the Israelite diet. Israelite families shared meals around the table; and wine, together with bread and olive oil, was not a luxury item but a gift that was enjoyed regularly.[46] Whether the Israelites drank wine in undiluted form or diluted it with water is impossible to reconstruct. Like the Romans (see Pliny's comment above), who did not use Greek wine for religious rituals because it was diluted with water, the prophet Isaiah compares Judah's corruption with "wine mixed with water" (Isa. 1:22), a clearly negative comparison. Dilution would certainly cheapen the economic value of wine: no one would want to buy diluted wine for the price of pure wine. This observation, however, does not exclude the possibility of occasional and even frequent dilution of wine for purposes of drinking in different social contexts.[47] And sometimes wine was added to water to purify it.

What we do know is that the Israelites were instructed to share this great gift with the poor and needy. The book of Exodus gives the Israelites instructions for working the land.[48] Every seventh year they were commanded not to work the land, including their vineyards (Exod. 23:11); they were to leave the fruit for the poor and for wild animals. They were also to share with the poor from each year's harvest (Lev. 19:10; Deut. 20:6; 22:9; 23:24; 24:21).

Wine as Medicine

Wine has always had a considerable role in medicine, and we shall discuss this in some detail in the second part of the book. The Old Testament often mentions wine with regard to the spiritual and emotional well-being of a person. When enjoyed in moderation, it can be helpful in soul care. The importance of joy and gladness for the well-being of life should not be underestimated. Wine can help elicit a sense of joy and delight in God, our Creator and Redeemer (Zech. 10:7; Ps. 4:7; Ps. 104:14-15; Eccl. 2:24; 8:15; 10:19). While bread strengthens the human heart, wine revives people, bringing joy and gladness. A good loaf of bread and a simple bottle of wine can work wonders.

While David makes music to lift King Saul's spirit in a time of depression (1 Sam. 16), Proverbs advises to give wine to the downcast and those in severe distress (Prov. 31:6-7; see also 2 Sam. 16:2). Earlier in Proverbs, wisdom is compared to a life of hospitality that includes wine (Prov. 9:2, 5). It is clear from Proverbs that wine has to be enjoyed with discernment. Those in power are discouraged from drinking too much wine lest they become arrogant and oppress the afflicted (Prov. 31:4-5; see also Prov. 23:20-21; Eccl. 10:17-19; Sir. 31–33).

The role of wine in daily life and medicine is deeply interwoven in the Old Testament. Family and community life around the table with the regular enjoyment of bread and wine ensured that the downcast were kept in good company. Here they were able to forget their sorrow for a little while (Prov. 31:7). As Martin Luther would observe much later, isolation and a false sense of asceticism will only drag the downcast further into the mud of depression.[49] The moderate enjoyment of wine in the context of family and community life can become a wonderful event for physical, emotional, and spiritual renewal (Ps. 128). Does one need wine to find these blessings? No, certainly not. And yet a glass of well-crafted wine can bring such delight that one needs to ask why somebody would refuse this great gift from our Creator. It is the New Testament that provides a window into how wine was used for purely physical ailments, and I shall discuss that shortly.

Wine in Cultic Practices and Religious Celebration

Given the important role that wine played in the life of Israel, it is no surprise that wine assumed a prominent role in their cultic practices and their religious and family celebrations. In Exodus and Numbers, the Israelites are instructed with regard to worship and sacrificial offerings. Only the choicest animals and agricultural products, including grain and wine, were permitted (Exod. 29:40; Num. 15:5, 7, 10; 18:12; 28:14). The fact that wine was chosen as a sacrificial offering also shows that it was highly regarded.[50]

To a modern reader, the sacrificial system of ancient Judaism seems foreign. However, in the context of the biblical narrative, it takes on a central role. God's initiative in redeeming his people has always involved sacrifices. The word "sacrifice" (from the Latin *sacrificium*) derives from a verb meaning "to bring near." It is an offering that enables humans to approach God.[51] Only through sacrifices, physical matter from God's good creation, are humans allowed to approach God. Through them the relationship between God and his people is restored, maintained, and celebrated. All sacrifices were meant to create and restore life-giving communication between God and humans and allow God's people to enter into the divine fullness of life.

The Israelites, by providing these sacrifices as offerings to God, were involved in this act of communication. They drew on all their spiritual, physical, and emotional senses in this important cultic practice, which was central to their faith and spirituality.[52] Different sacrifices served different purposes. As offerings, they functioned to solicit God's blessing, to receive forgiveness of sin, and to express gratitude to God for one's well-being. Offering up the first fruits of their harvest reminded the Israelites that all life, including the fruit of the earth, is a gift from God (Lev. 23:13; Num. 18:27; 28:14; Deut. 14:22-23; 15:14).

Wine also had a central place in feasts and celebrations. Hebrew life included many religious and family celebrations. One of the Hebrew nouns for feasts and banquets *(mišteh)* is derived from the Hebrew verb for drinking *(šātâ)*. Its etymology parallels the Greek word for banquet *(sumposion),* a compound of the Greek prefix *sun* ("with," or "together") and the verb *pino* ("to drink").[53] The Passover meal is a wonderful example of how feasting and drinking are intertwined in Jewish life. Four cups of wine were traditionally consumed, and this tradition is kept in many Jewish households to this day. To celebrate meant to gather, eat, drink wine, and be merry. Wine, together with music and dancing, helped establish a festive atmosphere, a sense of joy, conviviality, and celebration. Wine stimulated the guests, deepened the fellowship, and transformed a meal into a celebration.[54] Occasions for such celebrations were the grape harvest, also referred to as the vintage feast, and sheep-shearing. The vintage feast informs harvest celebrations to this day in traditional wine-growing regions in France and Germany.[55] Other occasions include the weaning of a child (Gen. 21:8), marriage feasts (Gen. 29:21-22), birthdays (Gen. 40:20), making covenants (2 Sam. 3:20), and the enthronement of a king (1 Chron. 12:40).

Jewish wedding feasts were particularly occasions of prolonged joyful celebrations. Some lasted for seven days.[56] It is unimaginable in contemporary Western societies to take off seven days of work in order to celebrate such an occasion. Jewish people placed great value on feasts precisely because they had deep religious meaning. The social expectation to leave work for seven days and celebrate gives expression to the high value they placed on marriage covenants. One must also not forget the weekly family celebration of the Sabbath. To a person who has grown up on a winery, the prominence of wine in regular family and religious celebrations seems normal and natural. In other contexts, however, where wine is a luxury item, such feasting may seem outlandish.

Within the Jewish agrarian world of the Old Testament, wine was a common drink; celebrations — in the best sense of the word — reminded the Israelites of their utter indebtedness to their Creator and Redeemer. Communal feasting gave occasion to pause, ponder, rejoice, and give thanks. No other drink in the world seems to be able to open up the human heart to such wonder, delight, and gratitude. But the Old Testament also addresses the abuse of wine. And because alcohol abuse is such an important subject matter both in the Bible and in contemporary society, I will devote a whole chapter to it.[57]

Abstinence

It is surprising how little the Old Testament encourages fasting from wine, but there are some notable exceptions: Israelites were to abstain from drinking wine in the case of certain special occasions and callings. In Leviticus, Aaron and his sons were commanded to refrain from wine and fermented drink whenever they would go and serve in the tabernacle in their priestly roles

(Lev. 10:9; Ezek. 44:21). The Nazirites (from the Hebrew *nāzar:* "to consecrate, to separate") dedicated themselves to God in a special way. They were commanded to abstain from consuming any aspect of the vine (including grape juice, grapes, seeds, and skin) for certain periods and services (Num. 6:3-4, 20; Judg. 13:4, 7, 14); but after the completion of the sacrificial offerings, the Nazirites were permitted to drink wine (Num. 6:20). Their vow of abstinence could extend for either a limited period (Num. 6:1-4) or could last a lifetime (Judg. 13; 1 Sam. 1:11).

Proverbs discourages kings from strong drink, including wine, lest they forget the laws of God and their responsibility to care for the poor and needy. Wine should be given to those in bitter distress so that they can forget their misery and be comforted (Prov. 31:4-9). Priests, Nazirites, and kings had a special vocation: they were set apart to administer the worship and rule of God, and too much wine would interfere with their holy vocations. It makes sense that their consumption of wine should be restricted for the sake of their calling and their ministry to others.[58]

The Figurative Use of Language Taken from Viticulture

For the Hebrews, whose culture was deeply embedded within an agricultural world and who were familiar with the process of making wine and with the enjoyment of wine, viticulture and wine were such a prevalent reality of daily life that they became sources of rich metaphors to describe God's relationship with his people. These metaphors were used to speak about Israel's identity, judgment, and redemption. The psalmist speaks of Israel as a vine that God brought out of Egypt and transplanted in fertile soil (Ps. 80:8, 14). Joseph is spoken of as a fruitful vine (Gen. 49:22). The metaphor of the vine would have brought to mind a whole range of associations — such as the need to stay rooted in God's garden; their dependence on God the vintner for pruning, watering, and protection; and their calling to become a fruitful nation and a blessing to others.

The sad oracles of the prophets, however, tell a different story. God's people refused to be fruitful, and they turned justice into violence. They neglected the poor and needy. Their grapes were sour, and the vine had become useless. Jeremiah exclaims: "Yet I planted you as a choice vine, from the purest stock.

How, then, did you turn degenerate and become a wild vine?" (Jer. 2:21; see also 6:9; 8:13; Ezek. 15:1-6; 17:1-10; 19:10; Hosea 10:2).

When Isaiah speaks about God's judgment on the leadership of Judah and Jerusalem, he accuses them of having "devoured the vineyard," referring in particular to the exploitation of the poor (Isa. 3:13-15). In his famous love song of the unfruitful vineyard, Isaiah speaks of God as a vintner who lovingly plants a vineyard and tends it. Yet the vineyard only produces bad fruit (Isa. 5:1-7; see also Joel 1:7; Mark 12:1-9). Bad fruit is a metaphor for the injustice and bloodshed done by God's people. It is for this reason that God withdraws his protection from his beloved vineyard and brings judgment upon it. When Isaiah declares God's judgment against the nations, he speaks of God as a vine-grower using his pruning hook to judge Ethiopia (Isa. 18:4-6). In Isaiah 63, God's wrath is compared to one treading the winepress and God's judgment to the pressing of the grapes (Isa. 63:1-6).

The prophet Joel speaks of God's judgment in terms of a winepress where the sour grapes (wickedness) are crushed (Joel 3:13; see also Lam. 1:15; Rev. 14:19-20; 19:15). This image comparing God's judgment to the winepress is important, because the Christian tradition began to interpret these particular passages christologically. The portrayal of Christ in the winepress became a popular motif in medieval Christian art, especially in the wine regions of France and Germany.[59]

When the prophets speak of God's restoration of his people, the vine and vineyard once more become powerful metaphors: "I will heal their disloyalty; I will love them freely. . . . They shall again live beneath my shadow, they shall flourish as a garden; they shall blossom like the vine, their fragrance shall be like the wine of Lebanon" (Hosea 14:1, 7). In Isaiah, God's people are called "a pleasant vineyard" that God the vintner guards, waters, and protects. God's redemption of his people will bring about a new season of flourishing, and "Jacob shall take root, Israel shall blossom and put forth shoots, and fill the whole world with fruit" (Isa. 27:2-6).

The ultimate purpose of God's redemption of his people is not self-serving. God's people are to become a pleasing "fragrance" and share their fruit with the whole world. This metaphorical use of the language of the vine and vine-yard for describing the relationship between God and his people in terms of identity, judgment, and restoration is important for understanding more fully the use of these metaphors in the New Testament. Jesus' pronouncement "I am the vine, you are the branches" (John 15:5), understood in light of its Old Testament background, opens up layers of potential meaning.

Wine and Eschatology

Viticulture and wine play a significant role when the Old Testament speaks of eschatology (from the Greek *eschaton:* "last things"). Scripture is replete with promises and warnings that God will complete the redemption of his people at a future time; therefore, his people look to a future age when he will come and fulfill his purposes. When Jacob prays over his sons in Genesis 49, just before his death in Egypt, his blessing of Judah specifically relates to a future abundance of vines and wine: "Binding his foal to the vine and his donkey's colt to the choice vine, he washes his garment in wine and his robe in the blood of grapes, his eyes are darker than wine, and his teeth whiter than milk" (Gen. 49:11-12). This beautiful vision of lush vineyards and wine in great abundance has paradisiacal overtones, recalling a lost paradise and instilling hope for a future abundance in God's presence. It will come to fruition when God leads his people out of Egypt through the desert into the Promised Land.

Once the Israelites settle into the Promised Land, however, they eventually turn away from God and are sent into exile. God's judgment follows a season of restoration, which brings about a more hopeful future. The judgment comes because of the Israelites' unfaithfulness and their neglect of the poor and vulnerable among them. God sends them into exile, away from the beloved Promised Land that he had once given to them.

Many of the prophets look to a future time when God will send an anointed one to fulfill his purposes. The blessing that Jacob gives to Judah becomes foundational for understanding how the Old Testament prophets envision a future age, a time when God will fulfill his purposes. It will be a time of redemption in which God will forgive the sins of his people and bring them back into the Promised Land. Here they will dwell once more securely and peacefully, and the land will flourish beyond its former glory, with an abundance of grain and wine. The mark of this age, often referred to as the messianic age (from the Hebrew *māšîaḥ:* "anointed by God"), is a renewed outpouring of God's Spirit and the curse of the Fall will be lifted. Wars will cease and God will renew all of creation — the heavens *and* the earth. God will usher in a peaceable kingdom where all of creation will blossom and experience God's shalom (Isa. 11).

Amos, whose oracles focus primarily on God's judgment, ends on a beautiful note of hope: "I will restore the fortunes of my people Israel, and they shall rebuild the ruined cities and inhabit them; they shall plant vineyards and drink their wine, and they shall make gardens and eat their fruit. I will plant them upon their land, and they shall never again be plucked up" (Amos 9:14-15). This passage envisions the future redemption once more between God and his people in their relationship to the Promised Land. The Israelites will be able to return to their land. The planting of vineyards and the enjoyment of wine in the Promised Land will be a sign of God's work of redemption. The prophet Joel expresses a similar hope as he envisions the redemption of God's people in the great community of God's creation, which includes the land (*'ădāmâ*), the animals of the field, and the children of Zion. Wine, together with grain and olive oil, are a sure sign of God's redemption (Joel 2:18-19, 21-24; see also Zech. 8:12).

The prophet Micah continues in a similar fashion, though his vision becomes more specific. Wars will cease, men will turn their spears into pruning hooks, and "they shall all sit under their own vines and under their own fig trees, and no one shall make them afraid" (Mic. 4:4; see also Isa. 2:4; Zech. 3:10; 8:12; Prov. 3:10). God's redemption includes Israel's return to the Promised Land and the freedom to till the soil and harvest its fruit. The soldiers will return to their land and literally forge their spears into pruning hooks. The Hebrew term used here refers to a particular knife that vintners use to prune their vineyards.[60] They will live in peace, without fear, and be able to work their vineyards once more. What was once true for families under the rule of Solomon (1 Kings 4:25) is now re-envisioned with respect to God's future redemption. It is a modest yet beautiful vision of small farmers with enough land to provide for their families and enough wine for daily use and a little extra for special celebrations. God's redemption does not envision a world ruled by grand and rich landowners, in which the poor and socially vulnerable are forgotten. Rather, it paints an ideal vision of a peaceable kingdom, where every family sits down in its own orchard and vineyard — enjoying a modest abundance.

The prophet Jeremiah speaks of a time when Israel will be able to return to their land with singing, dancing, merry-making, and vineyard-planting

(Jer. 31:5). God's goodness shall overflow in an abundance of grain, wine, and oil (Jer. 31:12; Joel 2:23-24). This is a complete reversal of the consequence of God's judgment, in which singing, celebration, and joy cease, gladness is banished, and a lack of wine becomes a sign of God's judgment (Isa. 24:7-11).

In Isaiah 25, God's redemption is envisioned as a great feast with choice wine for all peoples: "On this mountain the Lord of hosts will make for all peoples a feast of rich food, a feast of well-aged wines, of rich food filled with marrow, of well-aged wines strained clear" (Isa. 25:6).[61] It will be a time when God will swallow up death and wipe away the tears from all faces (Isa. 25:8). The prophet Isaiah even speaks of a new heaven and a new earth full of joy and delight. All weeping will cease and all suffering will end. God's people will plant vineyards and enjoy their fruit. Peace will reign on the earth, and even the wolf and the lamb shall feed together (Isa. 65:17-25).

The prophet Hosea envisions God's redemption as a wedding banquet that includes all living creatures (Hosea 2:18-23). The prophet Amos even speaks of a time when "the mountains shall drip sweet wine, and all the hills shall flow with it" (Amos 9:13; see also Joel 3:18). These images again evoke visions of great splendor, inspiring a yearning for a restored paradise. They instill in God's people a longing for a redemption in which the harmonious times of Eden, the garden of delight, will be restored. And this spiritual vision of God's restoration remains deeply anchored in Israel's embodied, personal, and communal lives, including the Israelites' relationship with the rest of creation. God's redeeming hand enables them to return to their homeland and live in peace. They will plant vineyards, receive their fruit as a blessing from God, and rejoice in him with feasting and celebration. Wine will flow in abundance.[62]

In the light of such profound promises for the messianic age, Jesus' first miracle, at a Jewish wedding in John 2, takes on multiple layers of meaning. Jesus shows himself Lord over his creation by performing the miracle of turning water, not only into wine, but into choice wine. But doesn't this miracle also become a sign that he has come to fulfill the messianic promises? He provides a choice vintage wine in abundance at a Jewish wedding, where singing, dancing, and merry-making are common practice. Is this the beginning of the fulfillment of God's promises as foretold by the prophets? For example, Isaiah envisioned God's redemption as a feast with an abundance of choice wine. Doesn't this miracle foreshadow the abundant age of which the prophets spoke so vividly? It is to the New Testament that we must turn to continue our study.

Wine in the New Testament

In light of the rich tradition of wine and viticulture in the Old Testament, it is not surprising that the theme of wine continues to be important in first-century Israel and in the New Testament. Of the New Testament books, wine-related language occurs most often in the Gospels (Matthew, Mark, Luke, John) and the book of Revelation. Wine is valued as an important commodity for trade (Rev. 18:13), and, since it is a staple of the culture, there is a fear that its cost will increase (Rev. 6:6).

Jesus is by far the most prominent person to deal with wine and viticulture in the New Testament. He assumes of his audience some knowledge of oenology (the study and science of wine-making), and he demonstrates his own knowledge. He is aware that the process of wine fermentation is powerful and can burst old wineskins that had already been stretched out by previous use (Matt. 9:17; Mark 2:22; Luke 5:37-38). He is also aware that aged wine is usually better than new wine (Luke 5:39). When he taught, Jesus often referred to the world of agriculture to teach about the nature of the kingdom of God, and vineyards in particular are featured quite prominently.

Apart from a brief warning against drunkenness in Luke 21:34, Jesus does not include it in his list of vices (Matt. 15:19-20; Mark 7:20-22). This seems to reflect the cultural context of Hebrew life in Israel: regular consumption of wine was normal, and excessive wine-drinking was frowned on — thus demonstrating that it was the exception.[63] On the other hand, the apostle Paul engaged with pagan cultures where excessive wine-drinking and drunkenness seem to have been more frequent — and more culturally acceptable — than in Hebrew society. Therefore, Paul felt it was necessary to include drunkenness in his list of vices (Gal. 5:19-21; Rom. 13:13; 1 Tim. 3:3).

Jesus himself seems to have enjoyed wine regularly. He must have done so often enough that his fellow Hebrews became uneasy with it. They accused him of being a drunkard: "Look, a glutton and a drunkard, a friend of tax collectors and sinners!" (Matt. 11:19; Luke 7:34). Jesus' enjoyment of wine and his first miracle at Cana affirm wine as a gift and blessing from God. He sees nothing intrinsically evil in it; rather, he argues, quite frankly, that the danger lies with the human heart and not with the gifts that God has given: "Listen and understand: it is not what goes into the mouth that defiles a person, but it is what comes out of the mouth that defiles. . . . Do you not see that whatever goes into the mouth enters the stomach, and goes out into the sewer? But what comes out of the mouth proceeds from the heart, and this is what defiles" (Matt. 15:11, 17, 18). While Jesus spoke these words in reference to the question of ritual hand-washing, they are also applicable to his attitude toward wine. The problem does not lie with the gifts of God but with the human heart. The apostle Paul also affirms wine as a gift from God (1 Tim. 4:3-4), singling out the health benefits of wine but also warning against drunkenness (1 Cor. 5:11; 6:10; Gal. 5:21).

Wine Used in Medical Contexts

Two important passages in the New Testament indicate that the early church, standing in a long tradition in the Ancient Near East, used wine for medicinal purposes. In 1 Timothy, Paul writes to his young friend Timothy about the false teachings of the Gnostics that had apparently crept into the church in Ephesus. The Gnostics denied the body and physical enjoyment as a gift from God, and thus they forbade marriage, certain foods, and wine. While Paul has addressed the issues of marriage and foods directly in an earlier section of his letter (1 Tim. 4:1-4), he deals with the issue of wine in more subtle ways. Timothy had been suffering from various physical ailments, including stomach problems. Paul advises him to cure it with the regular drinking of a little wine (1 Tim. 5:23). Here Paul shows his knowledge of the health benefits of wine. Implicitly, his medical advice also affirms wine as part of God's good creation in the face of the false teachings of the Gnostics.

The parable of the Good Samaritan (Luke 10:25-37) shows that wine, together with oil, was also used externally to treat wounds. Due to its alcohol content, wine works as an antiseptic and keeps wounds from inflammation and blood poisoning. Wine was also used, along with olive oil, to stanch the flow of blood.[64] No wonder wine had become such a highly valued cultural good in the Ancient Near East — including in Israel!

The Figurative Use of the Language of Viticulture

The New Testament uses the language of viticulture just as the Old Testament does to speak figuratively about God and his relationship with his people concerning their identity, judgment, and redemption. In the parables Jesus uses everyday scenarios, events, and traditions that reflect his cultural and agricultural context to teach about the kingdom of God/heaven, and the world of wine and viticulture features quite prominently. The parable of the laborers in the vineyard (Matt. 20:1-6), the parable of the two sons (Matt. 21:28-31), and the parable of the wicked tenants (Mark 12:1-12; Matt. 21:33-41; Luke 20:9-19) are three important examples where Jesus uses viticulture to speak figuratively about the kingdom of God. In the parable of the wedding banquet, Jesus compares the kingdom of heaven to a king who has prepared a wedding banquet for his son. While this parable does not make explicit references to wine-drinking, it would have evoked in Jesus' audience images of Hebrew wedding festivities that emphasized joyful celebration, which was expressed in music, dancing, and wine-drinking. (Matt. 22:1-14; see also John 2:1-11).[65] These are all marks of the coming of the kingdom of God. In all of these parables Jesus assumes that his audience is familiar with the world of wine and viticulture.

This familiarity is particularly important for understanding John 15:1-17. Jesus, in one of the "I am" sayings of John's Gospel, calls himself the true vine, his Father the vine-grower, and his disciples the branches off this one vine. The disciples are called to abide in him and to bear much fruit (John 15:1-6). In the perspective of its Old Testament usage, this is a provocative statement. It suggests that it is Jesus rather than Israel that is now the true vine of God. When the metaphors of the vine and vineyard are used in the Old Testament, God is always portrayed as separate and apart. In this metaphor, however, God in Jesus Christ is not only near, but also deeply intertwined with, his people. It suggests the most intimate union between Jesus and his disciples.

In this passage the disciples are repeatedly called to "abide" in Christ. The verb "abide" is used seven times in this short passage, and this rather frequent usage evokes the question of what this might mean for the disciples. Jesus explains this dynamic with regard to the vine and its branches. He assumes that his audience will understand this agricultural language and the implications of what it means for a branch to remain healthy and fruitful. It is the sap that the rootstock produces and brings up through the vine into the branches that sustains the branches of the vine and keeps them alive.

Does this potent metaphor perhaps suggest that it is only by continually drawing from the sap of the vine that one can remain alive in Christ? Could this passage, perhaps, hint at the importance of the Lord's Supper for Christian spirituality? John's earlier reflection on what it means to abide in Christ certainly seems to carry eucharistic overtones: "Those who eat my flesh and drink my blood abide in me, and I in them" (John 6:56). What Christ most certainly does emphasize in this passage is that those who abide in him abide in his love and do so by keeping his commandments. "As the Father has loved me, so I have loved you; abide in my love. If you keep my commandments, you will abide in my love . . ." (John 15:10). To abide in Christ means to love him by keeping his commandments.

Another important implication of this potent "I am the vine" metaphor is something that is often lost to the modern reader not familiar with viticulture. Of all the plants that serve as a source of food, the grape vine, like no other, can grow and be productive in the most adverse agricultural contexts. It thrives in stony soils and on the steepest hills and is most productive in places where little else can be grown. Christ's fruitfulness comes to a climax in a place where seemingly no life can be found: the cross. This self-sacrificial love of Christ is now to define how the disciples are to love: "This is my commandment, that you love one another as I have loved you. No one has greater love than this, to lay down one's life for one's friends" (John 15:12-13). The fruitfulness of the disciples depends on remaining in Christ and his self-giving love.

The metaphor of Christ as the vine and the disciples as the branches is profound and potent, and it hints at the organic unity between faith, human flourishing, and the call to love self-sacrificially. It is in this organic unity that Christians will find the fullness of joy (John 15:11). Before I draw this chapter to a close, I would like to point the reader's attention to a few more New Testament mentions of wine that deserve special attention.

Jesus, Feasting, and the Lord's Supper

Jesus affirmed the custom and importance of wine-drinking for Jewish celebrations when he performed his first miracle at the wedding in Cana. The host had simply run out of wine, and this shortage was as embarrassing then as it would be today. One does not run out of wine at such an important celebration.[66] Prompted by his mother, Jesus stepped in and rescued the hosts from this moment of potential humiliation. Not only did he turn the water into wine; he transformed it into choice wine. It was of such high quality that the sommelier responsible for the wine at that party commented to the groom about its quality — completely astonished by it (John 2:1-11).

However, the most theologically important occurrence of wine in the New Testament comes when Jesus celebrates the Passover meal with his disciples. The traditional Passover, as it was celebrated at the time of Jesus, included the enjoyment of wine. During the meal, four cups of wine were served in individual portions, relating to the four circumstances surrounding the deliverance out of Egypt.[67] Once again, Jesus partakes in the drinking of wine and affirms its goodness within the context of Jewish religious celebrations. But he not only partakes in the Passover meal; he now reinterprets it in light of his own life and mission. The God who brought Israel out of Egypt is the God who will now save his people in and through Jesus Christ, his death and resurrection, and his coming again in glory (Matt. 26:17-29; par. Mark 14:12-25; Luke 22:7-23; 1 Cor. 5:7). Even as they celebrate this important meal together, Jesus prepares his disciples for his departure. He announces to them: "I tell you, I will never again drink of this fruit of the vine until that day when I drink it new with you in my Father's kingdom" (Matt. 26:29; cf. also Mark 14:25; Luke 21:18). Just as the Old Testament, and particularly the prophets, envisions the *eschaton* in terms of feasting and an abundance of wine, so Jesus envisions the completion of all things in terms of festive celebration, the reunion with his beloved followers, *and* the drinking of wine.

Concluding Reflections

The theme of wine and viticulture in the Bible is a profoundly complex and important subject matter. I have only been able to offer a brief overview here. Rather than seeing a few comments regarding wine scattered here and there, we should perceive how the Bible unfolds a narrative in which God's creation and redemption are deeply intertwined. The theme of wine opens up an understanding of the Christian life that sees human life in a profound relationship with God and in deep fellowship with God's creation. Rather than understanding creation and salvation as two separate categories, the biblical narrative reveals that the two are profoundly intertwined. God's redemption encompasses all of creation, including the land and its fruitfulness. The Christian life calls us to recover our God-given place in this great community of creation by learning to treasure God's gifts and enjoy them faithfully and responsibly. Wine is, first of all, a gift from God and a sign of his blessing; as such, it has a very special role in our lives. It is to elicit a deep sense of joy and lead us toward an ever-growing posture of gratitude and thanksgiving to God, our Creator and Redeemer. It is with Saint Paul that we affirm that ". . . everything created by God is good, and nothing is to be rejected, provided it is received with thanksgiving; for it is sanctified by God's word and by prayer" (1 Tim. 4:4-5).

2

Wine in the History of the Church:
Its Rise and Fall

"Wine was given to make us cheerful, not to make us behave shamefully; to make us laugh, not a laughing-stock; to make us healthy, not sick; to mend the weakness of the body, not to undermine the soul."

Saint Chrysostom[1]

G iven the rich history of wine in the Bible and the central role of wine in the Lord's Supper, it should not be surprising that wine has always played an important role in the life of the Christian church, including the early North American church. This aspect of the church's history, however, is often forgotten. Today we find very little reflection on the importance of wine for the life of the church and Christian spirituality apart from brief comments about its use in the Eucharist. The health benefits of wine continue to be discussed and researched in great measure, but its spiritual significance often goes unnoticed. Many are surprised to hear that wine can actually enrich our spiritual lives; when consumed moderately, wine can bring much joy. Wine can also help foster a greater sense of wonder and gratitude and deepen our relationship with God and one another. Wine can also help us rethink our place in the community of God's creation and recognize the deep interdependence that exists between humans and the nonhuman creation in our pursuit of the knowledge of God.

Given the beauty and delight that a well-crafted wine can provide for those who partake, why are we so slow to recognize it as a gift from God with many spiritual benefits? At times Christians still have reservations about accepting and embracing wine as a gift to be enjoyed. The first impulse, especially in some traditions in North America, is to point out the dangers of alcohol and the problem of addiction.

The history of the church reveals a different attitude. It is a fascinating and surprising discovery to see how profound, constructive, and long-lasting the relationship between the Christian church and wine has been and continues to be. The subject is vast, and I cannot provide an exhaustive account here. Rather, I hope to give a taste of this rich history and to inspire further explorations.

In the following I will trace this theme chronologically and follow its trail primarily from the early church of the Ancient Near East to its expansion in the Western church of Gaul/Europe, and will conclude with its development in Central and North America. My account is indeed very limited, with significant omissions, but it helps focus our study. The relationship between wine and the Christian church has always been a rich one, and it needs to be remembered, recovered, and celebrated. The following account will also explain the historical roots of the rejection of alcohol and wine in parts of Christianity, prohibitions that are still prevalent today in certain small pockets of (primarily) Protestant groups. A brief sketch of the development of viticulture from the Greco-Roman world toward the Western empire will help set the stage.

Challenging Beginnings

The early church grew and spread throughout the Roman Empire, which considered wine a great cultural good and an important medical remedy.[2] Its economic significance increased as more vineyards were planted and the trade in wine became more prominent. According to the Greek historian Diodorus Siculus (ca. 80-20 BC), Roman wines had become so popular with the Gauls that the Romans were able to trade a jar of wine for a slave, a lopsided business deal indeed.[3] This would change dramatically in the second part of the first century AD: wine-growing had become more widespread, and this led, of course, to a rapid decrease in wine prices.[4] Emerging wine markets in Gaul (present-day France and Germany), Spain, and the Cyclades (Greek Islands) began to compete with Roman wines, so much so that John of Patmos, writing from a Greek island, prophesied that the Roman Empire would no longer be able to sell its wines (Rev. 18:13).[5]

The Romans learned viticulture from the Etruscans and the Greeks. While the Greek influence is well known and well attested, the Etruscan influence is less well known. To this day Italians are quick to point out that viticulture had been in what is now Italy long before the Romans came. How advanced Etruscan viticulture was we cannot say; but it appears that the Greeks were primarily the ones who taught the Romans about the advanced art of viticulture and viniculture. By the time of the early church, the Roman Empire had helped spread viticulture throughout what is now Italy, and by the fourth century to every province of the empire, including Gaul. The fourth-century Gallo-Roman poet Ausonius reflects on the beauty of the vineyards along the Mosel in Gaul in his poem "Mosella."[6] The Mosel River is one of the northernmost places in Europe where wine is produced.

The life of the early church was challenging, but in accordance with their beliefs, early Christians embraced wine as a gift from God. Following the example of Jesus, these brave Christians used wine in the Eucharist and enjoyed it with their meals. In the second century, however, voices emerged in the church that saw wine and women as a particular threat to Christian spirituality. These sectarian voices held that wine and women — rather than the desires and passions of men — were responsible for the violations of ethical codes.[7] Some sectarian groups even forbade the use of wine in the Eucharist, using water instead.

Saint Cyprian (AD 200-259), the bishop of Carthage in Africa, was one of the first church fathers to address this issue in great detail. He insists on the use of wine in the Eucharist in order to remain faithful to the teachings and practices of Jesus Christ, a striking and convincing argument that Saint Augustine highly praised. Cyprian develops his case from Scripture, arguing that not only Jesus, but also the apostle Paul, commanded followers of Christ to use wine in the celebration of the Eucharist. For Cyprian, this is a matter of obedience, not choice. He reminds his audience that Christ turned water into wine, and he sets forth a rather impressive theology of wine.

For Cyprian, wine was a sign of God's blessing, and the absence of wine was a lack of spiritual grace.[8] He insists that only wine can signify the blood of Christ, and he sees this signification foretold in the Old Testament. Noah,

Melchizedek, Abraham, Solomon, and the Psalmist all foreshadow the use of wine in the Eucharist. Cyprian argues that Jacob's blessing of Judah in Genesis 49:10-12 prefigures the eucharistic cup. The abundance of wine promised in Genesis 49, and "the blood of the grape" of which Jacob speaks, are fulfilled in the eucharistic cup. The prophets also foretell it: especially does the theme of the winepress in the prophets foreshadow Christ being crushed for our sake. The offering the church brings to the Eucharist, according Cyprian, needs to correspond to the suffering of Christ. The process of wine-making reflects Christ's sacrifice beautifully, and hence wine must be used in the Eucharist. Cyprian also recognizes that wine is a key symbol in Scripture for the eschatological age, when Christ will come again to renew the earth and drink wine with his followers. How could one abstain from wine and be prepared for this final feast?[9]

What is striking about Cyprian's argument is his profound grasp of wine's manifold functions in Scripture. He insists that wine must be used in the Eucharist in order to follow the commands and practices of Christ. The removal of wine from the Eucharist would lead to a great loss of meaning. It is worth quoting Cyprian at some length here:

> And you should understand that the warning we have been given is this: in offering the cup the teachings of the Lord must be observed and we must do exactly as the Lord first did Himself for us — the cup which is offered up in remembrance of Him is to be offered mixed with wine. For inasmuch as Christ says: *I am the true vine,* it can never be supposed that the blood of Christ is water; it is wine. And it is, therefore, obviously impossible that Christ's blood, by which we have been redeemed and quickened, should be present in the cup when in the cup there is no wine; wine signifies the blood of Christ.[10]

Cyprian goes so far as to argue that to depart from Christ's teaching in regard to the use of the wine is to depart from the gospel. He also praises the life-giving effect of wine in general, quite apart from the Eucharist. It puts the mind at ease and helps one relax in spirit and lay aside one's troubles and cares. This natural effect of wine is also mirrored in the eucharistic experience, where we are to cease from being burdened and troubled by our sins and find peace and joy in Christ — where God's merciful bounty is revealed.[11] Cyprian's careful

argument for the use of wine in the Eucharist is an important early document and has shaped the Christian tradition in significant ways, including the
thought of Augustine and Thomas Aquinas.

Saint Irenaeus (ca. 115-202), a contemporary of Cyprian who was minister-
ing in Gaul, defended the Christian faith against Gnostic heresies that denied
the gift and goodness of creation and did not believe in the salvation of the
human body. In Book V of *Against Heresies,* Irenaeus develops his argument
from the elements of the bread and wine used in the Eucharist. He reminds
his readers that God is the one who grants creation. Just as bread and wine,
as God's gifts, nourish and strengthen our physical bodies, so bread and wine
can be sanctified by God's word in the Eucharist and become the body and
blood of Christ for us. He continues to argue that, just as the body and blood
of Christ in the Eucharist nourishes our physical body, so can the physical
body receive the gift of salvation — which is eternal life. For Irenaeus, the
physical and spiritual are deeply intertwined, and Christians must not devalue creation but must trust that God wants to redeem all of it, including
our physical bodies.[12]

Clement of Alexandria (150-250) devoted an entire essay to the theme of
wine-drinking (*Paedagogus* 2). In that essay he repeatedly cautions against the
abuse of wine and advises his readers to keep it away from adolescents. He
recommends the enjoyment of wine especially for the elderly and during spells
of cold weather, since it warms the body. He suggests that wine can be drunk
for health reasons alone — or for the purpose of relaxation and enjoyment.
Drawing on the Jewish wisdom teacher Ben Sira, Clement affirms wine as a gift
from God that can bring joy if enjoyed in moderation. Wine probes into the
soul of humanity and functions in a revelatory way. Quoting Ben Sira, Clement
argues: "As the furnace proveth the steel blade in the process of dipping, so
wine proveth the heart of the haughty."[13]

For Clement, one's drinking habits reveal much about the state of one's
life. In contrast to sectarian voices that held wine (and women) responsible
for ethical violations, Clement emphasizes that it is man's own heart that has
to be held responsible. However, he seems more cautious than Cyprian and
Irenaeus are with respect to wine. While he affirms the benefits of wine, his
pastoral concern is to speak out against drunkenness and gluttony. Clement
advocates the virtue of temperance in the face of the substance abuse. His
goal is to affirm the goodness of creation, God's desire to redeem it, and the

importance of wine for the celebration of the Eucharist. The challenges that Clement addresses are different from those of Cyprian and Irenaeus, and thus he has a different emphasis.

In 313 an important event occurred that would change the fate of Christianity. With the Edict of Milan, Emperor Constantine legalized Christianity, and the (theretofore) ever-present threat of persecution fell away. Different challenges arose. Christians became more lax in their lifestyles, and drunkenness became accepted in some pockets of Christianity. Saint Basil of Alexandria (329/330-379) firmly spoke against it: like the other church fathers, he affirmed wine as a gift from God to strengthen the weak, but he insisted that it must not be abused. Basil was himself drawn to a monastic lifestyle and thus emphasized the importance of asceticism: he advised temperance and moderation in eating and drinking for those who wanted to progress in the virtuous life and grow toward union with God.[14]

Saint Chrysostom (347-407), on the other hand, had to contend once again with voices that believed wine to be evil. He affirms the positive benefits of wine and argues that drunkenness is the work of the devil. He writes: "Wine was given to make us cheerful, not to make us behave shamefully; to make us laugh, not a laughing-stock; to make us healthy, not sick; to mend the weakness of the body, not to undermine the soul."[15] For Chrysostom, wine is the work of God, and the problem lies, not with wine as such, but with those who abuse it. True abstinence, therefore, means abstaining from sin and drunkenness and enjoying the gifts of God's good creation in moderation.[16]

Saint Augustine (354-430) also felt the need to defend wine in the face of Manichaean heresies that viewed creation, including wine, as inherently evil. He argues that Christians honor their Creator by enjoying his gifts without abusing them.[17] They are to turn away from drunkenness and model their celebrations after Jewish banquets, where drunkenness was never accepted.[18] The wise person knows how to enjoy wine while also practicing restraint, and those who seek spiritual perfection need to learn not to be controlled and bound by substances but to enjoy them freely and to be able to refrain from them when necessary.[19]

Like Chrysostom, then, he argues that wine is not evil, but that a person's abuse of God's gifts is a sin. According to German oral tradition, Augustine summarized the benefits of wine as follows:

In many instances wine is necessary for human beings. Wine strengthens the stomach, renews one's energy, warms the body of the cold-blooded, poured onto wounds it brings healing. It chases away sadness and weariness of soul. Wine brings joy, and for companions it fuels one's pleasure for conversations.[20]

Depending on their context and the challenges they faced, the church fathers had different emphases. Some had to defend wine as part of God's good creation against heretical views that tended to degrade creation, which included wine, and saw it as inherently evil; others needed to speak out against the abuse of God's gifts that showed themselves in the form of drunkenness and gluttony, which was a different kind of degradation of the gifts of creation. Some of them did advocate a life of abstinence, but they never based it on the heretical teaching that wine itself is bad. All of them upheld a life of moderation as the ideal model of the Christian life. For the church fathers, the tensions inherent in a life of temperance bring about spiritual maturation. Temperance draws attention to the real source of life and happiness. Substances can never quench our deepest hunger and thirst. Only God can, and the role of fasting and temperance is to bring us into a fuller enjoyment of the giver of all good gifts.

Another important group worth mentioning is the desert fathers, the early monastic movement that developed alongside — but quite apart from — the mainstream church and the teachings of the church fathers in the fourth and fifth centuries. These Christians withdrew into the deserts of Egypt and Syria to leave all worldliness behind in order to seek the face of God and achieve purity of soul. Guided by severe ascetic practices, they sought to overcome the passions of the body; their primary strategy was avoidance and abstinence. Their stance toward wine and women was clear: Flee from temptation if at all possible![21] An exception in regard to wine was the celebration of the Eucharist.[22] While their collected wisdom is invaluable in regard to soul care and has seen a renaissance in both theological and psychological curricula, their severely ascetic lifestyle could not be upheld. At the time that this early monastic movement began to spread to the Western part of the empire, no one could have foreseen that it would be monks who would make such important and lasting contributions to the world of wine.

Pioneering Spirits: Christianity and Wine in Western Monasticism

Saint Martin of Tours (316-397) was an important advocate of the monastic life in the West and is credited with the development of viticulture in the Touraine region of France. Saint Martin grew up in what is now Italy and spent his adult life primarily in France. Both regions had a strong and long tradition in viticulture and wine-drinking. Tours, Martin's place of ministry, is happily situated on the fertile banks of the Loire River; the surrounding area is known to this day for its great wines. Legend has it that Martin not only spurred on the development of viticulture in his region but is also responsible for grafting the Chenin Noir vine from the wild Chenin vine found in the Touraine forests.[23] Martin was a great evangelist in Gaul, and many miracles were attributed to him, including the replenishment of empty wine jars at his grave.[24] Saint Martin's legacy was so great that Tours became an important pilgrimage center in Gaul. The legends surrounding his life deeply shaped the religious imagination of particularly the French, Germans, and Celts. An eighth-century Saint Martin's cross still stands on the Holy Island of Iona, Scotland. Martin Luther was named after Martin of Tours, and more than 3,600 churches in France were dedicated to him. Eventually, vintners adopted Saint Martin as their patron saint.[25] Pieter Bruegel's recently rediscovered painting *The Wine of St. Martin's Day,* commemorating the celebration of the feast day of Saint Martin, is a striking piece of sixteenth-century art witnessing to Martin's enduring impact on the religious imagination of Europe. He is remembered, not only for his generosity to the poor, but also for his view of wine as a gift from God to be enjoyed and celebrated.[26]

No monk has shaped Western monasticism as much as has Saint Benedict of Nursia (ca. 480-547). While our knowledge of Saint Martin's life rests primarily on tradition and legends, the contribution of Saint Benedict to the development of wine and spirituality is clearly documented in the rule he wrote for his monastic communities. The Rule of Saint Benedict, though influenced by the teachings of the desert fathers via the writings of John Cassian, was much more moderate. It is a very practical approach to the monastic life — with a strong emphasis on hospitality. It became the most popular rule for organizing monastic communities in the medieval world, and it has scarcely lost its appeal nearly 1,500 years later. Benedict wrote this rule to regulate the daily life of emerging monastic communities in Italy — into a rhythm of prayer, study, and manual labor.

The Rule regulates practical matters such as sleeping, eating, drinking, and clothing. Benedict recognized that it was unrealistic to forbid the drinking of wine in his Italian culture, which was so different from the life of the desert fathers in Egypt. Grape-growing and wine-drinking had a great history and tradition in Italy. The great wines of the Roman Empire had once come from Italy before emerging markets in Gaul challenged its reputation. While Benedict would have preferred for his monks to abstain from drinking wine for ascetic reasons, his Rule permits a daily allowance of wine, emphasizing the benefit it brings to the sick. Each monk is allowed one *herminia* a day. (In classical Rome, one *herminia* was half a *sextarius,* equivalent to .273 liters in today's measurements. Whether Saint Benedict's *herminia* contained exactly the same amount as did the Roman *herminia,* we cannot reconstruct, but it seems likely.) Benedict also permitted an increase in the daily allowance depending on places and circumstances. Hard manual labor of any kind or work during the hot summer months were two reasons he lists for the increase of a monk's daily allowance of wine. He spoke against drunkenness, just as he did against overeating; moderation in eating and drinking was the monastic ideal.[27] Whereas we would find this Rule rigid and overly ascetic today, it was much more balanced and moderate at that time — especially when compared to the desert fathers.

Saint Benedict's Rule came at a time when stability, structure, and rhythm were desperately needed. The gradual decline of the Western Roman Empire climaxed in the fall of Rome, and the last Western Roman emperor was deposed in 476, shortly before Benedict was born. Slowly but surely, Roman civilization and government, social and economic infrastructures changed. While many areas of civilized life suffered from barbarian invasion and domination, viticulture did not. The barbarians were quite fond of wine and furthered its development in the German and French lands.[28]

Amid the great collapse of the Roman Empire and the increasing chaos, the monastic communities slowly but surely emerged as centers of faith and learning. It was in these monastic communities that the agricultural insights of the Greco-Roman world would be preserved and cultivated, as the monks drew from the peasant knowledge around them.[29] In about 587 the king of Burgundy donated some of his land near Dijon, with its vines, to the Benedictine abbey of Saint-Bénigne. It was by way of such generous donations that the monasteries acquired land and were able to develop into powerful religious and economic centers. Indeed, some of the world's best wines today come from Burgundy. By the eleventh century, Benedictine monasteries owned all the (now famous) vineyards, such as those in Gevrey, Beaune, and Meursault.[30] The Benedictine abbey of Cluny, situated between Beaune and Mâcon, was richly endowed with vineyards and had an important role not only in advancing Western monasticism but also in advancing and improving the standards of viticulture.[31]

However, gifts from generous donors were not the only way monasteries acquired vineyards. The Latin poet Venantius Fortunatus (ca. 530–600/609) speaks of Benedictine nuns planting vines along the Main River in Franconia at Kitzingen and Ochsenfurt. Later, the Irish missionary Saint Kilian (640-689) is mentioned with regard to the development of viticulture in Franconia.[32] The codex of Lorsch (compiled between 1175 and 1195) lists manifold gifts given in the form of vineyards to the Benedictine abbey of Lorsch (founded in 764) in the Rhine-Hesse region.[33] The abbey was situated near the Rhine River, and to this day the region is known for its lovely wines. It also became an important center of learning with an impressive library. The illuminated Lorsch Gospels (written between 778 and 820) give witness to the cultural richness of this Carolingian monastery. The abbeys of Fulda, Saint Gall, and Reichenau (on the island of Lake Constance), Prüm, Hirsau, and St. Blasien all produced wine during the so-called Dark Ages and were richly endowed.[34] Arbeo (d. 784), the bishop of Freising, praises the agricultural bounty of Bavaria, including its vineyards, and mentions Saint Corbinian with regard to the development of viticulture.[35] Monks brought vines to Thuringia, Schlesia, and Prussia, among other regions.[36]

With the expansion of viticulture, wine increasingly became a staple in the German lands.[37] A papal document from the thirteenth century confirms that monasteries owned vineyards even as far north as Denmark.[38] These examples give a glimpse into the expansion of Christianity in Gaul and how often it was accompanied by the cultivation and expansion of viticulture. The bond between Christianity and wine had been sealed, and new ground was forged.

The Benedictine rhythm of prayer, study, and manual labor provided excellent conditions for the development of viticulture and viniculture in Gaul. Manual labor and study were prescribed aspects of the daily task of each monk/nun. This threefold pattern of life also had another implicit theological function: it placed the monastic community in that same theological context that I discussed above with respect to the creation story in Genesis. By working the land, the monks developed their relationship with God, not apart from the rest of creation, but by remaining deeply embedded in it through manual labor, study, and prayer.

Wine-growing and wine-drinking became an important aspect of daily life in many parts of Western Christianity, especially in the regions that are now France, Italy, and Germany. Monks also grew vineyards in Ireland and England, though their existence is often forgotten because little of it survived beyond the medieval period. Ale, beer, and mead remained the principal drinks in England, and wine seems to have been reserved primarily for monks and nobility and for consumption in the celebration of the Eucharist.[39] A new promised land opened up before these pioneering monks. They were responsible for advancing the gospel and converting barbaric tribes to Christianity, but they also had a key role in cultivating and expanding viticulture in Gaul and Britain. Did not the Old Testament prophets speak of God's blessings in terms of the land, and of an abundance of wine and grain as a sign of his blessing?

Wine, together with beer and mead, remained a primary source of safe fluids throughout the Middle Ages, especially in those regions where vineyards were cultivated. The water supply remained an unstable source of liquid and was often the principal carrier of disease.[40] Wine and beer were also important sources of calories and nutrients, especially significant if one considers the sparse diet, the hard manual labor, and the harsh living conditions of the average peasant at that time. Furthermore, wine continued to be used widely for medicinal purposes and was the only anesthetic known and available at that time.[41]

Drinking wine had an important social function. Peasant life in the early Middle Ages was extremely difficult, involving much harder manual labor than is borne today, uncertain political and economic circumstances, severe suffering, high mortality rates, and very little distraction or entertainment to ease the hardships of life. Community gatherings and celebrations that centered on food and wine were important ways peasants could escape the difficulties of life and find some distraction and merriment. Even the holy feast days of the church, along with other festivities, were celebrated with a great sense of conviviality.[42]

By the twelfth century, monasteries were the largest producers of wine in

Europe. They were able to make high-quality wine for reasonable prices. Their privileged position as religious centers in a deeply religious society enabled them to emerge as economic centers within their settings.[43] Viticulture and the wine trade became just one branch of the activities of these impressive medieval institutions.

Monks produced wine for many different purposes, but the primary purpose was their daily celebration of the Eucharist. The Sunday celebration was open to the public, and we should not underestimate the amount of wine that was needed to serve the peasants partaking in the Eucharist. In the early Middle Ages, peasants still received both the bread and the wine at communion.[44] In addition, wine was usually served after the church service. Many monks consumed wine daily with their meals. Wine was also exchanged among monastic communities. In 610, Saint Columbanus of Nantes shipped wine to the monks in Ireland, and the Venerable Bede (672/673–735) reports that vines were grown in Ireland.[45]

As the Benedictine commitment to hospitality and charity transformed monasteries into hostels and hospices for travelers — poor and rich alike — wine was needed to serve their guests.[46] And as monasteries developed their institutional roles, they also became important centers of learning. They established schools and hospitals and explored more carefully the healing agencies of natural resources, such as herbs, grains, precious stones, and, of course, wine. Hildegard von Bingen (1098–1179), designated a doctor of the Catholic Church, wrote extensively on this subject matter, especially in her works *Physica* and *Causae et Curae*. Her monastery, fortunately situated along the Rhine River, once again cultivates vines today, and the Benedictine rhythm of prayer, study, and manual labor draws many visitors and pilgrims into its hospitable arms.

Not all of the monasteries survived the onslaught of invaders such as the Vikings during the ninth and tenth centuries, but those that did emerged as centers of faith and learning once again — with significant land holdings. By the end of the Middle Ages, the monasteries were again thriving agricultural centers and the primary producers of wine in Western Europe.[47] Increasingly, wine also became an important factor in economic life, and monasteries played a key role in the medieval wine trade. Monasteries used the income from their vineyards to support their charitable hospitals and care homes.[48] Some of these hospitals, such as the Bürgerspital in Würzburg, Franconia,

Germany, have survived to this day — even in the face of the turmoil of secularization.

Over time, many Benedictine monks became rather lax in their adherence to the Rule of Saint Benedict, excusing themselves from the manual labor part of the Rule. Nor did the financial success of their enterprises always bode well for their spiritual well-being. In the twelfth century, reform movements such as those initiated by the Cistercians began to emerge. The Cistercians are named after the French village of Cîteaux, near Dijon, where the monastic reform movement began. Their goal was to return to a strict observance of the Rule of Saint Benedict, and they made manual labor mandatory for every monk once again. The movement emerged in the heartland of wine-growing in France, right along the now famous Côte d'Or, and it should not surprise anyone that viticulture became an important aspect of Cistercian life, despite their commitment to a rather severe ascetic lifestyle. Nuits-St-Georges, the main town of the Côte de Nuits wine-producing area, owes much of its history to the Cistercians. The Burgundian nobleman-turned-Cistercian-monk Bernard of Clairvaux remains to this day the most famous Cistercian monk and one of the most important medieval theologians.

While other monastic movements, such as the Carthusians, Franciscans, and the military religious orders, such as the Templars, also contributed to the development of viticulture, it was the Cistercians who greatly advanced viticulture in Europe.[49] Their commitment to manual labor and ascetic practices made them highly productive communities. A papal bull of the early thirteenth century decreed that undeveloped lands were exempt from tithing (taxes paid to the pope), and this spurred on the shrewd and hard-working Cistercians to focus on developing uncultivated lands.[50] They drained swamps, cleared woodlands, and did not shy away from strenuous manual labor in order to plant new vineyards.

It was the Cistercians of Cîteaux that first cleared and planted the still-famous Clos De Vougeot of Burgundy, one of their greatest contributions to the wine world. Over time the monks acquired several parcels of land, planted them with choice vines, and eventually surrounded the vineyard with a high stone wall. The grapes of these vines were small and brought low yields, but the quality of this wine was exquisite, and it is famous to the present day.[51] Cistercians developed special methods and took great care in cultivating the vines.[52] It was the Cistercians, for example, who first developed the concept of the *cru*.[53] The famous wine writer Hugh Johnson argues that the Cistercians made Clos De Vougeot "the laboratory of their pursuit of perfection."[54]

Dom Pérignon (1638-1715), a Benedictine monk and the cellar master at Hautvillers, needs to be mentioned here. Though he was not the first one to discover secondary fermentation, which is necessary to make champagne, his experimentation with grape varieties, vinification, and his genius in using cork to seal bottles led him to produce one of the first champagnes of the world. Legend has it that, when he summoned his fellow monks to sample his new concoction, he exclaimed, "Come quickly, I'm drinking stars!"[55]

The monks' pursuit of spiritual perfection included their vocation as vintners. Their love of Christ, the true vine, turned into a devotion to care for God's earthly vineyard. Their loving care allowed the blessed vines of God's good creation to become a noble wine. Tending the vines and crafting wine became a deeply spiritual practice that was often accompanied with recitations of the Psalms. They received this holistic vision of the spiritual life from Saint Benedict: in his Rule, Benedict not only had high standards for the character of the cellarer, the monk in charge of the business side of the monastery, but he also insisted that all utensils and goods of the monastery were to be treated with the same respect as the chalice of the altar. He wrote: "[Regard] all utensils and goods of the monastery as sacred vessels of the altar."[56] For Saint Benedict, earth and altar stand in profound relationship to one another; both belong to God and need to be treated with utmost respect. Clos De Vougeot and Dom Pérignon champagne remain two of the most famous witnesses to Christian perfection. In the film *Babette's Feast,* which explores the spirituality of food and wine, it is Clos De Vougeot that is served.

By 1790, the Cistercian monastery of Cîteaux still owned vineyards in Fixin, Gevrey, Vougeot, Aloxe, Pernand, Savigny, Beaune, Pommard, Meursault, and all of Clos de Vougeot. The abbey of Clairvaux cultivated extensive vineyards in Champagne, and the Cistercians of Pontigny are credited with the first plantings of Chardonnay vines in Chablis. The reform movement of the Cistercians expanded quickly, and from Morimond, France, 212 more abbeys were founded. One of them was the famous monastery of Ebrach in Bavaria, Germany, known for its leading role in developing viticulture in Franconia, where the monks introduced the Silvaner grape.[57]

In 1136, Saint Bernard of Clairvaux sent out twelve Cistercian monks to found the abbey Eberbach in the Rheingau. These monks first planted many of the vines along the Rhine River and introduced the pinot noir grape to the region. They also cleared the dense woodlands of the now famous Steinberg, planted it with vineyards, and enclosed it with a stone wall. The Steinberg site faces south toward the Rhine River and provides excellent wine-growing conditions. It became the most magnificent and impressive of all German vineyards and to this day is famous for its Rieslings. The Rhine River also provided easy conditions for trade, and the Cistercians took a prominent role in the wine trade.[58]

Baptized Imagination: Christianity and Wine in Western Art

It is not surprising that the world of viticulture, wine-making, and wine deeply influenced the theological imagination of these monks. While the church fathers were the first ones to reflect on Christ in the divine winepress, and explored the parallels between the wine-making process and salvation history, it was only in the twelfth century that this theme became popular in Christian art.[59] The oldest known depiction of Christ in the divine winepress dates from about 1108 and can be found at the abbey of Kleinkomburg, Germany.[60] While the theme of Christ in the divine winepress with various theological emphases was most popular in Germany and lasted well into the eighteenth century, it also become popular in France. Most depictions include the Scripture passage from Isaiah 63:3: "I have trodden the wine press alone." While the original Old Testament context speaks of Yahweh's battle against Israel's enemies as a time of redemption, the church fathers interpreted the passage typologically and believed this that Old Testament passage foretells the suffering of Christ on the cross.

Beginning with the church fathers, theologians developed the profound parallels between the wine-making process and salvation history first revealed in Scripture. The crushing and pressing of the grapes became a vivid symbol for the redemptive nature of God's wrath based on biblical passages such as Isaiah 63:3. The sacrificial death of Christ on the cross began to be beautifully depicted by artists who placed Christ alongside the grapes in the divine winepress in medieval art. Often the cross was also depicted; some depictions show the beam of the wine press in the form of the cross, and at times the cross is no longer depicted at all. While the idea of Christ in the winepress is not found in Scripture, it seems like a natural development of a very powerful and potent metaphor, especially for regions where wine-making was part of the culture. In these depictions Christ's suffering on the cross was also emphasized. It invited the onlooker to meditate on Christ's suffering and begin to understand one's own suffering in the light of Christ.

Toward the end of the fifteenth century, these depictions move toward a eucharistic interpretation of the divine press. The emphasis is now on Christ's presence in the Eucharist and God's grace flowing from the fountain of the divine winepress. While the sacrificial death is still depicted in terms of Christ in the divine winepress, the paintings now focus on the blood of Christ being poured out in the winepress and gathered up in the Eucharist cup at the bottom of the winepress. Streams of wine signify the unending fountain of God's grace flowing from the divine winepress and bringing cleansing and healing to the church.[61] Some depictions, such as Hieronymus Wieriz's engraving (before 1619) also beautifully reflect the church's Trinitarian nature by depicting the Father working the winepress, Christ on the cross being crushed, and the Holy Spirit in the form of a dove perched on top of the cross.[62]

Another important comparison between the world of wine-making and salvation history is to compare Christ to a noble grape. This beautiful image occurs in many poetic musings of the church fathers. Clement of Alexandria called Christ a crushed noble grape whom we receive in the wine of the Eucharist.[63] Saint Ephrem the Syrian (d. 373) and Saint Augustine called Christ a grape crushed for us to fill the eucharistic cup. Gregory the Great (d. 604) called Christ the mystical grape.[64] It is not surprising that these monks, who meditated on Christ as the noble grape, developed a deep concern to craft wines that would bring honor to Christ.

Many other art forms give witness to this rich tradition. Wood carvings, biblical commentaries, hymns and folk songs, sermons, mystical writings, and religious writings on viticulture all speak of the profound inspiration viticulture and wine had on the pastoral imagination of the Christian church.[65]

Tumultuous Times:
Christianity and Wine during and after the Reformation

The Reformation in Germany and the French Revolution in France would change the fate of monasticism and viticulture dramatically. Many monasteries were raided and destroyed — or simply dissolved. The attacks of the Reformers on monastic life, the peasant revolts of the sixteenth century, the Thirty Years' War in the seventeenth century (mostly fought on German lands), and the French invasions in the eighteenth century dealt an especially hard blow to the wine lands of Germany.

The Enlightenment brought increasing criticism of the monastic life, and imperial decrees ordered the closing of many monasteries. The biggest blow came during the French Revolution in France. In 1790, a systematic shutting down of abbeys and friaries began; the lands were sold, and the monks were persecuted. Later, Napoleon outlawed monasticism in every country he conquered. By 1810 most monasteries in Germany, Italy, and France had been shuttered. The cultural and agricultural loss was immense.[66] To this day, however, many of the wine labels, the names of cities and vineyards, remind us of the influence of monasticism on European viticulture, and the monks' contribution must not be underestimated or forgotten.[67]

The period of the Reformation dealt a terrible blow to viticulture in Europe. According to Hugh Johnson, "[The] divorce of church and land was a radical and permanent change."[68] The Reformers certainly enjoyed their wine when they were able to get it, but they were not engaged in cultivating vines.

Martin Luther (1482-1546), named after the patron saint of wine, Saint Martin of Tours, had been an Augustinian monk. His monastic order did not emphasize the importance of manual labor and agricultural endeavors. His wife, Katharina von Bora (1499-1552), however, was deeply shaped by life in the Cistercian abbey of Marienthron (Mary's Throne) and became an industrious businesswoman. She cultivated a large garden, brewed beer, bought fields around Wittenberg, and, with the help of many hands, provided for the increasing community gathering around the great Reformer.[69] Wittenberg was not a wine region, and thus wine had to come from elsewhere. The Luthers received wine as a wedding gift, and Martin Luther was paid for some of his preaching in Wittenberg in the form of wine. It is not surprising, then, that the Luthers had a substantial wine and beer cellar. Martin enjoyed wine daily and regularly expressed his love for good beer and wine. In a letter to his wife (July 1534) he muses: "You must wonder how long I am likely to stay, or rather how long you will get quit of me. . . . I keep thinking what good wine and beer I have at home, as well as a beautiful wife, or shall I say lord?"[70] Luther believed that wine was a wonderful gift of God and could bring a great sense of joy and comfort if drunk in moderation. He composed the hymn "A Mighty Fortress Is Our God" while drinking a glass of Rhine wine, on his way to Worms, in the wine tavern Zur Kanne in Oppenheim.[71] Luther had labeled monks "fleas on the fur coat of the Almighty"; unfortunately, he did not consider that some of these monks were also responsible for the lovely wines in the wine cellar that he enjoyed so much.

Luther, like some of the church fathers, had to deal with emerging voices in the Reformation that wanted to forbid the drinking of wine altogether. In typical Luther fashion, he made his point simply but clearly:

> Wine and women bring sorrow and heartbreak, they make a fool of many and bring madness, ought we therefore to pour away the wine and kill all the women? Not so. Gold and silver, money and possessions bring much evil among the people, should we therefore throw it all away? If we want to eliminate our closest enemy, the one that is most harmful to us, we would have to kill ourselves. We have no more harmful enemy than our own heart.[72]

Luther's pastoral insight is significant. He realized the problem does not lie with wine itself but with those who abuse God's good gifts. He also fiercely defended the use of wine in the Eucharist. At the same time, in continuity with Scripture and tradition, he severely condemned both gluttony and drunkenness.

Paul Gerhardt, one of the most important hymn writers of the Lutheran tradition, praised God's good creation in his hymn "Go Forth, My Heart, and Seek Delight." He encouraged the believers to seek out delight and joy intentionally in God's creation. In stanza six he exclaims:

> The strong juice of the vine each hour
> Is ever gaining strength and pow'r
> This glorious summer weather.[73]

In another hymn he muses:

> From hill-sides like a river
> Will wine and oil flow ever.[74]

The Lutherans enjoyed their wines, treasured by them as a gift of God, and gave expression to their gratitude in poetry, hymns, and spiritual writings. When John Wesley (1703-1791), the great founder of Methodism, first heard German Pietists sing Gerhardt's hymns on a boat to the Americas, he was entranced by their beauty and profound theology and began translating them into English.

Wesley was raised in the Anglican tradition, had a profound appreciation for the Eucharist, and used wine for its celebration. In his hymn "Author of Life Divine," he reflects:

> Author of Life Divine,
> Who hast a Table spread,
> Furnish'd with Mystic Wine
> And Everlasting Bread.[75]

Wesley discouraged his followers from consuming distilled beverages unless prescribed by a doctor, and he abhorred immoderate behavior, including drunkenness.[76]

The stance of John Calvin (1509-1564) toward wine was no different from that of Luther. While he is often thought of as a severe personality, his reflections on wine provide a rather different picture. In his *Institutes of the Christian Religion,* he muses: "And we have never been forbidden to laugh, or to be filled, . . . or to delight in musical harmony, or to drink wine."[77] He had a deep appreciation for creation and emphasized the importance of taking delight in it:

> Now if we ponder to what end God created food, we shall find that he meant not only to provide for necessity but also for delight and good cheer. . . . In grasses, trees, and fruits, apart from their various uses, there is beauty of appearance and pleasantness of odor [cf. Gen. 2:9]. For if this were not true, the prophet would not have reckoned them among the benefits of God, "that wine gladdens the heart of man, that oil makes his face shine" [Ps. 104:15]. Scripture would not have reminded us repeatedly, in commending his kindness, that he gave all such things to men.[78]

It is obvious that Calvin was not timid in embracing and enjoying the gifts of creation. He advocated drinking wine not only because it was a necessary source of liquid at the time but also for merriment, conviviality, and the experience of joy. It is worth quoting him at some length from his commentary on Psalm 104:15:

> In these words we are taught, that God not only provides for men's necessity, and bestows upon them as much as is sufficient for the ordinary purposes of life, but that in his goodness he deals still more bountifully with them by cheering their hearts with wine and oil. Nature would certainly be satisfied with water to drink; and therefore the addition of wine is owing to God's superabundant liberality. . . . Bread would be sufficient to support the life of man, but God over and above . . . bestows upon them wine and oil. . . . God shows himself a foster-father sufficiently bountiful in providing bread, his liberality appears still more conspicuous in giving us dainties. . . . As the prophet in this account of the divine goodness in providence makes no reference to the excesses of men, we gather from his words that it is lawful to use wine not only in cases of necessity, but also thereby to make us merry.[79]

For Calvin, the gift of wine reveals to us a remarkably extravagant and generous God. We experience God's goodness and care when we drink wine in moderation. It can deepen our sense of joy, gratitude, and wonder in our loving Father. Wine should "exhilarate" our minds toward a deeper sense of gratitude and spur us on in our service of God.[80]

Calvin firmly believed that it was unbiblical to forbid drinking wine under the pretext of preventing drunkenness. He called it an "inhuman philosophy" and believed that such "a malignant notion deprives us of the lawful enjoyment of God's kindness."[81] Calvin's concern was that the gifts of God should not be withheld but enjoyed in accordance with God's purposes. God has bountifully provided for us that we might not "voraciously devour his benefits" but to eat and drink so that "it may sustain, but not oppress us." Those who have bounty in life are to share with those in need.[82] For Calvin, abstinence will not protect us from abuse, but true gratitude toward God will.[83] He condemned the abuse of wine — just as Luther did — and upheld a life of moderation as the Christian ideal.[84]

It was quite common during Calvin's time for a minister to receive part of his income and gifts in the form of wine, and the town council of Geneva was certainly not stingy in providing generous allotments of wine for Calvin and his ministry of hospitality. John McNeill estimates that Calvin's allotment was "perhaps 250 gallons" annually.[85]

Like Luther, Calvin affirms that wine was to be used in the Eucharist. For Calvin, the physical, emotional, and spiritual benefits of wine parallel the benefits of Christ's blood for the soul. He argues: "By wine the hearts of men are gladdened, their strength recruited, and the whole man strengthened, so by the blood of our Lord the same benefits are received by our souls."[86] It is important to notice that Calvin singles out joy and strength as two important benefits of the Eucharist. The mark of the Christian life is a life of joy and gratitude directed toward God, our Creator and Redeemer.

John Knox and Ulrich Zwingli also affirmed wine as a gift from God, used it in the Eucharist, and condemned the abuse of it as a sin. Knox presumed in one of his writings that wine was drunk daily, and, just as in Geneva, wine was part of the Scottish minister's salary.[87] Zwingli even compared the word of God to "a good strong wine."[88]

The Reformers then, like the early church fathers, took a clear stance toward wine. In the face of emerging voices that wanted to forbid wine-drinking on biblical grounds, they affirmed wine as a gift from God to be enjoyed in everyday life and to be used in the Eucharist, and they condemned the abuse of wine or any of God's other gifts as a sin. As discerning theologians, they understood that the church has no right to forbid what God has sanctioned to be a gift and delight for humanity. In rethinking how the Christian life was to be lived and practiced, they wholly affirmed God as the generous and loving Creator who delights in bestowing gifts on his children, which make their hearts glad and their souls sing.

The early Puritans also enjoyed their wines, though the primary drinks of the English were beer and ale. There must have been a rather substantial wine-growing tradition in England during the Middle Ages, but it is difficult to reconstruct how much wine was grown and available for the peasant population during the various stages of the medieval period.[89] Imported wines from France, Germany, and Italy seem to have been mostly reserved for the British king and his court, the army, and, of course, the monks. Older Bordeaux wines, however, were sold off cheaply, and peasants may well have been able to afford them once the new wine had arrived on the market.

William Perkins (1558-1602), one the earliest Puritans, seems to have frequented the ale taverns quite often during his studies. He had the reputation of a drunkard before he experienced a religious awakening. The English, like the Germans, were known to be heavy drinkers. During the sixteenth and seventeenth centuries, as the influence of the church on society waned, the ale taverns took a more important role in society, and their numbers increased significantly.[90] The Puritans fought against the alehouses and the excessive drinking culture that went along with them. Perkins, once he came to his senses, did not reject alcohol altogether, and he did drink the wine served during the Eucharist.

John Bunyan (1628-1688) also affirmed wine as a gift from God. In his classic account of the Christian life, *The Pilgrim's Progress,* the protagonist, Christian, drinks wine as he meditates on Christ: "Now the table was furnished with fat things, and with wine that was well refined; and all their talk at the table was about the Lord of the Hill; as, namely, about what he had done, and whereof he did what he did. . . ."[91] When Christian finds himself in the valley of humiliation, a kind companion gives him "a loaf of bread, a bottle of wine, and a cluster of raisins. . . ."[92] When Bunyan paints a vision of the land of redemption, named Beulah, after Isaiah 62:4, the pilgrims discover that it is planted with beautiful vineyards, orchards, and gardens, just as the Promised Land was portrayed in the Old Testament. The pilgrims ask the gardener to whom they belong, and he responds, "They are the King's, and are planted here for his own delight, and also for the solace of pilgrims."[93] Bunyan, like the Reformers before him, emphasizes that wine brings delight and comfort to pilgrims. And just as the prophets of the Old Testament envision God's future redemption in terms of an abundance of grain and wine, so does Bunyan envision the country of Beulah as a place where there is "no want of corn and wine."[94] Bunyan's fictional story reflects his Puritan historical context. For example, when a group of English Puritans set sail in 1630 for Boston, they had ten thousand gallons of wine and three times more beer than water on their ship.[95]

New Frontiers: Wine in the Americas

The English Puritans, just like the French Huguenots and the German Pietists, affirmed wine as a gift from God and were eager to plant vines once they had arrived in the Americas. As early as 1524, explorers praised the rich growth of wild vines in North Carolina.[96] The French Huguenots are the first group that is mentioned as making wine in Florida in the middle of the sixteenth century (pp. 94-102). The abundance of wild vines in the Americas inspired the English imagination with visions of Eden and economic independence from France and Spain (pp. 12-13). The attempts on the eastern coast to make wine from the wild vines failed, however, and European vines *(Vitis vinifera)* were unable to grow in that climate because the intense humidity made the vines susceptible to fungus diseases, rots, insects, and bacterial infection. By the end of the seventeenth century, the hopes of making wine on the eastern coast of America had mostly disappeared, though new attempts were made repeatedly (pp. 24-25, 37, 54). The German Pietists began planting vineyards in Pennsylvania and North Carolina in the eighteenth century and were noted to be "especially anxious to advance the cultivation of the vine" (p. 103; see also pp. 62, 102). German Protestant refugees from the famous wine region of the Rheingau, called "Palatines," were also sent to grow wine in the Americas in the early eighteenth century (pp. 103-4). But their attempts also failed — due to the same difficult weather conditions. As a result, because wine had to be imported from Europe, it became a drink of the upper class. The cheapest alcoholic beverages available in the New World were rum and later whiskey, and the sociological impact of that reality would be severe.[97]

More attempts at planting vines were made before a wine industry finally began to be established after the American Revolution — primarily by Germans and French — in the early nineteenth century. Vineyards were grown as far west as western Indiana along the Wabash River, north around New York City, including on Long Island, and in the Finger Lakes region of northern New York state (Pinney, chaps. 5–8).

The Reformed theologian Jonathan Edwards (1703-1758) understood wine to be one of God's gifts and, if drunk in moderation, to be beneficial for the spiritual life and for physical well-being. In a letter to his daughter Esther, who suffered from stomach pains, he recommended that she try a recipe using ginseng stewed "in wine, in good Madeira or claret; or if these wines are too harsh, then in some good white wine. . . . And for a cordial take some spices steeped in some generous wine that suits your taste, and stomach."[98]

Thomas Jefferson (1743-1826) was a great wine enthusiast and became a patron and promoter of American wine and — more generally speaking — agriculture. He said that "no nation is drunken where wine is cheap," and he believed that agriculture was a God-given vocation.[99] For him, it was "the employment of our first parents in Eden, the happiest we can follow, and the most important to our country."[100] His five-year stay in France (1784-1789) and his visits to French and German wine regions must have taught him how important wine is in society for the development of a healthy and constructive relationship with alcohol. He firmly believed that wine, rather than abstinence, was the key: "No nation is . . . sober, where the dearness of wine substitutes ardent spirits as the common beverage. It is, in truth, the only antidote to the bane of whiskey."[101] Recent studies on alcohol dependence in the European Union seem to confirm this (see chap. 9 below).

The development of viticulture in the Americas became crucial for the survival of viticulture in Europe. A plant louse, native to America and now famous under the name phylloxera, was accidentally brought into Europe in the mid-nineteenth century. It nearly destroyed all viticulture in Europe. It was only by vintners' grafting a rootstock from a different vine species (which was imported from America and thus immune to phylloxera) to European vines that viticulture in Europe survived this devastating blow (Pinney, pp. 27-28).

The western coast of the Americas had a different story. Because this region was under the dominion of Spain, it was the Jesuit and later Franciscan monks who developed viticulture in Spanish California, though non–*Vitis vinifera* vines had been grown before their arrival. Desmond Seward argues that their experience was an exact repetition of what happened with the monastic expansion in Gaul during the Dark Ages. Inspired by the crafting of wine for the Eucharist and then for their everyday tables, they were finally followed and succeeded by secular wine growers.[102]

The Jesuits began to establish missions and develop viticulture in colonial New Mexico as early as 1590, and they expanded to lower Spanish California. In 1767 the Jesuit order was banished from Spain and its colonies, and the Jesuits handed over their mission to the Franciscans. Once the Spanish government decided to settle northern California, the Franciscan friars were ready and founded a new mission in San Diego in 1769. It was one of these brave Franciscan monks who brought the Christian faith and viticulture to the Bay Area, founding San Francisco de Asis in 1776. Twenty-one mission stations were eventually founded from there, the most northern one being San Francisco de Solano in the Sonoma Valley (1823).[103] They grew European vines (from the *Vitis vinifera* grapes), and the conditions were much more suitable than those of the eastern Americas, with which the Franciscan monks had no contact.

California today is a flourishing wine-growing region, and we should not forget that it was Franciscan friars who first established and developed viticulture in northern California. These brave friars followed the Rule of Saint Francis (1181-1226), one of the great reformers of European monasticism. Their devotion to a life of poverty was balanced with a deep appreciation for God's good creation. Saint Francis himself wrote in his *Canticle of the Sun*: "Be praised, my Lord, through our sister Mother Earth, who feeds us and rules us, and produces various fruits with colored flowers and herbs."[104] Saint Francis's vision of the Christian life was profoundly shaped by his creation spirituality, a life deeply embedded in God's creation and a desire to live in harmony with it.

Those Spanish Franciscan friars were a living witness to the tradition of Saint Francis as they developed viticulture in California and crafted wine for the Eucharist. A German traveler tasted the wine at the Mission San Jose in 1806 and noted that the wine is "sweet, and resembles Malaga," a rather impressive compliment (Pinney, p. 243). When Thomas Jefferson on the East Coast envisioned America as a new Eden and desired to make it into a wine-growing nation, he had no clue that Spanish California was on its way to becoming just that: a land where vines could grow in abundance and the hills could overflow with choice wine.

The success of these Franciscan friars, however, was short-lived. Mexico became an independent empire in 1821, and in 1833 the Mexican government decided to secularize all religious houses. By 1837 all missions were dissolved. Soon lay vintners took their place and continued to develop viticulture in California.[105] Surviving both secularization and Americanization, California viticulture blossomed into a thriving business with significant economic force (Pinney, p. 238). It had all the potential of becoming one of the leading wine producers on the world market. Though the development of viticulture in California experienced some severe blows, including the vicious phylloxera, by the beginning of the twentieth century, California was producing 45 million gallons of wine per year; it had doubled its production within a decade (p. 363). With the newly opened Panama Canal, all obstacles were removed for California to become a significant player in the world wine trade. Unfortunately, at the height of its success, its collapse was already dawning: the ratification of the Eighteenth Amendment to the American Constitution on January 16,

1919, which came into effect on January 16, 1920, forbade the production, consumption, importation, and exportation of intoxicating liquors in the United States of America (Pinney, pp. 1-3).[106] The impact of the American Prohibition on viticulture was devastating.

Prohibition was in effect for only fourteen years, but its impact on North American culture, including viticulture, has been profound, lasting to this day. How could this happen? One of the reasons was the failure to develop a significant wine-growing culture on the eastern coast of the Americas, which resulted in the predominance of distilled spirits as the cheapest alcoholic beverages — and their production increased rapidly. In 1792, according to temperance historian Daniel Dorchester, the United States had 2,579 distilleries; by 1810 there were 14,191 distilleries operating.[107] Distilled spirits, rather than wine, became the social drink of the lower classes and became a popular drink at funerals, ordinations, and military and political events. It is important to note that, at its beginnings, the temperance movement was not directed against wine and beer but against the unbridled use of distilled spirits. John Wesley had already recommended that his followers stay away from distilled spirits unless needed for medical reasons. With the abuse of distilled spirits becoming more prominent in the beginning of the nineteenth century, the temperance movement gained momentum and established an organized temperance society in the Americas in 1826. The great American revivals, including the Second Great Awakening, took up the cause of the temperance movement. The revivals made it part of their reform program, which focused on personal conversion and the moral perfection of individuals. The revival culture had many adherents among Presbyterians, Methodists, and Baptists, and it became a vast and powerful religious (Protestant) movement that deeply shaped the religious and cultural landscape of North America. While the original apostles of the temperance movement treasured their wines, increasingly shrill voices emerged that called for complete abstinence from intoxicating liquors.[108] Slowly but surely, all alcoholic beverages, including wine, came to be seen as evil, and abstinence from any alcohol, including wine, was elevated to the level of a superior mark of Christian spirituality. A crowning work of Prohibition propaganda was the depiction of the "serpent wine chalice," in which the use of wine in the Eucharist was damned as a work of the evil serpent.[109]

Thomas Welch, a Methodist minister turned dentist, discovered how to remove yeast bacteria in grape juice that naturally transforms grape juice into wine; that is, by removing or killing yeast bacteria, one can keep grape juice from fermenting. Welch's discovery made it possible to use grape juice, rather than wine, in the Lord's Supper. While monks had worked hard at refining the art of crafting good wine to the glory of God, Thomas Welch became a "counter apostle" who invented the art of unmaking wine, working against the rhythm of God's creation. While the Benedictine vision of the Christian life involved God, his community of people, and their working of the land, the emerging evangelical culture of the late nineteenth century focused on the salvation of the individual and the pursuit of one's moral perfection. With the absence of wine from the Eucharist, the antiseptic effect of alcohol disappeared from the communion cup. As a consequence, and for hygienic reasons, grape juice began to be served in individual cups, which helped deepen the emphasis on the formation of the individual. Drinking from the common chalice emphasized the communal nature of the spiritual life and helped symbolize that the believers are one in Christ, and the individual grape juice cups could no longer capture this important aspect of the Lord's Supper.

While Christians had had an instrumental role in developing and refining viticulture in Europe, Britain, and the Americas, it was also Christians who played a significant role in unmaking the emerging wine culture of North America. However, I should note that this unmaking was the work of a very particular though powerful Protestant movement. Catholics, Episcopalians, and Lutherans did not subscribe to this teaching. Prohibition in America, the result of complex cultural and political constellations, owes its birth in no small degree to this evangelical movement that had forgotten the voices of the church fathers and the great Reformers such as Martin Luther and John Calvin.

The consequences for American viticulture were devastating in multiple ways. The production of wine collapsed from 55 million gallons of wine in 1919 to 3.6 million gallons of wine in 1925 (Pinney, p. 436). The economic loss was severe: exporting wine onto the world market was impossible and would be for decades to come. The development of viticulture stalled and is still in the process of recovery. High-quality wine is still very expensive in the United States and unaffordable for many Americans.

The cultural and spiritual loss was also immense. This collapse of the wine industry left the United States without the opportunity to develop a healthy relationship with alcohol in the twentieth century on a broad social scale.

Many vintners in the United States have not been given the opportunity to discover and consider the rich relationship between wine and the Christian faith. Crafting wine is a remarkable spiritual experience, as vintners eagerly attest; however, little to no theological reflection is available to deepen their understanding of what they experience year in and year out in the vineyards, the cellar, and finally in the bottle. How the combination of sun, rain, soil, and vines can produce such a delightful liquid remains to this day a great mystery and should leave us in awe and wonder. It is this awe and wonder, delight and joy that we need to recover and give back to the church as an important way to foster a biblical and holistic Christian spirituality.

Concluding Reflections

The history of wine in the church shows that there once was a deep connection between the life of the church, the cultivation of the land in the form of viticulture, and the enjoyment of wine. Unlike grains and water, wine is not a necessity for human survival. Wine is a lavish and extraordinary gift to humanity. The biblical account and the great theologians of the church have always upheld wine as a very special gift from God that has specific roles in our spiritual lives.

The rejection of wine during the British and American temperance movement of the nineteenth century, and the secularization of Europe resulting in a split between the church and the land, have made us forget how important wine once was for the life of the church, both in the Lord's Supper and in Christian celebrations more generally. Over the course of the next chapters we shall continue to explore the spiritual benefits of wine and show how important it is to recover the connection that exists between the church and the land, between God's gifts of creation and the spiritual life. In the next chapter we shall consider the role of wine in the Lord's Supper and what this might reveal about a decidedly Christian understanding of the spirituality of wine.

3

Wine in the Lord's Supper:
Christ Present in Wine

*"For I received from the Lord what I also handed on to you, that
the Lord Jesus on the night when he was betrayed took a loaf of
bread, and when he had given thanks, he broke it and said, 'This
is my body that is broken for you. Do this in remembrance of
me.' In the same way he took the cup also, after supper, saying,
'This cup is the new covenant in my blood. Do this, as often as
you drink it, in remembrance of me.'"*

1 Corinthians 11:23-25

I n the Lord's Supper the spiritual benefits of wine become clear. All Christian denominations understand the Lord's Supper as a sacrament. The Lord's Supper is a more constant part of Christian life and worship than are other sacraments, such as baptism. While some denominations celebrate the Eucharist daily, others celebrate it weekly, monthly, or bimonthly. The Lord's Supper is an important Christian ritual that is set apart from ordinary life — but not over against it. In its elevated role it works toward the transformation of our ordinary lives. What we receive in the celebration of the Lord's Supper is meant to overflow into our daily lives and saturate our mundane living with the love and grace of God.

In what follows we shall explore the meaning of the Lord's Supper, in which bread and wine assume an important role. For nearly two thousand years the church has faithfully entered into this great mystery as an integral part of its worship. What is the meaning of the Eucharist in Christian worship? Why is wine used, and what is the theological significance of it?

The Lord's Supper is celebrated on Sundays, when the church gathers for worship. In Christian worship, as God's people, we hear and obey God's word and participate in the sacrament of the Lord's Supper. God's gift of salvation in and through the life, suffering, death, and resurrection of Jesus Christ is at the heart of all we do as Christians. In the Eucharist we receive the forgiveness of our sins and the gift of eternal life. It is in the gathered community of the church that we celebrate, live, and practice this gift of eternal life. This gift of grace (from the Greek *charis:* "favor, good will") comes to us not as an abstract idea or a mere intellectual pursuit. We have to receive it in faith as we gather as God's people, hear the word preached, and participate in the communal eating of bread and drinking of wine. Salvation becomes an embodied and communal experience.

In and through the celebration of the sacraments the grace of Christ becomes manifest in our lives so that all of life might become saturated with God's grace. The sacrament of baptism (from the Greek *baptisma:* "washing") is the rite of entry, where God and his people receive us into Christ's church. We receive the forgiveness of our sins, as God restores our relationship with him and with one another. The Eucharist (from the Greek *eucharistia:* "giving thanks") is the sacrament that sustains our Christian life. In the Lord's Supper, God continues to forgive our sins, comfort our sorrows, and transform our despair into the new hope we have in Christ's promise of eternal life. The Eucharist sustains the Christian pilgrim on this journey of eternal life. It is a life fully anchored on earth but oriented toward its consummation in the future, when Christ will return to judge and renew the earth and all its living creatures. But what is the theological significance of wine in the Eucharist?

The Eucharist: A Communal and Embodied Experience

Scripture encourages us to see Christ at work in all spheres of life and teaches us that Christ meets us in other people, especially those in need (Matt. 25). One particular place we are to look for and anticipate his presence is as we celebrate the Lord's Supper. Christ meets us in the gathered community of the church. By his word and the Holy Spirit, he blesses and sanctifies the offerings we bring in bread and wine. Christ brings to us not only the benefits of his work on the cross but his living presence in the celebration of the Lord's Supper. We receive spiritual sustenance through our physical and communal sharing in the Eucharist, by walking to the altar to stand or kneel, by opening our hands and our mouths to receive the physical matter of bread and wine. We chew, we taste, we listen, and we swallow. We digest. The Lord's Supper, central to our lives as Christians, is a wholly physical and communal experience. It calls on our mind, our senses, and our imagination to receive Christ and his work on the cross as a living presence in bread and wine, the fruit of the very earth that God made. This is a profoundly embodied and thus sensual experience and anchors our spirituality in creation. Christ modeled this for us: God took on human form in Jesus Christ and reconciled the world to himself by embracing creation. The earth has become his dwelling place, first in Jesus Christ incarnate (taking on human form), then in bread and wine and, as we eat and drink it, also among and in us. This is a great mystery.

It is a mystery that was offensive from the inception of the church. When outsiders first heard of Christians consuming Christ's body, they accused them of cannibalism.[1] First of all, drinking blood was an abomination in a Jewish mindset.[2] Furthermore, it was an offense to Gnostics, and their teaching has influenced Western Christendom to this day. Gnostics taught that matter is of little spiritual value; therefore, in order to mature spiritually, one has to remove oneself from created matter and transcend to a "higher" spiritual plane.[3] This dualistic understanding of the life of faith has haunted talk of the "spiritual" ever since and sees a deep divide between matter and spirit, the physical and the spiritual.

The Judeo-Christian faith has always held that God not only created this good world but also chose to manifest his glory in it. He reveals himself in and through creation and not apart from it. Creation and its materiality are a gift of God. The Lord's Supper is a defense against lingering Gnostic heresies with their strong tendency to devalue creation. Instead, it firmly anchors our life of faith in creation, upholding that God meets us in physical matter and our embodied and communal lives. As we bring ourselves, including our bodies, and as we bring the fruits of the earth in bread and wine (which includes our participation in labor and creativity in its production), God sanctifies them and meets us in bread and wine.[4] The fact that we bring ourselves together with bread and wine to God in the Lord's Supper and that we receive Christ in bread and wine solidifies our close kinship with creation in the world of salvation. Just as the Israelites offered the first fruits in gratitude for the land (Deut. 26:1-11), so God calls us to bring bread and wine with a deep sense of gratitude for the gift of the land and its fruit.[5]

The mark of a decidedly Christian understanding of the life of faith, then, is not a flight from creation and its physicality but a faith-filled embrace of it. We must trust that God is in the process of redeeming all of creation. The elements of bread and wine are therefore not "secular" matter, but, as fruits of God's good creation, are also spiritual realities. And the vintner and the baker deal with profoundly spiritual matter. Grains and grapes exist because God said, "Let the earth put forth vegetation: plants yielding seed, and fruit trees of every kind on earth that bear fruit with the seed in it" (Gen. 1:12; see also Gen. 1:29). Yeasts, key to making both bread and wine, are living and active fungi organisms. They transform grape juice into wine (and thus keep grape juice from spoiling), and they turn flour into edible bread. These living microorganisms, though invisible to the human eye, are invested with potent power to transform created matter. As such, they are gifts created by God. He lavishly placed these living micro-organisms into the world's atmosphere and continues to uphold them with love and care so that the fruit of the earth can become food for humanity.

In the Lord's Supper, then, we encounter Christ, the Creator and Redeemer. In it the bond between the spiritual and physical is experienced and practiced. Therefore, the Eucharist not only shapes and informs our renewed relationship with God and one another but also our renewed relationship with creation in general. It must now inform the way we view bread, wine, and the land as gifts from God to be treasured, respected, and handled with dignity and fidelity. The Eucharist must inform the way we treat and handle these things in practice.

While there were many disputes about the celebration of the Eucharist during the Reformation, the great Reformers Martin Luther and John Calvin continued to affirm the importance of the weekly celebration of the Lord's Supper. Traditionally, the Eucharist was celebrated at least weekly, and it was central to Christian worship.[6] With the Reformation, however, many different voices emerged, and the Lord's Supper became a place of theological dispute. As a consequence and over time, in some Protestant traditions it lost this central place and tended to be confined to the margins.[7]

Martin Luther, a strong defender of Christ's real presence in the Lord's Supper, argues this way:

God is in this flesh. It is God's flesh, the Spirit's flesh. It is in God and God is in it. Therefore it lives and gives life to all who eat it, both to their bodies and to their souls. . . . As we eat him he abides in us and we in him. For he is not digested or transformed but ceaselessly he transforms us, our soul into righteousness, our body into immortality.[8]

Luther's understanding of the human person seems to hold to a deep intrinsic relationship between body and soul. He continues to argue: "[T]he mouth, the throat, the body, which eats Christ's body, will also have its benefit in that it will live forever and arise on the Last Day to eternal salvation. This is the secret power and benefit which flows from the body of Christ in the Supper into our body, for it must be useful and cannot be present in vain. Therefore, it must bestow life and salvation upon our bodies, as is its nature."[9]

John Calvin believed that bread and wine have a rich symbolic function, representing to the believer the body and blood of Christ. He also emphasizes the vital link between ingesting physical and spiritual food. Calvin writes: "[S]ince, however, this mystery of Christ's secret union with the devout is by nature incomprehensible, he shows its figure and image in visible signs best adapted to our small capacity. . . . For this very familiar comparison penetrates into even the dullest minds: just as bread and wine sustain physical life, so are souls fed by Christ."[10] Both Reformers emphasized the physical and embodied nature of the Lord's Supper and that our grasp of spiritual realities is profoundly tied to created matter.

The Background of the Passover Meal

The Passover Meal

This physical and material understanding of Christian spirituality in the Lord's Supper is deepened as we consider its background among the Hebrews. When Christ first celebrated what we now call the Eucharist with his disciples, he did so in the context of the Passover meal (Matt. 26:17-29; Mark 14:12-26; Luke 22:14-20; John 13:1-4).[11] The Hebrew Passover meal commemorates and reenacts the historical event of the Exodus of God's people out of bondage in Egypt (Exod. 12:3-6). It is called the feast of Passover (from the Hebrew *pesaḥ*:

"passing over"), referring to God's "passing over" the houses of the children of Israel with his judgment and delivering them in his mercy (Exod. 12:7-13, 26-27). The Israelites were instructed to slaughter a lamb and mark their doorposts with its blood; the blood on the doorpost functioned as a sign for God to bypass the homes of the Israelite people. The smearing of the blood on the doorpost became a sign of one's faith in God's mercy.[12]

In the book of Exodus, God's people were commanded to commemorate and to observe this historic event as a statute with the Passover meal, not just for a time but for all times. They were given detailed instructions that included slaughtering and roasting the lamb, and eating it with unleavened bread and bitter herbs (Exod. 12:8). By the time of Jesus' ministry in first-century Judaism, the Passover celebrations had developed and included the drinking of four cups of wine. We cannot really reconstruct when wine was introduced to the Passover meal, but in the book of Jubilees, written in about 120 BC, wine is already presupposed as an old custom.[13] Each cup had a special role in retelling and reenacting the story of the Exodus. Abraham Bloch argues that the drinking of the four cups of wine was spaced in such a way as to produce joy but prevent drunkenness. The fact that a people not generally given to drunkenness are instructed to drink four cups of wine is unusual and, according to Bloch, highlights the extraordinary character of the Passover meal.[14] Wine, the fruit of the Promised Land — and enjoyed in the context of the Passover meal — became an important means by which Jewish pilgrims have lived into gratitude and joy for God's salvation from slavery and misery.

The annual celebration of the Passover meal was to be a memorial in the form of a feast for God's people (Exod. 12:14). This act of remembrance is not a mere mental recalling of ideas, dates, and moral values. Rather, it is a communal and embodied celebration that reenacts the events of the Exodus in the elaborate liturgy and festivity of the Passover meal. Through this festive reenactment, the celebrants receive anew God's saving presence in their midst. Bloch argues that this celebration is meant to keep alive the memory of the great struggle against slavery in Egypt. Celebrants do this via the physical taste of the bitter herbs; they remember God's mighty act of delivering his people from slavery by chewing and swallowing unleavened bread; and the celebration instills a great sense of gratitude and joy for the gift of deliverance by means of the literal tasting and drinking of the wine.[15] The slaughtered lamb is a sign of God's covenant with his people and thus frames the whole celebration.

The Passover meal is a wholly physical, embodied, and communal experience. Eating and tasting the bitter herbs, chewing the lamb, and drinking the wine call on the whole of the physical person to engage in this act of remembrance. There is no room given to develop a spirituality that defies creation and the importance of the human body for spiritual formation.

The Passover meal ends with prayers of praise and thanksgiving *(hallēl)*, in which Psalms 113–118 are sung. Then the fourth cup of wine is drunk and a brief prayer of thanksgiving completes the celebration: "Blessed art Thou, Lord our God, King of the universe, Creator of the fruit of the vine." In Israelite spirituality, the God who redeems and the God who creates and provides is recognized, named, and worshiped in the liturgy of the Passover meal. This last cup of the meal is traditionally called the "Cup of Elijah." It anticipates the coming of the prophet Elijah and emphasizes the season of watchful waiting (Exod. 12:42).[16] By the time of Jesus' birth, the Passover had come to be invested with increasing eschatological hopes. God's people were by then living under Roman rule and once again had the expectation that God would send an anointed one to redeem his people. They were yearning for a new exodus, an exodus that would deliver them from Roman oppression.

The Eucharist and the Passover Meal

In the celebration of the Passover meal Christ takes the place reserved for Elijah and fulfills God's purposes.[17] Just as God delivered his people from oppression in Egypt and called them forth to become his people in the Promised Land, so does God promise to deliver his people from sin and bondage through Jesus Christ. Both acts of deliverance involved a sacrifice and the shedding of blood. In the Exodus, the Israelites were instructed to slaughter a lamb; in the Lord's Supper we look to Christ himself, who became the sacrifice for us, "the lamb of God who takes away the sin of the world" (John 1:29). In Christ a new exodus happened, and a new covenant marks God's faithfulness toward his people.[18] Saint Paul calls Christ the "paschal lamb" (1 Cor. 5:7), and for him the eucharistic cup marks a new covenant sealed with Christ's blood (1 Cor. 11:25).

Just as the Israelites were instructed to celebrate the Passover meal as an act of remembrance, so does Jesus instruct his disciples to celebrate this Last

Supper as an act of remembrance. Jesus' celebration of the Last Supper includes prayers of thanksgiving; and as the Passover meal of the first century had strong eschatological overtones — the Israelites yearning for the coming of the Messiah to deliver his people — so does Jesus impress on his disciples that the Lord's Supper will find its consummation only in the future: "Truly I tell you, I will never again drink of the fruit of the vine until that day when I drink it anew in the kingdom of God" (Mark 14:25).

The commemoration of God's redemption in Jesus Christ becomes a primary way by which Christians live into this reality. We have briefly mentioned that the Hebrew-Christian understanding of "Do this in remembrance of me" is very different from a mere recalling of a historical fact and theological dogmas and morals.[19] The act of remembrance (from the Greek: *anamnēsis*, "remembering") is not a mere recalling of an event in the past but an active participation in God's faithful presence in the Lord's Supper. In this celebration Christ and the Holy Spirit continue to minister to us the benefits of Christ's death on the cross. In the sacrament of the Lord's Supper we recall God's faithful action in the past and thereby receive the benefits of the cross from God himself, who is present with us.

The Lord's Supper becomes a place where we cease to strive and we learn to receive the person of Jesus Christ, the forgiveness of our sins, and eternal life. Our spiritual and embodied journey to the altar, and the opening of our hands and our mouths to receive the elements, instill in us the important fact that the Christian life is given to us. This is something that Christ does and will continue to work within us until the end of days. We eat Christ's body and drink his blood. As we take into ourselves his living presence, he mysteriously forms and grows his very own life in us personally and communally. And as we commune with Christ in the Lord's Supper, we are being transformed by his very presence. The Christian life cannot be imposed from without. It has to grow from within through the very dear and real presence of Jesus Christ (John 15:4-10).

The very word "Eucharist" (from the Greek: *eucharisteō*, "giving thanks") emphasizes that one primary response to this gift of grace is thanksgiving. We give thanks for Christ, who sacrificed himself for us. The Eucharist, like Passover, involved a sacrifice, and it is for this sacrifice that we give thanks. And when congregants understand the role of sacrifice, the spiritual significance of wine in the Eucharist becomes apparent.

Sacrifice, Blood, and Wine

Sacrifice and Blood

The story of the Fall of man in Genesis tells us that sin came into the world and separated humanity from its Creator. From the beginning, God's initiative in reconciling to himself this fallen world involved a sacrifice, physical matter. While there were many different sacrifices for different purposes, such as thanksgiving and repentance (see the book of Leviticus), all of these sacrifices were meant to create life-giving communication between humanity and God and to allow God's people to enter into the divine fullness of life. One specific purpose was the forgiveness of sin, and this usually involved the sacrifice of an animal. As priests slaughtered the animal and shed its blood over the altar, God forgave sin and reconciled humanity to himself. Humans, however, were never to consume any of this blood. The first instance of the prohibition to consume blood is found when God makes a covenant with Noah after the Flood (Gen. 9:4).[20] It is remarkable that this covenant is not just between God and Noah and his descendants but also includes "every living creature that is with [Noah], the birds, the domestic animals, and every animal of the earth with you" (Gen. 9:10). God's redemption from the very beginning includes the nonhuman world. While God pronounces all living creatures and plants to be gifts of food for Noah and his descendants, they are under no circumstance to consume the blood of the animals (Gen. 9:4). Noah is the first to learn this. Noah is also the first to plant a vineyard (Gen. 9:20), though the connection between blood and wine will only become apparent later in the Hebrew narrative.

In the Hebrew mindset, blood is the center of life, both literally and metaphorically. It becomes a symbol of life that has its origin in God and thus belongs to God alone.[21] Blood is seen as the carrier of life and the seat of the human soul (Gen. 9:4; Lev. 17:11; Deut. 12:23).[22] For this reason it is set apart and not to be consumed by humans. In light of this Hebrew understanding of blood, Jesus' instructions at the Last Supper to drink "my blood of the covenant" (Matt. 26:26-28) seem offensive and in radical disjunction with a Hebrew understanding of blood and sacrifice.

Blood and Wine

The close association between blood and wine goes back to antiquity and is not unique to the Hebrew/Christian worldview. In antiquity much of the wine produced around the Mediterranean was red wine. Pliny the Elder mentions both red and white, but red seems to have dominated.[23] It is difficult to reconstruct why exactly blood and wine came to be so closely associated with one another.

Ben Sira wrote that "wine is very life to humans"; indeed, wine had an important role to play and tremendous value in Jewish life — both culturally and economically.[24] Wine was believed to stimulate the blood-forming organs of the body, and the Greeks called wine "life" because of its healing powers.[25] As I have noted above, wine was a primary safe source of fluid at the time, sustaining human life in the face of unsafe water supplies. In contrast to water and the dangers of contamination, wine could also be stored for long periods of time.[26] Furthermore, it was used widely as an antiseptic in medical practices, since its alcohol content is high enough to kill most bacteria. The parallel identification of wine with blood seems also to have derived from its similarity in substance and texture. The deep red color and thick smooth texture of red wine easily lent itself to the analogy with blood. Not surprisingly, wine was spoken of synonymously with blood and drawn on to explore spiritual realities, not only in the Hebrew/Christian religion but also more broadly in the pagan religions that surrounded Israel.[27] Hebrew practices, however, were distinct from those of their pagan neighbors.[28]

The close association of wine and blood can be seen in several passages in the Old Testament. On the one hand, wine is spoken of as "the blood of the grape" and understood as a gift from God the Creator and as a sign of his blessing. God's blessing on his people will be apparent in an abundance of choice wine here on earth (Gen. 49:11; Deut. 32:14; Sir. 39:26). The potent metaphor of "the blood of the grape" suggests that, just as blood was seen as the center and carrier of life, so wine was seen as the "very life to humans," as Ben Sira put it. On the other hand, the spilling of blood is spoken of in terms of drinking of wine. In Isaiah, God judges those who oppress his people and predicts that "they shall be drunk with their own blood as with wine" (Isa. 49:26; see also Zech. 9:15). In both the Old Testament and the New Testament, God's judgment is at times seen in terms of the crushing of grapes in the winepress of God's wrath, where "blood flowed from the winepress" (Rev. 14:20). The wine-making process became a symbol of God's judgment (Joel 3:13; Isa. 63:2-6; Lam. 1:15; Rev. 14:19-20). Just as grapes must be crushed in the winepress in order to be turned into fine wine, so must human life come under God's judgment in order for redemption and new life to take place. Climactically, this close relationship between wine and blood is present in the Lord's Supper, where Christ offers to his disciples the cup of wine and proclaims it to be his very own blood: "This is my blood of the covenant which is poured out for many" (Mark 14:24 par.). Christ took upon himself God's judgment, and our participation in the Lord's Supper allows us to enter into this great mystery.

As we approach the spiritual meaning of wine in the Eucharist, we must keep these two dimensions in mind. On the one hand, wine is a gift from God's good creation and a sign of God's blessing upon his people. It makes glad the hearts of men and women and elicits joy (Ps. 104:15). In the traditional celebration of the Eucharist the gratitude for God's good creation is explicitly expressed in the liturgy: "Blessed are you, Lord God of all creation, for through your goodness we have received the wine we offer you: fruit of the vine and work of human hands, it will become our spiritual drink. Blessed be God for ever." The vine and grapes are often seen as the best of creation in the Old Testament. The grape cluster that the scouts bring back from the Promised Land becomes a primary motif that this land is indeed blessed by God (Num. 13:21-27). As we consume the eucharistic wine, we are reminded that Christ the Redeemer is also Christ the Creator, and we eat and drink with deep gratitude, knowing that everything we consume is a gift from God. Wine then draws us into a more intentional appreciation of creation as a precious gift of God.

On the other hand, the drinking of wine in the Lord's Supper draws us into the world of sacrifice.[29] It is here that the spiritual meaning of wine takes on multiple facets that offer rich reflections for Christian life and practice. Just as grapes must be gathered, crushed, and turned into fine wine through the miracle of fermentation, so must human life come under the loving judgment of God. Our relationship with God, each other, and the rest of creation is broken and fractured. God's judgment, sometimes represented by the metaphor of a winepress in Scripture, brings about a season of redemption, healing, and renewal. As we sip from the eucharistic cup, we remember that Christ took upon himself God's judgment on the world. He stepped into the divine winepress and bore the sins and injustices of the world in order that all people might be reconciled with God.

There is an excess of meaning in a choice wine, in part due to its aesthetic beauty, which encourages further reflection. As we receive the cup and see the red thick liquid of wine (if red wine is used); as we smell its lovely fragrance; as we take a sip and feel the thick liquid on our lips and our tongue; as we taste and enjoy the complex flavors of wine enhanced by its smell — we can learn to allow our sensory experience to teach us something not only about the significance of Christ's blood but also about its preciousness. Christ's sacrifice stands out from all other sacrifices; it is sui generis. In the Old Testament the vine and the grapes are often used as a sign of the best of creation. In the Eucharist, we can reflect on Christ as the true vine and the noble grape. Just as the best grapes are used to produce a choice wine, so is Jesus the best of humanity — perfect and without sin. Through his death and the shedding of his blood, he has changed the fate of the whole world. We can now taste life in a way we have never been able to taste before. A choice wine can help us meditate and enter more fully into the great mystery of the Eucharist.

Wine also helps us remember that in the Lord's Supper we receive healing. Wine was historically known and used as medicine and especially as an antiseptic. With its approximately 11 percent alcohol, it can kill bacteria and has been used in healing people's bodies not only as an antiseptic but also through its moderate consumption. Wine nourishes, refreshes, and strengthens the body.[30] As we think of the healing capacities of wine while participating in the Lord's Supper, we can and should allow this reflection to help us ponder how Christ's blood functions as a spiritual antiseptic and how it brings healing. It cleanses us from sin and becomes a continual instrument for healing our relationship with God and with one another. In the church the healing of our relationship with God should overflow into the healing of our human relationships as we learn to forgive and accept one another in Jesus Christ. Some medieval depictions of Christ's sacrificial death capture this beautifully as rivers of blood flow from Christ's hands and side and signify the healing agency of his blood.

The use of wine as the blood of Christ in the Eucharist offers a rich fountain for reflection. It reminds us that salvation includes all of creation and in fact teaches us to be thankful for the gifts of God's good creation. Exploring the role of wine in the Lord's Supper also helps us reflect on the rich meaning of Christ's sacrificial death and the life that it brings to those who receive it.

Coming to Our Senses: Participating in Ritual

As we continue to ponder the significance of wine in the Lord's Supper, we need to keep in mind the context of the liturgy in which it is celebrated. The term "liturgy" derives from the Greek *leitourgia* ("to serve/worship"); it is a compound word of the Greek *laos* (literally "people") and *ergon* (literally "to work"). The term was first used by the apostles and denotes this act of formal worship in the church, the body of Christ (Acts 13:2).[31]

Christian spirituality must be anchored in our communal and embodied worship of the triune God. While Sunday worship is set apart from the other days of the week, it is to overflow into our ordinary lives and nourish it. The liturgy of our regular Sunday worship gives structure, meaning, and beauty to our worship. In it we sing praise, hear Scripture, listen to a sermon, offer thanksgiving and supplications, practice repentance, receive communion, and celebrate the seasons of the Christian church year (Advent, Christmas, Epiphany, Lent, Easter, Pentecost, etc.). While some would want to distinguish between liturgical and nonliturgical churches, I should point out that so-called nonliturgical churches still have certain structures by which they worship God — even though they might not be elaborate ones. The biblical term *leitourgia* would still apply to such churches.

The liturgy of Sunday worship is commonly described as a rite or ritual. Rituals, more generally speaking, are established practices that give form and transform the identities (including worldviews), relationships, and actions of persons within their particular social and cultural contexts. In a religious context, they work both vertically, shaping a community's relationship to the divine, and horizontally, forming the relationships among the members of a given community, the two dimensions being deeply intertwined.

A primary way by which this happens in ritual is that embodiment, communal action, and words work together to form an organic unity in addressing people holistically. Rituals do not speak one-sidedly to the intellect or to the emotions or to the spiritual sensibilities of a person, but they shape a person by addressing all of these fundamental human capacities. The embodied sensory experience of participating in communal rituals profoundly shapes our grasp of the truths expressed in action and word. Rituals can become catalysts that help integrate thought and action, bring order to chaos, and deepen our commitment to the beliefs we hold while encouraging transformation. Rituals place individuals within communal structures, and hold objective truth and subjective personal experiences in creative tension.[32]

In this regard, rituals are an important corrective to any culture that adopts a one-sided focus, whether it be an exclusively intellectual, a strongly emotive, individualistic, or disembodied spirituality. The post-Reformation church in particular developed an overemphasis on reason and scientific methods for the pursuit of knowledge and truth.[33] This imbalance was accompanied, in part as a reactionary movement, by the development of a spirituality that focused heavily on human interiority, leading away from a physical and embodied understanding of the Christian faith grounded in the incarnation of Jesus Christ.[34] This one-sided emphasis on reason and the scientific has deeply shaped the way we have come to understand human cognition in the modern world as primarily being a function of the intellect.

On the other hand, it must be noted that the rational has given way to an emotive spirituality in our culture that heavily focuses on the internal spiritual and emotional disposition of individuals as the primary locus of Christian formation. To this Dietrich Bonhoeffer exclaimed, "The flight from the created work to bodiless spirit, or to the internal spiritual disposition is prohibited."[35] In both cases, creation — our embodied lives and human senses — seems of little significance in relation to our faith in Jesus Christ. A reconsideration of the role of the body in the ritual of the Eucharist can help recover a more balanced perspective.

Another important aspect of ritual, drawn out by Catherine Bell, is that rituals strategically distinguish and privilege themselves with regard to other social actions, and a qualitative difference is made between them. In this way ritual seeks to accomplish something not apart from other social actions but precisely by being in a privileged relationship to them.[36] The Lord's Supper is distinguished from other meals by a range of symbolic actions and words, and we understand the meaning of it not apart from ordinary meals but precisely in its privileged position to them. The Eucharist shapes our identity as Christians and informs how we understand the rest of our lives, including ordinary meals, which stand at the center of human existence. While Jesus does not celebrate the Passover meal with his disciples in John 21, his invitation to share breakfast and the way he breaks bread have eucharistic overtones and connect this meal somehow to the Passover meal turned Eucharist. They are interrelated, and this seemingly "ordinary meal" receives a dimension of meaning precisely because of its inferior relationship with the Eucharist. A similar dynamic can be seen in Luke 24: the Emmaus road experience. This interrelationship will become important as we consider the role of feasting in Christian spirituality. The Eucharist — and Christian feasting more broadly speaking — are related to one another, but they are not the same.

A third and crucial part of ritual is that it keeps mystery at the center of our Christian life. When speaking about the Lord's Supper, it is tempting to reduce it to our understanding, our interests, and the theological problems and discussions that surround it.[37] In the end, the Lord's Supper remains a wonderful mystery. God has chosen to deal with the brokenness of this world through Christ's death on the cross. It is incomprehensible to the human mind, and we are called to embrace it in a posture of faith.

Tasting Christ in the Lord's Supper

Wine consumed in the Eucharist reminds us that we come to know and participate in this great mystery by being embodied people. We participate in a ritual that requires us to move our bodies, to think with our minds, to sing with our voices, to engage all of our five senses in our pursuit of the knowledge of God. Our whole being is called on to engage with the reality presented to us in the Eucharist. It is a deeply sensual experience that affirms our human bodies and our five senses as important means through which we come to understand how God meets us in the Eucharist. Intellect, sensuality in the positive sense of using our God-given senses in constructive ways, emotion, and spiritual vision (the eyes of faith) are called on to work together in understanding what we receive in the Eucharist.

The use of wine in Christian worship teaches us to pay attention to our embodied actions and how they aid us in our perception of the meaning of the Lord's Supper. In the fourth century, when the church saw a rapid increase in membership because Christians were no longer persecuted for their faith, the bishops of the time faced the challenge of educating the newly baptized about the meaning of the Eucharist. Surprisingly, they paid much attention to the physical nature of the Eucharist and the role of certain postures and gestures in human perception.[38] Though their use and interpretation of Scripture seems foreign to contemporary readers, their attention to the role of the body in Christian worship is helpful.

Cyril of Jerusalem (315-87) instructed those new Christians and pilgrims as they were faced with the great mystery and seeming paradox of Christ's presence in bread and wine. Cyril drew their attention to Scripture, arguing that Christ who had transformed water into wine at the miracle of Cana set a precedent for changing wine into blood.[39] He continued by providing them with mental images by which they were able to interpret their sensual experiences theologically. He encouraged them, for example, to imagine themselves dressed in white garments and promised that the bread would make "the face of their soul" cheerful. He instructed them in detail about certain bodily postures and gestures for understanding how we receive Christ in the Eucharist: "Do not have your wrists extended or your fingers spread, but making your left hand a throne for the right, for it is about to receive a King, and cupping your palm, receive the body of Christ." Likewise, he instructs them about drinking wine: "While it is still moist upon your lips, touch it with your fingers, and so sanctify your eyes, your forehead, and other senses."[40] By marrying mental images with physical action (postures, gestures) and sensory perception, Cyril affirms the importance of the body and sense perception for grasping spiritual truths.

John Chrysostom, presbyter in Antioch and contemporary of Cyril, also emphasized the importance of postures, gestures, and physical action (eating, drinking) in receiving the Eucharist. As the worshiper drinks the wine, according to Chrysostom, the devil becomes frightened by the mark of eucharistic wine on the believer's mouth: "If the devil merely sees you returning from the master's banquet, he flees faster than any wind. . . . If you show him a tongue stained with the precious blood, he will not be able to make a stand."[41]

In another instance he makes the analogy between the Eucharistic wine on the mouth of the believer and the blood of the lamb smeared on the Israelites' doorposts in Egypt just before the Passover. Here Chrysostom encourages the believer to pay attention to the physical and sensory experience of drinking wine and to turn it into a mental image of a domestic space. The worshiper is able, via these instructions, to see more clearly the spiritual benefit of Christ's death as the fulfillment of the Passover. Just as God passed over the Israelites because their doorframes were marked with blood, so are Christians spared and saved because of the "blood of the truth smeared on the mouths of the faithful."[42]

Both Cyril of Jerusalem and John Chrysostom had a profoundly integrated understanding of human beings, knowing that embodied experiences, including sense perception, mental image-making, and words work together in human cognition and are especially powerful when we speak of invisible, spiritual truths. The eyes of faith see the spiritual in the physical. In this understanding they follow the Hebrew tradition (Deut. 11:18-21). Rather than rejecting embodied experiences and the created world, both Cyril of Jerusalem and John Chrysostom realized that they needed to teach young believers how to understand their embodied experience of the Eucharist in light of the words spoken during the ritual of the Eucharist. They had a profound trust that human senses are a gift to be used in our pursuit of the knowledge of God.[43]

Our participation in the ritual of the Lord's Supper, with its emphasis on the movement of the body and different bodily postures and gestures, teaches us something fundamental about the Christian faith, something that is a very hard lesson to learn: that we are not in charge of our salvation and our spiritual growth. Eugene Peterson rightly asserts that the Eucharist "stands as a bulwark against reducing our participation in salvation to the exercise of devotional practices before God or being recruited to run errands for God."[44] Our participation in the Lord's Supper — our getting up from the pew to join the pilgrimage to the front, our postures and gestures of standing or kneeling, of opening our hands and holding them out to receive a piece from the one bread, bending our upper bodies forward and opening our mouths to be served wine from the one cup — has tremendous symbolic potential. Just as we partake by receiving Christ in the bread and wine, so must our fundamental posture in the Christian life be that of receptivity. It is an active willingness to remain poor and open at the center of our lives in order to receive Christ and his ongoing work through the Holy Spirit. We must learn to cease from striving and to trust that living consistently at the brink of exhaustion is not a mark of the spiritual life or a virtue for which we should strive. It generates anxiety and moves us away from a life rooted in Christ's action rather than ours.

We must learn to surrender our habitual tendency to brace against the love and grace of God and allow his presence to melt down our defenses. How do we brace ourselves against God? Alcohol abuse and addictive behaviors and disorders are one example by which we can radically seal ourselves off from experiencing God's love and grace. By opening ourselves up to God in our struggles with addictive behavior and disorders, we reveal our poverty and learn to become open to God's healing.[45]

In rituals like the Lord's Supper, believers learn to hold embodied action and words in creative tension and allow their baptized imagination to probe deeper into the mysteries of the Christian faith. Reality is reinterpreted for the worshiper, and a transformation of life happens through this very process of partaking in rituals. Old ways of seeing and being are rejected in favor of a new way of life revealed in the Eucharist. The spiritual meanings of Christ's body and blood are etched into our being by our embodied participation in sharing the bread and drinking wine from the one cup.

Concluding Reflections

The use of wine in the celebration of the Lord's Supper offers rich insight into the importance of wine for Christian spirituality. The Eucharist is an embodied and communal ritual and anchors our experience of the Christian faith in creation. Wine used in the Lord's Supper becomes a defense against lingering Gnostic tendencies that tend to devalue the importance of creation for Christian spirituality. The mark of a decidedly Christian spirituality is not a flight from creation but a faith-filled embrace of it. In the Lord's Supper we encounter Christ the Creator and Redeemer. Here we experience and practice the life-giving bond between material and spiritual realities. The Lord's Supper not only shapes and informs our renewed relationship with God and with one another but also with creation in general. The Lord's Supper instills in us the conviction that wine is a gift of God's good creation and a sign of his blessing. But wine will also draw us into the world of sacrifice. It reminds us that Christ stepped into the divine winepress and bore the sins and injustice of this world so that all people might be reconciled with God. Wine in the Eucharist also reminds us that God wants to heal us. The most appropriate response to the incredible gifts we receive at the table of the Lord's Supper is gratitude and joyful celebration, and the name Eucharist captures this well. It is to an exploration of the importance of feasting for Christian spirituality that we must now turn.

4

Wine and Communal Feasting:
The Joy of the Lord Is Our Strength

"Of all accusations against Christians, the most terrible one
was uttered by Nietzsche when he said that Christians had no
joy. . . . And we must recover the meaning of this great joy."
Alexander Schmemann[1]

The theme of wine in the Bible reveals that as human beings we are embedded in the community of creation. We have our origin in God, and we are to receive all that creation gives with gratitude and joy because it is a lavish and exuberant gift from God. Wine is a particularly lavish gift and a sign of God's blessing. It gladdens our hearts and elicits joy. In the Lord's Supper wine draws us into the world of sacrifice, making us keenly aware that all of God's creation is in need of redemption. Christ's work on the cross, the shedding of his blood, and our partaking by eating from the one bread and drinking from the one cup keep us rooted in a life of forgiveness. The Eucharist anchors our lives in the love and mercy of God and his desire to heal and restore broken relationships. Divisions are broken down in the Lord's Supper, and we find peace with God and each other as we eat the bread and drink the wine.

Grateful and joyful celebration are important ways by which Christians can respond to these exuberant gifts of creation and salvation. The Westminster Catechism (1647), summarizing the beliefs of Calvinism, begins with the question about the main and highest end of humanity. The answer it gives to this important question is that humanity is "to glorify God, and fully to enjoy him forever." If this is the case, why is there so little joy in this world — and especially in the life of the church? Exhaustion, anxiety, fear, and loneliness have become specters with which many of us are all too familiar, and joy seems hard to come by. The accusation that Christians have no joy is indeed a terrible one.

Alexander Schmemann understands this lack of joy as a severe crisis in Christian spirituality, and he calls the church to recover the Christian meaning of joy. Believing that the church has embraced the modern ethos of a joyless and business-minded culture, he argues that our frantic and pathetic hunger and thirst for perfection is the death of joy.[2] As a result, our engagement with the world has become too utilitarian and thus destructive. It focuses too much on human achievement rather than remembering the acts of God. It celebrates human progress rather than honoring and embracing God's sustaining and redeeming presence. Creation groans under this terrible burden, which eclipses the love, mercy, and sustaining care of God.

And in order to recover from the pressures and monotony of modern life, we have replaced rest with relaxation, fun, and passive entertainment. Rest in the Christian sense is a ceasing from work by actively seeking rest in God, who nourishes not only our bodies but also our souls. Relaxation and passive entertainment tend to be more indiscriminate in finding ways to relax, and they often have little awareness of our spiritual needs. Indeed, Schmemann diagnoses our modern culture as a "joyless rush . . . interrupted by relaxation."[3] We seem to be haunted by unceasing entertainment through mostly empty stimulation — a no man's land.[4] Jürgen Moltmann similarly paints a bleak picture of our modern existence: "Conditioned and regulated man needs his nightly whodunit on television. There he vicariously experiences adventure which has long since vanished from his monotonous world."[5] Schmemann goes so far as to suggest that we run into a serious crisis in understanding the very idea of a feast and its role in Christian spirituality.[6]

The film *Avalon* (1990), directed by Barry Levinson, gives testimony to the severe crisis that seems to have swept over the Western world. The film tells the story of a Polish family immigrating to the United States in the early twentieth century. In order to make a better life for themselves, they arrive in "the promised land" with the hope of a brighter future. The film begins by showing the extended family gathered around the Thanksgiving table, with the older relatives remembering and retelling their family story to the younger generations.

It is a depiction of a large and extended immigrant family joyfully feasting and celebrating around the table, eating delicious food and drinking wine.

The crisis begins when the family members wonder at that Thanksgiving table about whom they should give thanks to. The film then narrates the slow but steady disintegration of the family life of those seated around the table. Modern technology — first the radio and then the television — lures the family members away from the table. Financial success in the emerging and highly competitive market separates the extended family as they move further away from one another into suburban areas. The sons of the first-generation immigrants change their names in order to assimilate into American culture more easily, resulting in a further loss of family identity. The film ends on a most depressing note: the camera zooms in on one small family unit, parents and two children, sitting in front of the TV eating their Thanksgiving dinner on TV trays. The contrast between the opening portrait of the Thanksgiving meal and the last depiction of it could not be more stark. The extended family has disappeared: no ritual of sitting down together around the table, giving thanks, and engaging each other in conversation is in sight. The family does not remember the story of its history — and thus cannot share it with the younger generation. There is no sense of celebration or joy. The random entertainment presented on TV has taken family life captive.

Avalon is perhaps an overstated witness to the destructive aspects of modern technology. And yet the film depicts the very crisis Schmemann speaks about in a very moving way, and challenges us to confront it. How can we recover the meaning of this sense of joy and joyful feasting and its place in Christian spirituality? And does wine have a role in helping the church recover this great sense of joy?

Wine and Communal Feasting

Toward a Spirituality of Joyful Feasting

It is striking that Jesus' first miracle happens in the context of a joyous and lavish feast at a Hebrew wedding in Cana, where he turns water into wine (John 2:1-12). Why wasn't his first recorded miracle a healing miracle or feeding the hungry by supernaturally multiplying bread? Did he not come to redeem the world? Why would he "waste" his time partaking in an elaborate and long-lasting family celebration (a Hebrew wedding could last up to seven days) when he could be out there fixing the world's problems? In the Hebrew world that Jesus and his disciples inhabited, feasts and celebrations were important ways believers cultivated their spiritual lives. In them they remembered God's deeds of the past, embraced God's faithfulness in the present, and fostered expectant hope for God's redeeming intervention in the future.[7]

An abundance of wine as a sign that God's blessing had been firmly planted in the Hebrew imagination ever since Jacob first declared his blessing on his son Judah (Gen. 49:8-12). The prophets foretold that an abundance of wine would be a sign of God's future redemption. The book of Hosea, Matthew's Gospel, and the book of Revelation even envision the culmination of God's redemption as a wedding banquet (Hosea 2:18-22; Matt. 22:1-14; Rev. 19:6-7). In light of this expectation, Jesus' first miracle at a Hebrew wedding is profoundly revealing. It suggests that, in Christ, God's promises have come to fruition. An abundance of wine and joyful feasting will mark God's blessing and redemption. Jesus, by transforming the scarcity of wine into an abundance of it, begins to fulfill these promises and expectations.

What is striking about this miracle is that Jesus literally produces not only an abundance of wine but an abundance of choice wine! He directs servants to take six stone water jars traditionally reserved for the Jewish rites of purification and fill them with water (each jar would hold 80 to 120 liters of water, thus amounting to approximately 480 to 720 liters altogether). This was enough wine for a huge feast. How lavish and extravagant it was to offer an abundance of choice wine to a wedding party that was already tipsy and would not even be able to appreciate it properly (John 2:10)! We learn that Jesus reveals his glory in this miracle, a glory full of "grace and truth" (John 1:14-18; 2:11).[8]

The glory of God (Hebrew: *kabod*; Greek: *doxa*) is a central theme in Scripture, where it speaks of the great and bright splendor, majesty, dignity, and beauty of God's presence and activity among his people. God's desire is to dwell with his people and reveal his glorious presence to them. In both the Old and New Testaments, a great sense of awe and fear often accompanies an awareness of God's glory. When an angel first announced to the shepherds in the field the coming of the Messiah, Jesus Christ, we learn that "the glory of the Lord shone around them, and they were terrified," and the angel announced, "Do not be afraid. . . . I am bringing good news of great joy for all people" (Luke 2:9-10).

In John's Gospel we learn that "the Word became flesh and lived among us, and we have seen his glory . . . full of grace and truth" (John 1:14). The revelation of God's glory in Jesus Christ is an occasion for great joy. Jesus' first miracle at a Hebrew wedding reveals and affirms God's glory as a profoundly joyous occasion. The lavish and miraculous gift of an abundance of choice wine, as demonstrated in the Cana wedding, somehow draws us closer to understanding God's glory and splendor and his presence among us. According to Moltmann, the revelation of God's glory does not "merely manifest itself ethically in love to the neighbor but also aesthetically in festive play before God."[9]

The miracle at Cana reveals that Jesus affirms the importance of joyful feasting for Christian spirituality, and the miracle points to the reason for this joy. In Christ the messianic promises foretold by the prophets have come to fulfillment: he is our reason for joyful celebration. The riches of God's love and grace dwell in him, and these riches give sustenance and sustainability to our joy. John the Baptist points to this joy: "The friend of the bridegroom, who stands and hears him, rejoices greatly at the bridegroom's voice. For this reason my joy has been fulfilled" (John 3:29-30).

Jesus emphasizes the gift of joy several times in the Gospel of John: "I have said these things to you so that my joy may be in you, and that your joy many be complete" (John 15:11; see also vv. 16, 20-21, 24; 17:13). Mary's response to carrying the Savior in her womb expresses this great sense of joy: "My soul magnifies the Lord, and my spirit rejoices in God my Savior" (Luke 1:46-47). We magnify and praise Christ by giving thanks for and rejoicing in the gifts of created life and salvation. The apostle Paul repeatedly admonishes us to rejoice in Christ (Phil. 3:1, 4:4; 1 Thess. 5:16). The parable of the prodigal son reveals joyful feasting as a proper response to the return of a wayward child (Luke 15:32); but it also portrays the brother's inability to join in the festive celebration as a great disappointment (Luke 15:28-31).

Christian feasting becomes a place where we embrace and cultivate this posture of gratitude and joyful celebration. It is a deeply spiritual practice, and we must rediscover it as such. Joyful feasting becomes a place where we remember God and his gifts to us. Fostering a posture of gratitude through thanksgiving and rejoicing opens up our lives to God's presence and his abundant generosity. The Lord's Supper teaches us that we do so as a broken people always in need of grace and mercy. While we use worldly feasting to escape the pain, suffering, and boredom of our lives, Christian feasting becomes a place where we open up our lives to God's love and forgiveness. It is a place where the generosity of God's abundant love and grace forms and transforms. From here we can go forth into the world with gratitude and joy, affirming life as a gift to embrace, treasure, and share. The psalmist puts it this way: "You show me the path of life. In your presence there is fullness of joy; in your right hand are pleasures forevermore" (Ps. 16:11).

According to the biblical witness, wine plays an important role in helping us live into this posture of thanksgiving and joyful celebration, and it anchors our lives in God's generosity. Wine gladdens the human heart (Ps. 104:15) and allows us to experience God as the lavish giver. God delights in his creation and wants us to share in his delight. As fully embodied and communal creatures, we are called to use all of our God-given senses to enjoy him and his creation. Wine keeps us rooted in the sacrificial nature of our salvation and our call as Christians to live joyfully and sacrificially. Indeed, wine has a unique role in drawing us into the redemptive nature of Christian feasting, and it is surprising how little theological reflection has paid attention to this important subject matter. However, there are some notable exceptions, and *Babette's Feast*, a film that explores the redemptive nature of Christian feasting, is one of them.

Babette's Feast *and the Recovery of Joyful Redemptive Feasting*

While the film *Avalon* tells the story of the loss of feasting and joy in our modern Western culture, the film *Babette's Feast* invites us to ponder how we might recover the table of joyful celebration. The film tells the story of a small Lutheran Pietistic community in nineteenth-century coastal Jutland, Denmark. While the community is deeply religious and rooted in a life of thanksgiving and prayer, there is no sense of joy or joyful celebration. A flight from created matter in order to ascend to a higher spiritual realm defines spirituality as this community sees it. Their true home is the heavenly Jerusalem, and their understanding of the Christian life is about the salvation of one's disembodied soul. Asceticism and scarceness mark their existence. The founding dean and pastor does not allow his daughters, though beautiful and gifted women, to go to dances or parties. He turns suitors away because of his selfish desire (obscured behind his pious language) to have his daughters serve at his right and left hands. They are "pious melancholics," as one of their suitors calls them. The daughters, Martine and Philippa, named after the great Lutheran Reformers Martin Luther and Philipp Melanchthon, continue to lead the community after their father's death, living a sacrificial life of serving the poor and elderly.

Circumstances, however, repeatedly interrupt the melancholy existence of these sisters. Three strangers descend at different times upon the close-knit community; all of them have a keen sense for beauty. The first is young officer Lorens Löwenhielm, whose lifestyle is anything but pious. The sight of beautiful and pious Martine, however, inspires him toward a higher and purer life. It is the beauty of that "gentle, golden-haired angel" that touches him so deeply and allows him a glimpse into the spiritual realm.[10] However, he is unable to embrace the gifts set before him, and he returns to a life of strife and vanity.

The second visitor is Achille Papin, a Parisian opera singer who is visiting Jutland for health reasons. By chance he hears Philippa singing in church. While she sings of heaven and earth perishing and God's glory being revealed in human hearts alone, Achille becomes enchanted by the beauty of her heavenly voice. Achille convinces Philippa to take singing lessons from him, and he falls in love with the "beautiful soprano of the snow." Together they sing a duet from Mozart's opera *Don Giovanni*. They sing of the voice of joy calling, and Philippa responds, "I am fearful of my joy." It appears as though her fear of the sensual world and the temptations it brings make her decline any further interaction with Achille, and she seeks refuge in the safety of her ascetic home — to the great delight of her father. The contrast between the aesthetic and the ascetic could not be starker. Achille, greatly disappointed, returns to Paris, his spirit crushed.

Years later, another stranger arrives at the doorstep of the two sisters. Babette, a French woman, seeks refuge with them from the terrors of the civil war in France. Her pale appearance and a letter of recommendation from Achille Papin, however, warm their hearts, and they take her in. Babette is quiet, humble, and serves the sisters faithfully. Furthermore, her shrewd sense of business and ability to cook become indispensable gifts to the sisters and their ministry to the small and aging Lutheran community.

But not all is well. Though the pious believers meet regularly for Bible study, prayers, and hymn-singing, discord and dissension creep into the community over time. They bring up and recount old sins and hurts, they nourish bitter resentment, and one couple wonders whether God has forgiven them for the love affair of their youth. The burden of their guilt weighs them down. Could God's forgiveness possibly reach this far? The doubts about God's abounding grace and mercy and the poison of their unforgiving spirits reach deep into the crevices of their brittle souls. With their father now gone, the sisters are unable to restore the community to peace and harmony. This failure is especially disheartening as the founding dean's hundredth anniversary approaches. Babette watches all of this in silence.

It is an envelope from France for Babette that interrupts the strife and unrest of the pious Lutheran community. A lottery ticket has been the only connection that she still has to her native France, and the unlikely has happened: Babette has won 10,000 francs (about $60,000 in today's U.S. dollars) in the lottery. Though delighted for Babette, the sisters quickly realize that her unexpected fortune will turn into a great loss for their rapidly aging community. Surely Babette will, with this new fortune, return to her native France. They have no idea that the grace and mercy of God might be descending upon them in the most unexpected ways.

After days of silence and prayer, Babette, who has never expressed any wish to the sisters since her arrival some years before, begs them to let her cook a real French dinner in celebration of the dean's birthday. The sisters are stunned, but feel unable to decline this unusual request that so affronts their lives of asceticism and scarceness. It is at this point in the film that the repeated juxtaposition between a life of asceticism and aesthetics reaches its climax and comes to a point of crisis. When Martine and Philippa watch the goods from France — including living quails and a huge turtle — being delivered to their humble kitchen, they suddenly realize that they have opened their doors to great dangers. What if the anniversary dinner will turn into a witches' Sabbath? The huge living turtle stares at them like a demon from the underworld. Terror seizes their hearts. When they see wine bottles emerging in their pious home, they are horrified and ask if these bottles contain wine. Babette responds, "No. It is a Clos Vougeot 1846!" Indeed, it is not merely wine, it is a choice wine. Will Babette lure them into a feast with demons?

The very Clos de Vougeot that Cistercian monks had first cultivated many centuries earlier in Burgundy now appears in the kitchen of these pious Lutheran sisters and confronts their severe ascetic spirituality. While it is too late for the community to withdraw from the terrifying feast, they literally swear to one another that they will deny themselves all sense of taste and direct their tongue to its ultimate and higher purpose of praise and thanksgiving. Their shriveled up imagination has no room for fathoming that God's love and grace might come to them via a feast. They have no clue of the spiritual powers of a Clos Vougeot. The film narrates in the most moving way the role that food and wine can have in the formation and transformation of a Christian community.

As the sisters and brothers put up their defenses and brace themselves against the temptations that might befall them at the festive dinner, General Lorens Löwenhielm unexpectedly joins the festive occasion. The former prodigal son has returned and becomes the voice of a prophet. He recognizes, names, and praises the gifts of God that Babette has introduced to the ignorant and unreceptive saints tangled up in strife and bitterness.

Before they sit down at the table, Babette transforms the barren sitting room with its melancholy atmosphere into a place of festive splendor. A white tablecloth, carefully ironed, candles shimmering off a gentle and warm light, crystal glassware, beautiful fine china, and silverware all contribute to this festive atmosphere. After saying grace, the brothers and sisters remember their vow and remind one another that, just as the food at the wedding of Cana did not matter, so is this feast of no significance.

The first course served is Amontillado together with turtle soup. Amontillado is a Spanish sherry from the Montilla region, and when the general first samples the sherry and the soup, what he drinks and eats bewilders him. The sisters and brothers, their tongues somehow loosened, speak of spiritual things and remember their encounters with the dean. The next course served is Veuve Cliquot (1860) champagne with Blinis Demidoff, buckwheat pancakes with caviar. As they eat their caviar, one of the sisters recalls an Exodus-like story. The dean had promised a Christmas sermon to a village across the fjord, but the weather had turned so bad that it seemed impossible to cross the fjord by boat. But, as if it were a miracle, the weather became so cold that for the first time in known history the fjord froze, and the dean was able to cross the fjord on the ice and deliver his Christmas sermon. As they listen to this remarkable story, Babette serves them a glass of Veuve Cliquot champagne, once one of the finest champagnes in the world. This time the brothers and sisters know that the drink cannot be wine, since it is sparkling, and they take it for some kind of lemonade. The "lemonade" seems to perform wonders and elevates them to a higher sphere. The camera zooms in and focuses on their act of eating and drinking, on the facial expressions and the gaze of their eyes. Slowly but surely a transformation happens: "The convives grew lighter in weight and lighter of heart the more they ate and drank," and this newfound lightness somehow frees them from their interior entanglements, and they become more open and receptive.

The main course consists of the famous Burgundian choice red wine Clos Vougeot (1846) together with a beautiful but also disturbing main dish. Babette serves them *cailles en sarcophage,* quails stuffed with truffles and foie gras, served in a coffin made of puff pastry. Visually, the dish is a disturbing sight and rather suggestive in its symbolic quality. Quails in the Christian tradition remind us of the Exodus story in which God miraculously delivered the Israelites out of Egypt, and as they wandered in the wilderness, supernaturally provided them with food — quails in the evening and bread in the morning (Exod. 16:13). Babette serves her quails in a very unsettling way. They are entombed in their little sarcophagi with their heads hanging over the rim. Literally, "sarcophagus" (from the Greek *sarx*: flesh, and *phagein,* to eat) means "eating flesh." In the theological context of *Babette's Feast,* it seems highly suggestive of the Eucharist and the sacrificial nature of the Christian faith. Babette's artistic creation perhaps suggests that her meal somehow connects to the Eucharist.

It turns out that, before Babette fled to Denmark, she had been a famous chef in France. General Löwenhielm, who had enjoyed her culinary art at the famous Café Anglais in Paris, recognizes the dish and finds himself in a state of bliss. He recounts the reflection of his fellow diner, Colonel Galliffet, on the artistic skills of Babette: "[T]his woman is . . . turning a dinner at the Café Anglais into a kind of love affair — into a love affair of the noble and romantic category in which one no longer distinguishes between bodily and spiritual appetite or satiety." A theology of feasting could not be better described. It is a love affair between God and his people. For Babette, the physical and spiritual are deeply intertwined, and the grace of God comes to us *through,* not *apart from* our enjoyment of the physical world. But why did she serve the quails in a sarcophagus when she first created this stunning dish in France? Colonel Galliffet had been a fierce enemy of Babette: he had fought on the other side during the French civil war and was responsible for the death of Babette's husband and son. Despite this history, Babette cooked for and served her enemies with undivided devotion to her calling as a cook and artist. *Cailles en sarcophage* hints at this sacrificial service.

The feast Babette holds for her little Pietistic community in remembrance of their dean is also deeply sacrificial, though in a different way. While her sacrificial life at Café Anglais became incarnate by serving her enemies, her sacrifice for the Lutheran community consists of spending all she owns in order to create a feast such as she had not even done at the Café Anglais. Unlike Martine and Philippa's sacrificial life, which consisted of denying themselves the joy of their giftedness, Babette embraces her God-given gifts and through them reveals the glory of God. Sacrificial living lies at the heart of Babette's life, and it opens up a vision for all those who partake of it.

It is this beautiful and sacrificial feast that transforms General Löwenhielm from a prodigal into a preacher. He suddenly understands the nature of grace and is able to proclaim it to his fellow "convives":

> Man, my friends, . . . is frail and foolish. We have all of us been told that grace is to be found in the universe. But in our human foolishness and short-sightedness we imagine divine grace to be finite. For this reason we tremble. . . . But the moment comes when our eyes are opened, and we see and realize that grace is infinite. Grace, my friends, demands nothing from us but that we shall await it with confidence and acknowledge it in gratitude.

And as through a miracle, the gospel no longer falls on deaf ears. Suddenly the eyes and ears of the pious sisters and brothers are opened and they are able to hear and receive the grace of God. Their cheeks are reddened by the beautiful sherry, champagne, and wine, and their hearts are lifted to a loftier place — thanks to holy intoxication. The gifts of God's good creation soften their brittle souls, and they become receptive toward grace. What their weekly Bible study was no longer able to accomplish, Babette's sacrificial feast has. The choice food and wine, and the aesthetic beauty of the feast, break through all of their defensive walls and allow them to glimpse God's infinite love and grace. Beauty and grace belong to one another as the diners begin to reconcile. They share and forgive old sins, release bitter resentment, and embrace love. A fractured group of pious ascetics, completely entangled in strife and bitterness, transforms itself into a loving and forgiving community. The contrast articulated by this film could not be more stark or the transformation more moving. The Christians of this community finally realize that the Christian journey is not about enduring life on earth until they can escape to heaven. Babette's sacrificial feast teaches them that the Christian life is about welcoming and embracing heaven as it comes down to earth — paradise restored.

The next course consists of a beautiful arrangement of exotic fruits on a silver platter and a plate of savory cheeses. A huge cluster of grapes and fresh figs, so symbolic of the Promised Land in the Old Testament, features prominently in this course and expands the diners' Christian imagination. One of the brothers remembers the story of the Valley of Eshkol (Hebrew: "grape cluster"), in which scouts brought back a cluster of grapes, pomegranates, and figs as signs of the bountiful riches of the Promised Land (Num. 13:23). But obviously these pious sisters and brothers are not accustomed to such paradisiacal splendor. They have to learn from General Löwenhielm how to enjoy their figs properly. It is a humorous sight. Their spiritual exile seems over, and they recognize that God wants them to be joyful. The film ends with the brothers and sisters holding hands, singing and dancing under the starlit sky around the village water well, a symbol of Christ as the living water. The heavenly stars have moved closer to earth, Philippa says, and the members of this little Lutheran community are finally able to embrace their faith more fully. "Eternity is nigh" they sing, and the dry bones begin to dance.

Toward a Spirituality of Wine

What is so striking about the story of *Babette's Feast* is that writer Karen Blixen and filmmaker Gabriel Axel are able to capture the invisible movements of God's love and grace in the most vivid and beautiful way. They realize that wine in particular can have a powerful role in recovering a Christian understanding of joyful feasting, a place where God's deeds are remembered, his presence embraced and enjoyed, and hope for the future nourished. In a most moving way they show how champagne, which the Benedictine monk Dom Pérignon once compared to "drinking stars," and Clos de Vougeot, once a product of the Cistercian pursuit for spiritual perfection, can move the souls of men and women. The beauty of the wine and the gentle intoxication help soften the human soul and open it up to divine operation. Wine, in the context of this beautiful feast, allows the Jutland ascetics to see that the love and grace of God come to them as embodied and communal people embracing their God-given senses. God redeems our bodies as well as our souls: the two are deeply intertwined in the Hebrew/Christian understanding of persons, and wine makes us keenly aware of this connection. *Babette's Feast* also reveals that God pours out his love and grace without condition or discrimination, and he calls us to become open and receptive.

94

Wine has a unique way and amazing ability to open us up to one another, to help us put aside our defenses and masks, and to become more vulnerable, honest, and forgiving of each other. Wine can open up conversations and take them to deeper and more meaningful levels. Roger Scruton observes: "Just as you savour the intoxicating flavor of the wine, so do you savour its reconciling power: it presents you with the taste of forgiveness."[11] Just as wine helps the body relax, so does it help open up the soul, and the whole person becomes more receptive. *Babette's Feast* beautifully narrates this process in the lives of the pious brothers and sisters who slowly but surely open up, not only to the beauty of the wine but also to God and each other.

Another remarkable contribution of *Babette's Feast* is the detailed attention given to seeing, smelling, tasting, savoring, and naming wine. We shall take this up in greater detail in the next chapter. In Germany we have a saying that to drink is to pray, but to binge-drink is to sin.[12] The French mystic Simone Weil notes that attention in its highest form is prayer.[13] As we pay attention to what we eat and drink, we can turn it into a form of prayer. General Löwenhielm models the art of wine-tasting both in his attentiveness to the wine but also in his savoring. Awe, delight, surprise, and gratitude are all part of his appreciation of the highest-quality wines he is served. He becomes the teacher who embodies and expresses for us what is so difficult to put into words.

Speaking about wine is not easy. There are those who are so intimidated by the whole world of wine and its jargon that they do not want to say anything about it. And then there are those whose array of vocabulary for a given wine seems rather fanciful and outlandish. There are also cultural differences. Americans, for example, tend to be more outspoken in their appreciation of things, while Germans tend to be less outspoken and to understate their appreciation. The French have made an art of speaking about wine. But a certain amount of translation almost always seems necessary.

The only way we can speak about wine is via metaphor. We identify the flavor of a wine by means of association with familiar things we eat, drink, and smell. When we recognize that a wine smells like lemon, for example, we are said to discover its "citrus notes." But these associations are only partial, and thus our language is always limited in expressing what we fully experience in savoring a wine. This limitation is especially frustrating when we drink an exceptionally beautiful wine and want to share our experience by describing it. Quite often we are at a loss for words to describe what we taste, feel, and savor: it is often impossible to describe. This reminds us of our even greater inability to capture God's glory in human terms.

God's Gift of Choice Wines: Drinking Beauty

There does not seem to be another drink in the world with the potential to capture in concentrated form such a wide range of aromas and flavors. If crafted well, a wine can do so in an amazingly harmonious and even symphonic way. It can exude such beauty and delight that humans throughout the ages have tried to verbally capture their delight in drinking wine. The Song of Solomon speaks of the "best wine that goes down smoothly; gliding over lips and teeth" (Song of Sol. 7:9). George Herbert mused: "Love is that liquor sweet and most divine/Which my God feels as blood; but I, as wine." John Milton confessed: "Wine, one sip of this will bathe the drooping spirits in delight beyond the bliss of dreams. Be wise and taste." Goethe wrote: "Wine rejoices the heart of man, and joy is the mother of every virtue." Anthelme Brillat-Savarin, the great nineteenth-century food writer, argued that "a meal without wine is like a day without sunshine." And Robert Louis Stevenson called wine "bottled poetry." The songs in praise of wine seem to echo endlessly through the ages.[14]

One of the most beautiful aspects of a choice wine is its ability to reflect a specific place in specific ways. A well-crafted wine is like a mirror into the bounty of God's creation, much of it hidden from our sight. It is a remarkable — dare I even say miraculous — characteristic of a well-crafted wine. While we could argue about what we would identify as simple, good, or excellent wines, there is no question that some wines have an extraordinary beauty to them, an excess of meaning that evokes a sense of awe and delight. Any experienced wine-drinker will confess to this phenomenon. Some people have left highly successful careers after first encountering such wines and experiencing a sort of epiphany. The wine's beauty so deeply enchanted them that they found themselves on a quest to craft such wines in their homeland. They started learning to pay careful attention to land, soil, and climate, and they became more deeply embedded in the community of creation. Their quest was to gain the wisdom to participate in this process of allowing a wine to mirror in the best possible way a particular place. It gives vintners great delight when they see the enjoyment that their customers show as they drink their wine and recognize the craftsmanship that has gone into it. A choice wine reminds us that we are part of a deeply interconnected community of creation, a living organism that is highly mysterious.

So far, scientists have not been able to explain how all the aromas and flavors come to dwell in a wine. They can only explain certain aspects of it. The question of how subjective or objective wine-tasting can be is important.[15] But it is noteworthy that experienced wine-drinkers seem to look for very similar things in a wine: complexity, subtlety, intensity, structure, balance, and length of taste — that is, its ability to linger in the mouth. The aromas and tastes of a fine wine are intricate: layers of these aromas and tastes unfold in an elegant, balanced, and symphonic kind of way. Of all the liquids that humans drink in the world, wine is by far the most sophisticated one. And a fine wine leaves an undeniably strong impression on the taster. A low-quality wine tends to be either flat and empty or terribly unbalanced and loud — and there is not much that one can say about it. This lack of quality is not necessarily true of — indeed, can be very different from — simple wines, which can be rather beautiful in their simplicity. A choice wine does not need to be expensive, but finding choice wines that are affordable takes time and effort.[16]

Tasting wine is a very active process that demands a high degree of attention, patience, and a willingness to listen, reflect on, and contemplate what one has tasted. Gulping down wine is a waste of God's gifts. Wine should be reserved for contemplatives, people who are willing to slow down, to be attentive, listening, discerning, and reflective. A choice wine will usually unfold in rather subtle ways and often very slowly. Layers of meaningful taste take focused attention to be detected, discerned, and appreciated. Fine wines should not be drunk greedily but with respect and care. If wine is indeed a special gift from God, then it should be enjoyed prayerfully. Drinking wine at its best is like prayer. We respond to God by enjoying his gifts and allowing wine to instill within us a sense of wonder, not just for the wine but even more for the generous giver of such a lavish gift. Wine calls us to worship.

God's Gift of Choice Wines: Holy Intoxication

The beauty of a wine depends on many things, but one major contributing factor is the process of fermentation. Yeasts — microorganisms living in our atmosphere but also found on the skin of grapes — begin a process that converts natural sugars in the grape juice into alcohol. The yeasts, the process of fermentation, and the alcohol all shape the structure and beauty of a wine. Alcohol is an integral part of wine and deeply tied to its taste.

To many, however, the intoxicating effect of alcohol is seen as overwhelmingly negative — and that for good reason. Alcohol abuse has terrible consequences. But intoxication can also have very positive effects, and critics easily overlook these benefits. In places where wine-drinking is part of the culture, distinctions between mild intoxication and drunkenness are more naturally in place. For those cultures where these distinctions are not a given, it might be helpful to reflect on the difference between what I shall call "gentle" intoxication and severe intoxication and drunkenness.

Drunkenness and severe forms of intoxication can alter one's personality. Rather than opening a person up to conversation and conviviality, they shut down a person's ability to communicate, to be open and receptive. Signs of severe intoxication are either complete silence and an inability to communicate or obnoxious, aggressive, and often destructive behavior, accompanied by vulgar talk. Alcohol is too often used to escape reality rather than embracing it and engaging it in meaningful ways. It is to such drunkards that the apostle Paul writes admonishingly: "Do not get drunk with wine" (Eph. 5:18).

Gentle intoxication, however, enhances our festive play before God and knows its limitations. It creates a sense of exaltation, jubilation, and gladness. The steward at the wedding feast of Cana marvels at the fine wine being served "after the guests have become drunk" (John 2:10), and he seems to be referring to a very different form of drunkenness than the apostle Paul meant in the quote from Ephesians. *Babette's Feast* shows in the most moving way how gentle intoxication in the context of feasting can open up a community to conviviality and communal bonding. With its alcohol content, wine can warm and stimulate the body and help relax it. Cheeks turn rosy, and smiles and laughter come more easily. Alcohol also changes one's state of consciousness. While drunkenness makes one dull, inhibits one's motor and social skills, and can lead to destructive behavior and isolation, gentle intoxication can do exactly the opposite. It can heighten one's awareness and attention level, and it can bring artistic inspiration and unleash creativity. Martin Luther wrote the hymn "A Mighty Fortress Is Our God" while enjoying a glass of Rhine wine. One cannot overestimate the amount of creative thinking done with glass in hand. Wine can also enhance one's sense of delight and celebration. The Latin saying *in vino veritas* ("in wine there is truth") might just hint at a wine's ability to free one from self-conscious fear and care. Confessions come more easily — confessions of love, failure, regret, sorrow, and joy. Allowing conversations to go deeper creates more meaningful bonds between people and knits communities more closely together. The benefits are first of a relational and communal nature, but they flow into all spheres of society. In the fractured societies in which we live, the bond of holy intoxication might just be something we should consider more seriously.

Concluding Reflections

Wine is a gift from God and enhances our festive play before God. The accusation that Christians have no joy is a terrible one because joy should lie at the heart of the Christian life. Our belief in God, our Creator and Redeemer, calls us to a life of gratitude and joy; but somehow the church has forgotten about the importance of joy for Christian spirituality, and has forgotten how to embrace and cultivate it. The Hebrew/Christian tradition has traditionally understood feasting as a way to embrace and practice a life of gratitude and joyful celebration before the face of God. The wedding feast at Cana and the film *Babette's Feast* are profound reminders of this rich Christian tradition. The psalmist reminds us that wine's primary purpose is to bring joy to our lives here on earth (Ps. 104:15). Wine has the potential for profound beauty and can help stir our hearts toward heaven. The intoxicating effect of wine is often seen as purely negative. But *Babette's Feast* is a moving example of how gentle intoxication can enhance our festive play before God and can allow us to let go of our defenses and embrace a life of greater vulnerability and transparency with God and with each other. The wine in the Lord's Supper reminds us that God's greatest act of love occurred when he gave himself to us in Jesus Christ. He was crushed in the divine winepress so that we might be able to receive the forgiveness of our sins and the healing of our wounds. We no longer need to hide from God; we can freely open our broken lives before him, trusting with General Löwenhielm that God's divine grace is infinite. This is the reason for Christian joy.

5

Wine and Attentiveness:
Tasting God, Tasting Wine

"'Tasting is a way of life. We taste everything that comes into contact with our senses, be it a work of art, the present moment, the reality of existence; objects, people, the arts, love, life.' Looked at in this way tasting is a means of perceiving and understanding the outside world; it presupposes a state of mind that is constantly receptive to sensation."

Pierre Poupon[1]

A spirituality of wine and the recovery of a Christian understanding of joyful feasting prompt the question of what role the five senses play in our pursuit of the knowledge of God. Our human capacity for taste and savoring flavors is an extravagant gift from God: tasting brings to our existence a great deal of meaning, which we should pay attention to with gratitude and joy. Infinite combinations of flavors await those who are willing to be attentive tasters. The nineteenth-century food writer Jean Anthelme Brillat-Savarin put it this way:

> The number of tastes is infinite, since every soluble body has a special flavor which does not wholly resemble any other. Tastes are modified, moreover, by their combinations with one, two, or a dozen others, so that it is impossible to draw up a correct chart, listing them from the most attractive to the most repellent, from the strawberry to the griping bitter apple. . . . [W]e have been

forced to depend on a small number of generalizations such as sweet, sugary, sour, bitter. . . .[2]

Tasting wine is a much more sophisticated practice than one would think. The traditional conceptual framework of categorizing tastes into sweet, sour, bitter, and salty could easily mislead one to believe that tasting is a fairly simple activity.[3] What we recognize in our brain as flavor is made up of taste (gustation), smell (olfaction), texture (consistency, liquidity, structure), and temperature. We taste with our mouth, but we smell with our nose *and* our mouth. The human brain processes and evaluates the stimuli we receive from our nose and tongue and creates the impression that we call "flavor." A human tongue has between two thousand and five thousand taste buds (papillae), though in exceptional cases can have as few as five hundred or as many as twenty thousand. Papillae are of different types, with different distributions around the tongue. And each papilla has between 50 and 150 taste receptor cells; these give rise to nerve impulses to the brain. Indeed, God was generous in endowing us with such a multitude of taste buds. These taste buds undergo a regular cycle of regeneration as they grow, die, and are replaced by new growth.[4]

Our sense of smell is also richly endowed. Olfactory receptor cells are located both in our nose and at the back of our mouth (the retronasal passage). We have about one thousand different olfactory receptor cells, and these receptor cells expand from our nose to the back of our throat and deeply integrate the process of tasting and smelling.[5] Emile Peynaud argues that what we perceive as "taste" is actually primarily perceived by our sense of smell.[6] When we savor wine, we swallow it slowly so that the olfactory receptor cells in the back of our throat can also pick up the smell of the wine. This way we can enhance our ability to recognize the wine's flavor with its manifold nuances and enjoy it more fully. The flavor of a wine can linger for a long time, a phenomenon called aftertaste; it calls us to contemplate the wine long after it has been swallowed.

The Veil over God's Abundance

The complexity of flavors in our world is a gift of abundance; yet it often goes unnoticed and does not move us. This is a great loss. Peynaud rightly observes that life in the city cuts us off from the "profusion of tastes and smells" that occur in nature. We lose our instinctive curiosity about them and with it the potential to "have our memories and feelings stirred."[7] We are too busy getting and spending, as Wordsworth mused in his poem "The World Is Too Much with Us."[8] Our sensory powers are drained, exhausted, and shriveled by the likes of artificial flavoring, tasteless vegetables grown on Styrofoam and fed artificially — that is, without contact with real soil. Many consumers now prefer the strong and straightforward synthetic flavors to the more subtle and complex ones found in nature.[9] Homogeneous fast foods, with either very little flavor or strong artificial flavor, and overly sugary foods, including sodas, have created culinary deserts that are sealed off from the bounty of what creation has to offer. This decline seems ironic in view of the rapid increase in culinary programs on television and the popularity of cookbooks and culinary magazines that have accompanied this development.[10] Perhaps this renewed interest in the culinary aspects of life reveals a deeper longing in our culture to recover some of the richness we have lost.

Loud advertising screams for our attention and leaves us numb. Our economic engines have capitalized on the sensitivity of our senses. They seek to lure us into their agenda, and they steal our capacity to be truly attentive to the natural world around us. Commercial enterprises have long realized the power of smell and taste, and they create olfactory accents in order to sell their products. Some go so far as to argue that consumer capitalism has taken our olfactory imagination captive.[11] Who of us has not been lured into a shop just because a certain smell has wafted out, stirred our desires, and enticed us to enter?

In such a noisy and manipulated world it is difficult to contemplate and savor the great and subtle bounties that surround us in creation. Instead, we have become complicit by settling for food that is homogeneous, predictable, and lacking in variety. Too much food has either too little flavor or has too strong an artificial flavor. Unfortunately, the wine world has not been immune to this process, and the adding of artificial flavoring to wine is an accepted practice today.[12] Such foods perhaps feed our bodies (though their nutritional value is really quite questionable), but they no longer nourish our souls.

We have forgotten that eating and drinking can be deeply spiritual exercises that feed us as embodied and communal souls and root us in a particular place. As we enjoy the foods of our home with their very particular smells and tastes, eating and drinking instill in us a sense of belonging and rootedness. When I lived in Birmingham, Alabama, my family sent me gifts of wine and brandy. The taste and smell of these family-crafted drinks kept me rooted in what has always been my home, Franconia, even when I lived far away from it.

Carlo Petrini, the Italian founder of the Slow Food movement, rightly speaks of us as a people in exile when it comes to food production and the ability to enjoy locally produced foods that abound in variety and intensity of flavors. Petrini began locally, and his first project was to call the vintners of the Piedmont region to produce high-quality wines. He encouraged them to embrace their traditional grape varieties and allow the wines to reflect the local *terroir*. The Piemonte Barolo and Barbaresco wines, made from the Nebbiolo grape, are full of character. Their tannins soften over time and give the wines a lovely velvety feel. When crafted with care, these wines make a statement and defy the powerful international wine market.[13]

Noisy marketing machines propagate large-scale, profit-driven wine industries that tend to produce homogeneous wines without depth or character. These wines (though one could hardly call them "wine" if one were to apply the traditional definition of wine to them) eclipse the bounty of what creation has to offer and allow us to settle for less. It is a great loss.

But not all is lost. The transformation that the Piedmont region has undergone is remarkable and indicative of a larger, though quieter, movement. Many vintners have refused to give in to the pressures of producing homogeneous and popular wines. Others have awakened to the fact that crafting wine is more than a job to make money at — and possibly lots of it. Crafting a wine of high quality that reflects the *terroir* of a specific place is a vocation. The vintner's vocation is to produce, to the best of his/her ability, wines that reflect the bounty of their particular place.

As a living thing, wine conveys meaning: among other things, it can teach us about particular places. And it is the beauty and complexity of a well-crafted wine that will enliven and gladden the hearts of attentive drinkers. The mysterious process of fermentation not only transforms sugar into alcohol but also opens up the intricate flavors hidden in the grape juice; these are unleashed in the fermentation process. There is no other food in the world that has this capacity to reveal, with such intensity, a wide range of flavors in one single bottle. A well-crafted wine does this as it gives us a taste of the beauty and bounty of creation. A bad wine does the opposite, leaving us unfeeling, ambivalent, or even disgusted. A bad wine might be, technically speaking, correct, but it offers little to those who seek a wider and more subtle range of flavors and smells, a little complexity with balance, some variation and surprise that naturally come with different vintages. Bad wines can make drinkers decide that they do not like wine at all. They convey no meaning apart from perhaps quenching our thirst and giving us a little alcohol boost. There is a difference between savoring a well-crafted wine and drinking it merely for the purpose of consuming an alcoholic beverage.

Drinking, as we saw from our exploration of the Eucharist and of feasting, can become a deeply spiritual and transformative experience. The Christian life unfolds in the communal and embodied celebration of Christ's redemptive presence in our midst. In the ritual of the Eucharist we drink in order to remember, to be forgiven, and to be renewed. As we seek the renewal of our lives, why not let our sense of taste and smell be part of it? For this to happen we have to abandon some long-held prejudices.

Overcoming Prejudices

Bad wine and food eclipse the abundance of God's good creation, but this is not the only obstacle we have to overcome in developing a spirituality of wine. The church's relationship to the senses — and taste in particular — has been ambivalent, even though the Bible clearly affirms and celebrates the gift of God's good creation, including the sense of taste. In the second chapter of Genesis, God plants a garden of delight, and the fruit of the trees is a gift from God to humanity.

When the Israelites get a glimpse of the Promised Land, they understand God's blessing in terms of the land's agricultural richness, including lush vineyards and juicy figs and pomegranates (Num. 13:23). Feasting became an important means by which the Hebrews lived into their salvation narrative. In Ecclesiastes we learn that eating and drinking are God's gifts (Eccl. 3:13; 9:7). And the Song of Songs celebrates the enjoyment of the world through the senses, especially the sense of taste, as something fundamentally good. Jesus was known to attend dinner parties, and he continued the Hebrew tradition of embracing feasts as a means for spiritual formation. Eating and drinking with "sinners" became an important aspect of his ministry (Mark 2:16).

The human senses — and taste in particular — were so important that tasting became a metaphor for experiencing God. The writer of Psalm 34 speaks of God's deliverance and care, exclaiming, "Oh taste and see that the Lord is good" (Ps. 34:8). Psalm 119 speaks of the goodness and life-giving nature of God's decrees: "How sweet are your words to my taste, sweeter than honey to my mouth!" Proverbs personifies wisdom as a woman who invites pilgrims into her house: "Come, eat of my bread and drink of the wine I have mixed. Lay aside immaturity and live" (Prov. 9:5). Proverbs also compares the wisdom of God to the tasting of sweet honey: "My child, eat honey, for it is good, and the drippings of the honeycomb are sweet to your taste. Know that wisdom is such to your soul" (Prov. 24:13-14).

The prophet Ezekiel envisions the hearing and delivering of God's words to his people in the form of eating: "Oh mortal, eat what is offered to you; eat this scroll, and go, speak to the house of Israel. So I opened my mouth, and he gave me the scroll to eat. . . . Then I ate it; and in my mouth it was as sweet as honey" (Ezek. 3:1-3). In the book of Revelation, John, like Ezekiel before him, envisions the proclamation of the word of God in terms of eating a scroll. An angel speaks to him: "Take it, and eat; it will be bitter to your stomach, but sweet as honey in your mouth. So I took the little scroll from the hand of the angel and ate it; it was sweet as honey in my mouth, but when I had eaten it, my stomach was made bitter" (Rev. 10:9-10). The striking thing about this last passage is that it emphasizes not only the act of eating but also the digestive process that follows. Unlike seeing and hearing, the act of eating involves taking an object into oneself and digesting it. What one tastes, chews, and swallows will be digested and processed in one's digestive system and turned into energy. It seems that this far-reaching experience of eating, which deeply affects the life of the human body by nourishing it, lent itself particularly well to describing the often invisible experiences and effects of spiritual practices, including readings.

If eating and drinking are so important in the biblical worldview and even became a metaphor for our experience of God, why did the church develop such an ambivalent posture toward the senses — and particularly the sense of taste? The story is complex, but a few snippets of it will help provide a sense of what happened.

The Greco-Roman natural philosophers were the ones who began to distinguish between sense perception and a superior form of knowledge. Democritus (ca. 460-370 BC) writes: "There are two forms of knowledge, one genuine, one obscure. To the obscure belong all the following: sight, hearing, smell, taste, touch. The other is genuine and is quite distinct from this."[14] Aristotle (ca. 384-322 BC) continued this trend. For him the intellect (Greek: *nous*) is always right, while desire and imagination are imperfect.[15] He believed that the intellect is independent of sense perception, while the imagination is a movement resulting from actual sense perception.[16]

Aristotle's assessment betrays a deep suspicion of the five senses with respect to the pursuit of knowledge. Nevertheless, he did pay attention to the senses, discussed them individually, and explored their constructive role in human cognition. First he discusses sight, which he considers the sense par excellence; he understands taste to be a form of touch; and he discusses taste and touch last. Interpreters of Aristotle suggest that the order of his treatment of the senses implies a value judgment of them.[17] But Aristotle does recognize that both taste and touch involve a much more intimate engagement with the world around us. For example, he argues that taste is more accurate than smell because we touch what we eat, and taste is in fact the most accurate of all the senses.[18]

Aristotle profoundly influenced the Dominican friar Thomas Aquinas (1225-1274), who wrote a whole commentary on Aristotle's *De Anima*. Aquinas agrees with Aristotle that taste should be understood as a form of touch, but he goes one step further, suggesting that there are not five but only four senses, taste being merely a form of touch.[19] Thus, while Aristotle might have made an implicit value judgment by discussing taste and touch last, Aquinas suggests that taste should not be considered as a separate sense at all. In another context he discusses the senses with respect to aesthetics (from the Greek *aisthanomai*: "to perceive through the senses") and beauty. Aquinas distinguishes between those senses that have sufficient cognitive complexity and those that do not. In his *Summa Theologia* he argues:

> [T]hose senses chiefly regard the beautiful, which are the most cognitive, viz., sight and hearing, as ministering to reason; for we speak of beautiful sights and beautiful sounds. But in reference to the other objects of the other senses, we do not use the expression beautiful, for we do not speak of beautiful tastes, and beautiful odours.[20]

Aquinas believed that both taste and smell lack cognitive complexity and are thus not worthy of being considered as aesthetic experiences. While Aristotle adds value to the senses of taste and touch precisely because there is a more intimate engagement with matter, Aquinas does the opposite when he considers the role of the senses in aesthetic experiences. He argues that because touch and taste are the most material of all the senses, they are less "cognitive."[21] Aquinas seems to have made a value judgment about the taste, smell, and touch senses that would profoundly shape how Western civilization has understood those senses, especially Western Christianity. The effects of this value judgment have lasted to the present day.[22]

Increasingly, the senses of taste and touch fell into disrepute because of their close association with gluttony and sexual immorality, two of the seven deadly sins.[23] The pious adopted rigid fasting practices, and these were to keep them from giving in to the temptations of the flesh. Increasingly, people developed more ambivalent attitudes toward all the senses. They saw fasting and mortifications of the flesh as pathways to a higher and more spiritual life and understood faith to triumph over the allures of the senses.[24] In his rather graphic novellas, which are full of wit and irony, the Italian writer and religious critic Giovanni Boccaccio (1313-1375) mocks such approaches to the spiritual life.[25] But the ascetic practices prevailed. While these strict fasting practices were beneficial to many, they made the lives of the poor peasants, with their meager diet, even harder. The Reformers loudly protested against such spirituality. The question of the role of fasting has remained an important one in Christian spirituality, and a suspicion of the sense of taste and smell has prevailed to this day.

Solitary Voices in the Medieval Desert

There are notable exceptions to this trend. The medical world widely recognized taste as a superior sense.[26] Hildegard von Bingen (1098-1179), a Benedictine nun who was well read and experienced not only in theological but also in medical writings and practices, was also a remarkably gifted artist whose music and medical writings have seen a great renaissance in the present day. She also recognized the importance of the senses: in her allegorical interpretation of the parable of the laborers in the vineyard (Matt. 20:1-16), she compares the five different laborers to the five senses. God is the vintner who calls the five senses (laborers) into the vineyard of salvation. Hildegard calls the sense of taste the prince of the five senses and gives it a prime place in God's work of salvation.[27]

Another example is an early thirteenth-century manuscript entitled *Summa de saporibus* ("compendium concerning taste"). The unknown author describes the sense of taste as superior to all the senses.[28] While this text shows mostly a commonality with other medical texts of the time, the author argues that the sense of taste is the superior sense in our pursuit of knowledge, more generally speaking.[29] All in all, however, medieval thinkers considered the senses of taste and smell to be the most subjective of all the senses. For the most part, they did not believe that the sense of taste and smell could contribute much to our cognitive understanding of the world around us.

New Discoveries in Neuroscience

And yet, studies in anthropology and neuroscience have revealed a very different picture. Scientific studies have shown, for example, that a significant amount of the cerebral cortex (a layer of the brain responsible for thinking, perceiving, consciousness, memory, producing and understanding language) is devoted to sensing flavor. This particular part of the brain, the olfactory cortex, works to decode our sensory perception of flavor. It does so by comparing sensory perception with information stored in our brain from previous experiences. Once we recognize a certain flavor, we can interpret it, and it becomes a conscious cognitive perception.[30]

Our capacity to recognize and perceive flavor is deeply interconnected with other functions of the human brain.[31] Seeing, smelling, and tasting all operate when we taste wine, and the human brain works out a "multisensory integration" of all the stimuli we experience when tasting wine. Different regions of the brain work together to process the sensory information and produce the impression we call "flavor."[32] It is a highly complex cognitive process based on our sensory perceptions.

The impression of flavor in our brain in turn is deeply interconnected with other areas of our brain and elicits certain human behavior. Scientists have shown, for example, that those areas of our brain that process smell and taste also process emotions and memory.[33] These processes rely on widely distributed networks of neurons across many different brain structures and are profoundly interwoven. Our capacity to smell and taste somehow influences our capacity to remember. Neurobiologists are researching, in particular, the relationship between smell and memory. They have found that the loss of smell is one of the initial symptoms in degenerative neurological diseases such as Parkinson's and Alzheimer's. Scientists are now researching the hypothesis that there may be a connection between a lower ability to smell and the likelihood of developing such diseases.[34]

In light of such discoveries, we have to reconsider the theological importance of taste and smell. An "olfactory silence" marks our postmodern world, as public buildings suppress smell, and television and computers seal us off into a world without smell, away from the fragrances and stenches we encounter in creation.[35] We should not underestimate the effect that this "olfactory silence" has on our lives and perhaps even our health and well-being.

On a more positive note, scientists have also found that tastes and smells enhance our ability to remember, especially particular places, events, and people. Tastes and smells socialize us into our communities and give us a sense of belonging. Marcel Proust (1871-1922) reflected on the powerful impact that taste and smell have on our memory long before scientists paid serious attention to this question:

> But when from a long-distant past nothing subsists, after the people are dead, after the things are broken and scattered, taste and smell alone, more fragile but more enduring, more unsubstantial, more persistent, more faithful, remain poised a long time, like souls, remembering, waiting, hoping, amid the ruins of all the rest; and bear unflinchingly, in the tiny and almost impalpable drop of their essence, the vast structure of recollection.[36]

Proust was the son of a medical doctor and researcher, and perhaps he learned some of his insights into the power of smell from his father. Studies in neuroscience are now confirming some of his insights. Tasting and smelling can help us remember. Savoring a glass of wine can enhance our capacity to remember. It can and should intensify our experience of the Lord's Supper, for example, and aid us in our capacity to remember what we celebrate. Indeed, it is surprising that we have not paid more attention to it.

Only recently have theologians begun to reconsider the importance of touch, smell, and taste for the Christian faith and practice, following contemporary philosophers, anthropologists, and neuroscientists.[37] Increasingly, philosophers begin to consider tasting wine as an aesthetic experience.[38] This development is crucial, for it recognizes that the senses of taste and smell convey meaning, much more than we had previously imagined. It is time to pay attention.

To Drink Is to Pray: Savoring Wine as a Spiritual Practice

Savoring a well-crafted wine carries meaning and is both a science and an art form. It requires patient and devoted attention.[39] It reveals to us something of God's abundant generosity. God could have just provided water, but he also gave us wine. Christ could have just let the wine run out at the wedding of Cana; instead, he provided an abundance of choice wine. As Christians, we no longer look at wine as secular matter but learn to receive it as a gift from God. Wine calls us to a life of gratitude. To be grateful means to pay attention to what God has given us, to give thanks for it, to share it, and to appreciate it together. In this way savoring wine can become prayer.

Vintners often compare the life of a vine and its fruit to a human life because the parallels between them are so striking. The factors that make a well-crafted wine include the region and its topography, the climate, and the work of the vintner. The soil of the vineyard has an impact on the quality of the wine, but we do not know to what extent. Scientists are only just beginning to explore this. Some suggest that the depth of the roots of the vine adds complexity to the wine. The vintner also plays a significant role in determining the character and quality of a wine. She prunes the vines, and she makes choices about the quantity of grape clusters to be left on the vine, which in turn impacts the quality of the wine. The fewer grape clusters on the vine, the higher the quality (this is termed "low yield"). In determining the harvest time, she looks for a good balance between natural sugars and acidity in the wine. The weather conditions also have a remarkably important role in determining the wine's flavor. Sun, rain, fog, frost, the length of the summer, and the temperatures throughout the growing season — all these vary from year to year and give each vintage a distinct character.

Then there are the many ways the vintner can influence the wine's character and flavors during the time in the cellar. All of these factors make wine-tasting a fascinating experience; one has to be open to the unexpected and the unknown. Savoring wine is an adventure.

Praying with Our Senses

We can drink a glass of water without thinking about it. Artificially flavored drinks do not demand much attention or discernment from us either. They are simple, straightforward, monotonous, and predictable. A well-crafted wine, just like a well-crafted beer or well-grown and brewed tea, coffee, or hot cocoa, calls us to a life of attentiveness and contemplation. In his classic book on wine-tasting, Emile Peynaud (following Brillat-Savarin) argues that wine brings to us an infinite variety of natural flavors and aromas; it is complex and multifaceted, just as human beings are.[40] And wine evolves — in the bottle and as it is being poured into a glass. Even over a period of just one hour in the glass, a wine can open up and reveal different facets of its flavor, assuming that we taste our wine slowly.

Savoring wine at its best is like praying. It takes effort and a willingness to engage in something that is far more complex than what we are used to when we are simply consuming foods. The good news is that we can learn to savor wine if we are willing to make the effort. We can train ourselves to be more attentive to our sense perception. We can learn to notice and examine sensations, to evaluate them, and to learn the language to speak about them. We cannot communicate some — perhaps even many — of the sensations we experience while drinking wine, but we can still enjoy them (p. 17). We can train our senses to listen to the subtle and complex flavors of each wine.

Our senses of smell and taste become like workers in the land of salvation, laboring for a deeper appreciation of God's gift of wine and a more profound experience of joy and gratitude. And the more we savor a wine, the more we come to know it. Peynaud goes so far as to say that "[t]o taste effectively one must love wine, and to learn to taste it is to learn to love it more" (p. 15). Savoring wine is an affair of the heart, should always be done in moderation, and can enliven our relationship with God and with one another.

Learning to savor wine also helps us to train some of our senses. Peynaud reminds us that it keeps these senses active and engaged, improves their perception, and prevents their decline (p. 27). Savoring wine is like learning a new language. At first we might feel that we are stumbling along, but soon enough we find ourselves in a new world of new sensations, discovery, and delight.

One of the notable things about learning to savor wine is that it engages so many of our senses: sight, smell, and taste all work together. It also takes a great amount of concentration: focused attention, patience, and a willingness to slow down and know more fully what is before us. It teaches us to become more aware of — and to listen to and evaluate — what we see, smell, and taste. Tasting, as Peynaud wisely says, is "an act of self-examination" as we probe our memory and look for reference points in our past experience to identify what we smell and taste (p. 28).

Savoring wine teaches us to be more fully present to ourselves and the world around us. It also teaches us that we are part of a greater community, which includes the sun, the rain, the soil, the vines, the labor of the vintner, and all those who participated in bringing the wine to us. It reminds us that this world is a beautiful and mysterious place that we must not take for granted. It is a gift to treasure, celebrate, and care for. At its best, savoring a well-crafted wine teaches us to be grateful. To drink is to pray.

The Blessedness of Place

When we first see a bottle of wine and a glass before us, we notice the color, the level of clarity, and perhaps the fluidity (dessert wines, e.g., with their high residual sugar, are much "oilier," or "thicker," than other wines). The grape variety (such as Chardonnay, Riesling, Merlot, or Cabernet Sauvignon) determines the color of the wine and tells us much about the characteristics of the wine. Not all labels tell us what grape varietal is in the bottle. Italian wines may have a label identifying the name of the region, perhaps Barbaresco, or the name of the grape, perhaps Barbera.

Labeling varies from country to country, with each country having its peculiar wine laws and regulations. This variation can be very confusing, but there is a good reason for it. The French, with their emphasis on *terroir*, want to emphasize the importance of place. The specific region, the microclimate, and the soil have a significant impact on the quality of the wines. By informing us about the specific region, the producer wants to communicate the importance of *terroir*. Then there are countries where a specific site matters little, and their emphasis is on the grape variety. The United States does not require the wine industry to identify a specific site, but more and more vintners choose to do so.[41]

In Franconia, Germany, the wine label identifies the grape variety, the specific site and region, and the name of the winery. This practice seems to be the most consumer-friendly option, since it duly recognizes the importance of place, grape variety, and vintner — and it helps the consumer identify the wine.

A continued emphasis on place remains crucial if we want to save the wine world from collapsing into the ever-growing machine of industrially manipulated and manufactured wines that scarcely reflect a particular place or a specific vintage (year). The temptation is to settle for a homogeneous and predictable product that perhaps protects us from disappointment but even more from the unspeakable beauty, complexity, and surprise of a well-crafted wine.

Perhaps the world of wine can experience a revival just as the world of beer has. American beer, especially, had at one point become so industrialized, homogeneous, and bland that a significant grassroots movement of microbreweries had to rise up to reverse the trend. The world of microbreweries now offers a significantly wide-ranging and diverse range of craft beers. Though this is still a very small part of the total market, it is indeed an encouraging development.

Exploring the Terrain

Once you have read the label and seen the color and the level of clarity of a wine, you can now pay attention to the sense of smell and taste. The four primary tastes are sweetness, sourness, saltiness, and bitterness, though these descriptors are by no means exhaustive (many have now added the taste of umami). Korsmeyer observes that within these four categories "[a] multitude of tastes swarm on and within its four planes."[42] We must remember Brillat-Savarin's caution that these are merely categories for a wide range of impressions. Korsmeyer rightly bemoans our readiness to dismiss taste as an impoverished or limited sense, which is a remnant of the old hierarchy of the senses.

The mineral salts of wine are of a chemical nature and not discernible, though some wines might have hints of salt taste due to their vineyards' proximity to the sea. This elimination leaves us with three basic taste categories, and it is not too difficult to discern the level of sweetness, acidity, and bitterness in a wine — even for beginners. What is most helpful is to sample wines alongside other wines as the levels of different tastes become more apparent. Dessert wines, such as a French Sauterne, a German late-harvest Riesling, or a Rieslaner (a crossing between a Silvaner and a Riesling) have a high amount of residual sugar and taste very sweet. It is the interplay between the residual sugar and the acidity (sourness) that makes these wines so beautiful and interesting. If these wines do not have enough acidity, they can taste heavy or flat, overly sweet, and lacking in freshness. It is not easy to achieve this fine balance: it depends greatly on the right weather conditions and the craftsmanship of the vintner. Usually these noble grape varieties are low yielding and need to be planted in the best south-facing sites to achieve a high amount of sun exposure, since they mature late in the season. If the vintner picks the grapes too early, they might lack in sweetness; but if he leaves them on the vine for too long, the acidity might decline rapidly and leave the wine without shape. These wines are challenging ones to craft, but they also have the potential to become some of the most exquisite and aromatic wines.

In addition to their taste, these wines usually have a very rich bouquet. We perceive the bouquet with our olfactory sense (located in the nose and the back of the throat), and when speaking of the smell of a wine, we always have to compare the smell to something with which we are already familiar — and speak by way of association. We have to use metaphors. For example, these dessert wines usually have intense hues of subtle fruit, flower, and honey. The sweeter and fruitier wines are easier to describe because so many of their aromas compare to various fruit and flower smells we know. While we might not be able to identify each particular fruit or flower, we are familiar with such smells and can recognize them in a wine.

There are other dimensions of wine that are much more difficult to speak about because the corresponding flavors in other foods are few to none. Terms like "earthy," "minerality," or "mineral taste" have become popular to capture these notes that defy easy categorization. The Frankonian Riesling and Rieslaner have such notes, and they add an important dimension to the flavor profile of these wines, making them richer and more complex. These notes are probably related to the vineyard's *terroir*, though how exactly a wine can mirror the place where the grapes are grown is a question of considerable debate.[43] We do not eat soil and rocks, nor do the minerals in the soil affect the taste of a wine directly; so it is difficult to speak about their influence in more specific terms. The phrase "mineral taste" does not do justice to the rich and varied nuances that these notes add to the wine's flavor. Being at a loss for words, we literally stand speechless before such a wine. We have to learn to appreciate the richness and complexities of these notes without being able to put them into words. Thus wine has much in common with other areas of our lives, such as, for example, our emotional and spiritual experiences.

More often than not, it is the sweet wines that lure novices into the world of wine; drier wines are more of an acquired taste. It takes more effort to understand why these wines can be so beautiful. One has to pay more attention and become familiar with unknown and perhaps unexpected territory. Drier wines tend to be higher in acidity due to cooler weather conditions. Often, but not always, they have less fruit aroma and are more "minerally," "spicy," and "earthy" (for lack of better words). A Burgundian Chablis (made from the Chardonnay grape), a Frankonian Silvaner, and a pinot gris from the Alsace region, for example, are usually dry wines with a rather distinct flavor that popular wine writers now associate with the descriptors "mineral taste" and "spiciness." How these flavors get into the wine is still — perhaps fortunately — a mystery.

Some suggest that the soil in which these vines grow plays an important role in it. Vines can and should develop a dense and deep root system. Vintners have explained that when a vine lacks water and is under stress, it is forced to develop deeper roots in order to reach a new water supply. The deeper the roots grow, the more the roots can interact with and draw from different layers of soil, and the more complex the wines become. The soils of the Chablis, Franconia, and Alsace regions have a range of different soils, such as limestone, chalk, and clay. Limestone is a particularly important subsoil in all of these regions, and it is said to help soften the acidity of these wines.

If you are not familiar with such wines, it is important to listen and get acquainted with flavors you are unfamiliar with and for which you have no vocabulary. At first it might seem like a blur, and you will not be able to identify particular characteristics; but that will change over time. It takes time to get to know the wines and learn the language used to speak about them.

We call the Silvaner a shy wine because it does not impose its flavors on the taster. Rather, the wine unfolds in what the vintner hopes will be a subtle and elegant way. The fruit notes of a Silvaner are very subtle and often remind one of citrus notes. One learns to appreciate its acidity as it gives the wine good structure, a full body, and a lovely freshness. And yet the limestone seems to help soften the acidity. Franconian vintners now make Silvaner wines that are less dry and thus more popular in the world market. But I still like the lovely dryness of a traditional Silvaner: it is unique and defies homogeneity. A Silvaner is a bit like a shy or reserved person. Just because someone is shy does mean that he or she does not have profound things to say. It just takes a bit longer to get to know shy people. The Franconian culture, in which the Silvaner grape is cultivated, is a more reserved and understated culture, and the characteristics of a wine can and do reflect the culture in which it is cultivated.

A well-crafted Silvaner has rich "spicy" and "earthy" notes, and one enjoys them quietly; it is hard to find the right words for these notes and nuances. Vines have the ability to draw nutrients from the soil, and the concentration of different types of microorganisms in the soil affects the vine roots' capacity to draw out those nutrients. The fermentation process makes those nutrients more accessible to us. Perhaps this is why Pliny the Elder called wine the "blood of the earth."[44] Wine keeps us rooted in the reality that there are mysterious and wonderful things hidden deep down in the earth, and it allows us to appreciate those things.

The world of red wines is no different in this regard; fruity red wines are easier to talk about. A traditionally crafted and aged Chianti Classico or Chianti Rufina, made primarily from the Sangiovese grape in Tuscany, Italy, usually has a very distinct sour cherry bouquet, and the joy of that recognition is a delight because fruit notes are easier to recognize and name. Perhaps it is for this reason that New World wine regions try to emphasize the fruit notes of red wines much more than one would traditionally do. These wines are sometimes referred to as "fruit bombs" because they are overly fruity and often lack other important dimensions that are more difficult to discern and talk about. The fruit notes tend to be so strong and overpowering that it can make the wine somewhat one-dimensional. Unfortunately, as such "fruit bombs" age, the wine does not develop the classic "earthy" or "mineral" nuances but tends to develop a harsh medicinal taste. For the sake of technically "correct" wines, the vintners have minimized other aspects, such as the flavors that seem to come from the rich microbial life of the soil. Beginners appreciate it when they are able to recognize fruit flavors. But the wine-tasting world is a complicated place, and as one becomes more attuned to complex flavors in a wine, one looks for the more subtle nuances often associated with the *terroir*, particularly the topography, the soil, and the microclimate of a particular place.

As one grows in wine appreciation, one looks for more complexity. The more traditional red wines of Burgundy, such as those made from the pinot noir grape, or the French-style pinot noirs of Oregon and California, tend to have a lovely balance. Distinct and wide-ranging notes of mushrooms, or even stronger smells such as tobacco and leather, make these wines much more interesting and add to the fruit notes that they certainly have. These wines can bring a waft of rich and fertile countryside into our homes, hinting at soils with a strong concentration of microbial life. Do we have noses attuned to smell, and taste buds attuned to taste this great abundance that God has given us?

While both white and red wines can have bitter notes, it is usually only red wines that have tannins. Red wines are fermented "on the skin": rather than pressing the grape clusters and fermenting the grape juice only (as is the case with white wines), vintners mash the red grapes and put them through the fermentation process together with seeds, skin, and traditionally also the stem. These elements give off tannin extracts, and when the wine is young and the tannins have not been able to blend into the wine, they give off a rather distinct and strong sensation in the mouth. Over time, these tannin extracts break down and blend into the wine in the oxidation process, which is especially true when the wine ages in oak barrels. Our taste buds find the blending of the tannin extracts more agreeable. This process is why highly tannic wines, such as Cabernet Sauvignons, need to age in order to taste well balanced and elegant. It is amazing how grape skins, seeds, and stems can contribute so significantly to the taste of wine. However, sometimes these tannins taste more like an intrusion than a contribution. It takes real craftsmanship, skill, and patience to achieve a fine balance of the alcohol, fruit, and tannin. Without this balance, a red wine will not age gracefully.

The role of the vintners in crafting well-balanced wines is imbued with particular significance. They do not just make a generic product. The vintner has a vocation with an important goal: to craft a drink that can bring joy and delight, wonder and amazement, to those who have eyes to see, noses to smell, and taste buds attuned to taste with all their blessed might.

Concluding Reflections

Just as wine is a gift from God, so is our human capacity to smell and taste. Traditionally, the church has had an ambivalent stance toward the senses of taste and smell in particular. The vintner can help us recover these God-given senses and turn them toward a life of contemplation. While there will always be those who abuse the gifts of God in destructive ways, a well-crafted wine calls us to engage our senses in a prayerful way — listening, seeing, smelling, and tasting how wonderful this world that God has entrusted to us is. A well-crafted wine will teach us that "the world is indeed charged with the grandeur of God" and "it can flame out" and "gather to unimagined greatness." It takes a faithful and skilled vintner who will not spare the toil and will work the soil with care and love. The vintner can show us that "nature is indeed never spent" and can help us discover that there indeed "lives the dearest freshness deep down things because the Holy Ghost over the bent world broods with warm breast and with ah! bright wings."[45] It is to the vocation of the vintner that we must now turn.

PART II

SUSTAINABILITY

6

The Vintner as (Practicing) Theologian: Finder or Maker?

"Blessed are you, Lord God of all creation, for through your goodness we have received the wine we offer you: fruit of the vine and work of human hands, it will become our spiritual drink. Blessed be God for ever."

Eucharistic Liturgy

Wine's place in the celebration of the Lord's Supper can teach us that wine is not "neutral" ground, secular matter without sacred meaning. Wine draws us into a much broader, more holistic understanding of the Christian life. We are part of God's creation, and our Christian lives unfold in our relationship with God and creation.

As we think about the sustainability of that which sustains us, our life with and in God and with creation, both human and nonhuman, we must reconsider the work of the vintner. If the vintner participates in crafting wine that is both God's gift and the work of human hands, his or her vocation has profound spiritual meaning. Wine is not a generic drink. Like few other drinks in the world, it has the potential to develop a complex bouquet and intricate flavors that can leave our olfactory imagination in a state of bliss. Our taste buds and olfactory receptor cells find in wine one of the most challenging and engaging "landscapes" to discover, explore, and appreciate. A well-crafted wine can truly enhance our sense of joy to be alive in this beautiful world and to belong to a generous and forgiving Giver.

Do vintners recognize the important role they play in God's creation and redemption? Working day in and day out in this intricate play between "fruit of the vine and the work of human hands," do they discern that their vocation is not just a job in which they can earn a living, but also a calling? As part of this research project, I interviewed a number of vintners in order to explore their understanding of this vocation and their philosophy of wine-crafting. I began by interviewing vintners in Germany and France, representative of Old World wine. I sought out the older generation of vintners, most of them already retired but still rooted in the traditional Christian understanding of their vocation. I conducted interviews in the Rheingau and Franconia regions, both steeped in more than one thousand years of wine-crafting. From there I traveled to the United States, where I interviewed vintners in California and Oregon, those who represent the New World wine. Other than Tim Mondavi and Jason Lett, whose fathers played significant roles in developing viticulture in Napa Valley, California, and the Willamette Valley, Oregon, most of the vintners I interviewed in the United States were first-generation vintners. What most of these new vintners have in common is that they are part of small wineries that are dedicated to crafting wines of high quality and ones that reflect, as well as they can, the *terroir* of their given place and vintage. For the most part, they grow their own grapes and oversee the whole process, from planting and tending the vines, to harvesting the grapes, to the work in the cellar, to selling the wines to their customers.

The Vintner as Theologian:
Reflections from the Old World Wine Country

In the Rheingau, I interviewed Father Ralf Hufsky, a Catholic priest who tends his own vines, and Sister Thekla, the vintner at the Abbey of St. Hildegard (von Bingen). The Benedictine nuns are once again cultivating vines, just as they did during the time of Hildegard von Bingen (1098-1179). Sister Thekla and Father Hufsky know each other well, since Father Hufsky regularly celebrates Mass at the abbey. For Sister Thekla, life has been deeply shaped by her Benedictine order, and the rule of Saint Benedict in particular; Fathert Hufsky has carefully studied the works of Hildegard.

Father Hufsky emphasizes that wine is a symbol of joy and feasting and becomes a sign for the eschatological wedding feast between God and his people. When Jesus turned water into wine at the wedding of Cana he revealed that the time of the Messiah, the anointed one, had come. Wine becomes a symbol for the presence of the Messiah. This is why, according to Hufsky, Jesus was called a glutton and drunkard, by contrast to John the Baptist, who fasted. When Jesus then announced, "I will never again drink of this fruit of the vine until that day when I drink it new with you in my Father's kingdom" (Matt. 26:29), it suggested that the fulfillment of things was still to come, and that wine was pointing beyond this world to the existence of another world.

Father Hufsky appreciates some of the traditions of the Eastern Orthodox Church. He learned from Orthodox Christians in Iraq that the bride and groom at a wedding must drink a cup of wine directly after the completion of the ceremony. It reminds the couple that their marriage is a sacrament of joy. For Hufsky, joy in the Christian sense is about something that happens in us and is done to us. Joy is not something one produces but is a gift from God. On Sundays we celebrate this gift of joy in our salvation and drink wine both as a symbol for Christian joy and also because it enhances our sense of joy. We purposefully express this joy by setting Sunday apart from workdays, when we should drink less. Sundays are a time of celebration, though there are seasons of fasting as well.

The writings of Hildegard von Bingen inspired Father Hufsky in his work as a priest and a vintner. He recounts that Hildegard insisted that wine be used for Holy Mass since it is a symbol for the blood of Christ. At one point the Roman Catholic Church had to consider whether Chinese Christians could use rice wine for the celebration of the Eucharist; the Catholic Church decided against it. In the Eucharist the church does not merely recall an idea, but it remembers a specific historical meal — thus wine and wheat bread must be used.

Hufsky points out that Hildegard enjoyed celebrating with her sisters. He thinks that, while Saint Benedict tolerated wine, Hildegard affirmed the importance of the *Genuss* of wine, a German term that names the particular delight and joy one experiences when one eats and drinks. The English language has no equivalent for this term, though the word "savor" might cover some of its meaning.

For Hufsky, wine grows in the vineyard, is made in the cellar, and finds its ultimate purpose in the *Genuss* by humanity. Wine can be kept for hundreds of years: the oldest wine, from Johannisberg (Germany), is nearly five hundred years old and still drinkable. Johannisberg is one of the oldest sites for German Rieslings and was first developed by Benedictine monks over one thousand years ago. And yet wine is not meant to be stored for unlimited periods of time. As the fruit of the vine and work of human hands, wine achieves its goal when humanity savors it with a sense of joy and when it represents the blood of Christ in the Eucharist.

Father Hufsky believes that the role of the vintner is to reflect the gifts of God as faithfully as possible. The vintner unites the heavenly and earthly dimensions of life. In former times the vineyard was called a "wine garden," and it reminded people of paradise. Faher Hufsky believes that vintners should ensure that their vineyards look beautiful. Perhaps they could plant a peach tree or an almond tree, add a wayside shrine or a bench where people can sit and enjoy the place. Perhaps they could grow trees with winterberries to provide food for birds in the winter. The birds of the sky should receive their part because they are also members of the kingdom of heaven. By cultivating a wine garden, the vintner can show that the vineyard is not merely an agriculturally productive land that is there to produce profit; it is also there to delight and bring rest to humanity and to help us connect to the ultimate vintner, whom Saint John spoke of so beautifully (John 15).

On the feast day of Saint John the Apostle and Evangelist, December 27, the Roman Catholic Church in Germany celebrates the "Johannisweinsegnung," the Johannine blessing of the wine. According to legend, Saint John blessed a cup of poisonous wine and as a result the poisoned wine did not harm the drinker. Since then the Catholic Church has blessed and dedicated the wine on Saint John's feast day, showing that wine is meant to bring joy and well-being to humanity. The watering down and manipulating of wine has been a problem since ancient times, and Father Hufsky believes that this ritual reminds us that we need to protect wine from being spoiled, watered down, or overly manipulated.

Hufsky notes that the Catholic Church in Germany decided to use only the best wine for the celebration of the Eucharist. The liturgy of the Johannine blessing of wine includes a citation from John's account of the wedding feast of Cana: "You have kept the good wine until now" (John 2:10). Hufsky explains that in the liturgy this citation has a dual meaning: the best wine comes last, and it is a symbol of the appearance of Jesus Christ as the climax of God's revelation. Hufsky points out that Johannisberg has several wayside shrines depicting Christ in the winepress. In the old medieval winepresses, the cross-beams conform to the shape of a cross, and the analogy seems natural. Christ in the winepress teaches us even today that the active embrace of suffering, rather than fighting against it, can bring about great fruit. The formation of human life happens in the tensions, challenges, and even suffering of life if we learn to trust God and allow him to do his work within us. The theme of Christ in the winepress addresses this important question of human suffering and invites believers to ponder their own experience of suffering in light of Christ's suffering.

Hufsky recognizes that wine is ambivalent in that it has another side to it; but he argues that we cannot protect ourselves from everything. We would cease to live. He argues that it is much harder to get drunk on wine (if it is a well-crafted wine) than it is on beer or hard liquor. In the Rheingau the cultural rule is to drink no alcohol before six o'clock in the evening.

When Father Hufsky has church meetings whose purpose is for people to get to know each other, he serves wine. Hufsky believes that when we drink a bottle of wine with someone, we make ourselves vulnerable, as wine loosens the tongue and we speak more openly. When the purpose of the meeting is to accomplish a task or to discuss a church issue, he does not serve wine. Hufsky concludes his reflections by emphasizing the importance of sharing the wine from one's vineyard. One can harvest — but one should not exploit — the vineyard, and it is important to share the bounty that one receives. This is what we learn from viticulture in the Old Testament. When the church celebrates and the poor participate, we share the wine with them as a sign of the eschatological wedding feast.

Sister Thekla has also gleaned much from Hildegard von Bingen, especially the way Hildegard cultivated her creation spirituality. Hildegard understood that we are embedded in creation, and our relationship with creation deeply shapes our relationship with God. The activities of working the land and cultivating the vines have taught Sister Thekla how dependent she is on creation: the interplay between the climate, the vine, and our human participation. One has to learn to become highly attentive to the dynamics in the vineyard, and the eucharistic prayer regarding wine — "fruit of the vine and work of human hands" — has become very important to her. The power of creation and the work of human hands are deeply intertwined and interdependent, and this dynamic demands a watchful eye.

Sister Thekla had to accept that there are powers in creation that she cannot control, but she can respond to them actively and creatively. Each year is different, and each year brings forth an exciting wine that is shaped by that year's unique conditions. Some years are more challenging than others, but often the wines of "bad" years actually might just need some time to mature in the bottle. Wine is a living thing, and though we cannot control it, Sister Thekla is often pleasantly surprised by what she discovers as the wine matures in the bottle.

Sister Thekla understands the commission in Genesis 1 for humans to rule the earth, not as an excuse to oppress and exploit, but to use what creation has to offer in a responsible way. She believes that she has been entrusted with these vineyards, and it is her responsibility to pass them on so that the next generation can continue to work the land. When humans become too far removed from creation, they forget how dependent they are on creation. For her, the modern idea of the "wine-maker" has more to do with the modern food industry and technology than with the interplay between "fruit of the vine and work of human hands." Sister Thekla does not think that she is "making" wine. Her role in the wine-crafting process is that of protecting, caring for, and watching over the various stages.

Since the sisters at the Abbey of Saint Hildegard are concerned to care for creation, they considered the question whether they should become biodynamic in their wine-growing and only use natural fertilizers to enrich the soil of the vineyard. The abbey, however, only owns small parcels of land, which are surrounded by other vineyards that do not farm biodynamically. The sisters decided that it would be dishonest to call their wines "organic," since fertilizers go deep into soil and their vineyard would be affected by the fertilizing of the adjoining vineyards. It is important for the sisters to be honest with their customers.

A well-crafted wine costs more than does a mass-produced wine with no particular distinction, those so often found in the aisles of large supermarket chains. For Sister Thekla, spending a bit more money (eight to ten euros rather than three euros) on a well-crafted wine has to do with one's philosophy of life. Germans in general tend to invest more in their houses and cars. But life is short. Once in a while we should allow ourselves a good glass of wine with a meal. Sister Thekla believes that, in order to enjoy and savor life, it takes *Gelassenheit* (another important German word that is difficult to translate into English). The German mystics used *Gelassenheit* to express our ability to trust God and thus be able to let go of the cares of life and find peace and joy in God despite — even in the midst of — those cares.

Sister Thekla usually chooses the wine that is used in the Eucharist at the abbey. On weekdays she chooses a more simple wine, and on feast days she chooses a special wine. Sister Thekla believes that Jesus purposefully chose wine for this celebration. The reality of wine encompasses a wide range of notions, such as violence and stress, transformation and maturation — which draws us into an understanding of the cross. Wine can only become wine when the grapes are crushed, and this reminds us of Christ in the winepress and the suffering he had to go through. Pain and suffering are also part of the Christian life. Wine undergoes a fundamental transformation in the fermentation process, and what exactly happens in that process is beyond our current understanding; but we do know that a good wine matures over time.

And wine creates conviviality. One usually does not drink wine alone, but together with another person or other people; wine enhances our relationships with one another. All these ideas are present in the Eucharist, and wine helps us grasp the meaning of the Eucharist and its purpose in our lives.

The last person I interviewed in the Rheingau was the cellar master at the winery that is still called Kloster Eberbach, named after the former Cistercian monastery. Kloster Eberbach is now a government-owned winery, but it has a long history of wine-growing. The monastery dates back to the twelfth century, when Bernard of Clairvaux sent out twelve monks to found it. Mr. Bernd Kutschick no longer has any connection with the Christian faith, but he bemoans these modern times, in which the development of certain technology has led to a loss in vine varieties and thus wine quality. For him this circumstance is a significant cultural loss; we shall hear his concerns more fully in the next chapter, on technology and wine-growing.

The wine region of Franconia, which I can affectionately call "my home," has an even older recorded tradition than does the Rheingau of Christians expanding viticulture. As I have observed above, the Latin poet Venantius Fortunatus wrote in the sixth century about Benedictine nuns planting vines along the River Main in Kitzingen and Ochsenfurt. One of the vintners I interviewed is Sister Hedwig, now a retired Augustinian nun at the Vogelsburg winery, by Volkach. The Vogelsburg is a happily situated winery that sits on a hill overlooking one of the most scenic wine regions in Franconia. The winery now belongs to the Juliusspital, a charitable hospital and winery. The Vogelsburg was first given to the Benedictines in 906, and Sister Hedwig emphasizes that vines have been grown here, with little interruption, for 1,100 years.

Sister Hedwig grew up on a farm, learned early in life to care for creation, and has always been concerned about working with creation in harmonious ways. She asks herself regularly whether she takes the commission of Genesis 1 seriously, not in the sense of overburdening creation, but in the sense of Genesis 2, where God plants a garden and places humanity in it to till it and care for it. Sister Hedwig believes that Genesis 2 interprets the command in Genesis 1 to rule, fill, and subdue the earth (Gen. 1:26-28; 2:15). It is a positive ruling of the land in that humans take responsibility for the land that is entrusted to them by God. We are allowed to participate in what is happening in creation and can affect it in positive ways. In light of her beliefs, Sister Hedwig has to ask herself over and over again whether her beliefs inform her work in the vineyard. This is especially poignant when it comes to the way vintners treat the soil on which they grow their vines.

A Short Excursus: Understanding Vineyard Soils

An important aspect of viticulture is caring for the soil and the land. In order for a vine to flourish, it needs healthy soil. But what is a healthy soil, and how do we best care for it? This question is an important one not only for the vintner but also for all those involved in agricultural endeavors around the world. I think it appropriate to go on a brief excursus for the purpose of understanding vineyard soil, to show why an important part of a vintner's vocation is to understand and care for the soil.

Vines are sturdy plants and can thrive where no other fruit-bearing plant can. They do need soils that drain well; and in cooler climates, stony soils are very important because the stones help retain heat and give off warmth to the vines during the night. Some suggest that vines with deeper root systems tend to develop better wines. A study of the vineyards of the great wines of Bordeaux showed that the best wines come from vineyards with well-drained soils and with water levels just within reach of the vine roots. The stress that the vines experience in drawing water from the ground seems to help them focus on producing higher-quality grapes.[1]

The presence of living organisms and organic matter generally distinguishes soil from rock material. Living organisms can still be found in depths of several kilometers. A range of inorganic minerals provides the structural framework for these living organisms. Robert White explains:

> Life in the soil is a struggle, but the cycle of growth, death, and decay is essential for healthy soil functioning in cultivated fields, forests, grasslands, and vineyards. Organisms ranging from bacteria (invisible to the human eye), to insects, earthworms, and burrowing animals feed on the residue of plants and other organisms, and themselves become food for subsequent generations.[2]

Over time, particular soil profiles develop. When a vine is planted, it interacts with the soil and extracts nutrients from it. Different pieces of land have different soil variations and structures, and these soils interact with the local climate (microclimate) and particular vines in specific ways, giving wines their distinct characters. It was the achievement of the Cistercian monks of Citeaux in Burgundy, along the Cote d'Or, to discover — probably over hundreds of years — the particular character of the Clos de Vougeot vineyard. They winnowed out vine varieties until they decided that the pinot noir was most suitable for this site and climate. The Cistercian monks at Eberbach, Rheingau, in turn, discovered the Steinberg and began, after another long period of trial and error, to plant Riesling grapevines there.[3]

The task and the challenge of the vintner is not only to keep the soil living and healthy but also to learn, by trial and error, what vine varieties grow best in a particular soil and microclimate in order to craft a wine that reflects a particular place (*terroir*). The choices and the interaction — and the culturally conditioned personality — of the vintner with soil, microclimate, and vine varieties represent a complex and mysterious process that science has not been able to understand fully up to the present day.[4]

When vines are planted, they draw nutrients from the soil, and the soil fertility declines.[5] An important task of the vintner is to make sure that the soil remains well balanced and is refertilized when necessary. It is here that Sister Hedwig had to make choices: what fertilizers and pesticides to use to keep the soil, the vines, and her surroundings healthy and productive, not only in the short term but for future generations of vintners. And it is here that her faith informed her decisions. She wanted to take care of the soil, and to work as much as possible in harmony with creation. So Sister Hedwig became an organic vintner.[6]

While organic and biodynamic viticulture is much more popular today, it was not when Sister Christa, Sister Hedwig's predecessor at the Vogelsburg, began her vocation as a vintner in the late 1950s. The development of chemical fertilizers and pesticides marked twentieth-century agriculture, and — especially since the 1960s — these chemicals have been used extensively in modern viticulture.[7] Sister Christa, new to the job, also used them to spray the vineyards. But one day in the early 1960s, the pesticide got into one of her boots and she became sick. After much thought, she decided that something that was not good for her body would also not be good for the vineyard, and she tried organic wine-growing. The Vogelsburg winery has been organic ever since. Sister Hedwig has great respect for Sister Christa because it took great courage to strike out and try organic wine-growing when the trend at that time was moving in the opposite direction. Embracing organic viticulture was a struggle that brought many challenges. The vines around the Vogelsburg did not always look the healthiest. But the tendency in Franconia today is toward a much more natural and organic way of farming the land, and the two Augustinian sisters quietly pioneered it.

*   *   *

Prince Albrecht Castell-Castell and his ancestors have been involved in crafting wines since the thirteenth century, and he understands viticulture as part of his family tradition. The Castells also brought the Reformation teaching into their region in the sixteenth century. Prince Castell-Castell is firmly rooted in his Protestant faith. He has been married for over sixty years and has eight children, and his trust in God has carried him through life. His faith profoundly shapes the way he views his vocation as a vintner. Under the influence of God's creation mandate to humans to till and care for the earth, Prince Castell-Castell believes that God has entrusted us with parcels of land, and we are to plant fruit that is useful for humanity. What he can offer to his customers is thus a gift. The role of the vintner is to choose the best vine variety for a particular parcel of land, to care for the vine, to protect it from pests and parasites, and to find the right balance between quantity and quality. Too much emphasis on quantity will reduce the quality of the wine; on the other hand, the goal is not to focus solely on the production of elite wines either. The Castells' primary emphasis is to take the fruit of the vine and to craft, with much patience, care, and experience, high-quality wines that are affordable.

The account of the wedding feast at Cana in John has left a deep impression on Prince Castell-Castell. In John's account, Jesus joins in a festive celebration and shares the joys of humanity. John tells us that God wants to celebrate with us. He wants us to be joyful and to savor life, not only with water but also with wine. Jesus could have turned stones into bread, but instead he revealed his extravagant generosity and turned water into wine. Wine belongs to feasting; it crowns a festive occasion. The miracle of the wedding feast at Cana is also an invitation to believe in Jesus Christ as the Messiah and to learn to live in him. The Lord's Supper allows us to taste Christ in the most intimate way when we eat the bread and drink the wine. For Prince Castell-Castell, this is very special. When we eat and drink, we take something completely into ourselves, and this is what we do in the Lord's Supper. We take Christ into ourselves by eating his body and by drinking his blood, and we experience something profoundly intimate and meaningful. It is a life-giving event that nourishes us on our journey of faith.

Mr. Edi Krammer used to be the cellar master for the Castell winery. He is now retired and continues to grow his own vines, which he lovingly cares for. To him, crafting wine is an affair of the heart, and one has to approach viticulture with much love. Mr. Krammer speaks with, and cares for, each vine as a mother does for her children. Just as a mother hopes that her children grow up well, so does the vintner hope that the vines grow up to be healthy and strong. Mr. Krammer describes his role in the wine-crafting process as analogous to midwifery. He calls the yeast the "mother" of the wine, and his role is to make sure that the conditions for giving birth are clean and healthy. He helps direct the grapes to their ultimate goal of becoming a well-crafted wine. Each vine variety and each vintage has its own unique way of being birthed, and the vintner needs to be attentive to the unique demands of each vintage, each of which has different challenges. There is no set formula for crafting wine; it is a living thing and needs the attention and care comparable to the care one gives to one's children.

One of the questions I asked every vintner was: Where is wine made? Is it primarily made out in the vineyard or in the cellar? With the advances of technology, much can be done to vines in the vineyard and to the grape juice/

wine in the cellar. Different countries have different laws that protect wine from being overly manipulated. Old World wine countries, with a longer history of wine manipulation, tend to have much stricter wine laws than those in New World wine countries. In general, the vintner is still left with many choices with respect to how he or she crafts the wine.

Herbert Müller and my sister, Gertrud Kreglinger-Müller, work as a team at the Kreglinger winery. Herbert is a rather traditional vintner and calls "wine-making" an "unword." He sees himself much more as a finder and craftsman. For him the foundation for a wine of quality is laid in the vineyard. The work he does in the cellar involves protecting the quality of the grapes and allowing them to develop into a well-balanced wine. It is in the cellar that Herbert uses his skills, knowledge, and experience as a craftsman to allow the wine to find its final form. Herbert's philosophy of crafting wine sets limits on how much technology he will use in the cellar. (We shall hear more about those technologies and their limits in the next chapter.)

The emphasis of Herbert's work is in the vineyard, and this emphasis has taught him how utterly dependent he is on nature — and ultimately on God. Franconia is one of the northernmost wine-growing regions in Europe, and the weather conditions are more extreme than in other regions. Late frosts in the spring and sudden heavy rains or hail in the fall can cause devastating damage to the harvest. This feeling of utter dependence has deeply shaped Herbert's identity as a vintner and has taught him to be humble. Most humans in advanced societies are no longer involved in working the land and have forgotten how dependent humanity is on creation.

Each autumn the Lutheran church celebrates a harvest thanksgiving service, and Herbert has noticed that this service used to be so much more important than it is today. If the farmers did not harvest enough food, the population would starve. Today people buy their fruit and vegetables in a supermarket, and they forget how dependent they ultimately are on creation. Creation offers us such a bounty and amazing variety in herbs, fruits, and vegetables; in the supermarket we often find only a fraction of this great abundance. We have forgotten and no longer sing the wonderful hymns, such as the famous Paul Gerhardt hymn "Go Forth, My Heart, and Seek Delight," which teach us to foster a sense of wonder and awe for this incredibly beautiful creation.[8]

Armin Störrlein from Randersacker grew up in a Catholic home and is now semiretired and has passed on the responsibility of the winery to the next generation, though, of course, a vintner rarely retires. The rhythm of nature and life in the vineyard has deeply shaped Störrlein's life. Every year he watches new things come into existence: the first budding of the vines, the first blossoms, the first bees and insects, the summer in all its glorious majesty, and the phases of growth. He experiences the maturation of the grapes, the harvest, and the dying of a vintage. Everything looks dead and seems to be without life. And then everything happens all over again. For Störrlein, the life of grapevines and how they self-pollinate is a new act of creation each year.

A good vintner needs sensitivity and a deep sense of responsibility, and Störrlein believes that a great responsibility toward the land and the vineyards has been entrusted to him and his family. He wants to work the land and harvest its fruit, but he must not exploit it. Instead, he hopes to pass it on to the next generation in at least as good a condition as, or even better than, he received it. When he thinks about Christian spirituality with respect to his own work, he believes that wine is a gift and product of nature, and nature, in turn, is a gift from God. He feels strongly that his work as a vintner includes the conservation and protection of this natural and cultural gift we have received. Today, however, the food-manufacturing industry, with its many technological advances, poses a great threat. The "food" that is produced today with the help of technology and chemicals has little to do with the natural product of the farming world.

When Störrlein was younger, he thought humanity was brilliant and that, with the help of technology, everything was possible. But as he got older he realized that humans fail. The older he gets, the more he realizes how small he is in relation to the vastness of what we find in creation and beyond, and that he must not take himself too seriously. Everything we do is accompanied by human frailty. It is not always meant for evil, but we have to realize that we are not in heaven yet. Nature has its own laws, and we can be thankful that it still has its own secrets. We cannot comprehend nature completely. If we were able to grasp and know everything, we would try to control it, and humanity would become very dangerous. Knowledge has enriched humanity, but there is always the danger of the abuse of knowledge.

Störrlein was also quite enthralled with the use of technology when he was younger, but he has evolved as a vintner and has joined a movement in Germany that seeks to craft wines as naturally as possible. He believes that "technological" wines lack "soul." There is something indefinably beautiful about crafting a natural wine that reflects place. Störrlein wishes to craft wines that bring joy and health to his customers — and are at the same time affordable. In Franconia, well-crafted wines are affordable to the average person. But there are wine regions in the world, especially in the New World, where the average person cannot afford the artisanal wines produced in their neighborhood, region, or even country. Störrlein thinks that this circumstance is problematic and borders on blasphemy. Wine should not be understood as a luxury good. He cannot think of one family in his village that would not drink a good glass of wine at least once a week.

Störrlein believes vintners should work together with their governments to create economic structures in which family businesses can thrive and offer affordable wines. It is usually the family businesses that take care of the land best because they feel a much greater sense of ownership and responsibility toward the land. Corporations focus too much on profit and not enough on the sustainability of the land. Störrlein once met the owner of such a corporate wine company in Australia, and he was surprised to learn that the owner did not even drink wine. The only reason he owned the wine corporation was to make money.

The last person I interviewed in Franconia was Mr. Wolfram König from Randersacker, a retired vintner who is deeply steeped in his Catholic faith. He was instrumental in the recovery of the ritual of the blessing of grapes in that region of Franconia. It is a tradition that goes back to the Old Testament: the offering up of the first fruits (see chap. 1). For König, wine is a symbol of joy and a sign of reconciliation in the Eucharist. When there is reconciliation, there is peace; and when there is peace, there is joy. Joy is the expression of a profoundly felt gratitude toward God. For König, marveling and rejoicing are the most beautiful prayers, and wine can enhance people's sense of joy. We must never forget that this is part of the purpose of wine.

König points out how easy it is to forget this lesson. When the people of Israel wanted a king to rule over them (Judges 9), they were told a parable. In the parable Israel turns to the vine and asks it to rule over God's people, and the vine responds, "Shall I stop producing wine that cheers gods and mortals and go to sway over the trees?" (Judg. 9:13). For König, this parable emphasizes that wine is provided to bring joy. In the parable the vine refuses to be used to rule and hence to oppress; rather, it remains faithful to its calling to bring joy. Let us never forgot that this calling is the biblical mandate for the vine: to bring joy not only to its owner but also to the neighbor — whether poor or rich.

The Vintner as Theologian:
Reflections from the New World Wine Country

The two wine regions I visited in North America were in Northern California (the Sonoma and Napa valleys) and Oregon (the Willamette Valley). Most of the vintners I interviewed did not have any particular ties to their Christian upbringing, though when it came to the subject of the spirituality of wine, they had fascinating insights. Most striking were the repeated comments by several vintners that the Christianity they had grown up with was far too narrow for what they experience day in and day out in the vineyard. They said the world of the vintner is far too mysterious to be captured by what they had come to know of the Christian faith.

Jason Lett, of Eyrie Vineyard in Oregon, grew up on a vineyard. His father, David Lett, helped pioneer viticulture in Oregon; he discovered that certain Northern European varieties, including the pinot noir variety, grow very well in the Willamette Valley. Some very fine pinot noirs now come from this young wine-growing region. When I first approached Jason Lett about the spirituality of wine, he was hesitant because he did not think he had anything to contribute to this subject matter. Little did he know.

Amid all the excessive wine talk that seems to have taken over the commercial wine world, Jason Lett has stopped taking notes when he tastes wine. It is hard to put into words what one experiences when one drinks a well-crafted wine. But there is one thing that Jason knows when he tastes a good bottle of pinot noir: the energy of a conversation will improve with a good bottle of wine, and it will enhance the conversation. Jason believes a wine picks up and reflects the attitude of the people who craft it, and the wine can transmit that attitude to those who drink it. It is a form of communication, and it works much like music. Music evokes an emotional response without depicting anything directly emotional. Wine does it in the same way.

Just like his father, Jason enjoys experimenting with his wines, and one area of experimentation that fascinates him is music. That music affects humans deeply is well recognized and accepted; but that music can also affect the process of crafting wine has only recently become an area of exploration. For the last few years Mr. Lett has filled two fermenters of the same size with grapes from the same site. Each fermenter is exposed to a different music. One fermenter "listens" to the music of Hildegard von Bingen, while the other is exposed to the music of John Coltrane. When I asked Jason Lett why he chose those two musicians, he responded that he wanted good music, but two very different styles of music, and music that had a spiritual/mystical dimension to it.

Jason feels that a traditional conception of God is far too simple to explain all the mystery that he encounters in crafting wine. One of the reasons he crafts wine is that he feels that he is being exposed to a much greater reality. His concern about the traditional understanding of faith as he had come to know it, is that it tends to be very hierarchical and locked into a *human* understanding of things, that its adherents are often unaware of the greater reality he experiences in the vineyard — a reality that is miraculous.

A woman from a local church comes to visit the Eyrie winery regularly. She is a Christian and wants to learn about the vine, since it is such a common metaphor in the Bible. Jason thinks that this woman believes that drinking wine is a sin, but at least she is willing to learn a bit more about the vine as a metaphor for human life. Jason also knows the pastor at First Baptist Church in town, and has become quite friendly with him. He does not usually think of Baptist churches as having a deep, ecological understanding of spirituality, but Kent Harrop, the pastor, is very much in tune with the fact that we live in a miraculous place and should take care of it. Jason himself has a deep sense of the interconnectedness of life and believes that we humans are far less important than we often think we are. Each year he is almost pleasantly surprised by how he is supported by the grapes he grows. Perhaps the church can learn from vintners like Lett, allowing him to teach us something about God's creation and what it means to recover a more humble and harmonious relationship with it.

Russ Raney, now retired, started up Evesham Wood Vineyard in Oregon. He is an Episcopalian and understands, first of all, that wine is a gift from God. When he first planted vines in 1987, an Episcopal priest blessed those vines in a ceremony. Raney has taken great care to farm organically and to leave the wines as natural as possible. He sees a great temptation in the North American wine world to alter wines in order to appeal to a small but influential group of wine writers. Since North America was not able to cultivate a cultural knowledge of what makes a well-crafted wine (because of the devastations of Prohibition), a relatively small group of popular wine writers have filled the void. They freely offer their opinions to a consumer market that often feels at a loss in the face of such an overwhelming range of wines from all over the world. The power that these wine writers have had is considerable, but this influence is changing. Wine blogs with writers who specialize in specific regions can offer more nuanced insights and help guide those in search of a good bottle of wine.[9]

A vintner has to make choices about how much his or her wine will reflect a particular place, and to craft a wine that reflects each vintage in unique ways. But a vintner also has to sell the wine — and thus must consider the market and its preferences. Russ Raney is thankful to see an increasing market emerging that is no longer content with wines that have overripe fruit flavors and are high in alcohol content. He observes that the more people drink wine with their meals, the more they look for more subtle and nuanced wines. For Raney, understanding the land and the vine is a God-given mandate and calls him to a life of gratitude. He sees himself as a mediator who has a responsibility to preserve this gift and allow a wine to reflect the land as well as possible. This sense of responsibility has kept him from intervening too much with the wine and using invasive technology that alters the wine significantly. It takes centuries to figure out what vine variety will thrive best in specific parcels of land. And the less invasive technology one uses, the more one can explore what wines will become most typical of the area.

Adam Lee, of Siduri Wines in Santa Rosa, California, grew up Southern Baptist but no longer identifies with this particular expression of Christianity. He is the only vintner I interviewed who does not grow his own vineyards; but he does try to be involved with his vintners and their vines as much as possible. *Terroir* and the uniqueness of parcels of land in crafting wine are very important to him. But most people do not seek out this extra meaning and deeper engagement that *terroir* is capable of providing. They are happy to drink a wine that tastes like pinot noir, for example, but are not interested in a particular expression of this grape variety stemming from a particular *terroir*. But Lee thinks it is important: he feels that his culture has lost the memory for the land, for the gift of the land, and for the particulars of the land. No piece of land is the same, and in order to recover a sense of place, we need to recover the particulars of place. Wine can do that for us like no other drink in the world.

Lee has read in Genesis that, before the Fall, there was a complete harmony between humanity and creation. This circumstance changed after the Fall, and he feels that this desire for natural wines where humans do not have to intervene is really a desire for the complete harmony between humans and creation. It is an ideal that we should uphold, but we must also realize that in this world this ideal can never be achieved. While he works hard to craft wines as naturally as possible, Lee does have to intervene and use technology where necessary. He also points out that this tension is an ancient one. Pliny the Elder already complained about salt water being mixed into the wine and called it a "bastardization" of real wine.

Crafting wine is a great mystery, and Lee has read many books on the technical aspects of wine-making. Scientists cannot find a direct correlation between the minerals in the wine and the minerals in the soil, for example: Where does the flavor come from? We don't know — at least not fully. What strikes Lee most is how little of the whole process of crafting wine is actually understood. It is a great miracle, just as so much of life is mysterious and we need to take the time to ponder it.

Ted Lemon, of Littorai Wines, is a biodynamic vintner with vineyards in Sonoma and Mendocino counties, growing primarily pinot noir and Chardonnay.[10] Lemon learned his craft in Burgundy and is deeply shaped by the traditional French approach to crafting wines of *terroir*. He understands his role in making wine to be as a guide and shepherd. The types of soil along the coast moving inward toward Sonoma and Napa are remarkably varied and exciting for the world of the vintner. We know that soil does shape the wine in profound ways, but we do not know how it does so. Lemon feels that the older he becomes, the less he knows.

He does know that three factors go into making a great wine: the site, the right vine variety on the right site, and the management, which is culturally conditioned. He believes that wine is a mirror of society. California has gone through a cultural moment where the wines have been very big, brash, and high in alcohol content. When we look at the last twenty years of American society, whether in the film industry or the polarized political landscape, we see a culture that is loud — with people shouting at one another — and thus our wines have shouted because they reflect the society in which they are being produced. But we can be thankful that matters are changing. In the 1960s and 1970s the wines were not like that, and increasingly Americans want wines of balance, subtlety, and finesse where the fruit aromas do not overpower other more delicate aromas in the wine.

For Lemon, the earth is imbued with spiritual meaning, but for some reason we do not have the spiritual capacity anymore to hear the song of the earth. Often we are too far removed from it. If wines are to provide truly unique songs of the earth, then we need to allow them to sing their songs. Lemon wants to help his customers understand these wines and the songs they sing. The role of a wine of place is to be a reminder to humans that there is a spiritual world and wine is an expression of it. There is a surplus of meaning in a well-crafted wine that takes it beyond a mere drink we use to quench our physical thirst. Peaches or bananas cannot reflect place in the way wine can. Wine allows us to get a glimpse for how amazing this world really is, and Mr. Lemon believes that he has a priestly responsibility. He feels a profound sense of wonder and awareness for what has been entrusted to him, and he wants to ensure that his wines reflect this spiritual dimension. He also feels a strong responsibility to care for the land that has been entrusted to him.

Joe Davis, of Arcadian Winery in Santa Barbara, had a "conversion" experience of sorts as an undergraduate student. He was working in a wine shop, and one of his customers gave him a very special bottle of Domaine Dujac 1978 Clos de la Roche Grand Cru from Burgundy. Mr. Davis opened the bottle and remembers vividly the wonderful aromatics that were wafting out of the glass, like frozen dry ice smoke. It was very heavy and very beautiful. And then he tasted the wine, and he felt as though he were levitating off the ground. It was as if he had been transported into another place, and he remembers vividly thinking that this wine was the most incredible thing he had ever tasted.

It was then that a vision grew within him to re-create such a pinot noir in the unique conditions of his own home in California. It is Davis's life mission to craft wines of place that reflect as well as they can the unique conditions of each parcel of land. The Burgundian philosophy of crafting wine, first developed by Benedictine and Cistercian monks, has profoundly shaped his own approach, and one can taste the very particular song of Californian *terroir* in his wines.

Mike Officer, of Carlisle Wine Cellars in Santa Rosa, Sonoma County, loves old vines and crafts lovely Zinfandels from these old vines. His mother and her sister started up an Episcopal church once, but he no longer identifies with their faith. Before turning to the craftsmanship of a vintner, Officer was a computer programmer. But he left life in the big city to pursue his passions. He understands his role to be that of a shepherd, a steward of the old vines, and he hopes that these vines will do well beyond his time on this earth. His mission is to protect old vine varieties, not giving in to the latest fashion trends on the world wine market by replacing old vine varieties with new and more fashionable ones.

Officer does not really see himself as a wine-maker. Rather, he emphasizes that it is natural yeasts that cause this transformation from grape juice into wine. Yeasts have about three hundred different metabolic pathways, and one of those pathways is glycolysis, where a carbon source, sugar, is taken to produce ethanol. In the fermentation process, so much more is going on than the transformation of sugar into alcohol, and we really do not understand much of what is transpiring. There are so many more microbiological organisms that are interacting with the yeasts, and they all have their own metabolic processes.

Every year Officer is filled with a sense of awe — and is also humbled — to be able to take part in such an amazing craft. He feels deeply attached to old vineyards, to the people who have gone before and tended those vines, their struggles, and their labor. He feels as though these old vines are reaching out to him and wanting to tell him their story. Officer gets very emotional about these things and feels that this might be rather silly. I told him that it was quite human to feel connected to the land, to time, and to history. Recovering our relationship with the land, and not viewing in it terms of its economic value only, is a deeply spiritual affair. What Officer is striving for in his emphasis on biodiversity, his protecting of old vines, and his keeping alive the memory of those who have gone before sounds to me like a profoundly spiritual quest.

Tim Mondavi grew up at a winery. His father, Robert Mondavi, played a major role in developing viticulture in Napa Valley. The elder Mondavi's interest in the Cabernet Sauvignon grape led him to visit Bordeaux, France, where he was profoundly inspired by the "fine wine and gracious living" mentality.[11] Eventually, wine tourism and cultural events at the Mondavi winery helped introduce wine as a cultural good in Napa Valley and California more generally. The Mondavi vineyard grew to be one of the largest wine producers in California, sourcing grapes from all over the region, and Tim worked there from the time he was fifteen years old. In 2004 the Mondavi family sold the winery, together with the family name, to one of the largest wine corporations in the world. Today the Mondavi winery reflects the passions of a large corporation, while the family returned to their original vision — to craft fine wines.

Like a monk in pursuit of perfection, Tim retreated to Prichard Hill in the eastern hills of St. Helena, where he is on a new mission to craft a wine of distinction. For the first time in his life he makes wine solely from grapes grown on his own property. The small-scale winery allows him to tend to each vine, each parcel of land, and to work with his team in a single effort to craft something of which they can be proud.

The Mondavi family has roots in the Catholic tradition, and Tim attended a Jesuit boarding school. His family has always made wine for the Eucharist. For Tim, the meal around the table is the single most important institution for our families, since it is at the table where we share our sorrows and joys, and show respect for the fruit of the land. Father Gordon, a Catholic priest, comes to do the blessings of the grapes at the vineyard, and a long-standing family tradition continues. Tim believes that our faith should find expression in showing the land respect. He now only crafts wines from a single site because he believes that the best wines are reflections of that single site where one can harmonize wines — as those monks did way back when. He believes that his work is imbued with spiritual meaning as he seeks to craft something great, a wine with finesse and nuance that can help transform a meal, just as in *Babette's Feast*.

Concluding Reflections

A well-crafted wine has the unique capacity to allow us to get a glimpse into the splendors of particular places like no other food can. It can have a surplus of meaning that can delight and bring great joy to humanity. Such wines can rekindle within us a sense of wonder and awe for God, a deep gratitude for creation and all its rich blessings, and can enhance our joy and festive play before God. Therefore, the vintner has a great responsibility to ensure that such *terroir* wines continue to exist.

Corporations and the food-manufacturing world have not stopped their advance in the world of wine. They are powerful forces in a highly competitive world wine market. The source of their grapes, grape juice, and wine is often unclear and plays a minor role. These wines move much closer to the world of generic products — those with no particular distinction. They have little to teach about the recovery of our connection to a particular place. With the help of modern technology, corporate wineries have been able to increase the quality of their products for sure, but whether those wines have anything in particular to contribute to a conversation about the spirituality of wine, where place, particularity, complexity, and nuance are important, is questionable. Nor do they, for the most part, challenge and expand our olfactory imagination. Most of the wines have left me indifferent at best, if not disappointed, or even worse, disgusted. Because I know the potential that lies in crafting a wine of *terroir*, it seems discouraging that these generic wines threaten to take over the wine market. Therefore, we call on the faithful and faith-filled vintners to continue to craft wines of *terroir*, and we plead with local governments to work with their vintners to make these wines more affordable.

7

Technology, Spirituality, and Wine

"We shall not cease from exploration. And the end of all our
exploring will be to arrive where we started and know the place
for the first time."

T. S. Eliot, "Little Gidding"

There is no wine without the help of technology. The vintner needs a vintner's knife to prune the vines, containers to collect the grapes, shears to harvest the grapes, and vats to crush and ferment the grapes. Technology is indispensable not only for crafting wine but for human life in general; yet it is a hotly debated subject in the twenty-first century. Technology profoundly shapes our daily lives, whether it is at work, or in school, medicine, recreation, entertainment, travel, economics, politics, or the home.

The development of technology over the last three hundred years has placed incredible power into human hands, but humans have not always used it wisely. Modern technological inventions such as nuclear weapons and nuclear power, and information and biomedical technology, have raised important ethical and moral questions. Technological disasters, environmental exploitation, and pollution in particular have justifiably given rise to loud outcries against an unbridled use of certain technology.

In light of such complex issues surrounding the realm of technology, it seems best to begin by establishing a definition of the term as it relates

143

to crafting wine. Different people mean different things when they use the word "technology." With the explosion of technological productions of everyday items such as electronic and digital devices (televisions, computers, smartphones, etc.), many people use the term to speak about those devices in particular. The English word "technology" derives from the Greek word *technologia,* which deals with the knowledge, discourse, and study of art or craft. (The Greek word *technē* is usually translated as "art," "craft," or "skill.") Like any other craftsman, such as a carpenter, seamstress, doctor, or engineer, the vintner draws on his/her knowledge of *technē* to work the land and to craft wines. The artist, too, draws on *technē* to paint a picture, to form a sculpture, or to compose and play music. Like the German language, English distinguishes between "art" (German: *Kunst*) for decorative things and "craftsmanship or artisanship" (German: *Handwerk*) for practical or functional things, though the line between those two is often blurred and permeable.[1] This is especially true when it comes to the world of crafting wine; it is also true when we create the artifacts used in worship, such as a chalice.

The knowledge, discourse, and study of technology do not evolve in a vacuum. The technology and techniques, the practices and artifacts that we develop out of this knowledge always emerge in particular cultural contexts, values, and needs and are deeply embedded in them. The technology a vintner draws on to craft wine is an expression of the history and values of his/her culture. Technology and culture are profoundly intertwined and deeply affect one another. It is not surprising that philosophers and sociologists have taken on technology as an important aspect of their research.[2]

As we think about the role of technology in Christian spirituality, we need to realize that technology in its most fundamental sense (as *technē*) is profoundly linked to human creativity. If we believe that God created the world and that we are made in the image of God, we can understand that this basic human impulse and capacity toward creativity is a gift from God that we must treasure, cultivate, and share.

The vintner has a unique vocation in this regard. Few drinks in the world have so great a capacity to reveal in one small glass the beauty hidden in creation as wine does. When crafted well, it is like a poem that praises the bounties of God's goodness found in creation.

Living in Tension: The Vintner as
Craftsman or Industrial Food Engineer?

The way a vintner uses technology is crucial for crafting a wine. She or he must make ethical, aesthetic, and economic choices in selecting the technology for crafting wine. With the rise of the Industrial Revolution in the nineteenth century and the rapid development of modern technology since then, the world of wine has expanded and changed dramatically. The wine world has become vast and complex, and the use of technology is equally wide-ranging. While the 1960s through the 1990s saw a huge rise in the use of pesticides and herbicides in vineyards, the trend today is to move toward more sustainable practices, at least in some parts of the world. New technological inventions pose different questions and challenges. On this wide-ranging spectrum we shall look briefly at the challenges of industrial food engineering and what theological considerations might add to the question of the use of technology. Most vintners today live in the tensions of a technologically minded world that is profoundly tied to the global wine market.

When the wine-maker's goal is merely to make a cheap and decent wine with only the underlying utilitarian goal of maximizing profit, then she or he will use technology to this end. With little or no understanding of the earth as a sacred place, a wine-maker can readily use modern technology for the efficient mass-production of wine. It is a profoundly modern affair devoid of faith or aesthetics. Wine is easily degraded into becoming just another generic drink, a commodity in the globalized market. Its goal is to be pleasing to the palate of the relatively uninformed consumer who wants to have a stable and consistent product. Such wines offer little surprise and certainly do not seek to challenge and develop the palate of the people who drink it. They have introduced many to the world of wine, and perhaps that is their benefit. What we do not know is how many people decided that wine is not for them on the basis of such wines. The quality of these mass-produced wines is certainly better than it was even twenty years ago. But while such wines have become much more drinkable, the deeper spiritual significance of the particulars of the land and its fruit is obscured at best and completely eclipsed at worst. Wine's ability to stir our souls toward wonder and gratitude is easily lost in such mass-produced wines.

This approach to making wine fits well with the ethics behind much of modern technology, the ethics of a "society dominated by technical or instrumental rationality . . . strongly utilitarian in its cultural biases."[3] It leaves little room for wonder, mystery, and surprise. It is a demystified world, and its manufactured wines reflect the absence of wonder and mystery. The documentary *Mondovino,* directed by Jonathan Nossiter, is probably the most accessible, albeit somewhat overstated, witness to this approach, an approach deeply influenced by rapid globalization of the wine market.[4]

Alongside the rather complex development of globalization, and its particular use of technology determined by its particular set of values, there is another tradition reaching back to premodern times, profoundly shaped by Christian values. This tradition emerged in the monastic communities of France and Germany, where Benedictine and Cistercian monks, just like modern vintners, had to make use of *technē* available to them in order to craft their wines.

Thanks to the Rule of Saint Benedict, these monks developed a deep regard for the land and its fruit; they also learned that their use of technology was not a "neutral" or secular matter but was imbued with spiritual meaning. Saint Benedict wrote: "[Regard] all utensils and goods of the monastery as sacred vessels of the altar."[5] Saint Benedict understood creation to be sacred and insisted that the technology the monks used to work the land had to harmonize with their Christian beliefs and practices. The Cistercians, in particular, understood the crafting of wine as a profoundly spiritual affair. They made themselves at home wherever they went and got to know their land well. With the monastic rhythm of prayer, study, and manual labor, they used *technē* to improve the quality of their wines by focusing on the particulars of the land.[6]

The vintners of Burgundy, renowned for their excellent wines, owe much of their craftsmanship, their understanding of *terroir,* and their Grand Crus to those dedicated monks. In their devotion to God, those monks turned to crafting wine with love and zeal. Prayer and patience accompanied the monks' use of *technē,* since they were deeply committed to drawing out the best that creation had to offer. For the Cistercians, crafting wine was a spiritual pursuit, and their hope must have been that their wines would be like the spire of a church "reaching out towards a meaning which it acquires only if we have the culture and the faith to provide it."[7] This caring hand of the Cistercians is perhaps one reason why Burgundy, where the Cistercians cultivated the land and vines so prayerfully, is to this day one of the world's most renowned places for wines of *terroir.* Roger Scruton sensed this heritage on his many travels to Burgundy when he wrote:

Visitors to Burgundy . . . will sense all around them the history and religion. . . . They will know that this soil is hallowed soil: it has been blessed and
cajoled and prayed over for centuries, many of the vineyards being worked
by monks for whom wine was not just a drink but a sacrament. . . . Even in
this skeptical age their vine is, for the Burgundians, something more spiritual
than vegetal, and their soil more heaven than earth.[8]

Scruton's description of his love affair with Burgundy is perhaps a bit
over-romantic, and the history of Burgundy and its wines is a bit more complex and sobering. Burgundy does indeed have a rich heritage, but Burgundian vintners also went through a period of overusing fertilizers and pesticides. Commercialization and industrial food technology have impacted
Burgundy just as they have any other region in the world, and Burgundian vintners, like any other vintners, have had to make discerning choices
about technology.[9]

There are two extremes on the wine-producing spectrum today. On the
one hand, there are the mass-produced wines that are affordable to most
people; on the other hand, there are the premium wines of the world that
are unaffordable to the ordinary person.[10] Some critics suggest that both of
these styles of wine have deep ties to the global wine market. The former is
a cheap product that is readily available in supermarkets around the world.
The latter has become an object of high aesthetic appreciation — and also of
speculation — that appeals to a wealthy group of international collectors and
investors. Many vintners, wine writers, and experienced and sophisticated
wine-drinkers believe that mass-produced wines and premium wines have
suffered a similar fate: the increasing homogenization and lack of diversity
in flavor.

Tyler Colman, who has a doctorate in the political economy of the wine
industry in France and the United States, explains that Michel Rolland, one
of the most sought-after consulting oenologists worldwide (portrayed as the
bad guy in *Mondovino,* the documentary on the globalization of wine), helps
create a certain style around the world, and Robert Parker, perhaps the most
influential wine writer in the United States, likes that style.[11] Wine chemist
David Bird argues: "The great joy of the wines of the world is their infinite
variety, and there can be no doubt that wines have moved closer in style since
the advent of modern winemaking."[12] While modern technology has certainly

helped vintners and wine-makers make better wines in many respects, it seems to have brought about a considerable loss as well.

There are many vintners — perhaps most vintners — whose lives and work exist in the tensions between these two extremes of industrial food engineering and the Grand Cru–style wines of the world. Their wines are neither overly manufactured nor are they devoid of the help of modern technology. Their values and/or financial limitations determine how much of, and what kind of, modern technology they use in order to craft their wines. They neither mass-produce wine nor craft wines of such elite status that only the richest people in the world can afford them. Often these wineries are family-owned and -run. The vintner and his/her family take special pride in crafting wines because they still have personal contact with their customers and find it deeply satisfying when their customers delight in their wines and come back for more. I grew up in such a winery.

These wineries and their vintners seem to be the best places to explore a spirituality of wine and the role of technology in it. They tend to have a very profound understanding of, and relationship with, the land that they farm and care for themselves. Many of them work very hard for their wines to express the particular places that they have come to love and respect. They do not view vines merely as plants for the utilitarian goal of economic gain but as living organisms in need of care and attention. This care is why many vintners say that crafting wine is an affair of the heart.

If Christian spirituality also involves understanding how God is at work in this world, then creation and our relationship with it is an important aspect of Christian spirituality. Modern society has changed the way, philosophically and morally, it thinks about God, creation, and our relationship to both. The belief that creation is a gift from God to be treasured and cared for has been eclipsed, and nature has been reduced to a "resource" in service of modern progress. Modern technology, a result of these modern values, has profoundly altered our relationship with creation. More often than not, it has made our lives more detached from creation. Perhaps these conscientious vintners, deeply involved in understanding and working with the land, might be able to give us some insight into the positive and negative influences of technology and how we might think about it. But before we allow these vintners to voice their perspective, we need to consider one more dimension that has shaped the world of wine: the global wine market.

The Haunting Global Wine Market

When we think about the spirituality of wine, particularly how wine can help us connect with God, each other, and the wonder of particular places, we need to consider the impact of globalization. Globalization as we know it today is an incredibly complex phenomenon that is built on modern values. The desire for economic growth and profit drives globalization, and it tends to have little concern for the earth as a sacred space that needs to be respected, cared for, and protected. Globalization allows for free trade and exchange of goods worldwide, and it has shaped and transformed our eating and drinking habits radically.

The good news of globalization is that you can now enjoy a local wine such as the Gewürztraminer from Alsace, France, in a small restaurant on the east coast of Scotland or a Slow Food restaurant in Birmingham, Alabama; or you can find it on the shelf of a wine shop in Vancouver or Beijing. North Americans, Europeans, Russians, and Asians now eat and drink some of the same things.

Supermarket chains such as Tesco in Britain, Aldi in Germany, and Trader Joe's in the United States (owned by one of the Aldi brothers) offer very cheap wines — and at times even good wines — to a clientele that previously did not drink wine at all.[13] What is so disturbing is that many of these supermarket wines seem to have very little connection to any particular place. This seems to be true of all manufactured goods made for the global market.[14] In many cases one never knows where, specifically, the grapes for these wines are grown and what chemicals have been added to the wine. Globalization certainly has made wines much more accessible and affordable worldwide, but globalization has also introduced some bitter notes to the globalized palate. The rapid change of taste, homogenization, and the decreasing significance of place are some of the many side effects of globalization.[15]

Chasing after the Popular Taste:
The Globalization and Homogenization of Taste

One of the significant side effects of globalization is rapidly changing preferences in taste. As people are urged to desire what is fashionable, they become more detached from what is local and more dependent on global taste trends. Whatever the popular taste at any given time, it holds great power, since consumers readily spend their money according to what is fashionable. Mike Veseth rightly suggests that "[t]he battle for the future of wine is all about power — whose idea of wine will dominate and whose tastes and interests will prevail."[16] With the increasing globalization of the wine market, the latest taste preference has a powerful impact on wine producers because they need to be able to sell their wines.

Since this global wine market is still young and its consumers are mostly new to the world of wine, their palates are only beginning to develop. They tend to have little confidence in their own ability to judge what they taste in the glass, and thus they have relied on a few wine specialists to guide them in their taste and choices. In addition, the issue of extensive comparative wine tastings seems to be a relatively recent phenomenon and has added to the complexity of the wine world. Newcomers understandably are often at a loss as they encounter the sheer volume of choices and are forced to rely on those who seem to have mastered the extraordinarily complex world of wine. These specialists, in turn, have a significant amount of power as they make their ratings of wines according to their own value systems. Because vintners' livelihoods depend on getting high scores on the rating systems of these specialists, many vintners feel that they need to mold their wines to those rating systems in order to sell them.[17]

The preferences of taste that have developed with the rise of the global world wine market are deeply influenced by the culture in which these preferences have emerged. Ted Lemon, biodynamic vintner from California, suggests that the popular wine taste in California mirrors the society and its cultural expressions. Heavy red wines with overly ripe fruit flavors and high alcohol content are still very fashionable, though their popularity is waning. The impressions one gets from such boisterous wines are immediate, predictable, easily recognizable, and very loud. Often they are rather one-dimensional. Rarely do such wines give way to the more subtle flavors of "minerals" and "earthiness" that seem to come from a vibrant microbial *terroir*. The flavors we associate with "earthiness" are much more challenging to discern and even more difficult to talk about. These flavors open different levels of delight and profoundly remind us of the earth from which we are all taken and to which we all shall return. When wine-makers forget these flavor profiles to fit fashion, a surplus of meaning has been lost, and we have forgotten just a little bit more how important the soil, with its microbial life, is — not just for crafting wine but for our lives in general.

Burgundian monks took many vintages of trial and error to select Chardonnay cultivars and figure out where they flourished. The focus on sites and their microclimate has remained central in Burgundy to this day. When Chardonnay wines suddenly became popular on the world wine market in the 1980s, wine-makers began growing them everywhere, without much discernment of whether the land was suitable for this particular vine variety. Older and less popular varieties had to give way to a fleeting taste. Many of those Chardonnays had very little in common with their Burgundian ancestors. The modern wine-makers focused less on the land and more on their own personal vision, deeply infused with a desire to please the current — and quickly fading — consumer palate.

True to the modern worldview, creation and what it has to offer often vanished from the scene, and the vision of individuals became the guiding factor in making wines. Their use of technology became more invasive. They saw technology as a way to manipulate and control nature rather than learn how to draw out the best in nature. The selection of high-yielding Chardonnay varieties, newly developed aromatic yeast strains, 100 percent malolactic fermentation, and the intense use of oak barrels transformed the role of the vintner from midwifery and craftsmanship to that of an actual maker or inventor. These wine-makers were able to hide the thin, mass-produced Chardonnays behind the "makeup" of artificially induced fruit flavors and an overuse of oak barrels. Robert White puts it this way: "Technological wines that rely on dial-a-flavor yeasts and additives to make up for dead soil don't taste distinctive or real."[18] Of course, there were and are exceptions, and New World regions now produce some lovely Chardonnays. Indeed, many New World wines are much better today as consumers become more educated and prefer more nuanced wines.

Fortunately, these highly manipulated Chardonnays have fallen out of fashion, and for the time being, Sauvignon Blanc and other white varieties such as pinot grigio seem to be quite popular. But what has become of all those huge Chardonnay vineyards now that New World–style Chardonnays have fallen out of fashion? Have they been uprooted and replanted with vines that are more popular now? And how long will the new fashion in wine taste last?

Another thing that is troubling about the globalization of the wine palate is that globalized tastes can change quite rapidly. A small vintner cannot easily change his/her wine production with the coming and going tides of globalized taste. Growing vines and crafting wine does not lend itself to such fast-paced change to accommodate fast-changing, fashion-oriented palates. It takes years for a vineyard not only to produce fruit but also to put down significant root systems to draw nutrients from the soil matrix. It takes a great deal of time and patience to figure out what vine varieties grow best on a given parcel of land.

The financial instability that comes with these tidal waves of wine fashion is deeply disturbing. The small vintner will always be the most vulnerable member of the globalized wine market, while big corporations such as Gallo or Constellation Brand can absorb those tidal waves more easily.[19] Relying on mass production, heavy use of modern technology, and large-scale marketing strategies, they are able to invent wines and adapt more easily to the fashion of the day — which they themselves help to create.[20]

The Decreasing Significance of Place

Another significant side effect of globalization is that the importance of place increasingly recedes into the background. Mike Veseth argues that most "products and services we buy and use today are pretty *terroir*-free — they could come from anywhere and go to anywhere."[21] As the popularity of mass-produced wine — with little connection to any particular place — increases, the importance of the particularity of place recedes into the background. This matters because, for one thing, there is a spiritual and aesthetic loss. For those who do not care so much about a wine of *terroir* and the surplus of meaning it can bring, this loss might not be severe; however, for those who believe that the earth is not neutral matter but is imbued with spiritual significance, this loss is substantial. It robs us of the joy of tasting a wine that reflects a particular place and a particular vintage — the charm associated with a particularity of taste and a particularity of origin.

Such wines can connect us with particular places and with the vintner's ability and creativity to allow these particulars to shine through in the wine. Such wines often surprise us. Each vintage tastes a bit different and teaches us that wine, like human life, goes through seasons and is deeply affected by its surroundings. Such an approach to crafting and enjoying wine assumes that we are not detached individuals whose primary identity is that of consumers. Rather, it teaches us that we are persons deeply embedded in a community of creation. We are dependent not just on each other as human beings but utterly dependent on creation as a living organism with a finely balanced ecosystem. It is a great gift, and the joy of being drawn into this community of creation by tasting well-crafted wine should not be underestimated.

Even if some of us do not care about this spiritual and aesthetic dimension, we all should and must care for the earth as the only home we have. Going hand in hand with the decreasing significance of place for the production of wine is a decreasing interest in the care for the land. Corporations whose primary goal is economic gain do not seem to have earth's sustainability as high on their priority list as they should. But questions about sustainability specifically in wine-making are crucial. It is interesting that Veseth, an expert on the global wine market, only raises questions about global warming with respect to the changing face of where wines will be grown in the future. But how much do agrarian practices, with the aid of modern technology, further the destruction of particular places and the finely balanced ecosystem in them? How can we develop sustainable practices that will help heal the earth rather than continue to contribute to its destruction? It is time to allow vintners to reflect on these important questions.

The Vintners' Perspectives on Technology: Old World

With the development of modern technology, the crafting of wines has become easier, and many argue that the quality of wines has become much better. Mr. Bernhard Weissensee, a retired oenologist, advised vintners throughout the Franconia wine region for the better part of the second half of the twentieth century, a time when the advancement of modern technology took great strides. Weissensee closely observed the rise of modern technology and its impact on the crafting of wine in Franconia. He repeatedly emphasized how many benefits modern technology has brought to the wine world.

For a season Weissensee worked in research, seeking to winnow out vine varieties that would flourish better in the cool wine region of Franconia. The Rieslaner, a late-ripening and highly sensitive vine variety, was not performing very well and stood on the brink of extinction. With the help of modern technology, a group of researchers began a selection process and developed a Rieslaner vine that was more resistant and had a greater capacity to produce. The Rieslaner vine is not a high-yielding vine variety by any stretch of the imagination; but the loss of this lovely wine would have been very sad. Under ideal weather conditions the Rieslaner grape can produce some beautiful dessert wines. The unique interplay between fruit, sweetness, and significant levels of acidity adds a special voice to the often very dry Franconian wines.

Another important success of modern technology came in the face of an impending disaster in the wine industry in Europe. Quite suddenly, in the middle of the nineteenth century, vines began to die; this first occurred in France, but it quickly spread throughout Europe. It was a great tragedy, and it seemed that vineyards would disappear from the landscape of Europe for good. Over time, researchers discovered that the grape louse, better known today as phylloxera, had been accidentally imported from the Americas and was responsible for this terrible devastation. The phylloxera feeds on the roots of the grapevines and slowly kills them.

Weissensee recounts that the first phylloxera was discovered in 1907 in Franconia. Researchers looking for ways to save the vines came upon the idea of grafting European vines onto American vine species — since the rootstocks of the latter are resistant to phylloxera. Today almost all European and North American vines are grafted onto rootstocks from American vine species.[22] Weissensee still marvels at those smart early-twentieth-century researchers who, with the help of technology, were able to save European viticulture. But as Weissensee sees it, this rescue came at a loss. He does not think that the quality of the wines produced from these grafted vines is as good. Weissensee is of a generation that was still able to drink wines from nongrafted vines. Today these wines have become very rare, found only in cellars of old wine regions such the Rheingau, where, according to Father Hufsky, five-hundred-year-old wines from the Johannisberg are hidden away.

König, another vintner whose working life spanned the second part of the twentieth century, also believes that the grafted vines do not produce the fine quality that the ungrafted vines did before the phylloxera plague. In general, König has reservations about the popularity of cloning in the wine world. With the help of modern technology, a certain vine is singled out because of its high quality, its disease resistance, or its high-yielding capacity.[23] This particular vine is then reproduced over and over through vegetative reproduction. Traditionally, a vineyard would have a considerable range of Riesling vines, for example, but with the cloning of one particular vine, a certain variety in the vineyard is getting lost. König is not of the currently popular opinion that wines are always "better" today. They do have more breadth and variety in flavor, but he feels that the beautiful interplay of different nuances in the wines is often lost.

Mr. Bernd Kutschick, of Kloster Eberbach, has similar concerns. He argues that wine is the most multifaceted drink in the world and that the wide range of vines used to be considerable. With the regular practice of cloning one particular vine, however, this variety is getting lost. He feels that this is a considerable cultural loss, a loss that we do not just experience in the wine world but in the cloning of vegetables and fruit as well.

My father, Peter Kreglinger, helped shed some light on the role of yeast in the making of wine. He believes that what grows in the vineyard determines the quality of a wine, even as modern technology has helped considerably to ensure that the quality grown in the vineyard can be preserved and cultivated in the cellar. The most important process in the actual crafting of wine is the fermentation process, and the vintner's role is to ensure a safe and successful fermentation. With the help of yeasts, living microorganisms that belong to the fungus realm, grape juice is transformed into wine. Yeasts have many metabolic pathways, and one of them is glycolysis, in which yeasts feed on sugar and transform carbohydrates into carbon dioxide and alcohol. People often forget that this is only one of many transformations that happen in the process of fermentation. We do not know how many other metabolic pathways are at work and how they help shape the flavor and structure of the wine. But yeasts are profoundly powerful, and it is no surprise that fermentation was a deep mystery to the ancients, who believed that the gods were at work in it.

The presence and potency of yeasts vary from place to place and year to year, and they make natural fermentation a rather unpredictable and at times even volatile venture. Not all yeasts have a positive impact on the wine, and some can actually introduce flaws into the wine. Relying on natural yeasts can also lead to "stuck fermentation," a phenomenon in which the fermentation process unexpectedly comes to a halt. It is a vintner's nightmare because it can completely spoil the wine.

Peter Kreglinger remembers that, after vintners began using more pesticides to fight diseases in the vineyard, it affected the cycle of yeast cultures. Some yeast cultures have completely disappeared (because of the use of pesticides) and have made natural fermentation more difficult. The use of pesticides, another phenomenon of modern technology, has helped fight diseases in the vineyard; but, as is so often the case, it comes with a loss, not the least being the disappearance of healthy yeast cultures.

In order to help vintners stabilize the fermentation process and guarantee a safe fermentation, researchers began collecting yeast strains from around the world. They selected high-quality yeast strains, multiplied them, and made them readily available to vintners. Peter Kreglinger remembers that, in the beginning, the vintner had one or two cultured yeasts to choose from. Today a vintner can choose from hundreds of different cultivated yeast strains. While the initial incentive behind cultivating yeast strains was to ensure a stable and safe fermentation process, the cultivated yeast strains developed today do a lot more than guarantee a stable fermentation: they purposefully alter and profoundly shape the flavor of the wine.

Increasingly, the use of cultivated yeast strains raises the question of to what extent such wines still reflect a particular place and to what extent the wine becomes the invention of the wine-maker and his use of highly selected yeast strains, what White sarcastically calls "dial-a-flavor yeasts." Yeast companies even advertise on the package of the yeast the specific aromas and qualities a given yeast strain will add to a wine.[24]

Depending on the vintner's philosophy, modern technology has made it possible to control the flavor profile of wine in ways not possible before. While the initial idea for cultivating yeast strains was to ensure a safe and successful fermentation and thus the quality of the wine, cultivated yeast strains have come under attack because they are increasingly used to control and alter the more natural flavor profile of wines.[25]

The development of genetically modified yeast strains poses even more questions. At this point they are authorized for use in the United States, but they are still illegal in the European Union. Sister Hedwig, our pioneer biodynamic nun/vintner, has great reservations about genetically modified products in general and their use in the production of wine in particular. As a Christian, she never saw herself merely as a vintner; beyond that, she is one who has felt called to care for and protect creation. We have yet to find out how the genetically modified products influence our finely balanced ecosystem and how they affect human beings. Too many questions remain unanswered, and Sister Hedwig believes that we need to be very cautious about uncritically embracing such advances in modern technology. She believes that questions about the sustainability of our agricultural practices should always accompany the work of a vintner.

The line between technology being helpful in protecting and enhancing the craftsmanship of wine and becoming too invasive and manipulative is often blurry. Many feel that wine is not merely a generic product made to please the consumer palate, but that it is part of creation and that its beauty and diversity are thus a great gift to humanity. They tend to enjoy wine because it is a natural product that reflects some of the wonder of creation and can offer them an emotional and spiritual connection with particular places. They view the vintner as the person who can help create this link.

The Vintners' Perspectives on Technology: New World

The more vintners use highly invasive technology that enables them to impose their own vision on the wine, the more questions arise concerning how natural the wine remains and whether the traditional understanding of wine still applies.[26] Different vintners express different concerns. Should one irrigate a vineyard? How does regular drip irrigation affect the vines when they are no longer forced to develop a deep root system? Many vintners believe that vines with a deeper root system produce more profound wines.

Traditionally, many wines are aged in oak barrels. Oregonian Jason Lett discovered in a wine museum in Germany that the Romans learned from the Celts to store wine in wooden barrels. Storing wines in oak barrels has a long tradition in the world of wine: it helps soften the tannins in red wine, and if done well, can add a lovely component to the wine. But some wines handle aging in oak better than others do, and it is a costly process: oak barrels are expensive and the aging takes time. The vintner has to watch the wine carefully because just a little oxygen exposure in the oak barrel — and not too much — enhances the slow integration of flavors. Today a wine-maker can order oak chips or oak powder online, sprinkle them into the stainless-steel tank, and artificially create an oak flavor with much less financial cost and personal effort. In craftsman circles this practice is frowned on; indeed, many shudder at the very thought of it. The oak flavor is surely present, but integration and subtlety are often lacking.

In very hot climates, such as can be found in California, Australia, and South Africa, many wineries use a "spinning cone" column to separate out alcohol from a wine in exceptionally hot years. German engineers from the nuclear industry first developed the spinning cone column, a sophisticated piece of modern technology. With the help of a centrifuge, vintners "take apart" the wine so that some of the alcohol can be removed from it. While some use the spinning cone only for those exceptionally hot years, others use the spinning cone regularly. They follow a vision of what they want their wines to be, usually a full-bodied red wine with strong overripe fruit flavors. In order to achieve this vision, the vintners pick grapes very late in the season. With overripe fruits come high alcohol levels in the wine, and the spinning cone column is used to "spin out" some of the alcohol from these wines. The spinning cone here serves to help create a wine that creation would not naturally produce.

The use of the spinning cone column is in dispute in the wine world because it represents a highly interventionist approach to wine-making.[27] It raises ethical questions about its inherent tendency to shape human engagement with nature in very particular ways. Long gone are the days when technology was seen as "neutral ground." The technological tools provide humans with an autonomy from nature that has significant implications.[28] Rather than using spinning cones only for those exceptionally hot years, they can easily become a tool that allows a wine-maker to override the conditions of the natural world and create something artificially. Not only do such practices estrange us from the rhythm and potential that creation has to offer; they also provide humanity with a vision of reality that seeks to supersede and sidestep the limits and boundaries of creation. Philosophers in particular have raised serious questions about this highly interventionist use of technology, calling for restraint and "self-learned self-limitation."[29] If the spinning cone column is part of a trajectory, where will this lead us ultimately? It is the opposite of organic and biodynamic viticulture that seeks to respect and work closely with nature's natural rhythms and limitations.

How do vintners think about these modern artifacts of technology? I have asked vintners in California and Oregon about this. Eyrie Vineyard's Jason Lett is concerned that the regular use of the spinning cone indicates that the wrong varieties are planted in some places. David Lett, his father, made a significant contribution to the wine world by experimenting with wine varieties in Oregon. One of the most important uses of *technē* in crafting wine is exploring what variety grows best in a given parcel of land. With the help of this *technē*, David Lett discovered that pinot noir grapes grow exceptionally well in the Willamette Valley. This somewhat fickle vine has flourished so well there that the Oregon pinot noirs have gained worldwide recognition as wines of *terroir*. Jason thinks that the overuse of high-tech tools heightens the problem of the human ego. He believes that, as a vintner, you have to get out of the way of your own ego. Once you allow your ego to start making decisions about your wine, you become a beverage manufacturer. Jason does not want to be a wine-maker, but a *vigneron* (a French term usually translated as "wine-grower").

Jeremy Seysses, of Domaine Dujac, is from Burgundy; but since his wife is from California and was trained there, they inhabit parts of both worlds. Domaine Dujac is now farmed completely organically, but one year Jeremy wanted to try out the reverse-osmosis machine to see how it would influence the wine. The reverse-osmosis machine is a piece of modern technology that can be used to remove unwanted components from wine. One of Jeremy's wines had a little too much volatile acidity, and he wanted to experience firsthand what the reverse-osmosis machine could do. He was told that it was miraculously surgical and could remove only those compounds the vintner wishes to remove from the wine. He did a trial run, and the wine dropped half a percent in alcohol content — something he had not wanted to do. And afterwards, the wine was never the same: it had completely lost its structure, and it did not come together. It is difficult for Jeremy to describe what happened. Before the intervention, the wine simply had a slightly high amount of volatile acidity; afterwards, the wine was no longer cohesive. It took Jeremy's wine ten years to mature back to what it was before he used the reverse-osmosis machine.

Steve Doerner, of Oregon's Cristom Vineyards, has nothing against technology per se; he believes that it works for him to have a technological toolbox to help him avoid issues when they arise. Steve understands his role in crafting wines as guiding rather than forcing the wine into particular pathways. He steers it a little but does not want to make it do just anything. With this philosophy for crafting wine, Steve seeks to use technology with discernment rather than rejecting it altogether. Just because some wine-makers have used 100 percent new oak barrels and have produced overoaked Chardonnays does not mean that a vintner needs to throw out oak barrels altogether.

The same is true for irrigation: if it is used judiciously, it can be very beneficial. Doerner does not usually irrigate his vineyards, but during one exceptionally hot and dry year he irrigated about 10 percent of the vineyards because the vines were suffering too much. Doerner does believe that vines need to be stressed in order to produce good wine; when vines are stressed by growing in soil that is somewhat dry, the vintner can make wines with more interesting flavors. The vines' main goal is to produce fruit, and if they are not stressed a little, they become merely vegetative and do not concentrate on producing fruit. The stress on the vine signals to the plant that it is time to think about reproducing rather than just growing more leaves. Steve believes that the soils in the Willamette Valley do just that to the vines.

A vintner has to find the right balance between a little stress and complete health. Vines do have to be healthy in spite of the stress, and the vintner needs to supply them with the nutrients they require. But if one has to rely on high-tech tools all the time, then one probably has that particular grapevine growing in the wrong place. Steve likes to work in a region where he does not have to rely on high-tech tools much. He chose to come to Oregon from California because Oregon is cooler, and the grapes never produce too much alcohol. He does not need to think about using the spinning-cone column or the reverse-osmosis machine, and this circumstance suits his philosophy of crafting wines using as little intervention as possible.

Mike Officer, of Carlisle Winery and Vineyards, tends old vines in the Sonoma Valley, some of them over 120 years old. He is dedicated to preserving these old vines. While Sonoma is not as hot as Napa Valley, it is much warmer than the Willamette Valley in Oregon. And water shortage is a significant problem. Mike's overriding preference is to use as little invasive technology as possible. There are times, however, when he does need to resort to certain kinds of technology in order to provide his customers with the highest-quality wine possible. Officer uses drip irrigation for younger vines — but not for the more mature ones. He makes fifteen different Zinfandels from old vines and has used the spinning-cone column only on very rare occasions and only for very small amounts of wine. He used it once to remove volatile acidity, and it turned an undrinkable wine into something serviceable and pleasant. Still,

Mr. Officer believes that the wine suffers a bit when the spinning cone is used, and he prefers not to use it.

When his Zinfandels do have too much alcohol in them, he uses a much gentler process to remove alcohol than the spinning cone.[30] Sometimes he has to dig into his repertoire of tools and occasionally resort to them, especially with the older Zinfandels, since the ripening of the grapes varies a great deal and makes it difficult to determine the perfect harvest time. If a wine is horribly out of balance because of the alcohol content, he does have to intervene, though he prefers not to have to do it. Vintners live a life of tension, just as the rest of us do, facing challenging issues and having to make discerning choices.

Ted Lemon's Littorai winery is only ten miles away from Mike Officer's Carlisle winery. Many of his vineyards are closer to the coastline, where the microclimates are very different — some considerably cooler. Ted believes that there is a wide range of diverse soil types in Sonoma County, especially along the coast, where the intersection of the North American and the Pacific plates has created a wide range of soil types. In Occidental, for example, there are five distinct geological origins within five acres of land. The potential of these sites for wine-growing has yet to be explored. A French writer once wrote that great wine is the constant reminder that we are the children of the earth, and we separate ourselves from our mother at our peril.

Lemon's approach to crafting wine is profoundly influenced by his training and experience in Burgundy. He had farmed conventionally for twenty years before turning to biodynamic farming; so he is very well acquainted with the use of modern technology in farming. He believes that the bottom line of modern technology has three outcomes: it makes one's job easier; it costs less money; and it has the (more hidden) consequence that one will have to spend less time on the farm. Whether it is irrigation monitoring from the computer screen or using infrared technology for spotting the weak spots in the vineyard, every new technology is designed to have the vintner out in the vineyard less, removing him/her from the natural world more and more.

For Lemon, getting to know a place well and finding the right wine variety for the right site are crucial. The love, care, and intuition a vintner develops for his or her work will be reflected in the vineyard. Lemon believes that place is not merely a question of physical matter but is a living and spiritual reality. He believes that humans have a unique capacity to bring those two together as they work the land. He even believes that "certain sites have a spiritual predisposition which allows them to create great wines, which in turn creates a spiritual reaction within us."[31]

Lemon rejects the use of modern technology, such as the spinning cone, on his winery. For him, such pieces of technology are like filters on a camera lens. The more filters one uses, the more the vineyard recedes into the background, until ultimately the taste of place itself disappears.[32]

Concluding Reflections

The question of the role of technology — and especially the use of certain modern technology — is a complex one. On the one hand, it has given vintners tools that can be extremely helpful, especially in the challenging and difficult years. But when does certain modern technology become a crutch whose use keeps vintners from developing some of the most basic skills or *technē* they need to learn? The most important element — and the highly determinative use of technology — is when the vintner learns to discern what grape variety to plant on a given parcel of land. This process takes time, because vintners have to make themselves at home and get to know a place well.

It is here that the experience and knowledge of the vintners/craftspeople come into play and enable them to use their *technē* with creativity and wisdom. While big wine corporations use place to produce wines that sell well, a vintner's calling is more profound. Embedded in creation, he/she seeks to reflect the particulars of place as well as possible. Vintners are keenly aware that creation is full of mystery, and a well-crafted wine has the capacity to move us to a place of wonder. It takes craftsmanship to discover it.

At the beginning of this chapter I raised the question of the role of technology in Christian spirituality. I suggested that technology in its original sense, as *technē*, is profoundly linked to human creativity. When we understand creation as a gift from God and the particulars of the land as a concrete expression of God's abundant love, then the vintner has a unique vocation. Technology can now be seen as "a sacred vessel of the altar," as Saint Benedict put it so eloquently. Very few drinks in the world have the capacity to mirror the beauty hidden in creation as does one small glass of wine. This capacity is why Robert Louis Stevenson called wine "bottled poetry." Wine, when crafted well, is like a poem that praises the bounties of God's goodness hidden in earth, wind, rain, sun, and the vine. The vintner has a profoundly sacred vocation: to reveal to us the splendor and bounty that God placed into his creation for us to discover and enjoy.

In light of this belief, vintners should use technology with discernment, self-restraint, and creativity to discover the bounties found in the places they call home. While the New World of wine still has much to discover as "new land" continues to be developed, explored, and rediscovered, the Old World of wine has to reconsider its tradition in light of changing climate conditions. Both worlds need to remember that this world is our only home, and the best way to take care of it is to work with the rhythms and limitations of creation rather than seeking to ignore and transcend them. It is for this reason that we must "not cease from exploration. And the end of all our exploring will be to arrive where we started and know the place for the first time."

8

Wine and Its Health Benefits

"No longer drink only water, but take a little wine for the sake of your stomach and your frequent ailments."

1 Timothy 5:23

The apostle Paul was neither the first nor the last one to understand that wine has significant medicinal value if enjoyed in moderation. The health benefits of wine have been known since antiquity, and wine was a prime medical agent in ancient, medieval, and early modern times, up to the nineteenth century.

Wine is a highly complex, rich, and nutritious beverage. It is an important source of caloric intake and is abundant in minerals such as iron, magnesium, calcium, iodine, copper, sodium, and potassium. Wine contains many vitamin B complexes, such as thiamine (vitamin B1), riboflavin (vitamin B2), pantothenic acid (vitamin B5), pyridoxine (vitamin B6), niacin (vitamin B3), cobalamin (vitamin B12, only in red wine), and folic acid. The process of fermentation releases additional amounts of some of these vitamins. Red wine also contains the rich polyphenols such as resveratrol. These polyphenols are extracted from the skin, seeds, and stem of the grape as the wine undergoes fermentation, and their medicinal value as antioxidants has been widely studied and recognized. It is thus no surprise that wine has played a significant role historically not only as a food but also as medicine.

With the rise of modern medicine, however, more natural remedies became less important; many were forgotten and then they disappeared from the general consciousness. The advances of modern medicine have been remarkable, and the development of pharmaceutical drugs has revolutionized health care in the Western world. Many aspects of modern medicine have increased our standard of living, and we would not want to live without modern medicine.

And yet these advances and the shift toward using pharmaceutical drugs have led to a cultural amnesia of sorts. We have forgotten and neglected the wisdom and insights of a long medical tradition. Overdependence on pharmaceutical drugs and conventional modern medicine has eclipsed the traditional knowledge that creation offers an abundance of "natural" remedies for many human ailments: the use of wine for medicinal purposes is one such example. In addition, modern medicine has tended to focus on isolating and treating physical problems rather than seeing the whole person, and understanding how physical illness might be related in a holistic way to our emotional and spiritual needs. Traditionally, the Christian tradition has used wine to minister to the spiritual, emotional, and physical needs of a person. Wine used in the Eucharist reminds us that we are spiritual beings and that our cure can never be reduced to our physical needs. Humans are living souls with profound spiritual, emotional, and physical needs, and we need to be treated and healed in more holistic ways.

The Health Benefits of Wine: A Historical Perspective

Ancient Times

Ancient cultures such as the Egyptians, Babylonians, Persians, Greeks, Romans, Indians, Chinese, and, of course, the Hebrews and early Christians — all give witness to the medicinal value and use of wine.[1] Some of the first written comments on the healing properties of wine can be found in Homer's *Iliad* and *Odyssey* (ca. eighth century BC). Wine is the most frequently mentioned medicament in these narratives. These ancient narratives reveal that wine was known and used as a stimulant, an antiseptic, a sedative, and a painkiller (pp. 20-22).

The ancient Greek physician Hippocrates (ca. 460–ca. 370 BC), often called the father of Western medicine, lived during one of the most prolific stages of Hellenistic civilization and contributed significantly to the flowering of intellectual life during that period. His writing on medicine and the medicinal value of wine was extensive: it would influence medicine for centuries to come. He carefully observed how patients responded to various medical treatments, and he employed strict hygienic rules (pp. 37, 40); he also used wine extensively in his medical practice, prescribing it for the external treatments of wounds and ulcers.[2] He also recognized the nutritional value of wine and recommended it as a nourishing dietary beverage. He prescribed it as a cooling agent for fevers, for purgative purposes, and as a diuretic; he carefully observed how different kinds of wine have different effects and meticulously directed their uses for specific conditions. He advised when wine was to be diluted with water and when the use of wine should be avoided. Hippocrates carefully observed the effect of various wines on the digestive system and understood the impact of wine on the gastrointestinal tract: he knew which wines accelerate and which delay bowel movement and urinary flow. He recognized wines that help hydrate the body and ones that dehydrate the body, and how different wines affect the brain in different ways (pp. 37-40). Hippocrates' knowledge of wine's health benefits was and remains impressive, and no one would state them so clearly again until the time of Galen (AD 131-201) — some six hundred years later. While modern medicine has not confirmed some of Hippocrates' observations, many of them still hold true today.

Hippocrates' famous contemporaries, such as Socrates, Plato, and Aristotle, all gave witness to the medicinal benefits of wine. Reading a few snippets of their wisdom might help cure our cultural and medical amnesia. Xenophon quotes his teacher, Socrates, whose musings on wine are much more poetic and philosophical than the rather matter-of-fact writings of Hippocrates:

> Wine moistens and tempers the spirits, and lulls the cares of the mind to rest, . . . it revives our joys, and is oil to the dying flame of life. . . . If we drink temperately, and small draughts at a time, the wine distills upon our lungs like sweetest morning dew. . . . It is then the wine commits no rape upon our reason, but pleasantly invites us to agreeable mirth.[3]

As a philosopher, Socrates emphasized the aesthetic, emotional, and cultural benefits of wine. Wine brings joy, settles a restless spirit, and brings comfort to those who face death. When enjoyed in moderation, it enhances human conversation and fosters conviviality.

Plato discourages the young from drinking too much wine but argues that wine brings comfort to the elderly, renews their strength, helps them forget their sorrow for a little while, and softens their disposition.[4] Theophrastus (370-285 BC), whose name literally means "divine orator," was a student of Aristotle and would become the leading botanist of ancient times. He discussed how medicinal plants decocted in wine might be used for medical purposes. Theophrastus also provided recipes for perfumed and honeyed wines and discussed their effect on the sense of taste (Lucia, p. 42). Mnesitheus (320-290 BC), a physician of Athens, wrote that red wines aid bodily growth and white wine helps the digestive system, medical insight that would be confirmed in modern times (p. 42).

The famous Roman encyclopedist Celsus wrote quite extensively on medicine during the beginning of the Christian era. He made distinctions between the health benefits of various wines from different wine regions, such as Italy and Greece. While some wines have a laxative effect, he informed his readers, others have constipating effects. He carefully recorded the healing properties of different wines for digestive-tract ailments and recommended certain wines for stomach problems (pp. 53-54).

Pliny the Elder (AD 23-79), the famous Roman naturalist, had an impressive knowledge of wine and its health benefits. He writes: "As for medicines, grapes hold such an important place among them that they act as remedies in themselves, merely by supplying wine."[5] Pliny recommends honeyed wines (mulsum) in particular: mulsum stimulates the appetite, and when drunk cold, relaxes the bowels. Salt mixed with wine gently purges the bowels and expels intestinal worms (Lucia, p. 59). He recommended saffron in wine to relieve itching sensations and wild marjoram taken in white wine to counteract the stings of spiders and scorpions. Pliny recommended wine flavored with anise and bitter almonds as a mouthwash, arguing that it removes all bad odors and sweetens the breath (pp. 60-61). The medicinal use of wine seemed to stretch into every area of health care.

The famous second-century Greek physician Galen summarized and systematized the medical knowledge of ancient times. His writings were preserved in the Byzantine and Arabic periods and influenced Western European medicine for over a thousand years.[6] Galen based his medical knowledge on careful observation and experience, and he used wine extensively in his medical practice. He served as a physician to the Roman gladiators, cleaning their wounds with wine. It has been said that none of the gladiators died from in-fected wounds (Lucia, p. 69). He also cleansed fistulous abscesses with wine; he recommended that patients suffering from insomnia should drink wine. He advised the use of different kinds of wines for different fevers, though he did not recommend that all fevers be treated with wine. His preferred prescription for a weak stomach was warm wine. His recipes for antidotes to poisoning include a rather complicated discussion of the kinds of wines that should be used in the mix. Only the best Falernian wine, high in alcohol content, was suitable (pp. 70-71).[7]

As I observed above, the Hebrews were familiar with the health benefits of wine and emphasized the spiritual and psychological benefits of drinking wine (Prov. 31:6-7). The Bible also documents Jesus' recognition of the antiseptic healing properties of wine when applied externally (Luke 25:29-37), and the apostle Paul believed that wine helps an upset stomach and "various other aliments" (1 Tim. 5:23). But overall — and first in importance — the Bible emphasizes that wine is a gift from God, a sign of God's blessing and benev-olence that brings joy to his people. Wine's primary purpose thus remains a spiritual one and must not be reduced to its physical and emotional healing properties. Anne Morey, a Catholic vintner from Burgundy, reminds us that in the Christian tradition, wine is first of all medicine for the soul.[8]

The Medieval Period and the Rise of Monastic Hospitals (Infirmaries)

As a result of the decline and collapse of the Roman Empire, medical research stagnated; at that time the Byzantine and Arabic cultures contributed to the preservation and passing on of ancient medical knowledge.[9] With the emer-gence of monasticism in late antiquity and the early Middle Ages, caring for the sick took on a new social form.[10] Monasticism developed as an alternative social institution that sought — in its original intent — to renounce and tran-scend traditional social bonds. The Rule of Saint Benedict was and remains a radical subversion and reorientation of traditional hierarchical social orders. In Christ all are the same, and Saint Benedict worked out a very practical rule for community living that would embody this belief in the daily lives of the monks. Whether from noble or peasant background — whether rich or poor — everyone now wore the same clothes, ate the same food, had to partake in manual labor, and shared the same rhythm of life. When the Benedictine monks of Cluny began to stray from this original vision, and certain monks began to excuse themselves from manual labor, they abandoned an important aspect of Benedictine spirituality. A key concern of the Cistercian reform of Benedictine spirituality, then, was to emphasize once more that all are the same in Christ and no one was to be excused from the humble task of manual labor.

From its very beginning, the monastic movement concerned itself not only with the spiritual but also the physical well-being of its followers. In Greco-Roman times, medical care was primarily a privilege reserved for the wealthy, for soldiers, and to ensure that slaves remained healthy laborers.[11] Both Old and New Testaments consistently emphasize the importance of caring for the destitute, such as widows and orphans, as well as beggars and travelers.[12] The emergent monastic communities, away from the support system of their families, began to establish their own social structures. It is in these early monastic communities that the foundation for an organized health-care system emerged in order to replace the familial support structures that they had left behind.[13] Saint Benedict (ca. 480-543) made caring for the sick a mandate of good works in his Rule:

> Care of the sick must rank above and before all else, so that they may truly be served as Christ, for he said: *I was sick and you visited me* (Matt. 25:36), and, *What you did for one of these least brothers you did for me* (Matt. 25:40). . . . Let a separate room be designated for the sick, and let them be served by an attendant who is God-fearing, attentive and concerned.[14]

Before Benedict, Basil of Caesarea (ca. 329-379) had founded an impressive hospital in the East where the poor, strangers, homeless, orphans, elderly, infirm, lepers, and other sick persons received charitable care.[15] Saint Benedict solidified this Christian commitment to care for the sick and poor by making it a mandate for his monastic community. He also insisted that each abbot establish an infirmary in the monastery.[16] These hospitals and infirmaries were, of course, very different from our modern idea of a hospital. They were closely tied to the religious and social dimension of monastic life, and, as a result, the care for the sick became an important part of the Benedictine and later Cistercian mission in the world.

Hospitals such as the infirmaries at Kloster Eberbach in the Rheingau (built about 1220), the well-preserved infirmary at Monastery Ourscamp near Noyon in the north of France (built around 1210), and S. Spirito in Rome, founded in the twelfth century by Pope Innocent, still give witness to this important emphasis of monastic spirituality.[17] The Rule of S. Spirito Hospital speaks of the importance of "the feeding and giving hospitality and clothes to the poor, looking after and housing the sick, pregnant women and abandoned children. . . ."[18] In Florence, monastic communities founded forty-one hospitals and pharmacies before the Black Death of 1348.[19]

The well-preserved hospital and hospice in Beaune, Burgundy, is an important witness to how a late-medieval hospital might have looked. It was built to care for the poverty-stricken population of the town, and it was run by a monastic order. The religious artwork in the hospice miraculously survived the tumults of the French Revolution and gives witness to this integrated concern of caring not only for the physical but also for the spiritual and emotional needs of the patients. Beautiful Christian artwork fostered the patients' hope for eternal life, and it brought comfort to the sick, the destitute, and the dying.[20] The building of hospitals and hospices — as we now know them in the Western world — was, first of all, a monastic mission before it became secularized in the modern period.[21]

Slowly but surely, monasteries emerged out of the Dark Ages as centers of healing and learning. Alongside the establishing of hospitals, monasteries had their own pharmacies where they made medicines for the sick. They also had their own plant nurseries. Monks and nuns were remarkably skilled in cultivating medicinal herb gardens and vineyards, and they used herbs and wine extensively to make their own medicines.[22] It is not surprising that medical knowledge was developed, practiced, and preserved in the context of such monastic communities. Wine continued to play a significant medicinal role. Many medical texts have been preserved, and they give ample witness to the medicinal use of wine in medieval times.

Byzantine and Arabic Traditions

The most important contribution of Byzantine physicians was their preservation of Greek and Roman medical knowledge through their writings, though only a handful of their writings have survived. Aëtius of Amida (ca. 502–ca. 575) was a Christian Byzantine physician who discussed the medical uses of wine in his *Tetrabiblion*. Aëtius was educated at the Alexandrian medical school and used wine extensively in his medical practice. For women who suffered from frigidity, he ordered not only strenuous work but also that they drink some wine. He prescribed potions for contraception, which were to be drunk with wine to be effective. Those suffering from diphtheria had to drink wine instead of water. Alexander of Tralles (525-605) seems to have offered some original observations, but in general the Byzantine period remained a period of preservation rather than development of new medical knowledge (Lucia, pp. 73-75).

Even though the Koran forbids the drinking of wine, some physicians in Islamic territories continued to advocate the medicinal value of wine. The famous Jewish physician Rhazes (860-932), who lived in Persia, brought to Islam his cultural knowledge of the health benefits of wine; he also recommended treating wounds with wine. Another Persian, the renowned physician Avicenna (980-1036), wrote *Canon of Medicine,* a medical book that would profoundly influence not only Islam but also Western Europe until well into the seventeenth century. The *Canon* includes an entire section on the medicinal use of wine. Avicenna's depth of knowledge regarding the health benefits of wine seems to suggest that he was familiar with the medical writings of Greece and Rome (Lucia, pp. 73-75, 79-82). Ibn Butlan (1038-1075), an Arabic Christian physician in Baghdad, wrote *Tacuinum Sanitatis (The Maintenance of Health),* a medieval handbook on health and well-being that focuses on diet, exercise and rest, and mental health. His work was translated into Latin and became a popular medical text in the late Middle Ages in Western Europe.[23] Another important and celebrated Jewish physician of the Arabic world was Rabbi Moses ben Maimon (1135-1204); he was the court physician to Saladin, the sultan of Egypt and Syria. In one of his letters to the sultan's son, who struggled with indigestion, he wrote:

> It is well known among physicians that the best of the nourishing foods is one that the Moslem religion forbids, i.e. wine. It contains much good and light nourishment. It is rapidly digested and helps to digest other foods.... The benefits of wine are many if it is taken in the proper amount, as it keeps the body in a healthy condition and cures many illnesses.[24]

Even *Arabian Nights* features a reflection on the health benefits of wine. All this evidence reveals that, even though the Koran forbids the drinking of wine and sees it as a gift reserved for life in paradise, the medicinal use of wine during the Middle Ages in Muslim countries is well attested.[25]

The Rise of Medical Schools in the Middle Ages

Monastic communities began to preserve, translate, and copy Greco-Roman — and later Byzantine and Arabic — manuscripts on medicine from Greek into Latin. They were able to glean from and develop ancient medical knowledge and pass it down to future generations. The *Geoponica,* or *Agricultural Pursuits,* is one important example. It is an anonymous collection of twenty books assembled in Istanbul (then called Constantinople) for the Byzantine Emperor Constantine VII and dates back to the tenth century. Book III includes an extensive discussion of the healing properties of wine.[26]

Just ninety miles south of Monte Cassino, one of the most important medical centers of the Middle Ages emerged. In the tenth century, Benedictine monks founded the medical school of Salerno. Clerical and lay physicians worked together, and the Benedictine brothers at the monastery of Monte Cassino made all the collected and translated medical writings available to them. The school was able to accumulate, systematize, and develop a significant body of medical knowledge. It is not surprising that this school continued to explore and emphasize the medicinal benefits of wine. Wine was prescribed as a nutrient, as an internal antiseptic, and as a restorative. The *Regimen sanitatis salernitanum* (or Salernitan Rule of Health) is credited to this school, which prescribed wine more frequently than any other therapeutic agent (Lucia, p. 92).

It is noteworthy that the medical school of Salerno also admitted women to the school. Though we have no record that the Benedictine nun Hildegard von Bingen (1098-1179) attended this school, her writings suggest that she may have been aware of their teaching and may have used it in her own medical practice at Rupertsberg in the Rheingau. The early thirteenth-century manuscript *Summa de saporibus* (or Compendium Concerning Taste), for example, is credited to the medical school of Salerno. Contrary to tradition, it elevates the sense of taste to be superior to all the other senses (see chap. 5). Hildegard was one of the few medieval theological writers who also elevated the sense of taste over all the other senses.

Hildegard's medical writings include *Physica* (Medicine) and *Causa et Cura* (Causes and Cures). She saw moderation as the key to good health; she advocated a balanced diet, sufficient rest, and alleviation of stress. She discouraged eager ascetics from being too strict in their practices: "Do not lay on more strain than the body can endure. Immoderate straining and abstinence bring nothing useful to the soul."[27] Like the medical tradition before her, she used wine extensively in her medical practice, sometimes on its own but often together with herbs, honey, and other additives. In *Physica* she prescribes the internal and external use of wine for a wide range of ailments. Those who have problems with the chest, heart, stomach, and digestive system should drink good, pure, and mild wine. Hildegard advises women who suffer regularly from heavy menstrual bleeding not to work too much, not to get worn out by too much travel, and to drink beer and wine for strength.[28] She recommended drinking cooked herbs in wine not just as a deterrent to bad breath but also to counteract the underlying problem of "rottenness" in body and chest. She advised drinking wine infused with herbs to kill worms in the stomach and recommended using wine as an antiseptic ointment for inflamed gums, ulcers on the body, and to diminish pus on wounds.[29] While many of her medical recipes seem obscure to the modern reader — and cannot be substantiated by modern medicine — many of her insights into the health benefits of wine are remarkably current.

The later Middle Ages saw a continued interest in the health benefits of wine. Arnau de Vilanova (ca. 1235-1311), of the medical school of Montpellier, was a well-known and highly respected academic medical practitioner. His *Liber de Vinis* is a whole book dedicated to the therapeutic use of wine. Vilanova's great reputation turned this book into a medieval "bestseller" and helped establish the use of wine as a recognized system of therapy in the late Middle Ages. He lists some forty-nine different medicinal wines and prescribes their use for many different diseases, such as malaria, tuberculosis, gout, epilepsy, intestinal parasites, seasickness, sterility, and loss of memory. He prescribes wine to prevent hair loss, to straighten the tendons, to improve complexion, to increase appetite, and to quicken the mind.[30] Distilled spirits had only recently been discovered, and Vilanova called brandy *aqua vita* ("water of life") because of its healing properties. Applied to wounds, it inhibits infection; Vilanova seems to have been the first physician to record the use of distilled wine as an antiseptic for wounds (Lucia, p. 108).

The antiseptic treatment of wounds was not universal during the Middle

Ages. It was common practice to provoke the generation of pus in wounds. Innumerable victims died in torment from such infections. It seems that Arabian commentators had first provided faulty translations of ancient material, and it had become popular belief that the promotion of "laudable pus" would help heal wounds. It was only in the early thirteenth century that medieval surgeons such as Hugh of Lucca from Bologna and Theodoric Borgognoni (1205-1298) challenged conventional medical practices (p. 111). Borgognoni was a Dominican friar, bishop, and medical surgeon who challenged the idea of "laudable pus" and parted with traditional practices handed down from Arabic medicine when he promoted the use of wine as an antiseptic in surgery (p. 113). Henri de Mondville (ca. 1260-1316), a French surgeon and lecturer at the University of Montpellier, praised wine as a "wound drink," emphasized its disinfectant qualities, and advised the use of wine for washing wounds.[31] The use of wine as a disinfectant continued throughout the Middles Ages, though the notion of "laudable pus" did not completely disappear.

The Renaissance Swiss physician and surgeon Paracelsus (1493-1541), of Basel, was a pioneer in chemical pharmacology. A contemporary of Martin Luther, he radically questioned traditional medical practices and specifically the idea of "laudable pus." Instead, he taught that nature, the "natural balm," heals wounds, and he promoted the use of tinctures and alcoholic extracts in his medical practice (p. 117).

The external and internal use of wine for medicinal purposes continued throughout the Middle Ages. The great contribution of Western monasticism to medicine was the recovery, preservation, and cultivation of medical knowledge from ancient Greece, Persia, and Rome. The reader should also remember that it was Christian monasticism that began to institutionalize medical care by building hospitals. It was in these monastic infirmaries that monks and nuns, whom Martin Luther had sweepingly called "fleas on the fur coat of God Almighty," made medical care available not only for its members and the well-to-do but also for the poor, vulnerable, and marginalized of society.

Modern Times and the Brief Eclipse of Wine as Medicine

Wine continued to be used as medicine well into the modern period. The official European pharmacopoeias (books describing drug preparations) during the seventeenth, eighteenth, and early nineteenth centuries included wine and alcohol. The *London Pharmacopoeia* of 1836 prescribes wines for stomach and digestive problems, as diuretics, and for patients suffering from gout. The *Pharmacopoia Universalis* of Heidelberg (1835) lists 170 different wines, and the *Pharamcopée Universelle* in Paris (1840) lists 164 wines. The first *Pharmacopoeia of the United States* (1820) contains nine recipes for wine-based medicines, and a subsequent edition (1850) adds port, sherry, and brandy (pp. 145-47).

The rise of the temperance and Prohibition movements, which climaxed in the Prohibition period in the United States (1920-1933), challenged the use of alcohol and wine for medicinal purpose. The 1883 edition of the *U.S. Pharmacopoeia* eliminated port and sherry, and the 1893 edition eliminated "stronger white wine." Though the 1905 edition still listed twelve medicinal wines, the Pharmacopoeial Convention of 1916 voted to delete all wines from the list. When the British revised their *Pharmacopoeia* in 1932, they followed this lead and eliminated all wines from their list (pp. 148-49).

American Prohibition, however, did not completely erase the medicinal use of wine; it allowed the production of alcoholic beverages for medicinal purposes. Salvatore Lucia suggests that never before, or after, did physicians prescribe alcoholic beverages in such quantities, more often for "festive" rather than "therapeutic" purposes (p. 150). But wine never made it back into the official American and British pharmacopoeias, and thousands of years of the knowledge of and experience with the medicinal benefits of wine were forgotten. The French, the Italians, the Germans, and even the Japanese continued to list medicinal wines; so the cultural amnesia and silence concerning the health benefits of wine was never complete. And yet, with the rise of pharmaceutical drugs toward the end of nineteenth century, wine as medicine increasingly receded into the background.[32] Ancient and traditional wisdom on the healing properties of nature came under scorn, sometimes for good reason, since superstitious beliefs had led to the popularization of strange recipes for medicinal cordials that defied any scientific examination.

The latter part of the twentieth century, however, saw a renaissance of interest in natural medicines that has lasted to the present. The popularization of the writings of Hildegard von Bingen, for example, reminded the German people of a rich heritage to be rediscovered. A recent documentary on her life was released on DVD in 2010; the German edition includes a booklet that lists and explains the medicinal value of various herbs that Hildegard had explored in her writings.[33]

The rediscovery of the health benefits of wine on an international scale, however, came through different channels. Though medieval writings such as Hildegard's remind us of this forgotten medicinal gift, it was a French study that drew international attention to the health benefits of wine in contemporary society.

An Overview of the Modern Scientific Perspective

It is rather ironic that the popularization of just one medical study by a Frenchman, Dr. Serge Renaud, helped counteract our cultural amnesia with regard to the medicinal value of wine. An American reporter stumbled on French wisdom concerning the health benefits of wine and found it confirmed in the study by Renaud. A popular CBS television program then introduced these findings to the general American public in 1991. Since then, medical research into the health benefits of wine has skyrocketed, and reports on new discoveries and theories regarding those benefits appear in the news on a regular basis.[34]

Serge Renaud had studied the relationship between moderate wine-drinking and low-rate cardiovascular diseases (diseases of the heart and blood vessel system). This study revealed that the French had a much lower rate of cardiovascular disease than that of other industrialized countries such as the United States and the United Kingdom. In most countries the high consumption of saturated fats is positively related to an increased risk of heart disease. Paradoxically, this tendency is not true in France: though the French have a high intake of saturated fat (they love their cheeses) and smoke cigarettes, they nonetheless have a low mortality rate from heart disease. Today this finding is referred to as the "French paradox." Renaud found that the French drink a moderate amount of wine with their meals daily (they also eat and drink more slowly). Scientific studies revealed that the consumption of alcohol at the level of consumption in France (approximately one to two glasses of wine a day) can reduce the risk of heart disease by at least 40 percent. Renaud suggests that wine drunk in moderation may be one of the most efficient "drugs" to prevent heart disease.[35]

Since then, many scientific studies have confirmed Renaud's findings and suggest that the moderate consumption of any kind of alcohol (1-2 drinks per day) can reduce the risk of cardiovascular disease by an average of 30-35 percent in comparison to nondrinkers.[36] Given that cardiovascular diseases are the leading cause of death in many industrialized countries, especially in the United States, this medical finding is exceedingly important. Strokes, which constitute one form of cardiovascular disease, are the third-leading cause of death and a major cause of disability in the United States. A daily glass of wine drunk in a leisurely way can significantly reduce the risk of stroke. This is good news indeed.[37] Studies around the world have shown that moderate drinkers tend to have a lower mortality rate than either nondrinkers or heavy drinkers.[38] Heavy drinking and binge drinking, on the other hand, increase the risk of heart disease and stroke.

Researchers are still exploring why alcohol has such a positive effect; a certain amount of uncertainty remains. Different hypotheses exist. Medical studies have shown that the HDL (high-density lipoprotein, also called "good cholesterol") concentration is increased in people who consume alcohol moderately.[39] Good cholesterol reduces the risk of hardening of the arteries. One very popular theory is that red wine, in particular, has antioxidant effects and prevents plaque formation in the arteries. It is supposed that components such as flavonoids in red wine reduce one of the most dangerous forms of LDL (low-density lipoprotein, also called "bad cholesterol," or oxidized LDL). In its oxidized form, LDL contributes to atherosclerotic plaque formation and hardening of the arteries. Researchers have also discovered that the human body can absorb antioxidants in red wine more easily than those in grape juice.[40] One study suggests that red wine — and no other source of alcohol — decreases the risk of atherosclerosis, a disease of the arteries characterized by the depositing of fatty materials on the inner wall of the arteries.[41] However, earlier in this chapter we pointed out that all kinds of alcohol have beneficial effects. It remains uncertain whether wine is more protective with regard to cardiovascular diseases than other types of alcohol. It seems likely that the type of alcohol is not as important as the amount of alcohol consumed and the pattern of intake.

Other studies suggest that resveratrol, a molecule in red wine produced by plants in response to stress, protects against cardiovascular diseases. One study also revealed that resveratrol might even improve motor skills with age.[42]

These studies are based on feeding mice high amounts of resveratrol in powdered form, and we should consider them with caution. The levels of resveratrol in moderate amounts of wine are minimal in comparison.[43] These findings are derived from animal data and can therefore not be directly applied to human health. However, there are multiple studies suggesting that resveratrol might even protect against cancer, particularly prostate and breast cancer.[44]

Another fascinating study explored the effect of alcohol on the cognitive function in women. While it is well known that excessive drinking impairs one's cognitive abilities, a recent study showed that moderate drinking (up to one drink) might actually decrease cognitive decline in women. In particular, older women who drank up to one drink per day had consistently better cognitive performance than nondrinkers. The most plausible explanation is that wine may help preserve the circulatory system of the brain and thus not only prevent strokes but also cognitive decline.[45]

Despite all these promising findings, scientific research on the medicinal benefits of wine is still in its early stages. The main area of research has been on the preventive aspects related to cardiovascular diseases because they are the number-one cause of death in the Western world. Historically, however, there are many other areas where wine has played an important medicinal role — such as in its antibacterial effects, quite apart from its alcohol content (Lucia, pp. 177-80). Since the middle of the twentieth century, scientific studies have been conducted on the possible value of moderate wine or alcohol consumption in controlling obesity, diabetes, stress, and dementia.[46] Though wine was traditionally prescribed for stomach problems, current medical practice tends to limit alcohol use in patients with gastric/stomach problems. Some research has shown that alcohol consumption increases the risk of some types of gastrointestinal cancer and also breast cancer. But the increased risk was largely found in individuals who drank more than the recommended upper limit.

Concluding Reflections

The question of the health benefits of wine remains a complex one and will occupy the medical world for many years to come. Research certainly should not be limited to the positive effect it has in preventing cardiovascular diseases, but should explore other areas of health as well. One very fascinating area of research would be the positive effects wine has on the emotional and spiritual dimensions of human life. Most studies of the social role of wine have focused on the abuse of alcohol and its destructive impact on patients and their families. Few studies have actually explored and evaluated how the regular and moderate use of wine affects the quality of life in positive ways. It is more difficult to measure scientifically how an increased level of joy and conviviality can affect one's overall well-being or how drinking a moderate amount of wine in old age can help keep depression at bay.

Arnold of Villanova emphasizes both the physical and emotional benefits of wine:"Now the time has come to prepare the wines that are used for medicinal purposes. . . . And its goodness is not only revealed in the body but also in the soul, for it makes the soul merry and lets it forget sadness."[47] It is no wonder that Louis Pasteur called wine "the most healthful, the most hygienic of beverages."[48]

Wine is a beautiful gift that can add tremendously to our well-being, but only if we enjoy it in moderation. As soon as wine, and alcohol in general, are consumed beyond moderate amounts on a regular basis, they can severely damage our own and other people's health. It is to the abuse of wine and alcohol that we must now turn.

9

Wine and the Abuse of Alcohol: Rescuing Wine from the Gluttons for the Contemplatives

*"In whatever you do, be moderate, and no addiction will afflict
you. . . . Wine is very life to humans, if taken in due measure.
Does one really live who lacks the wine which was created from
the first for his joy? Joy of heart, good cheer, and delight is wine
enough, drunk at proper times. Headache, wormwood, and disgrace is wine drunk amid anger and strife."*

Jesus Ben Sira[1]

The abuse of alcohol has been a serious problem historically and in
contemporary society. The destructive force of alcohol abuse and
the damage that comes with addictive behaviors and disorders can
be horrific. Films like *Days of Wine and Roses* (1962), *When a Man Loves a
Woman* (1994), and the documentary *Prohibition* (2011) depict how addiction
to alcohol can destroy not only the lives of individuals but also their extended
families and entire communities. Its destructive effects can reach into and be
felt by many future generations.

Contemporary psychology discusses and treats alcohol abuse under the
general umbrella of "addictive behaviors and disorders." Addiction to alcohol
is one of many substance-focused addictions, such as those to heroin, cocaine,
marijuana, prescription and over-the-counter medications, tobacco, caffeine,
energy drinks, and food. Behavioral addictions include those to gambling,
shopping, exercise, work, sex, the Internet, cybersex, video games, cell phone

use and texting, and social networking.[2] Research into the nature of addiction has grown rapidly over the last twenty years, and it reveals that addictive behaviors and disorders have become a major problem in contemporary society.

In light of such developments, would it not be best to avoid alcohol altogether? Certainly the temperance movements in both Great Britain and the United States advocated this approach. The abuse of alcohol in the form of strong and cheap spirits such as gin and whiskey brought incredible suffering, especially to working-class people. Industrial workers would collect their meager earnings and take them straight to the pubs and bars, while their wives and children would go without food and clothing. It is understandable that in such cases of widespread social evil, the only possible solution seemed to be to advocate complete abstinence. The Salvation Army, for example, was the first organization founded to reach out and minister to people addicted to alcohol and morphine. These peculiar historical situations called for a radical response in order to bring sanity and healing.

In the wake of the temperance movement, some readers of the Bible argue to this day that the Bible does not encourage the consumption of wine at all. While it is understandable that, in certain historical and personal situations, individuals and groups might choose to abstain from wine and alcohol altogether, the Bible does not support total abstention.[3] Though Martin Luther did not have to respond to that particular abstemious reading of Scripture (it only emerged in the aftermath of the American Prohibition), he did have to counter Christian voices in his own day that wanted to forbid the drinking of wine. It is worth quoting Martin Luther again, since his response is so poignant and brings to the fore important concerns about a generalized response to the role of alcohol in Christian spirituality:

> Wine and women bring sorrow and heartbreak, they make a fool of many and bring madness, ought we therefore to pour away the wine and kill all the women? Not so. Gold and silver, money and possessions bring much evil among the people, should we therefore throw it all way? If we want to eliminate our closest enemy, the one that is most harmful to us, we would have to kill ourselves. We have no more harmful enemy than our own heart.[4]

What Martin Luther saw so keenly was that the removal of one substance would not eliminate the problem, but would transfer it into other areas of our lives. The German people of Luther's time were heavy drinkers, and Luther severely condemned drunkenness and the abuse of alcohol. Instead of forbidding wine and alcohol altogether, however, Luther challenged believers to take responsibility for their behavior. He had learned from his own experience that true freedom only comes by honestly facing in the presence of a loving and merciful God the things that imprison us. But how does the Bible speak about alcohol abuse? And does it offer any constructive ways of dealing with it?

Alcohol Abuse and Drunkenness in the Bible

The biblical narrative always portrays drunkenness and the abuse of alcohol in negative terms. The judgment of such behavior is often implicit rather than explicit. For example, Noah was the first person in the Bible to plant a vineyard, and he was also the first person to get drunk, according to the biblical narrative. Though Noah is not judged, his drunkenness exposes him to great shame (Gen. 9:20-26). The story of Noah's drunkenness makes clear that all facets of human life are affected by sin and in need of God's redemption, including our wine consumption.

Films such as *Days of Wine and Roses* and *When a Man Loves a Woman* are nothing in comparison to the horrific story of Lot and his daughters in Genesis 19. Lot and his family had barely escaped Sodom and Gomorrah, cities of profound immorality and brutality. Lot and his two surviving daughters had fled into the hills, where they stayed in a cave. The daughters, without the prospect of any descendants, decided to get their father drunk on wine in order to seduce him and secure for themselves offspring (Gen. 19:30-38). This account is not for the faint of heart and leaves the modern reader with a sense of horror at Lot's daughters' calculating and immoral behavior.

The priest Eli's account of watching Hannah, a barren and troubled woman, behave suspiciously in the temple is important in a very different way. Eli thought Hannah was drunk and began accusing her: "How long will you make a drunken spectacle of yourself? Put away your wine" (1 Sam. 1:14). But it turns out that Hannah was not drunk at all. She replied, "Do not regard your servant as a worthless woman, for I have been speaking out of my great anxiety and vexation all this time" (1 Sam. 1:16). Rather than drowning her sorrow and anxiety in alcohol, Hannah was praying to God in the temple. It is in prayer before

God that she found relief and comfort in the midst of her troubles. Implicit in this story is a clear rejection of drunkenness as acceptable behavior. But the story also upholds Hannah as a model for the spiritual life. Hannah was unable to conceive a child, and this inability not only made her a social outcast but also caused her great anxiety and turmoil. She exemplifies the believer who is able to trust God with her troubles. She turns to him rather than wine in her time of great distress, which is all the more admirable because many in her situation would turn to the comfort of alcohol.

The story of King David, Bathsheba, and her husband, Uriah, is another heart-wrenching story of how wine can be abused — and to destructive ends. Uriah faithfully served King David in his army. While Uriah was away fighting for the king in battle, David was at home watching Bathsheba bathe and lusting after her. King David used — or better, abused — his power and privilege as king by ordering Bathsheba into his palace, where he committed adultery with her. Bathsheba conceived a child, and a cover-up action was required. David called Uriah home from battle, hoping that Uriah would make love to his wife. But Uriah was an honorable man and refused to go home when all of his fellow soldiers were still out on the battlefield. At that point, David invited Uriah to a feast and got him drunk, presumably with the hope that Uriah would then return home to his wife and sleep with her. Again, Uriah did not go home, and David sent him to the battlefront, where, by David's orders, he was placed in the front rank and his death in battle was inevitable (2 Sam. 11).

The Old Testament prophets consistently spoke out against drunkenness and alcohol abuse. Though the prophets firmly upheld wine as a gift from God and understood an abundance of wine as a sign of God's redemption of and benevolence toward his people, the abuse of wine would lead to a disregard for God and his purposes. God's people would forget to be a blessing to others, and would be unable to exercise justice and govern wisely. The prophet Isaiah says: "Ah, you who rise early in the morning in pursuit of strong drink, who linger in the evening to be inflamed by wine, whose feasts consist of lyre and harp, tambourine and flute and wine, but who do not regard the deeds of the Lord, or see the work of his hands!" (Isa. 5:11-12; see also 5:22; 28:1-3, 7-8; 56:12; Hosea 4:11, 18; 7:5; Joel 1:5, 3:3; Amos 2:8; 4:1; Hab. 2:15).

While the book of Psalms only praises the positive effects of wine, the book of Proverbs also warns against the abuse of wine and drunkenness. Proverbs teaches the ways of wisdom to the young, and those who are given to drunkenness are not wise (Prov. 20:1). It is important to note that Proverbs frames its discussion of the negative effects of drunkenness and alcohol abuse with two positive affirmations of wine as a gift from God and wine as medicine for the dying, suffering, and poor (Prov. 3:10; 31:6).

Proverbs 23, in particular, warns against drunkenness and gluttony and encourages the young to embrace a life of seeking truth, wisdom, and understanding (Prov. 23:23). It gives a surprisingly vivid and detailed description of the state of severe drunkenness and the following hangover (Prov. 23:31-35), probably in the hope of deterring the young from even trying to get drunk. Proverbs admonishes kings and rulers to abstain from wine and strong drink lest they forget their responsibilities, act unjustly, and cease to care for the poverty-stricken and marginalized of their communities (Prov. 31:4-5, 8-9).

The Hebrew worldview, while clearly receiving wine as a gift from God with gratitude and thanksgiving, consistently rejects the abuse of alcohol and drunkenness as inappropriate and destructive behavior leading to disregard for God and his good purposes for humanity. While God wants his people to enjoy the gifts that he has given them, their purpose as God's people extends beyond their own well-being and enjoyment to be a blessing to others.

It seems that this religious and cultural norm had established within Israel a firm moral code with respect to drinking practices. Perhaps this background is why we find very little in Jesus' teaching that addresses this particular problem. Jesus ministered primarily to Jewish people, and the Torah had deeply engrained in them the view that alcohol abuse was unacceptable. The Gospels only contain three brief exhortations against drunkenness or drinking with drunkards, and exhortations to be watchful and prayerful follow them (Matt. 24:45-51; Luke 12:45; 21:34). Jesus apparently drank so much wine, especially with the socially outcasts and "sinners," that his own Jewish people became uncomfortable with it and even called him a glutton and drunkard (Matt. 11:19; Luke 7:34).

The apostle Paul, on the other hand, ministered in an entirely different cultural setting. He preached the gospel to churches that had many pagan converts to Christianity. These members had been raised in Greco-Roman cultures, where drunkenness and alcohol abuse were much more prevalent. Places like Corinth, the island of Crete, Ephesus, Thessaloniki, and Rome were deeply steeped in religious and cultural practices that not only allowed but also encouraged drunkenness — in both religious and social settings. It is thus not surprising that Paul's pastoral writings contain serious admonitions against such pagan practices. In his Epistle to the church in Corinth he asked the members not to associate with drunkards (1 Cor. 5:11; see also 1 Cor. 6:10; 11:21). For the church of Galatia he provided a long list of vices to avoid, among them drunkenness (Gal. 5:19-21). He admonished the church in Thessaloniki to stay sober and avoid drunkenness, living, instead, in faith and love and the building up of one another (1 Thess. 5:6-11).

Apparently, the older women on the island of Crete were given to heavy drinking, and Paul taught Titus how to deal with that specific problem. Rather than forbidding wine altogether, he encouraged Titus to teach them to embrace a life of temperance (Titus 2:3). Paul encouraged the Ephesians to live wise lives; for him, this meant learning to pray and worship rather than getting drunk with wine (Eph. 5:18-20). Paul admonished the church in Rome to live honorably, and this lifestyle included avoiding drunkenness and debauchery (Rom. 13:13). He even advised the believers in Rome to abstain from eating meat and drinking wine if it was causing other Christians to stumble. He wrote:

> Let us then pursue what makes for peace and for mutual upbuilding. Do not, for the sake of food, destroy the work of God. Everything is indeed clean, but it is wrong for you to make others fall by what you eat; it is good not to eat meat or drink wine or do anything that makes your brother or sister stumble. (Rom. 14:19-21)

Paul makes an important pastoral point here. Christians are called to be deeply concerned about the well-being of others. When they find themselves in settings where the eating of certain foods and the drinking of wine will be offensive or hinder the advance of the gospel, then they are to abstain in those settings for the sake of keeping the peace and building up others. Rather than insisting on the members' right to eat and drink what they wanted, Paul called Christians to a life of love and compassion. The care and concern for others has priority over the desires of one's stomach.

In light of such strong teaching against drunkenness and gluttony,[5] the church has a special responsibility in a world that increasingly struggles with addictive behaviors and disorders. Before turning to the question of how the church can respond to these challenges, we need to explore more carefully how contemporary psychology understands and addresses these problems.

Alcohol Abuse: Contemporary Perspectives

Alcohol abuse can take on many different forms. While the Bible warns against drunkenness, it does not deal with the problem of addiction as we know it today. The ready availability of hard liquor such as gin, vodka, rum, tequila, or whiskey allows a level of drunkenness and addiction in our culture that was unknown in the ancient world. Only since the Industrial Revolution has it been possible to produce distilled forms of alcohol on a large scale and distribute it cheaply to the general public.

As one considers the nature of alcohol use and abuse, one has to differentiate between normal use without any sign of intoxication, light intoxication (also called tipsiness), drunkenness, severe drunkenness, social drinking, drinking for relaxation, regular heavy drinking, binge drinking (popular among the younger generations, also called coma-drinking), and a clear addiction to alcoholic beverages. People who experience severe drunkenness or drink heavily on occasion are not necessarily addicted to alcohol, and those who drink socially or for relaxation must be careful not to develop addictive behaviors. A clear distinction between use, heavy use, and abuse is not easy. When does use turn into heavy use and heavy use into abuse? Medical research into the health benefits of wine shows quite clearly what levels of alcohol are beneficial and what levels become harmful to our bodies, and perhaps it should be our guide.

What we do know is that addictive behaviors and disorders of all kinds have increased rapidly in Western cultures. Alongside this trend, and related to it, is an astronomical increase in clinical depression and many other varied and complex — often vaguely defined — psychological states. These psychological states often include depressive components such as anxiety disorders and phobias.[6]

Alcohol abuse and addiction remains an area of great concern. The National Survey on Drug Use and Health of the USA (NSDUH) from 2013 reports that approximately 51.1 percent of Americans aged twelve and older drink alcohol (at least one drink during the past thirty days); 23 percent of Americans aged twelve and older have practiced binge drinking (five or more drinks on the same occasion); 6.5 percent of the population reported heavy drinking (five or more drinks on the same occasion on each of 5 or more days in the past 30 days).[7] The NSDUH study of 2010 reports that 3.5 percent of people aged twelve or older nationwide were estimated to be dependent on alcohol. The highest rate of binge drinking and alcohol addiction is found among young adults between eighteen and twenty-five.[8] The rate of alcohol dependence and alcohol abuse declined slightly between 2002 and 2012, from 7.7 percent to 6.8 percent.[9] The survey also revealed that there remains a significant treatment gap — that is, not enough treatment for those in need of it — for problems related to drugs or alcohol.[10]

Surprisingly, these studies do not specify what kind of alcohol is being consumed. How many of the 3.5 percent of people aged 12 years or older in the United States who are dependent on alcohol do actually get drunk on wine? Most addiction to alcohol comes in the form of hard liquor such as vodka, tequila, whiskey, schnapps, and cheap beer rather than wine. It would be beneficial if future studies included a discussion of the type of alcohol that is being consumed. We know that the drinking problems that emerged during the industrialization and urbanization of society in Ireland, Scotland, England, and the United States were due to the ready availability of cheap hard liquor.

It is also important to note other studies that have shown that alcohol use varies among Americans of different ethnic and socioeconomic backgrounds. For example, abstention in the United States is inversely associated with social status: the lower the social status, the higher the abstention.[11] The more educated people in the United States are, the more likely they are to drink.[12]

The Health and Social Care Information Centre in England reports similar statistics — except in those regarding alcohol dependence. It classifies drinking habits as hazardous (24.2 percent: 33.2 percent in men and 15.7 percent in women), harmful drinking (3.8 percent: 5.8 percent in men, 1.9 percent in women), and alcohol dependence (5.8 percent: 8.7 percent in men and 3.3 percent in women) as one manifestation of harmful drinking. It is noteworthy that the prevalence of alcohol dependence seems to be much higher in England.[13]

Alcohol dependence in the European Union is estimated at 5.4 percent in men and 1.5 percent in women. It is worth noting that alcohol dependence is lowest in Southern Europe (1.7 percent in men and 0.6 percent in women). These are primarily Mediterranean wine-producing and wine-drinking countries. They have the lowest overall consumption rates and the most favorable drinking patterns: wine is primarily drunk with meals. Nordic countries and the Central-East and Eastern European counties have notably higher rates of alcohol dependence. This stems in part from the high overall consumption rates and detrimental drinking patterns, including heavy binge-drinking.[14]

Understanding Alcohol-Use Disorders

Research into the nature, causes, and treatment of alcohol-abuse disorders has increased rapidly over recent decades, and many theories concerning the cause of alcohol abuse and addiction exist. These disorders are complex and chronic, and they include psychosocial, environmental, and genetic factors. The consequences of alcohol-abuse disorders are severe: they include injuries caused by vehicle accidents, physical health risks, psychological effects, and financial costs. While there are many different treatment approaches, so far no unifying theory has been developed, nor is there any empirical evidence to show that one treatment approach might be superior to others.[15]

Of the statistics cited above, alcohol abuse and alcohol dependence are the two patterns that are of particular concern. Alcohol abuse is officially defined as a recurrent pattern of alcohol overconsumption that results in significant impairment in at least one domain of a person's life — such as failure to meet commitments at work, relationship problems, legal problems, financial problems, or occasions when alcohol use leads to dangerous situations that place the drinker and others at risk, such as driving while intoxicated.[16] Alcohol dependence is defined as a markedly maladaptive pattern of alcohol use. Alcohol-dependent persons may not be able to control their drinking: they feel cravings to drink, and they continue to consume alcohol even after experiencing adverse consequences, such as relationship breakup, job loss, or poor health. Increasingly higher tolerance for alcohol and withdrawal symptoms are also defining features of alcohol dependence.[17]

Any discussion of the causes of alcohol abuse and addiction must include a wide range of considerations.[18] Studies have shown that males have a much higher risk of developing an alcohol-use disorder compared to females. One study explored how men and women respond to marital dissatisfaction. While men tend to drink, women tend to become depressed.[19] Race and ethnicity are also important. Alcohol abuse in the United States is highest among Native Americans and lowest among African Americans and Asians. The risk of alcohol abuse and dependence generally decreases with age. Environmental factors are also significant: social attitudes within a given society influence both the availability of alcohol and how it is consumed. The home and family life has a profound impact on the risk of alcohol-use disorders. Poor parental monitoring and a modeling of heavy alcohol use contribute to the likelihood of adolescent drinking and binge drinking.

Studies have also shown that lifetime alcohol abuse is significantly linked with traumatic childhood experiences such as the loss of a parent, parental divorce or separation, parental psychopathology, parental aggression, and sexual molestation. Other studies have shown that childhood sexual abuse, physical abuse, emotional abuse, and physical neglect increase the risk of adult alcohol dependence.

Genetic factors also play a significant role in developing alcohol-use disorders. Scientists suggest that the heritability of alcohol dependence is about 50 to 60 percent. But knowledge of specific genetic causes of alcohol dependence is still limited, and research is currently underway to better understand the genetic contribution to alcohol-use disorders and how to treat them.

An important concern with regard to alcohol-use disorders is that substance-dependent individuals often display either a lack of awareness or a denial of their addiction. Recent neuroscientific studies have linked these symptoms to cognitive and emotional disorders. These insights will have important implications for the rehabilitation of individuals who abuse alcohol and/or drugs, and perhaps the insights will also help others understand and feel more compassion toward those who struggle with addiction.[20]

Sociocultural Perspectives

Scientific research into the nature, causes, and treatment of alcohol-abuse disorders is invaluable as our societies seek to confront such disorders. And yet it is important to ask more fundamental questions concerning the rapid increase of substance-focused and behavioral addictions in our Western societies. What are the undercurrent values that shape our societies and communities? Are there beliefs, values, and patterns of conduct in Western societies that nourish addictive behavior and disorders? Sociological research and philosophical reflection on the larger social context of substance use suggest that many Western societies have become more substance-dependent. Positive beliefs about drug use and its effects have helped to turn us into a drug-oriented society. Patricia Jones-Witters and Weldon J. Witters write about the United States:

> We are a drug-oriented culture. We use a host of different drugs for a variety of purposes: to restore health, to reduce pain, to induce calmness, to increase energy, to create a feeling of euphoria, to induce sleep and to enhance alertness. A multitude of substances are available to swallow, drink, or inhale in order to alter mood or state of consciousness.[21]

Some suggest that the increased acceptance of drug use is positively linked to a decline in religious belief and practices. Research has shown that persons actively engaged in religious practices are less likely to get involved in drug use. Jewish communities, for example, introduce children to alcohol through their rituals. Their first religious education includes teaching them the proper benedictions for food and drink, and wine is understood as something sacred. Children learn to understand drinking as an act of communion, and drunkenness as a profanity, a perversion of the sacred use of wine. In the family home, children are taught by example how to drink, and simultaneously how not to drink. The more the consumption of alcohol is tied to the socialization process within a given culture, the less likely it is that members of that society will abuse alcohol.[22]

When a given culture develops an ambivalent attitude toward alcohol, or when alcohol is completely forbidden, as it was during Prohibition in America, then a culture loses the ability to model and foster a constructive use of alcohol.[23] According to David J. Hanson, Prohibition "encouraged the rapid consumption of high-proof drinks in secretive, non-socially regulated and controlled ways."[24] By removing alcohol from the socialization process, Prohibition created a void in which alcohol abuse was able to flourish, profoundly affecting generations to come.

During Prohibition, Ernest Hemingway was based in Paris, and he made some striking observations about the different social attitude of the French toward alcohol as compared to the American attitude:

> In Europe then we thought of wine as something as healthy and normal as food and also as a great giver of happiness and well-being and delight. Drinking wine was not a snobbism nor a sign of sophistication nor a cult; it was

as natural as eating and to me as necessary, and I would not have thought of eating a meal without drinking either wine or cider or beer.[25]

In France, just as in Italy and Germany, the enjoyment of wine to this day is deeply integrated into society and shaped by cultural norms. As the influence of Christian faith on society is waning in Europe, however, the attitudes toward alcohol have become more ambivalent, and alcohol abuse is on the rise. Binge- and coma-drinking, especially among adolescents, have become considerable problems in Europe. As societies consider how to face the problem of alcohol abuse, we must heed the studies of sociologists. We must consider the under- lying beliefs, values, and practices of our Western societies, since they have a profound effect on how alcohol is being consumed.

What roles do governments and pharmaceutical industries and their mar- keting strategies play in stimulating use of some substances? Questions are be- ing asked whether or not physicians prescribe drugs too easily, too frequently, and in dosages that are too high. What are the social messages about what is appropriate behavior? What special needs and motivations are associated with substance use?[26] Research into substance use by adolescents in the United States shows that there are at least two groups using drugs. One group shows no serious social or psychological disturbance: they seek sensation and social fit and respond to peer pressure. The other group shows some social and emo- tional disturbance, and they are more likely to become addicted to drugs.[27]

One of the recurring themes in sociological studies is the use of alcohol as anesthesia.[28] When faced with stress situations in life, people turn to addictive behavior and disorders to cope. Then they begin to justify their behavior to themselves, ending up in a cycle of denial and/or lack of awareness. Why is it so common today for people to turn to substances to anesthetize themselves? Has our society lost the knowledge and ability to cope with stress, anxiety, loss, pain, and suffering without resorting to addictive behaviors and disorders? Does our society even foster such coping patterns? What are the social causes of addiction?

Bruce Alexander, a Canadian psychologist, has explored the structure of our Western societies to see how these social structures might foster addic- tive behavior and disorders. He suggests that the globalization of free-market cultures fosters a high degree of dislocation. Alexander understands disloca- tion as a lack of psychosocial integration: for him, psychosocial integration includes an inward experience of identity and a meaningful set of outward social relationships in which individuals develop a healthy sense of belonging within a given community. Dislocation does not necessarily imply geographic separation but denotes psychological and social separation from one's culture and leads to a sense of alienation, fragmentation, and disconnection.[29]

Alexander argues that a free-market society is based on intense and unrelenting individual competition and tends to view humans primarily as individual economic actors. He suggests that the more Western civilizations embrace free-market ideals, the more dislocation will occur. When socially and psychologically integrated societies are fragmented, it provokes a desperate response from individuals, and addictive behavior and disorders increase dramatically. Free-market societies, with their emphasis on consumerism, help people adapt to their dislocation by developing addictions to the consumer products offered to them.[30]

Alcohol Abuse: Engaging the Church with Contemporary Perspectives

How should the church engage with and respond to the problem of addictive behaviors and disorders and the possible underlying social patterns that nourish them? Many lay ministries, such as Alcoholics Anonymous (AA), have emerged outside, alongside, and within the church to address the staggering challenges of addictive behaviors and disorders that have so profoundly penetrated our societies.[31] Programs modeled on AA have spread throughout the United States, where it began, and around the globe. AA has extended its ministry to a wide range of other addictive behaviors and disorders through programs such as Gamblers Anonymous and Workaholics Anonymous. Many members have found solace and healing in these strongly communal ministries, and their contribution should not be underestimated. Though scientists cannot measure AA programs scientifically, since they are faith-based and their participants remain anonymous, most of them recognize that AA is an effective treatment for alcohol abuse.[32] The church must continue to support and encourage these ministries as important ways to bring healing to those shackled with addictive behaviors and disorders.

As we consider the challenges that addictive behavior and disorders bring, not just to individuals but also to their families and communities, we should ask whether the church can do more. While ministries like AA have brought much healing and recovery to individuals, these programs do not seem to address and challenge the underlying values and patterns of our Western societies that foster addictive behaviors and disorders. We could well insist that the church do more than help individuals manage their addictive behaviors and disorders. While the church has always had a calling to bring healing to the sick, and must continue to do so, its calling is much greater. It must always remember its identity as the body of Christ and become the good leaven that seeks to transform its surroundings, and this includes the way we consume.

William Cavanaugh explores the underlying structure of free-market cultures and how they shape our lives — and especially our habits of consumerism — from a theological perspective. He suggests concrete alternative practices that can reshape our lives and help us consume in ways that become redemptive rather than destructive. Cavanaugh shows that a free-market society understands individuals as autonomous consumers who should be free to pursue and consume what they want as long as they do not harm others. A free market has no unifying or common end to which the desires of individuals are directed. Cavanaugh writes: "To claim that desires can be ordered either rightly or wrongly to objectively desirable ends has no place in a free market."[33] It is a profoundly consumption-oriented vision of human life with no particular end or purpose. It can include the transcendent and faith in God, but only insofar as the autonomous individual freely embraces it as part of his or her desires.[34] Cavanaugh shows that this orientation stands in direct opposition to the Christian belief that our lives are directed toward God — and find their ultimate meaning only in him. To be truly human in the Christian sense means to be in life-giving relationship with God and one another; it is a profoundly relational understanding of life.

Addictive-Behavior Disorders and the Theological Language of Sin

In this section we shall explore addictive behaviors and disorders from a theological perspective. In particular, we shall investigate the theological language of sin and how it might help the church think about addictive behavior and disorders. Sin is first of all a theological category that includes, of course, moral and psychological dimensions but must not be reduced to them. The Bible presents the reality of sin to us mostly in storied and concrete forms, while dogmatic formulations tend to define sin in highly abstract and generalized form.[35] In order to be in a constructive dialogue with the intricate concerns and challenges of addictive behavior and disorders, we must offer an understanding of sin that can address these concerns and challenges.

Sin is a complex, multidimensional, and often very subtle reality that calls for a nuanced theological understanding that includes the moral, social, psychological, and physical dimensions of human life. One important question with regard to a theology of sin is how free human beings really are. Free markets fundamentally understand humans as free to choose, pursue, and consume what they desire. Christian theology, on the other hand, does not understand humans to be fundamentally free. Different faith communities have taken different views on this question of human freedom, but all of them agree that human freedom has been compromised.

The theological language of sin identifies human beings as alienated and estranged from God and from one another and in need of redemption. Thus sin is first of all a relational reality, a breakdown of relationships and an active resistance to the presence and work of God in our lives. The theological concept of sin then seeks to capture the pathological dynamics that break down and destroy our relationship with God and consequently with one another and the rest of creation.

Sin is a profoundly hopeful theological category because it identifies and names the pathological in the face of a loving and merciful God, who wants to redeem his creation. The corollary of the bleak reality of sin is the bright radiance of God's superabundant love and forgiveness. In a society where competition, perfectionism, and displacement drive people to the brink of exhaustion, isolation, and despair, Christians are called to humbly confess their sin to God and receive mercy, grace, and healing.

Too often we picture the autonomous individual at the center of what it means to be human, and it is tempting to reduce sin to the guilt that comes from the "free" acts of individuals. Individual sin, however, only touches on some aspects of the complex reality of sin. It is common in some Christian circles, for example, to reduce addictive behaviors and disorders to the moral failing of individuals. The sad reality that genetic and social factors can play a significant role in developing alcohol dependence shows that human beings are not autonomous and free individuals but deeply intertwined with their family of origin and their social environment.[36] Such a perspective does not diminish the reality of individual sin and its moral dimensions; but it does recognize that sin is much more complex, multidimensional, and subtle in real life, and that it calls for a more nuanced theological understanding.

Christian theology does not understand the human as an autonomous individual. Rather, it understands humans as profoundly relational — in relationship with God, with one another, with the rest of creation, and even with the history of humanity. Therefore, sin as a theological category cannot be reduced to acts of individuals since these acts only scratch the surface of the complex reality of sin. Sin as a theological category encompasses much broader social, communal, and historical dimensions. Sin transcends the acts of individuals and can become a complex force or dynamic at work in institutions, communities, and whole structures and systems of societies.[37] The very structures of our societies, institutions, and communities can be profoundly pathological and work toward alienating us from God, from each other, and from creation.

As we think about how the theological language of sin can help us understand addictive behaviors and disorders, we have to turn to the more fundamental question of consumption; we need to consider the underlying structures and dynamics at work in our society and how they form our habits of consumption. Free-market economics is based on intense competition. What does this competition do to individuals and societies at large? Living in a culture of constant competition instills in individuals the impression that they are always working against others. It fosters a sense of isolation and estrangement from others, and leads to great loneliness. When competition contributes to the erosion of relational life and the breakdown of relationships, then we must consider competitiveness as a form of sin among individuals and in society at large.

Overemphasizing the economic output of individuals subtly suggests that our identity as human beings is primarily anchored in our economic achievements and our value as economic actors. It reduces human beings to utilitarian and functional roles rather than spiritual and relational ones. It undermines our identity as spiritual beings with profound spiritual, relational, and emotional needs that transcend the material. All this, according to Bruce Alexander, leads to the fragmentation of our societies and provokes desperate responses from individuals. To put it in theological language, those individuals fall into sin.

The truly tragic aspect of free-market societies is that they help individuals adapt to their sense of dislocation by developing addictions to the consumer products that they themselves offer. This addiction, in turn, causes individuals to look for solutions not outside of themselves but by focusing on themselves and the desires that the marketing world has implanted in them. A vicious circle begins, and once addictions are developed, it is extremely difficult to free oneself, especially when one is not willing to seek outside help. This is yet another form of sin that is present in the very structures of our societies; but it becomes individual sin once consumers find themselves entangled in various addictions.

There is another dimension to this dynamic that is worth calling attention to. What is so disturbing about this vicious circle is that it operates in hidden and subversive ways that are difficult for the consumer to identify. The prevailing business model, especially of large corporations, is to communicate their marketing to the wider public as the transfer of information about their products and our need for these products. It gives the consumer the false impression that he is autonomous and rational, that he can make free choices that are both informed and voluntary, that he is free to choose the products that he desires. On the other hand, marketing strategists are utterly aware of their power to create and manipulate consumer desires and guide them to their proper economic destination, the consumption of their products.

Cavanaugh argues that one reason marketing strategists are so successful in manipulating desire is their success in convincing the broader public that they are *not* manipulating their desires. They freely use the latest psychological and neuroscientific research to create consumer desires by targeting their subconscious impulses. Most contemporary marketing, says Cavanaugh, is not based on providing information. Rather, it is built on associating products with evocative images and deeply personal and vulnerable goods, like self-esteem, love, sex, or success, that have little or nothing to do with the product itself.[38]

Neuromarketing, in particular, specializes in appealing to persons in ways that will then affect the pleasure center of the human brain. They seek to tap into the subconscious minds of consumers.[39] Feeling pleasure motivates humans to repeat behaviors. Neuromarketing seeks to identify the right triggers that associate their products with the feelings of pleasure in their target consumer audience. In this way they are able to establish a profound emotional bond between the consumer and the products that they offer.

What becomes clear from exploring and understanding the sinful, pathological patterns at work in the broader society is that the internal dynamics that shape a person's actions, such as addictive behavior and disorders, are deeply influenced by and cooperate with sinful pathological dynamics at work in interpersonal relationships and in the wider society.[40] Though we do have freedom and are not wholly determined, the idea that we are completely and unconditionally free is an illusion. This is important to remember as we seek to understand addictive behaviors and disorders from a theological perspective. When Jesus warned his disciples, "Watch out, and beware of the yeast of the Pharisees and Sadducees" (Matt. 16:5), he did not address the sin of individuals but the sinful pathologies at work in a subgroup of religious teachers. The metaphor of yeast suggests that this group works like a complex microorganism with sinful patterns that are powerfully at work but hard to identify because these sinful pathologies are invisible and hidden under the veneer of religiosity.

The theological language of sin seeks to identify and name these complex and multifaceted pathologies and calls individual believers and the church as a whole to take responsibility in and for them before God. By doing so we open up our lives to God's love and forgiveness, trusting that he is present by his Spirit to heal and restore our relationship with him, with each other, and with the rest of creation. God's intention for humanity is the vital flourishing of our lives. Addictive behaviors and disorders take us in the opposite direction: they imprison us and separate us from God and one another. Furthermore, addictive behaviors and disorders also completely warp our relationship with creation.

Concluding Reflections

God's gift of wine was particularly given to bring joy, and the moderate enjoyment of wine can indeed bring great joy, enliven and deepen conversations, relieve stress, bring comfort to the aging, and be beneficial to our health. *Babette's Feast* portrays, in the most moving way, how feasting, including the enjoyment of wine, can stimulate emotional and spiritual renewal. When we use wine or food or any other substance as an anesthetic to cope with the stress, suffering, pain, and perhaps boredom of our lives, we not only abuse God's gifts but also close ourselves off from the possibility of receiving comfort and healing that comes from being in a relationship with God and one another. It is for this reason that we need to rescue wine *from* the gluttons *for* the contemplatives, because wine was meant to draw us nearer to God and each other rather than alienate us even further from his loving and healing presence. In the words of the German proverb, "To drink is to pray, to binge-drink is to sin."

10

Wine, Viticulture, and Soul Care

"I am the true vine, and my Father is the vine-grower. He removes every branch in me that bears no fruit. Every branch that bears fruit he prunes to make it bear more fruit. . . . Abide in me as I abide in you. Just as the branch cannot bear fruit by itself unless it abides in the vine, neither can you unless you abide in me. I am the vine, you are the branches. Those who abide in me and I in them bear much fruit, because apart from me you can do nothing. . . . As the Father has loved me, so I have loved you; abide in my love."

John 15:1-2, 4-5, 9

"A vine is like a human life and the vintner like a mother who tends to her children."

Wisdom from the world of vintners

In the preceding chapter we explored alcohol abuse and the increasing problem of addictive disorders and behaviors in our society. Their widespread occurrence suggests that more profound challenges face the church than the isolated problems of individuals alone. There are fundamental pathological structures in our society that evoke addictive behaviors and other disorders, and the church needs to address these underlying structures. While most alcohol abuse and addiction are related to hard liquor and cheap beer, we cannot

199

deny the sad reality that people do get addicted to wine as well. And yet a biblical understanding of creation does not allow the church to reject the gifts God has given. Though most recovering alcoholics will have to abstain from alcohol, the church is called to live in the tensions, temptations, and failures of life — and to embrace God's forgiveness and healing in the midst of it. The Latin proverb *abusus non tollit usum* ("the potential for abuse never takes away the legitimacy of proper use") will be upheld.

Meanwhile, the church must find ways to embrace those souls who are like untended gardens and bring them to the only true gardener. It is in God that we can find life in abundance, but not without some pruning of our addictions (John 15:1-3). The figurative language of agriculture in Scripture — particularly viticulture — offers a rich and organic vision of the Christian life. It can baptize anew our Christian imagination as we seek to understand what it means to be the church in the context of contemporary society. Insights from vintners and from their work in the vineyard further enrich our understanding of these potent metaphors. The parallels between life in the vineyard and life in the church are striking.

Viticulture and Soul Care

Comparing God to a gardener and a vintner and the church to a vineyard or the branches of a vine conjures up a whole range of associations that cannot be applied merely to the individual. These associations place believers in interdependent relationships with each other, and they envision human life in a profound relationship with and utter dependence on God.

This vision of the Christian life is in stark contrast to the values of many aspects of Western contemporary society. The media tell us that we are autonomous consumers who should be free to pursue and consume what we want. Contemporary society allows consumers to be "spiritual" in the sense that they are free to pick and choose the spirituality that appeals most to them and fits their individual preferences. The corollary of this consumption-oriented approach to life is that it tends to view people primarily as individual economic actors who have to learn to prepare for and survive in this world of intense and unrelenting competition. It tends to reduce human life to functioning in an economic web that undermines some of the most basic human values — such as love, trust, and mercy.

The figurative language of viticulture in the Bible challenges us to re-envision and contemplate a life that is rooted in God's economy, an economy not based on competition and maximum profit but on love, forgiveness, and mercy. It envisions God as a vintner who wants his vines and vineyard to flourish and to produce abundant fruit. When the psalmist prays, "Restore us, O God of hosts; let your face shine, that we may be saved. You brought a vine out of Egypt . . . and planted it. You cleared the ground for it; it took deep root and filled the land," he expresses his faith that God can still act and restore even when the vineyard seems barren and is laid waste (Ps. 80:7-9). When Isaiah complains that God's vineyard has been devoured, he uses this metaphor to bring to light how the neglect of the poor affects the whole vine-yard (Isa. 3:14-15). When the poor, vulnerable, and marginalized are forgotten — or worse, oppressed — this treatment will affect the health of the whole vineyard. God's vineyard will only flourish when the stronger and more pow-erful will reach out to the weaker and more vulnerable, and when they learn together what it means to flourish in God's vineyard. A biblical understanding of human flourishing is very different from a contemporary emphasis on max-imizing productivity and profit. Living souls cannot be reduced to economic actors, nor can they flourish spiritually as isolated individuals.

Identity

One of the great gifts of the Christian faith is that it gives the believer a strong sense of identity. As we learn to re-envision what it means that our identity is in Christ, it is tempting to remain in the abstract. Scripture, how-ever, is replete with tangible ways of envisioning what it means to belong to Christ. The Gospel of John introduces Christ as the one who was with God in the beginning creating the world (John 1:1-4). It takes us right back to the beginning of Genesis. The creation account envisions the created world as a deeply interconnected community. Scripture portrays God's creative and redemptive purposes not just between God and his people but also including the land and all living creatures. Our identity as human beings is deeply tied to the land. God the potter formed Adam from the dust of the earth (Hebrew: *'ādām 'ădāmâ*), breathed into his nostrils the breath of life, and Adam became a living soul (Gen. 2:5, 7, 15). We must remember that this Hebrew wordplay emphasizes Adam's — and thus our — close kinship with the earth. As God's creatures, we are taken from the earth, belong to the earth, are utterly dependent on the earth's fruitfulness, and are called to work and care for the earth. We are earthlings.[1] The creation account envisions the fruit of the earth as a gift from God not only to humanity but also to every living creature. We are to share it with the animals of the earth. God's promise to Noah to sustain seedtime and harvest reminds us that it is God who upholds the earth's fruitfulness; it is a gift and promise of God (Gen. 1:29-30; 8:22). Keeping in mind this fundamental interconnectedness and human dependence on the earth and its fruitfulness, the figurative use of viticulture both deepens our understanding of our dependence on the earth and takes us beyond it.

When Christ says, "I am the vine, you are the branches," he grounds our being in a spiritual dimension that will always transcend the physical reality we experience in a world dominated by marketing, a world in which we consume the goods offered and secure our place as economic actors. Christ's words teach us that we are profoundly spiritual beings who draw life and nourishment from spiritual realities. This truth does not mean that we remove ourselves from the material world and escape into an otherworldly spiritual reality. Rather, it teaches us to recognize that the material world and what it has to offer can never be sufficient to address us as spiritual beings and offer us the spiritual food that can nourish and sustain us.

In Christ we are drawn into the life of God that gives us our identity as human beings. Christ invites us to see one another not as isolated and autonomous consumers but as branches held together and nourished by Christ, the vine, and tended by a caring vintner, God the Father (John 15). The metaphor of the vine and the vineyard suggests that the spiritual life is organic and not easily compartmentalized. It also suggests that our life source is not the product of human hands. Rather, it comes from our vintner (father) who sustains his vineyard by watering, pruning, and protecting it day and night (Isa. 27:2-3). God's intention for his vineyard is for it to blossom, flourish, and be fruitful (Hosea 14:7; Isa. 27:5). God does not seek to enslave his people to achieve maximum profit; rather, he offers the conditions for the vital flourishing of his people that will lead to a life of fruitfulness.

Wisdom from the Craftsman Vintners

It is striking that many of the vintner craftspeople I interviewed understand their relationship with their vines in parental terms. They see themselves as motherly and fatherly guardians of their vines, and they view the vines as children in need of care, nourishment, and pruning. Perhaps their lifelong experience of tending to the vines and the vineyard will shed more light on these potent metaphors for the life of the church and what it means to root our identity in Christ the vine and God the vintner/father.

Michael LaFarge is a Catholic vintner from Burgundy and comes from a long family tradition of vintners. He decided to move away from the modern agricultural techniques he learned in his university training, especially those that rely heavily on interference with the natural organisms by using chemicals and fertilizers to manipulate the soil for more intense growth. LaFarge explained that the chemicals destroy the microorganisms that exist in a vineyard, and the wine-maker exerts a position of control over the vineyard when he uses them. The posture the wine-maker takes is always "against" something: against nature, against illnesses, against problems. It is a relationship of power and opposition toward the vineyard.[2] LaFarge believes that we live in a world based on fear, and that informs our training and education.

Michael LaFarge, instead, wants to work with creation. Nature is alive, and he wants to learn to understand the living organisms in his care and what it means to work with them. He believes that the Cistercians who first planted vineyards in Burgundy had a sense for *terroir*. They had a profound sense of belonging to and being connected with the land where they lived. The Cistercians had the ability to feel the great *terroirs*. They knew where to tear out the great forests and where to leave them standing. Their knowledge of and familiarity with a wide variety of plants and how they interact with one another was profound. They knew how other plants could strengthen the vines and influence the vineyard in positive ways.

LaFarge wants to see himself as *part* of creation rather than standing *against* it. By relearning to work this way, he feels that he not only brings his own contribution to this living organism but also joins in the work of previous generations. He is relearning what it means to be in continuity with them and to add to their work. He feels, through his work, a profound relationship with his ancestors — his father, grandfather, and great-grandfather. His ancestors selected many of the vines that Michael tends today; they are not clones that he has brought in from the outside, which is a rare exception in the wine world today. The connection he has with the past happens on many levels, two of which are the soil and the vines he cultivates. There are many elements to the living organism of the vineyard that we just do not think about and often ignore. Viticulture is ancient, but the modern world has forgotten about it.

LaFarge believes that the work and prayers of the Cistercians still affect his life and work today. The world of the Spirit is not the same as the temporal dimension of the physical world; the work in the vineyard makes LaFarge keenly aware of that. But for LaFarge, the well-being of the vine and the vineyard is directly linked to the loving posture he has toward the vines. It is important to him to go to the vines often, to feel the vines, to stay connected with them, and to learn what they need. In a world that is based on fear rather than love, LaFarge works hard at being loving toward his vines and not acting out of a sense of fear. He believes that his posture of love helps the vines flourish and produce a wine that is vibrant. LaFarge is not the only vintner who approaches his vines this way. The vintner-craftspeople whom I interviewed have developed a posture of love as they continually learn how to better care for their vines.

Sylvain Pataille, a Burgundian oenologist turned vintner — with deep roots in the Catholic faith — regularly goes to see his vines alone, and he listens to them. When I asked him whether his vines speak to him, he said, "No, it is much more concrete." They do not speak to him but, like small children and pets, who cannot speak, they have other ways of communicating to him what they need. By taking the time to listen to them, Pataille learns what they need and hence understands better what work he has to do in the vineyard. Living with the plants and the earth, he feels a deep connection to them. Rather than using some kind of agricultural technique or science, he is part of a profoundly interconnected and dynamic reality to which he is still learning to become more sensitive.

A wine-maker who is only interested in the vineyard as an economic investment — with the expectation of maximum profit — will not understand LaFarge or Pataille, nor will he appreciate their spiritual and emotional commitments. LaFarge and Pataille have to make a living, as any other vintner does; but their vocation cannot be reduced to economics. They love their vineyards and their vocation as vintners, and they care for their vines like fathers and mothers care for their children. LaFarge wants to craft a wine that is vibrant and unique, a wine that gives a strong sense of perception and expresses the living energy of the vineyard and can bring joy to those who drink it. Pataille remembers that in France wine used to be something sacred: the monks understood the value of their work and of creating something beautiful, and they wanted to honor God by being artistic.

When we hear vintners like LaFarge and Pataille speak about their beloved vines and vineyards, it is not difficult to see the connections to the life of the church and to what it means to be in God's vineyard, a branch of the vine Jesus Christ. The church is a living organism and its vitality, its life source, comes from God himself. God's love, grace, and mercy sustain the life that grows in this organism. The role of the pastor should never be one of power and control, one that uses fear to control and "protect" the vineyard from possible diseases. Rather, the pastor is called to come alongside and be part of this living vineyard, attentively tending to each vine or branch with love and care.

LaFarge reminds us that each vineyard's history, as well as the work of its former vintners or wine-makers, affects the life of the vineyard. The same is true for each church. A pastor and his or her congregation must learn to understand the vineyard's history, test the health of the soil, and become attuned to the unique microclimate in which a congregation lives. A pastor must be cautious about grasping for the newest fertilizers on the market that promise maximum growth quickly. To ensure long-term health and growth, a pastor must be willing to get to know the vineyard well, listen to each vine and branch, and discern what the vines and vineyard needs. The pastor must regularly walk into his vineyard, learn to be present to his vines, and respond with love and care.

Koinonia

When Christ speaks of himself as the vine and his disciples as the branches, he speaks of God's closeness. God the Father no longer just leaves others in charge of the vineyard; he promises to be near and present in Jesus Christ and by his Holy Spirit. This presence is a great promise and an unfathomable gift, but it does not automatically guarantee the fruitfulness of God's vineyard. In order for the branches to bear fruit, they must learn what it means to remain in Christ the vine. They do so by loving one another. The Christian call to *koinonia* (Greek: "fellowship, joint participation, communion") in Christ lays the foundation for a decidedly Christian understanding of and commitment to life in community.

It is difficult today to speak about the church as a community because in many places community in the traditional sense of the word does not exist anymore. More often than not today, the term "community" is used to speak of modern attempts to bring people together in our deeply fragmented societies. The very fabric of our modern lives keeps us isolated and makes building *koinonia* difficult. Life itself is so compartmentalized into family life, work, school, leisure, shopping, eating out, travel, and church attendance that these different aspects of our lives do not often intersect anymore. The film *Avalon* movingly depicts the disintegration of traditional family structures as the family members make way for progress and individual autonomy. Many people do not know their neighbors anymore, nor do they know where their food comes from, how it has been produced, or whether the farmers receive an appropriate amount of compensation for their labor and produce.[3]

All these developments have affected the life of the church. How can we recover this sense of mutual love and care when we live such fragmented lives? It is a great challenge and vocation for the church to embrace anew this call to *koinonia* — that is, to grow out of our lives rooted in Christ's presence. Can the insights of the vintner once more help us re-envision this organic and deeply interdependent understanding of the Christian life? Perhaps these reflections might not offer concrete ideas for how churches can cultivate *koinonia* in the very particular situations in which they find themselves. And yet a renewed vision of our calling to a life of *koinonia* might inspire churches to become creative and seek out ways to foster *koinonia* despite all the odds of our deeply fragmented societies.

Wisdom from the Craftsman Vintners

Jeremy Seysse from Domaine Dujac in Burgundy seeks to craft wines with a "soul," wines that are unique, dynamic, and complex.[4] I asked him why he thinks complexity is so important. With the increasing industrialization of wine production around the world, he says, come standardization and homogeneity. Why are so many people drawn to standardization? Seysse thinks that people look for standardization because there is something deeply reassuring about it. He believes it is a choice of security. But his vocation as a vintner is to craft the best wine possible, perhaps even a great wine, and greatness is not based on security. When customers sample his wines and find great delight in them, they are unaware of how challenging it is to craft such a wine. At times wine-lovers romanticize Jeremy's work, having little grasp of what it means to work with nature and seek to bring forth the best in it. It is difficult and grinding work.

When we think about the life of the church, we can see similar dynamics. The church can easily become a place where individuals gather to find comfort and security in homogeneous groups. These groups can be based on stages in life: singles, young professionals, young families, divorcees, or retirees. People look for churches whose members might share similar educational backgrounds, professional occupations, or ethnic origins. When the unity of the church is reduced to homogeneity of opinions and habits, stages in life, economic status, or educational background, then the vital flourishing of life in the Christian sense is more difficult.

In Christ, the church is called to transcend economic, cultural, and ethnic differences and barriers and grow into a oneness that is based on God's abundant love and forgiveness (John 17:20-25; Gal. 3:27-29). *Koinonia* grows out of the joys, tensions, and pains of a diverse and complex community. In the church, persons of different backgrounds with unique gifts and vocations are called to live and share for mutual enrichment and delight. We must learn, like the vintner-craftsman, to see diversity as a gift rather than a threat.[5] It enriches our understanding of God as our Creator and challenges us to trust that God's love and grace work to redeem us precisely in those differences and the challenges that they bring. In that sense the church is not a "safe" place to which we can retreat for the affirmation and comfort of "sameness." Rather, our call to *koinonia* challenges us to embrace the vulnerability that comes from allowing and nurturing diversity. It calls us to love those who are different from us. Surely, the wine that comes forth from such a vineyard is richer, more complex, and inspiring to a world that suffers from increasing homogenization, on the one hand, and fragmentation, alienation, and isolation, on the other.

Oregonian Jason Lett is another vintner who reflects on the importance of complexity and richness in a wine and on how this development happens.

There are many different components to crafting such a wine. One important factor is the life of the soil and the vine's ability to draw nutrients from it. Jason explains that grapevines are wonderful sugar factories but are very bad at drawing minerals from the soil. Fungi living in the soil, on the other hand, are bad at producing sugars, but they are good at breaking down stones in the ground. In order for the grapevines to draw minerals from the soil, the vine's roots have to form symbiotic associations with the fungi that live in the soil around them. In fertile soil a wide range of fungi grow, colonize around the vine's roots, and form just such nurturing symbiotic associations with them. The diverse microorganisms that form associations with plants are collectively called "mycorrhizae." Jason explains that mycorrhizae need a very complex environment so that not just one or two but hundreds and thousands of different kinds of mycorrhizae can flourish. The vintner can nourish these complex associations between soil and fungi by allowing other plants, such as grasses and flowers to grow in the vineyard. This biodiversity encourages a deeper community of organisms in the life of the soil. The force of life in the soil increases, and this allows the vine to draw more nutrients from the soil.

It is quite remarkable that Scripture often compares the spiritual life to the life of plants and their need to become rooted in fertile soil in order to flourish. The psalmist writes: "You brought a vine out of Egypt. . . . You cleared the ground for it; it took deep root and filled the land" (Ps. 80:8-9). The parable of the sower in the Gospels makes a similar comparison but warns us against unfruitfulness and encourages us to become attentive to the soil matrix of our lives: "A sower went out to sow. . . . [S]eeds fell on rocky ground, where they did not have much soil, and they sprang up quickly, since they had no depth of soil. But when the sun rose, they were scorched; and since they had no root, they withered away" (Matt. 13:3-9). The health of the soil and the depth of roots in the soil are indispensable elements for the survival and flourishing of plants. But life in the soil is a struggle. The living microorganisms that make up the life of the soil undergo a regular cycle of growth, death, and decay in order for new growth to happen. When Scripture invites us to imagine our lives as plants rooted in rich soil, it invites us to understand our lives in this cycle of growth, death, decay, and renewed life. Jesus explains his own suffering and death in light of this cycle of death and decay that leads to new life and multiplied growth (John 12:24-26).

This vision of the spiritual life is deeply unsettling and disturbing to our

Western societies, where we work so hard to avoid suffering and pain. The farmer and vintner, of course, understand and trust in this cycle of death, decay, and renewed life. But the suggestion that this same cycle works supernaturally to transform our lives into a life of fruitfulness seems paradoxical. The temptation to anesthetize when faced with stress, suffering, loss, anguish, and pain is great, and the range of available anesthetics seems endless. And yet "curing" oneself with alcohol, overeating, shopping, taking drugs, or escaping into a virtual world, for example, is neither life-giving nor does it lead to a fruitful life. It fossilizes our inner lives and leaves us resistant to the love and grace of God that seek to transform our lives into fruitfulness.

In the parable of the sower, the plant superficially rooted in rocky and stony soil stands for the person who, in the face of affliction, anguish, and persecution, is unable to grow in faith (Matt. 13:20-21). But in Christ's suffering, death, and resurrection our own suffering and sorrow find new meaning. Rather than seeing them as destroyers of life that take away our joy, we are called to trust that God can transform our suffering and sorrow and bring forth new life and fruitfulness. The parable of the sower warns us that our natural tendency is to give up on the life of faith as we experience suffering. When Christ speaks of himself as the vine and his disciples as the branches, he reminds us that this life of faith is a gift from God. We can learn to endure suffering with patience and hope as we remain in Christ, and learn to love one another and share the suffering we face. This endurance, too, is an important aspect of *koinonia*. Christ is to the life of the church what the living fungi are to the soil, breaking down the rocks and stones of suffering and sorrow in our lives and transforming them into minerals that can nourish us. As we allow Christ to surround and colonize our root systems, and as we learn to form organic coalitions with him in all seasons and situations in life, we can learn to draw nourishment and strength in and sometimes despite all life circumstances. Scripture repeatedly calls us, rather than turn inside and anesthetize ourselves with things that will only suffocate the spiritual life, to turn to God in prayer. Hannah, the barren and deeply troubled woman in 1 Samuel, becomes a model of the life of faith. In her suffering and sorrow she turns to God in prayer, and by doing so she opens up her life to God (1 Sam. 1:15-16). Just as a vintner is deeply involved in taking care of his vines, so are we called to open our lives to God the Father/vintner in order to allow him to care for us and make us into a fruitful vineyard.

The Vintner Prunes His Vines

Vines are sturdy plants. They can grow and thrive in the most adverse circumstances and produce fruit where no other fruit-bearing plant can grow. They grow on the steepest hills, and their roots slowly work themselves through rocky soil and draw nutrients from it, where other fruit-bearing plants would only wither. Left to themselves, however, they grow like weeds and are not particularly concerned to produce fruit. An important role of the vintner is to cultivate the vines in the direction of healthy growth and fruitfulness. Part of cultivating the vines is to prune their branches and tie them onto wires, along which they then can grow. The vintner does this to expose the leaves and the growing clusters of fruit to the right amount of sunlight to ensure that the fruit ripens properly. This process is complex, and crucial for growing grapes. The vintner is highly involved in discerning what the vine needs. Depending on the weather conditions of a given growing season, she will adjust the branches and the growth of leaves so that the fruit can ripen steadily — neither too fast nor too slow.

When Christ compares God the Father to a vintner who prunes every branch toward fruitfulness, he speaks of God as a loving Father who is concerned about his vineyard and its calling to be fruitful. This comparison also implies that God is intimately involved in enabling each branch to become more fruitful (John 15:2, 9, 15-16). The call to love one another grows out of Christ's love for us. As we open ourselves up to God's love in Christ, as we allow God the Father/vintner to prune our lives toward fruitfulness, we become free to love one another. It is an organic cycle where the love of Christ nourishes our love for the other, and the only way we can remain in Christ's love is to continue to love one another. It is a profoundly relational understanding of the Christian life that sees the maturation of our friendship with God and one another as the ultimate fulfillment of our lives here on earth. This friendship is where true joy is found (John 15:8-11, 15). Just as a vineyard is meant to produce good grapes for choice wine to gladden the hearts of humanity, so are members of the church called to love one another, find true joy, and share it with the world.

Wine, Viticulture, and Soul Care

Wisdom from the Craftsman Vintners

The vintner understands the work of pruning well and regularly: it is an important part of every vintner's work in the vineyard. I have asked vintners to reflect on this important part of their work. Sister Hedwig (whom we met in chap. 6) sees in the pruning of the vines profound parallels to her life as a Christian. It challenges her to reflect on her own life. Does she welcome direction from the outside? Whom does she allow to prune her life? Sister Hedwig asks herself whether she is willing to hold back voluntarily, and to relinquish things in her life despite all the possibilities that life brings. If she pursues everything that interests her, then her energies will be divided and she will not do one thing well. Sister Hedwig reminds us that the purpose of pruning is not the cutting back itself but the hope for more abundant and beautiful fruit.

Once the vines are pruned, they are tied to wires spanned across the vineyard and held up by poles. This wiring structure gives the vines support and directs them in their growth (the technical term for which is "trellising"). Sister Hedwig admits that it is hard to allow someone else to bend one's life and firmly tie it down. She suggests that the wire systems in the vineyards are like the structures and rules in a community. We need them for the common life, and they give us support and stability. When we live too independently and grow without such structures, we become more vulnerable and live without direction. We can easily wither away and do not bear fruit.

Father Hufsky (also introduced in chap. 6) sees the work of pruning as the vintner's active parenting of the vines toward their potential. As he prunes the vines, he seeks to minimize negative tendencies, and he encourages the positive and strong aspects of the vine. After he prunes the branches, he binds them to a wire to direct their growth. Father Hufsky discovered in the writings of Hildegard von Bingen her use of the same Latin term, *infixi,* to speak about this work of binding the branches to a wire and the way that was used for Christ's being tied to the cross. It seems that Hildegard understood God's work of pruning human lives in light of Christ's death on the cross.

When Hufsky ties vine branches to the wire, he has to bend them, and sometimes they crack a little. There is an element of force in it, but ultimately it gives the branches support and enables them to grow. Hufsky sees parallels here to the Christian life. We need to let go of aspects of our lives that are not necessarily bad but that hinder us from being tied to Christ and his sacrificial death. This is one of the ways in which we can find freedom and bring forth rich fruit. The Christian life does not consist in hyperactivity — branches growing like weeds with little fruit on them — but in choosing a single-minded path directed toward Christ.

The metaphor of pruning branches for the Christian life suggests that we grow spiritually by being cut back, by allowing our lives to be restrained. This restraint seems paradoxical and perhaps even frightening. While the vintner quite naturally understands the importance of pruning and knows that the proper pruning of his vines will only enhance their fruitfulness, in contemporary society such an understanding of human flourishing seems disturbing. It is much more common to think that in order to develop our potential, we should not be cut back and tied down, but we should be allowed to soar on the winds of freedom and make the most of every opportunity. In the realm of consumerism this attitude means that we should be free to consume what and when we want and as much as we want.

As we think about the life of the church, and what it means that God wants to prune our lives, we need to ask what it means to step out of the pathological patterns of our society that hinder, injure, or even suffocate the spiritual life. The church cannot silently stand by and watch as increasing numbers of people find themselves imprisoned by substance-focused and behavioral addictions. Our relationship with the material world has become deeply broken and fractured. Many have lost the most basic understanding and wisdom of how to eat and drink in ways that nourish not only our bodies but also our souls.

William Cavanaugh reminds us that how we relate to the material world is a spiritual practice.[6] We have to relearn together, as the church, that the earth is a gift from God and thus a sacred place imbued with spiritual meaning. How can we recover a sense of awe and wonder for the material world? How can we learn to treasure and care for the material world that is not ours alone but the home of future generations? One way we can do so is by becoming more thoughtful about our consumer habits. We all have to consume every day to stay alive. How can we consume in ways that honor God and his creation and allow human life to flourish?

Pruning Consumerism

Cavanaugh argues that for many, consumerism has a spiritual dimension to it, even if they do not recognize it as such. He argues that it is a way of pursuing meaning and identity and a way by which we connect with other people.[7] As we know less and less about where products come from, we feel no connection with their producers or the places where products are grown or made. As the relationships between producers, places, and consumers fall away, consumers develop stronger attachments to the products they buy. Marketing strategists no longer offer mere information about a product, but they work hard to associate certain feelings with a product. They seek to create relationships between people and the things they buy. When we associate ourselves with a certain brand, for example, it gives us a sense of identity and comfort. Brand names can also provide a sense of community with all the people who associate with a particular brand.[8] Some people deal with depression by going shopping, a kind of "retail therapy" that unfortunately leaves consumers spiritually and emotionally malnourished. Marketing often works in hidden and subversive ways: it steadily forms and transforms the way we think of ourselves and those around us. It works to create desires in us and encourages consumer habits that promise to meet our deepest needs as human beings — in which, of course, they do not succeed.

From the Virtual to the Real

One way the messages of the marketing world reach us consistently and relentlessly is through the media of virtual places. Television, radio, the Internet, smartphones, and computer games are just a few examples of media that shape our imagination to think and act in certain ways. Just as vintners must use discernment and self-restraint as they use certain technology for the crafting of wine, so must we be more intentional and discerning about our use of electronic devices in our daily lives. The virtual world — and the marketing we encounter through it — is not neutral ground. It profoundly shapes our lives. Children with little capability for discernment are especially vulnerable to its messages. The regular use of electronic devices shapes their brains toward frantic activity, and the constant flow of marketing trains them in the ways of consumerism as a lifestyle. Public spaces, such as supermarkets, shopping malls, movie theaters, and so on, have all become places where advertising bombards us; these bombardments help us slip into the roles of consumers and form consumer habits. As we think about the pruning of our lives, the virtual world is one place where we can exercise restraint by limiting our exposure to it. Doing so opens up time and space for spiritual practices that can nourish and sustain us.

From the Lord's Supper to the Common Table

The church has an important role in helping us relearn to consume in ways that are life-giving and honor God and his creation. To return to examples already discussed, in the Lord's Supper we practice a way of consuming that helps us see that eating and drinking are indeed spiritual practices, ones that we must learn to cultivate. Some Protestant churches have missed a significant opportunity for teaching when they dropped the following prayer out of their liturgies: "Blessed are you, Lord God of all creation, for through your goodness we have received the wine we offer you: fruit of the vine and work of human hands, it will become our spiritual drink. Blessed be God for ever." How are we to remember that wine, like bread and all that we eat and drink, is a gift from God and work of human hands to be consumed gratefully and responsibly? Fewer and fewer churches today celebrate the annual harvest thanksgiving service, in which we also remember that the fruit of the earth is God's gift, and we learn to receive it and share it with thanksgiving. These are aspects of our worship that the church needs to recover; indeed, we need regular reminders that eating and drinking are spiritual practices.

The Lord's Supper also helps us remember that God wants to heal our relationship with food and drink. As we offer our lives, together with the bread and the wine, to God, we must find the courage to own up to disorders and addictions that imprison our eating and drinking habits. The journey of pruning and healing is often a difficult and painful one, but the cross of Christ reminds us that this pain is exactly where life can grow anew. We must trust that God can redeem our relationship with food and drink. He wants us to enjoy and share freely what creation offers to us. Those who habitually use food and drink as forms of anesthesia cannot enjoy them properly. They also close themselves off to the possibility of receiving comfort and healing from God and from those who want to help them. When families have become too fragmented and dysfunctional to be a place of healing, then the church has a responsibility to become family and offer hope, comfort, and guidance.

As we learn that eating and drinking are indeed spiritual practices, nourishing our souls as well as our bodies, we begin to think differently about "common" meals. For many, the common meal around a communal table has all but disappeared. The virtual world has drawn us away from the table. What if families and communities made the common table the central piece of furniture in the home once more? What if we were to relegate the television and/or the computer to a small corner of the house and restricted the time spent in front of it? Our daily need for food and drink might again become a daily opportunity to turn eating and drinking into a spiritual practice — one in which we learn to open our lives to God and to one another. We have to relearn to discern between physical, emotional, and spiritual hunger and how they can be nourished in different ways. In *Babette's Feast* the thoughtfully crafted meal, the atmosphere around the table, and the physical act of eating and drinking begin to break down emotional and spiritual barriers that have been decades in the making, and it opens up possibilities for healing and reconciliation. As we open our bodies to food and drink, we can open our lives to one another, nourish conversation, and allow more meaningful friendships to grow. While food and drink can satisfy our physical appetite, they cannot quench our spiritual thirst and our emotional hunger. But as we become more thoughtful about what we eat and how we eat, we can call forth an atmosphere of openness and receptivity toward one another and toward God. Our lives are ultimately oriented toward God, and it is only in him that we find the rest and peace for which we all yearn.

To Drink Is to Pray

Wine as a gift from God and the work of human hands is there to make our hearts glad. As we prayerfully sip a glass of wine, we can reverse the trend of detachment from producer and place. We can learn about the vintner who crafted the wine and the unique place where it was grown. We can learn to make room for wonder as we meditate not only on the wine but also on the ultimate giver of this precious gift.

As we begin to understand that to drink is to pray, we can learn to restrain ourselves and not gulp down wine. Rather, we can learn to allow wine to lift our hearts to God and open our lives toward one another. When Babette shared the gifts of creation so sacrificially with her adopted family, that act brought about the transformation of the whole community. The beautifully set table, the carefully crafted meal, and the choice wines were tokens of her love for a community lost in strife and bitterness. Slowly but surely the sisters and brothers opened up their lives to one another and began to forgive. In the sheer presence of so much generosity and beauty, they could no longer remain in their poverty of spirit; they could once again experience the flourishing of their *koinonia,* as love and mercy surrounded them in such tangible ways.

Concluding Reflections

The language of agriculture — and particularly viticulture — in Scripture opens up a vision of the Christian life that profoundly challenges contemporary understandings of human beings as individual economic actors and autonomous consumers. This vivid imagery invites us to reimagine our Christian lives rooted in God's economy, an economy that is not based on competition and maximum profit but on love, forgiveness, and mercy. It challenges us to rediscover our identity in Christ and calls us to a life of *koinonia,* where that love, forgiveness, and mercy can grow out of our rootedness in Christ's presence. In Christian community the personal is not swallowed up by the communal; rather, we bring our diverse gifts and backgrounds and offer them up for mutual enrichment and delight. The metaphor of pruning encourages us to trust that restraint — being cut back — can become a life-giving practice. When God prunes our lives and as we embrace practices of restraint and moderation, new spaces unfold in which our lives can flourish anew and bring forth an abundance of fruit. And as we prune our consumer habits and learn to open our lives to God's loving and redeeming presence, we can rediscover what it means when we say, "To drink is to pray."

Conclusion

Life on my family's winery has changed. My parents passed on the winery to my sister Gertrud and her husband, Herbert. Two of their children are now training to become vintners. They have to learn the ways of craftsmanship just as my father and my sister and brother-in-law did. It takes many vintages and decades of experience to gain the wisdom and knowledge one needs to tend the vines and to craft wines well. The younger generation can draw from the knowledge and wisdom of the older generation; at the same time, members of the younger generation have different ideas about what a well-crafted wine might be. They bring in new ideas and sometimes recover some old ones. Some things change and others do not. Our family home, rebuilt during the Thirty Years' War in the seventeenth century, still stands, silently witnessing to the generations that come and go. Our mother, who loved being in the vineyard and the garden so much, has gone home to her Creator. Nowadays we must, as a family, find new ways and new rhythms of gathering the extended family around the table. The memories linger, but the life of the winery continues as the hustle and bustle hurries it along.

The life of faith also continues. Those in the younger generation have to discover for themselves the life of faith and learn the ways of God. We still attend the (Lutheran) St. Martin's church in our village, the same small sanctuary where our ancestors have worshiped for many generations. Our rich Lutheran rituals and traditions still provide the rhythms within which we learn to live life in light of our beliefs and our understanding of God our Creator and Redeemer.

But not all is well in the world of wine. Many vintners of the younger generation in Franconia find it difficult to connect their lives and their work in the vineyard with the Christian faith of their ancestors. The wisdom of the past and the understanding of how our Christian faith can inform our work in the vineyard seem to be getting lost. In this book I have discussed how the insights of the vintners do shed light on and deepen our understanding of the spirituality of wine. These vintners also help us grasp more fully the potent scriptural metaphors for the Christian life from the world of wine. The dialogue between Christian spirituality and the world of wine is an important one. We must not forget the rich insights that the vintners can offer, and we must trust that Scripture and the Christian tradition can still be meaningful and life-giving to those involved in crafting wine for the delight and enjoyment of humanity.

* * *

Jesus' very first miracle, at the wedding in Cana, challenges modern sentiments. When Jesus turned water into wine, he interrupted the natural flow of creation. This miracle invites us to believe that creation as God's gift is not a closed system but open to God's creative and redemptive presence.[1] Rather than seeing God over against creation, this miracle helps us see that God in Jesus Christ entered into creation to reveal God's glory. What is quite remarkable about this first miracle is that Jesus came into the world to share and intensify the joy of ordinary people.

In his great novel *The Brothers Karamazov,* Fyodor Dostoevsky reflects on this in the chapter entitled "Cana of Galilee."[2] The character Alyosha had wanted to become a monk in the Russian Orthodox tradition and to follow in the footsteps of his spiritual father, Zosima. Earlier, however, Father Zosima had challenged Alyosha not to stay in the monastery but to sojourn in the world, to live like Christ among the Russian people. In the chapter "Cana of Galilee," Alyosha returns to the monastery after Father Zosima has died — to keep watch at the priest's coffin. Father Zosima holds an icon of the Savior in his arms. Alyosha's feelings of sorrow are intermingled with a sweetness, and even a joy, as he sits and prays by the coffin of his beloved teacher. Half in slumber he hears Father Paissy read from the Gospel of John. Recognizing that the reading is the story of the wedding at Cana, Alyosha perks up, listens attentively, and exclaims:

> I love that passage: it's Cana of Galilee, the first miracle. . . . Ah, that miracle, ah, that lovely miracle! Not grief, but men's joy Christ visited when he worked his first miracle, he helped men's joy. . . . "He who loves men, loves their joy." . . .[3]

Alyosha marvels at Christ, who came to share in the joys of ordinary people. It is this story of the Lord's superabundant generosity in providing choice wine at a peasant wedding in Cana that gives Alyosha a renewed vision and hope for God's desire to redeem this world. He now recognizes what his vocation in the world might be. He ponders the choice wine that was kept until last, and with the eyes of faith he begins to understand the deeper meaning of this miracle. Without neglecting or minimizing the literal meaning of this first of Jesus' miracles, Dostoevsky, through the eyes of Alyosha, moves on to explore its meaning more fully. This wedding feast and the miraculously provided abundance of superior wine point to the heavenly wedding banquet where the wine of salvation will flow in great abundance and make glad the hearts of the people. Alyosha hears Father Zosima speak to him as out of a dream, encouraging him to embrace his vocation in the world:

> We are rejoicing . . . we are drinking new wine, the wine of new and great joy. . . . Begin, my dear, begin, my meek one, to do your work! . . . Do not be afraid of him. Awful is his greatness before us, terrible is his loftiness, yet he is boundlessly merciful, he became like us out of love, and he is rejoicing with us, transforming water into wine, that the joy of the guests may not end. . . .[4]

Alyosha is filled with dread, but he now understands that in a broken world his vocation is to proclaim God's forgiveness. He has to help the people embrace it so that the wine of salvation can flow freely.

*   *   *

The vision of the prophet Isaiah that God will swallow up death, wipe away the tears from all faces, and remove the disgrace of his people and instead provide a feast of rich food and well-aged wine has begun in the life and ministry of Jesus Christ (Isa. 25:6-8; Rev. 21:4). The Old Testament prophets instilled in God's people a longing for a future redemption, where the harmonious times of Eden, the garden of delight, will be restored. Wine will flow in great abundance. When Christ transformed water into a great abundance of wine at the wedding of Cana, he provided a powerful sign that in him these promises of old have come to be fulfilled.

Rather than seeing the miracle of Cana as mere symbol or picturesque illustration hinting at greater spiritual realties, however, we can and must see in it the manifestation of God's presence with his people and his desire to re-deem all of creation. The gift of wine will always remain a tangible expression of God's blessing and his desire to rejoice with his people and make them glad.

Wine in the Lord's Supper will always remind us that Christ is the choice wine that God poured out for the life of the world. He is the noble grape that was crushed in the divine winepress so that the world might be reconciled with God and receive everlasting life. Even when Christ celebrated the Passover meal with his disciples, he prepared them for his departure and taught them that the fulfillment of his mission will only come in the future. And like the Old Testament prophets, who envisioned the *eschaton* in terms of feasting and an abundance of wine, so does Jesus envision the completion of all things in terms of festive celebration, the reunion with his beloved, *and* the drinking of wine: "I tell you, I will never again drink of this fruit of the vine until that day when I drink it new with you in my Father's kingdom" (Matt. 26:29; see also Mark 14:25; Luke 21:18). Meanwhile, as we enjoy a glass of wine prayerfully, it should always fill us with hope and the longing for a future time when Christ will return to renew the heavens and the earth. Life will then be like a grand wedding banquet where we no longer see God through a glass darkly but see him face to face (Rev. 21:1-4; 1 Cor. 13:12).

Appendix 1

Hebrew and Greek Wine Terminology in Scripture

Hebrew Terms

Term	Meaning	Frequency[1]
אגר (*'gr*)	to gather	1 (Deut. 28:39)
אדם, hith. (*'dm*)	to be red, redden, to glow or look red	1 (Prov. 23:31)
אוב (*'wb*)	skin-bottle	1 (Job 32:19)
ארה (*'rh*)	to pluck, gather	1 (Ps. 80:12 [80:13 MT])
אשישה (*'šyšh*)	raisin-cake	5
אשכול (*'škwl*)	cluster (of grapes)	9
באשים (*b'šym*)	stinking or worthless things, wild grapes	2
בלע, niph. (*bl'*)	to be swallowed up, to be engulfed by wine	1 (Isa. 28:7)
בסר (*bsr*)	unripe or sour grapes (collective)	4
בציר (*bṣyr*)	vintage	7
בצר (*bṣr*)	to cut off (grape clusters)	7
געש, hithpo. (*g'š*)	to reel to and fro (said of drunken men)	1 (Jer. 25:16)
גביע (*gby'*)	cup, bowl	1 (Jer. 35:5)
גדר (*gdr*)	wall (esp. enclosing a vineyard)	4
גפן (*gpn*)	vine (always grape-bearing [2 Kings 4:39])	54
גת (*gt*)	winepress	5
דבש (*dbš*)	honey	53
דלית (*dlyt*)	branch, bough	1 (Jer. 11:16)

221

Term	Meaning	Frequency[1]
דרך (*drk*)	to tread a wine- (or oil-)press	11
הידד (*hydd*)	shout, shouting, cheer (esp. in harvest)	7
הלולים (*hlwlym*)	a vintage-rejoicing, merry-making connected with thanksgiving; or holiness of praise, i.e., a consecrated thing in token of thanksgiving for fruit, offered in fourth year	2
הלל, hith. (*hll*)	to act madly, or like a madman; of nations, to act as drunken men, figurative of the terror brought on by Yahweh's judgments	2
המה (*hmh*)	to be boisterous, turbulent, as with wine	1 (Zech. 9:15)
זג (*zg*)	name of some comparatively insignificant product of the vine, the eating of which was included in things prohibited to Nazirites; the skin of the grape	1 (Num. 6:4)
זלזל (*zlzl*)	(quivering) tendrils	1 (Isa. 18:5)
זמר (*zmr*)	to trim, prune	3
זמורה (*zmwrh*)	branch, twig, shoot (esp. of grape vine)	5
זקק, pu. (*zqq*)	to be refined, purified	1 (Isa. 25:6)
חמה (*ḥmh*)	excitement, wrath[2]	1 (Jer. 25:15)
חלל, pi. (*ḥll*)	to treat a vineyard as common by beginning to use its fruit[3]	4
חמץ (*ḥmṣ*)	vinegar	5
חמר (*ḥmr*)	(n.) wine	3
חמר (*ḥmr*)	(v.) to ferment, boil, or foam up	1
חמר (*ḥmr*) and חמרה (*ḥmrh*)	wine (Aramaic)	6
חקר (*ḥqr*)	to search	1 (Prov. 28:30)
חרצן (*ḥrṣn*)	some insignificant vineyard product, usually taken as grape kernels, grape stones, from acrid taste	1 (Num. 6:4)
יין (*yyn*)	wine[4]	141
יקב (*yqb*)	wine vat (a trough or hollow excavated in the rock for receiving the juice trodden out in the גת); sometimes also winepress (the trough in which the grapes were trodden out)	16

Term	Meaning	Frequency[1]
כוס (*kws*)	cup (esp. for wine)	31
כרם (*krm*)	vineyard (often figurative of Israel under YHWH's care); vine-dresser	97
ליץ (*lṣ*)	scorner	1 (Prov. 20:1)
מגל (*mgl*)	sickle (vine tool)	2
מזג (*mzg*)	mixture, i.e., mixed wine	1 (Cant. 7:3)
מזמרה (*mzmrh*)	pruning knife	3
מזרק (*mzrq*)	bowl for wine	1 (Amos 6:6)
ממתקים (*mmtqym*)	sweetness, sweet things (said of drinks)	2
מסך (*msk*)	(n.) mixture, i.e., wine mixed with spices	1 (Ps. 75:9)
מסך (*msk*)	(v.) to mix, produce by mixing, i.e., to make a choice drink by mixing with spices, etc.	6
משרה (*mšrh*)	juice, esp. the juice of grapes	1 (Num. 6:3)
משתה (*mšth*)	feast, banquet (occasion for drinking, drinking bout); drink	44
נאד (*n'd*)	skin-bottle, skin	5
נבל (*nbl*)	skin of wine	5
נזיר (*nzyr*)	untrimmed vine[5]	2
נוע (*nw'*)	to quiver, wave, waver, tremble, totter, stagger like a drunkard	2 (Ps. 107:27; Isa. 29:9)
נסיך (*nsyk*)	libation; drink-offering	1 (Deut. 32:38)
נסך (*nsk*)	(n.) drink-offering	60 (explicitly mentioned as a libation wine, 5)
נסך (*nsk*)	(v.) to pour out libations	5
נצה (*nṣh*)	blossom (of vine)	4
סבא (*sb'*)	to imbibe, to drink heavily	9
סכה (*skh*)	booth; rude or temporary shelter, esp. for watchers in vineyards	2 (Isa. 1:8; Job 27:18)
סמדר (*smdr*)	blossom of grape	3
סרח (*srḥ*)	overrunning, spreading (vine)	1 (Ezek. 17:6)
עבר (*'br*)	to pass, go over[6]	1 (Jer. 23:9)

Term	Meaning	Frequency[1]
עללות (*'llwt*)	gleaning (going over a second time)	6
ענב (*'nb*)	grape(s)	19
עסיס (*'sys*)	sweet wine	5
פורה (*pwrh*)	winepress	2
פיק (*pyq*)	tottering, staggering	1 (Nah. 2:10)
פרט (*prṭ*)	the broken off, i.e., fallen grapes	1 (Lev. 19:10)
צמוקה (*ṣmwqh*)	bunch of raisins (dried grapes)	4
קיא (*qy'*)	(n.) vomit	3
קיא (*qy'*)	(v.) to vomit up, spew out, disgorge	1
קיץ, hiph. (*qyṣ*)	to awake from stupor (of drunkenness)	2
קשׂוה (*qśwh*)	a kind of jug, jar, utensil of tabernacle and temple; jars of the drink-offering	4
רעל (*r'l*)	reeling	1 (Zech. 12:2)
רקח (*rqh*)	spice (i.e., spiced wine)	1 (Cant. 8:2)
שׂריג (*śryg*)	tendril, twig (of vine)	3
שׂרק (*śrq*)	choice species of vine	4
שׂרקה (*śrqh*)	choice vine	1
שׁגה (*šgh*)	to swerve, meander, reel, or roll in drunkenness; to be intoxicated	1
שׁדמה (*šdmh*)	field	2
שׁכור (*škwr*)	drunken	14
שׁכר (*škr*)	(v.) to be, or become, drunk, drunken	18
שׁכר (*škr*)	(n.) intoxicating drink, strong drink	23
שׁכרון (*škrwn*)	drunkenness	3
שׁמר (*šmr*)	lees, dregs	5
שׁקה, hiph. (*šqh*)	to cause to drink water, to give to drink	7
תירוש (*tyrwš*)	must, fresh or new wine	38
תעה (*t'h*)	to err (of intoxication); to be made to wander about (as a drunkard)[7]	3
תרעלה (*tr'lh*)	reeling	2

1. Frequencies provided indicate occurrences *only as they pertain to viticulture, wine, wine-making, etc.* Many of the words listed are much more common in Scripture and have a broad range of meanings, but for the purposes of this appendix, I have counted only those occurrences related in some fashion to wine. In some cases of infrequent words/meanings, Scripture references are provided.

2. "In view of the meaning of the root, the basic meaning of *ḥēmâ* may indicate "being hot" (from excitement), thus, e.g., "boiling," then "wrath": cf. Hosea 7:5, which mentions the "effects of wine." See Ernst Jenni and Claus Westermann, eds., *Theological Lexicon of the Old Testament,* 4 vols. (Peabody, MA: Hendrickson Publishers, 1997), 1:435.

3. "In the hi. the meaning 'to begin' dominates alongside 'to desecrate' (in addition to ho. 'to be begun' and *teḥillâ,* 'beginning'); the connection between the two groups is clarified by the use of *ḥll* pi. in the sense of 'to place in profane use' (Deut. 20:6(bis); 28:30; Jer. 31:5, of the beginning of the use of a vineyard at the end of a period of consecration in which the harvest was forbidden for one's own use. Cf. Lev. 19:23-25: see *ILC* 3-4:271)"; Jenni and Westermann, *Theological Lexicon,* 1:427.

4. Ranges of meaning include "common drink, for refreshment," "tonic," an "art(icle) of commerce" kept "among supplies in strongholds" for "making merry." It could serve cultic purposes: "used for rejoicing before YHWH . . . as drink-offering in prescribed ritual." As such it was kept "among temple stores." It was "used also in heathen ceremonial." It was "intoxicating" and "forbidden to Nazirites . . . Rechabites . . . (the) mother of Samson . . . (and) to priests entering the sanctuary." It was also deemed "unfitting for kings." Many compound words include this word, and it carried many figurative meanings. See Francis Brown, S. R. Driver, and Charles A. Briggs, eds., *A Hebrew and English Lexicon of the Old Testament* (Oxford: Clarendon Press, 1952), p. 406.

5. "*nāzîr* referred originally to something removed from everyday life, elevated above the customary and set aside for something special. The old blessings in Gen. 49:26 and Deut. 33:16 describe Joseph as *nāzîr,* hence as one who assumes a special, extraordinary position among his brothers" (cf. also Lam. 4:7, if one does not prefer to emend the text; cf. Hans-Joachim Kraus, *Klagelieder: Threni,* vol. 20 of *Biblischer Kommentar, Altes Testament* [Neukirchen-Vluyn: Neukirchener-Verlag, 1968], p. 67). "This usage provides the basis for understanding the figurative use of *nāzîr* in Lev. 25:5, 11, to indicate the 'untended and unpruned vine': it is the vine removed (in the Sabbath and Jubilee year) from normal usage (Noth, *Lev,* OTL, 186)." See Jenni and Westermann, *Theological Lexicon,* 2:727.

6. Cf. Jer. 23:9: ". . . over whom wine hath gone (= overcome with wine)"; Brown et al., *Hebrew and English Lexicon,* 717a.

7. "Comparisons with lost sheep (Isa. 53:6; Ps. 119:176, etc.) or with the groping around of drunks (Isa. 19:14; 28:7; Job 12:25) lead to the fig. meaning 'to go astray' (causatively, 'to lead astray, mislead, seduce'), with the subj. 'heart' or 'spirit' also 'to be confused' (Isa. 21:4; 29:24; Ps. 95:10). . . . The sinner is compared to lost sheep (Isa. 53:6; Ps. 119:176), while the ignorance and folly of the wise (Isa. 19:13f.), the prophets and priests (28:7), and the leaders of state (Job 12:24) are equated with the staggering of drunks." See Jenni and Westermann, *Theological Lexicon,* 3:1432.

Greek Terms

Term	Meaning	Frequency[1]
ἄκρατος (*akratos*)	unmixed	1 (Rev. 14:10)
ἄμπελος (*ampelos*)	vine, grapevine	9
ἀμπελουργός (*ampelourgos*)	vine-dresser, gardener	1 (Luke 13:7)
ἀμπελών (*ampelōn*)	vineyard	23
ἀσκός (*askos*)	leather bag, esp. a wineskin	12
ἄψινθος (*apsinthos*)	plant of the genus Artemisia, proverbially bitter to the taste, yielding a dark green oil (the rendering wormwood derives from its association with medicinal use to kill intestinal worms)	1 (Rev. 8:11)
βότρυς (*botrus*)	bunch of grapes	3
γένημα τῆς ἀμπέλου (*genēma tēs ampelou*)	of wine as the product of the vine	3 (Matt. 26:29; Mark 14:25; Luke 22:18)
γεύομαι (*geuomai*)	to partake of something by mouth; to taste	1 (Matt. 27:34)
γεωργός (*geōrgos*)	one who does agricultural work on a contractual basis, vine-dresser, tenant farmer	17
γλεῦκος (*gleukos*)	sweet new wine	1 (Acts 2:13)
δρέπανον (*drepanon*)	agricultural implement consisting of a curved blade and a handle, used for a variety of purposes; sickle	2
κεράννυμι (*kerannymi*)	to mix liquid components, mostly of water with wine (to dilute high alcoholic strength); mix	1 (Rev. 18:6)
κλῆμα (*klēma*)	branch, esp. of a vine	4
κραιπάλη (*kraipalē*)	unbridled indulgence in a drinking party; drinking bout	1 (Luke 21:34)

Term	Meaning	Frequency[1]
κῶμος (kōmos)	excessive feasting[2]	2
ληνός (lēnos)	term for something hollow, such as a vat or trough, hence also winepress	5
μέθη (methē)	drunkenness	3
μεθύσκομαι (methyskomai)	to become intoxicated	5
μέθυσος (methysos)	drunkard	2 (1 Cor. 5:11; 6:10)
μεθύω (methyō)	to drink to a point of intoxication; to be drunk	5
νηφάλιος (nēphalios)	pertaining to being very moderate in the drinking of an alcoholic beverage; temperate; sober	2
νήφω (nēphō)	to be well-balanced, self-controlled[3]	6
οἰνοπότης (oinopotēs)	wine-drinker, drunkard	1 (Matt. 11:19)
οἶνος (oinos)	beverage made from fermented juice of the grape; wine[4]	34
οἰνοφλυγία (oinophlygia)	drunkenness	1 (1 Pet. 4:3)
ὄξος (oxos)	sour wine; wine vinegar[5]	5
πάροινος (paroinos)	pertaining to one who is given to drinking too much wine; addicted to wine; drunkard	2 (1 Tim. 3:3; Titus 1:7)
πότος (potos)	social gathering at which wine was served; drinking party	1 (1 Pet. 4:3)[6]
πύργος (pyrgos)	tall structure used as a lookout; tower (esp. in a vineyard, for watchmen)	3 (Matt. 21:33; Mark 12:1; Luke 14:28)
ῥήγνυμι (rhēgnymi)	to cause to come apart or be in pieces by means of internal or external force; to tear in pieces, break, burst (used of wine bursting wineskins)	2
σίκερα (sikera)	an alcoholic beverage;[7] beer	1 (Luke 1:15)

Term	Meaning	Frequency[1]
σταφυλή (*staphylē*)	(a bunch of) grapes	3 (Matt. 7:16; Luke 6:44; Rev. 14:18)
τρυγάω (*trygaō*)	to harvest (grapes)	3 (Luke 6:44; Rev. 14:18-19)
ὑπολήνιον (*hypolēnion*)	trough placed beneath the winepress to hold the juice trod from the grapes; wine trough; vat	1 (Mark 12:1)
φραγμός (*phragmos*)	structure for enclosing an area; fence; hedge (frequently enclosing a vineyard)	2 (Mark 12:1; Matt. 21:33)

1. Frequencies provided indicate occurrences *only as they pertain to viticulture, wine, wine-making, etc.* Many of the words listed are much more common in Scripture and have a broad range of meanings; but for the purposes of this appendix, I have counted only those occurrences related in some way to wine. In some cases of infrequent words/meanings, Scripture references are provided.

2. "Orig. a festal procession in honor of Dionysus (cp. our festival of Mardi Gras), then a joyous meal or banquet, in the NT . . . only in a bad sense." See Walter Bauer, Frederick W. Danker, William F. Arndt, and F. Wilbur Gingrich, eds., *A Greek-English Lexicon of the New Testament and Other Early Christian Literature* (Chicago: University of Chicago Press, 1979), p. 580.

3. "Prim. 'be sober'; in the NT only fig. = be free fr. every form of mental and spiritual 'drunkenness,' fr. excess, passion, rashness, confusion, etc." See Bauer et al., *Greek-English Lexicon*, p. 672.

4. Secondary meanings include the figurative "punishments that God inflicts on the wicked, *wine*" and "the plant that makes the production of wine possible, *vine* or *vineyard,* eventually the product *wine,* effect for cause." See Bauer et al., *Greek-English Lexicon*, p. 701.

5. "It relieved thirst more effectively than water and, being cheaper than regular wine, it was a favorite beverage of the lower ranks of society and of those in moderate circumstances . . . , esp. of soldiers. . . . Given to Jesus on the cross." See Bauer et al., *Greek-English Lexicon*, p. 715.

6. "Here prob. in the sense of 'carousal.' In the Gr-Rom. world it was customary for literati to hold banquets at which topical discussions were featured, with participants well lubricated with wine (see the dialogues of Pl. and esp. X., Symp.). These would not properly be rendered 'carousals.' It is prob. that the Petrine pass. has less sophisticated participants in mind." See Bauer et al., *Greek-English Lexicon*, p. 857.

7. "As a rule σ. was differentiated fr. wine and mentioned w. it. . . . It is not possible to determine whether σ. was considered any stronger than wine; the rendering 'strong drink' (so in many versions) may therefore be misleading." See Bauer et al., *Greek-English Lexicon*, p. 923.

Appendix 2

Crafting a Church Service for the Blessing of the Grapes

In Germany this church service is traditionally celebrated in August (depending on the ripeness of grapes) and is based on the Old Testament's injunction to offer up the first fruits to God in gratitude and festive celebration before God (Deut. 26:1-11).

It can be applied to other fruit and vegetables as well, depending on where you live.

These are just suggestions and can be modified according to your tradition and culture.

Following the church service there would be a celebratory meal whose purpose would be to encourage the congregation to live into a posture of gratitude and joyful celebration.

Opening Hymn Suggestions

"Go Forth, My Heart, and Seek Delight" (Paul Gerhardt, translated by John Kelly). This is a beautiful hymn that specifically mentions the fruit of the vine. It is my favorite hymn because it leads the congregation into a prolonged sense of wonder and adoration for God our Creator. It can be found online at http://www.hymnary.org/hymn/PGSS1867/63.

"Sing to the Lord of Harvest" (John Monsell). This is a hymn that is especially appropriate for a grain harvest.

"We Plow the Fields" (Matthias Claudius, translated by Jane M. Campbell)

Welcome

Prayer for the Day

> God, Creator of all life, grant our hearts to grow in gratitude and joy as we receive and share with one another all the good things that you give to us. Grant that we may grow in love and care for one another — just as you love and care for us.

Suggested Readings:

> Deuteronomy 26:1-11
>
> Proverbs 3:9-10
>
> Psalm 104 (especially verses 1, 13-15)
>
> Ben Sirah 35:7-10
>
> John 2:1-11
>
> John 15:1-12

Intercessory Prayers

> Intercessory prayers are offered especially for the vintners, farmers, and workers, the vineyard and the vines, the land, the soil, the harvest, and — not least of all — for the hungry of this world, that they might be fed.

Sermon

Presentation of the Grapes to the Altar

Prayer of Blessing over the Grapes

> Bless, O Lord, these new grapes, the grapes that you, Lord, with heavenly dew, with rain, and in mild and steady weather have allowed to ripen by your grace. You gave them for our grateful use in the name of our Lord Jesus Christ.[1]
>
> Or

Bless these grapes through the grace of the Holy Spirit in the name of the Father and the Son and Holy Spirit. Amen.

Hymn

"Now Thank We All Our God" (Martin Rinkart, translated by Catherine Winkworth)

The Lord's Supper (also called the Eucharist,
Holy Communion, or the Breaking of the Bread)

Include ancient prayer: "Blessed are you, Lord God of all creation, for through your goodness we have received the wine we offer you: fruit of the vine and work of human hands, it will become our spiritual drink. Blessed be God for ever."

Prayer of thanksgiving and/or Postlude:

Schubert's German Mass (Deutsche Messe in F.D. 872), 4th movement:

"You Gave Me, Lord, My Life and Being" (The English translation can be found at http://www.cpdl.org/wiki/images/d/do/German_Mass_complete, _English.pdf.)

Be creative and inventive and allow your own church tradition and culture to inform this service.

---

1. This prayer is based on a prayer from the German *Missale Bambergense* of 1490.

Notes

Preface

1. Each interview was transcribed. Rather than quoting vintners word for word, however, I have woven their reflections into a narrative in order to give flow and coherence to the material. The vintners were allowed to look over the material and give their consent before publication.

Introduction

1. Richard Bauckham, *Living with Other Creatures* (Crownhill, UK: Paternoster, 2012), p. 111.

2. Bauckham, *Living with Other Creatures*, p. 112.

Chapter 1

Wine in the Bible: God's Gift and Blessing

1. All Scripture quotations in this chapter are taken from the New Revised Standard Version unless otherwise indicated.

2. Lothar Becker, *Rebe, Rausch und Religion: Eine kulturgeschichtliche Studie zum Wein in der Bibel* (Münster: LIT Verlag, 1999).

3. Becker, *Rebe*, p. 98. See appendix I for a list of these Hebrew and Greek terms and their translations.

4. Robert Forbes, *Cosmetics and Perfumes in Antiquity*, vol. 3 of *Studies in Ancient Technology* (Leiden: Brill, 1955), pp. 80, 193. Gustav Dalman, *Arbeit und Sitte in Palästina: Brot, Öl und Wein*, vol. 4 (Hildesheim: Georg Olms Verlagsbuchhandlung, 1964), pp. 382-85. Nathan MacDonald, *Not Bread Alone: The Uses of Food in the Old Testament* (Oxford: Oxford University Press, 2008), pp. 54, 60-61.

5. Robert Curtis, *Ancient Food Technology,* vol. 3 (Leiden: Brill, 2001), p. 184. See also Tim Unwin, *Wine and the Vine: An Historical Geography of Viticulture and the Wine Trade* (London: Routledge, 1991) p. 63.

6. Becker, *Rebe,* p. 49.

7. Becker, *Rebe,* p. 50; Unwin, *Wine and the Vine,* p. 64.

8. Unwin, *Wine and the Vine,* pp. 68-71.

9. For archaeological evidence of the importing of wine from Palestine into Egypt, see Patrick E. McGovern, *Ancient Wine: The Search for the Origins of Viniculture* (Princeton, NJ: Princeton University Press, 2003), pp. 94-101.

10. Curtis, *Ancient Food,* pp. 145-46.

11. Curtis, *Ancient Food,* pp. 152-59. For a careful discussion of the role of wine in ancient Egypt, see Mu-Chou Poo, *Wine and Wine Offering in the Religion of Ancient Egypt* (London: Kegan Paul International, 1995).

12. For a careful discussion of the theme of wine in antiquity, see Gregory Austin, *Alcohol in Western Society from Antiquity to 1800: A Chronological History* (Santa Barbara, CA: ABC-CLIO, 1985), pp. 1-50.

13. Austin, *Alcohol,* p. 16. He also established a law that would punish an offense with twice the severity if the offender was intoxicated.

14. *The Wisdom of Ben Sira: A New Translation with Notes by Partrick W. Skehan,* trans. Patrick W. Skehan (New York: Doubleday, 1987), p. 385.

15. Pliny, *Natural History IV,* trans. H. Rackham, 10 vols. (Cambridge, MA: Harvard University Press, 1968), 14.139-48. For a helpful introduction to the Roman Empire and wine, see Curtis, *Ancient Food,* pp. 372-80.

16. Pliny, *Natural History,* 14. For a discussion of other Roman writers on viticulture and vinification, see Unwin, *Wine and the Vine,* pp. 101-7.

17. Pliny, *Natural History,* 14.10, 14, 28. For a discussion of the role of geography and how it was understood to influence wine in ancient times, see John Varriano, "Regional Tastes," in *Tastes and Temptations, Food and Art in Renaissance Italy* (Berkeley: University of California Press, 2009).

18. Curtis, *Ancient Food,* pp. 294-95.

19. With Burnham and Skilleås, I will restrict our use of the definition to wine made from grapes only, in contrast to the definition in *The Oxford Companion to Wine.* See Douglas Burnham and Ole Martin Skilleås, *The Aesthetics of Wine* (Oxford: Wiley-Blackwell, 2012), p. 36.

20. See Philip Whalen, "'A Merciless Source of Happy Memories': Gaston Roupnel and the Folklore of Burgundian Terroir," *Journal of Folklore Research* 44, no. 1 (2007): 21-40.

21. For scientists exploring the *terroir*-specific nature of wine, see, e.g., V. Renouf et al., "The Wine Microbial Consortium: A Real Terroir Characteristic," *Journal International des Sciences de la Vigne et du Vin* 40, no 4 (2006): 209-16. Just because many notions of *terroir* and its taste cannot be captured by a modern scientific approach to objective knowledge does not negate the existence of *terroir*. For an excellent article on this question, see Geneviève Teil, "No Such Thing as Terroir? Objectivities and the Regimes of Existence of Objects," *Science, Technology and Human Values* 37, no 5 (2012): 478-505.

22. Richard Bauckham argues for this understanding with respect to a biblical understanding of creation care. See Richard Bauckham, *The Bible and Ecology: Rediscovering the Community of Creation* (Waco, TX: Baylor University Press, 2010).

23. Wendell Berry, "Christianity and the Survival of Creation," in *Sex, Economy, Freedom and Community: Eight Essays* (New York: Pantheon Books, 1993), p. 103.

24. C. Schultz, "עֵדֶן," *TWOT* 2:646-47.

25. L. J. Coppes, "אָדָם," *TWOT* 1:10-11. Gerhard von Rad, *Genesis: A Commentary*, trans. John H. Marks, OTL (Philadelphia: Westminster, 1972), p. 136.

26. Various terms have been used to describe this hierarchical dimension of humanity's relationship with the rest of creation. In order to correct a false sense of lordship over the earth that contributed in significant ways to an oppressive and exploitative posture, contemporary theologians have gravitated toward the idea of stewardship. Richard Bauckham argues that what is needed in our time is a reconsideration of the place of humans within the larger community of creation from a much broader biblical perspective. See Bauckham, *Living with Other Creatures* (Crownhill, UK: Paternoster, 2012), pp. 1-13; see also Bauckham, *Ecology*, pp. 1-17.

27. Bauckham, *Living*, p. 17.

28. For a reflection on Noah as a conservationist, see Bauckham, *Ecology*, p. 24.

29. L. J. Coppes, "נוּח," *TWOT* 2:562-63.

30. It is striking that most commentators see Noah's vineyard as a direct fulfillment of Genesis 5:29. See, e.g., von Rad, *Genesis*, p. 136; Claus Westermann, *Genesis 1-11: A Commentary*, trans. John Scullion (Minneapolis: Augsburg Publishing House, 1984), pp. 360, 484, 487; Victor Hamilton, *The Book of Genesis: Chapters 1-17*, NICOT (Grand Rapids: Eerdmans, 1990), pp. 259, 321; Gordon Wenham, *Genesis 1-15*, WBC (Dallas, TX: Word Books, 1994), pp. 128-29; Bruce Waltke, *Genesis: A Commentary* (Grand Rapids: Zondervan, 2001), p. 115; and Joseph Blenkinsopp, *Creation, Un-Creation, Re-Creation: A Discursive Commentary on Genesis 1-11* (New York: T&T Clark, 2011), p. 154. Waltke points out that while Cain's descendant Lamech repaid wrong with revenge and continued the spiral of violence (4:23-24), Seth's descendant Lamech waits for God's deliverance from the curse. He trusts in God.

31. Wenham, *Genesis 1-15*, p. 198. See also Manuel Dubach, *Trunkenheit im Alten Testament: Begrifflichkeit-Zeugniss-Wertung* (Stuttgart: Verlag W. Kohlhammer, 2009), pp. 83, 85.

32. Westermann, *Genesis 1-11*, p. 487.

33. Unless otherwise noted, all Scripture citations are from the New Revised Standard Version.

34. J. N. Oswalt, "בָּרַךְ," *TWOT* 1:132-33.

35. Dalman, *Arbeit und Sitte*, p. 229.

36. I owe this insight to conversations with Dr. Allen Ross. The blessing of Joseph could also refer to a vine, though the Hebrew leaves it more open (Gen. 49:22).

37. The biblical narrative emphasizes the contrast to Egypt, where the Israelites were burdened by the toil of their hands; this land is irrigated by God himself (Deut. 11:10-15; see also Lev. 26:3-5).

38. In some translations the Hebrew word *'ĕlōhîm* used here is translated as "gods." The word *'ĕlōhîm* (pl.) is used in Judges both for Israel's God and the pagan gods. Since the question in this chapter is about who is going rule over God's people, it seems more likely that *'ĕlōhîm* refers here to Israel's God. The Hebrew word for "men" used in this passage is *'ănāšîm* and refers to men in contrast to women.

39. Walsh interprets archaeological evidence of ancient Israel and suggests that these small family-owned vineyards produced around 183 gallons (approx. 694 liters) of wine per year, amounting to 2.5 bottles a day and some extra wine for special celebrations. These are rough

guesses but help envision what these oracles might hint at. See Walsh, *The Fruit of the Vine: Viticulture in Ancient Israel* (Winona Lake, IN: Eisenbrauns, 2000), pp. 111-12, for images and his discussion.

40. Magen Broshi, *Bread, Wine, Walls, and Scrolls* (Sheffield, UK: Sheffield Academic Press, 2001), pp. 154-55. Walsh, *Fruit of the Vine*, pp. 21, 25. Walsh emphasizes that it was only the elite that were able to afford these expensive imported wines. The lower class had to settle for beer instead, a byproduct of grain farming. Recent excavations in 2013 of an extensive 3700-year-old Canaanite wine cellar in Northern Israel (Tel Kabri) confirm that Canaan had a rather sophisticated understanding of viticulture.

41. Walsh, *Fruit of the Vine*, p. 209. For biblical references, see, e.g., Num. 18:27; Deut. 11:14; 15:14; 16:13; Judg. 9:13; 1 Chron. 27:27; Neh. 5:11; Prov. 3:10; Isa. 16:10; 62:8-9; Jer. 40:12; Joel 3:18; Amos 9:13-14.

42. Pliny, *Natural History*, 14.6.55.

43. Walsh, *Fruit of the Vine*, p. 210.

44. Broshi, *Bread, Wine, Walls, and Scrolls*, pp. 147-48.

45. For a careful discussion of viticulture in ancient Israel, see Walsh, *Fruit of the Vine*; see also the German classic by Gustav Dalman, *Arbeit und Sitte in Palästina: Brot, Öl und Wein*, vol. 4 (Hildesheim: Georg Olms Verlagsbuchhandlung, 1964). On how to evaluate various evidence in regard to the Israelite diet, see MacDonald, *Not Bread Alone*, chap. 2.

46. Walsh, *Fruit of the Vine*, pp. 209-19; Becker, *Rebe*, pp. 132-33. Nathan MacDonald concludes from his research that wine was a "principal drink" for the Israelites. MacDonald, *Not Bread Alone*, p. 61. Whether wine was enjoyed daily is a disputed question, though the majority of scholars conclude from their research that it was enjoyed daily by most families. For scriptural references, see, e.g., Num. 18:12; Judg. 19:19; Ruth 2:14; 1 Sam. 16:20; 25:18; Pss. 104:15; 128:3; Prov. 9:5; Eccl. 9:7.

47. Pliny, *Natural History*, 14.5.54; see also MacDonald, *Not Bread Alone*, p. 61; Broshi, *Bread, Wine, Walls, and Scrolls*, pp. 161-62.

48. It is remarkable how ethical instructions relating to people are interspersed with instructions relating to working the land. These two are deeply intertwined in the Hebrew mindset.

49. Theodore G. Tappert, ed., *Luther: Letters of Spiritual Counsel* (Vancouver: Regent College, 2003), pp. 85-86, 88, 95.

50. Becker, *Rebe*, pp. 134-35.

51. Jacob Milgrom, *Leviticus: A Book of Ritual and Ethics* (Minneapolis: Fortress Press, 2004), p. 17.

52. For a helpful introduction, see Milgrom, *Leviticus*, pp. 17-20.

53. Becker, *Rebe*, p. 142.

54. Walsh, *Fruit of the Vine*, pp. 185-86, 225-26. Becker, *Rebe*, p. 142. For scriptural references, see Gen. 21:8; 26:30; 29:22; Deut. 14:26; 2 Sam. 3:20; 1 Kings. 4:20; Esth. 2:18; 8:17; 9:17-22; Ezra 6:22; Eccl. 9:7. On the role of music and dancing, see Exod. 15:20-1; 1 Sam. 18:6; 2 Sam. 6:16; Ps. 30:11; Jer. 31:13.

55. The vintage feast is included in the festival calendars of ancient Israel: Exod. 23:14-19; 34:18-26; Lev. 23:1-44; Deut. 16:1-17 see also Judg. 9:27; 1 Sam. 25:2-36; 2 Sam. 13:23-28. Cf. Walsh, *Fruit of the Vine*, pp. 228-47; Becker, *Rebe*, p. 143.

56. Craig S. Keener, *The Gospel of John: A Commentary,* vol. 1 (Grand Rapids: Baker, 2003), pp. 498-99.

57. See chap. 9.

58. Another group to mention are the nomadic group of the Rechabites. Though they are invited by the prophet Jeremiah to drink wine, their commitment to their traditional nomadic lifestyle forbade them to drink it (Jer. 35:1-11).

59. Only one monograph is dedicated to this important tradition: Alois Thomas, *Die Darstellung Christi in der Kelter* (Düsseldorf: Schwann, 1936).

60. See Becker, *Rebe,* p. 98. The *TWOT* defines it as a "pruning knife" and notes occurrences here and in Isa. 2:4; 18:5. The word is related to the verbal root *zāmar,* meaning "trim, prune" (see Lev. 25:3-4; Isa. 5:6). L. J. Wood, "זָמַר," *TWOT* 1:245-46.

61. The Hebrew word used here *(šemer)* can denote purified wine, i.e., wine without yeast. After wine has gone through the fermentation process, the yeast needs to be strained from the wine. This is a common practice. Yeast in the Old Testament is primarily but not always a sign of impurity and would imply here a time when sin and corruption exist no longer.

62. Literature written between the times of the Old Testament and the New Testament also incorporate the fecundity of the vine as a sign of the coming of the Messiah. See, e.g., 2 Baruch 29:5 and 1 Enoch 10:19. Papias is cited in Irenaeus, *Against Heresies* 5.33.3-4 (*ANF* 1:562-63). Martin Hengel, *Studies in Early Christology* (London: T&T Clark, 1995), p. 316.

63. This pattern is in contrast to their pagan neighbors, particularly the excesses of the Roman Empire and the Herodians (Becker, *Rebe,* p. 169).

64. Dalman, *Arbeit und Sitte,* p. 260.

65. For a short but helpful introduction to Jewish wedding celebrations during Jesus' time, see Keener, *John,* pp. 498-501.

66. Keener, *John,* pp. 502-3.

67. Becker points out that the Jewish blessings spoken at the Passover meal included the praise of God as Creator: "Praised be the Creator of the fruit of the vine" (German: Gelobt sei der Schöpfer der Frucht des Weinstocks). Becker, *Rebe,* p. 177.

Chapter 2

Wine in the History of the Church: Its Rise and Fall

1. Irving Woodworth Raymond, *The Teaching of the Early Church on the Use of Wine and Strong Drink* (New York: AMS Press, 1970), p. 110.

2. See Pliny, *Natural History IV,* trans. H. Rackham, 10 vols. (Cambridge, MA: Harvard University Press, 1968), 14.7.58; see also Pliny, *The Greek Herbal of Dioscorides,* trans. John Goodyer, ed. Robert T. Gunther (New York: Hafner Publishing, 1959), pp. 601-23.

3. Diodorus Siculus quoted in Edward Hyams, *Dionysus: A Social History of the Wine Vine* (London: Sidgwick and Jackson, 1965), p. 134.

4. The rich merchant Trimalchio, living during the time of Nero's reign, comments on the decline of wine prices (Hyams, *Dionysus,* p. 138).

5. Hyams, *Dionysus,* p. 138.

6. Hyams, *Dionysus,* p. 147.

7. Irving Woodworth Raymond, *The Teaching of the Early Church on the Use of Wine and Strong Drink* (New York: Columbia University Press, 1927), p. 94.

8. *The Letters of St. Cyprian of Carthage III*, ed. G. W. Clarke (ACW 46; New York: Newman Press, 1986), p. 104.

9. *Letters of St. Cyprian III*, pp. 98-103.

10. *Letters of St. Cyprian III*, p. 98; see also pp. 98-109.

11. *Letters of St. Cyprian III*, p. 104.

12. Irenaeus, *Against Heresies*, 5.2.2-3 (*ANF* 1:528).

13. Clement of Alexandria, *Paedagogus*, 2.2, ed. M. Marcovich (Leiden: Brill, 2002), p. 83, quoting Sir. 31:26-27.

14. Raymond, *The Teaching of the Early Church*, pp. 106-8.

15. Chrysostom quoted in Raymond, *The Teaching of the Early Church*, pp. 106-8.

16. Raymond, *The Teaching of the Early Church*, p. 115.

17. Augustine, *Contra Faustum* 30.5 (CSEL 25.1:753-54).

18. Augustine, *Epistolae* 17.4 (CSEL 34.1:43); 34.4 (CSEL 34.2:25).

19. Augustine, *De bono coniugali* (Oxford: Clarendon Press, 2001), pp. 47-49.

20. This is a frequently quoted saying in Germany, but no specific reference to any of Augustine's work is given.

21. For specific references to wine, see Benedicta Ward, *The Desert Fathers: Sayings of the Early Christian Monks* (London: Penguin Books, 2003), pp. 7, 24-26, 28.

22. John Cassian, *The Conferences*, ed. Boniface Ramsey, ACW 57 (New York: Paulist Press, 1997), 23.21, pp. 812-13.

23. Desmond Seward, *Monks and Wine* (New York: Crown, 1979), p. 21. According to Seward, the Chenin Blanc developed from the black grapes of the Chenin Noir.

24. Seward, *Monks and Wine*, p. 21.

25. Daniela-Maria Brandt, *Heilige Helfer für Winzer und Wein* (Würzburg: Echter Verlag, 1993), pp. 168-69; Seward, *Monks and Wine*, p. 21.

26. It should not surprise us that Saint Martin is mentioned several times in the classic text on the history of wine in France: Roger Dion, *Histoire de la vigne et du vin en France des origins aus XIX siècle* (Paris: L'auteur, 1959), pp. 249-51.

27. Timothy Fry, ed., *The Rule of St. Benedict in Latin and English with Notes* (Collegeville, MN: Liturgical Press, 1981), chap. 40, pp. 238-41.

28. William Younger, *Gods, Men, and Wine* (London: The Wine and Food Society Limited, 1966), p. 231.

29. William Younger tries to downplay the role of monastic communities in the development of viticulture, but his lack of engagement with the rich monastic tradition makes his argument unconvincing. His emphasis, however, on the important role of laymen passing on agricultural wisdom to monastic communities is important (Younger, *Gods, Men, and Wine*, pp. 232-33). Austin, Dion, and Schreiber, on the other hand, affirm the important role of monasticism in this regard: Gregory A. Austin, *Alcohol in Western Society from Antiquity to 1800: A Chronological History* (Santa Barbara, CA: ABC-Clio Information Services, 1985), p. 54; Dion, *Histoire*, pp. 171-87; Georg Schreiber, *Deutsche Weingeschichte: Der Wein in Volksleben, Kult und Wirtschaft* (Köln: Rheinland-Verlag, 1980), pp. 71-72.

30. Younger, *Gods, Men, and Wine*, p. 233.

31. Seward, *Monks and Wine*, p. 40; Robert White, *Understanding Vineyard Soils* (Oxford: Oxford University Press, 2009), pp. 14-15.

32. Venantius Fortunantus, *Die Moselgedichte*, in Younger, *Gods, Men, and Wine*, p. 231; Alois Thomas, *Die Darstellung Christi in der Kelter* (Düsseldorf: Schwann, 1981), p. 24.

33. Seward, *Monks and Wine*, p. 30.

34. Seward, *Monks and Wine*, p. 30; Schreiber, *Deutsche Weingeschichte*, p. 75.

35. Schreiber, *Deutsche Weingeschichte*, p. 72. For more information on the role of the Benedictines in developing viticulture in Germany, see Seward, *Monks and Wine*, chap. 4.

36. Thomas, *Christi in der Kelter*, p. 24.

37. Friedrich Bassermann-Jordan, *Geschichte des Weinbaus* (Neustadt an der Weinstrasse: Pfalzische Verlagsanstalt, 1975), p. 1164; Thomas, *Christi in der Kelter*, p. 25.

38. Thomas, *Christi in der Kelter*, p. 24.

39. For the development of viticulture in Britain, see Seward, *Monks and Wine*, chap. 9; Austin, *Alcohol*, pp. 55-56, 77.

40. Austin, *Alcohol*, p. 54.

41. Austin, *Alcohol*, pp. 54-55.

42. Austin, *Alcohol*, p. 55.

43. Seward, *Monks and Wine*, p. 35; Austin, *Alcohol*, p. 500; Dion, *Histoire*, pp. 175-87.

44. Seward, *Monks and Wine*, p. 33.

45. Seward, *Monks and Wine*, p. 26.

46. Schreiber, *Deutsche Weingeschichte*, p. 76; Seward, *Monks and Wine*, p. 29.

47. Schreiber, *Deutsche Weingeschichte*, pp. 73, 76; Seward, *Monks and Wine*, p. 33.

48. Schreiber, *Weingeschichte*, p. 73; Seward, *Monks and Wine*, pp. 120-21.

49. On the contribution of the Carthusians and Templars, see Seward, *Monks and Wine*, pp. 78-110

50. Schreiber, *Weingeschichte*, p. 84; see also Dion, *Histoire*, p. 185.

51. Dion, *Histoire*, p. 186.

52. Seward, *Monks and Wine*, pp. 68-69.

53. *Cru* is a French term usually translated into English as "growth," designating a particular parcel of land in relation to its qualities for growing vines. To this day this term is used to classify French wines.

54. Hugh Johnson, *The Story of Wine* (London: Mitchell Beazley, 1989), p. 130.

55. Deborah Vess, "Monastic Moonshine: Alcohol in the Middle Ages," in C. K. Robertson, ed., *Religion and Alcohol: Sobering Thoughts* (New York: Peter Lang, 2004), p. 167.

56. Fry, *Rule of St. Benedict*, 31.10, pp. 228-29.

57. Schreiber, *Weingeschichte*, p. 89; Seward, *Monks and Wine*, pp. 65-66.

58. Seward, *Monks and Wine*, pp. 73-74; Johnson, *Story of Wine*, p. 136.

59. Thomas, *Christi in der Kelter*, pp. 53-66.

60. Thomas, *Christi in der Kelter*, p. 103.

61. Thomas, *Christi in der Kelter*, pp. 139-40, 169-70.

62. See http://metmuseum.org/Collections/search-the-collections/383698?rpp=20&pg=2 &rndkey=20121009&ft=*&what=Prints&pos=34.

63. Clement of Alexandria, *Paedagogus* 1.6.47, p. 30, discussed in Thomas, *Christi in der Kelter*, p. 56.

64. Thomas, *Christi in der Kelter*, pp. 58-60.

65. It is surprising that only one monograph is devoted to this rich aesthetic tradition. See Thomas, *Christi in der Kelter.* A chapter can also be found in Schreiber, *Weingeschichte,* pp. 439-58.

66. Seward, *Monks and Wine,* pp. 168-75.

67. Schreiber, *Deutsche Weingeschichte,* pp. 85-86.

68. Johnson, *Story of Wine,* p. 309.

69. See here Roland Bainton, *Women of the Reformation* (Minneapolis: Fortress Press, 1971), pp. 23-44.

70. Martin Luther to Katherine Luther, July 29, 1534, in *The Letters of Martin Luther,* trans. and ed. Margaret A. Currie (London: Macmillan, 1908), p. 299. On the daily drinking of wine, see AE 37: 150.

71. Hans Jörg Koch, *Wein: Eine literarische Weinprobe* (Leipzig: Reclam, 2002), p. 85.

72. Martin Luther, WA 10/III. Translation mine. See also Roland Bainton, *Here I Stand: A Life of Martin Luther* (New York: Abingdon, 1950), p. 214. For a discussion of these emerging voices that wanted to forbid alcohol altogether, see Mark Holt, ed., *Alcohol: A Social and Cultural History* (New York: Berg, 2006), pp. 25-40.

73. Paul Gerhardt, "Summer Song," in *Paul Gerhardt's Spiritual Songs,* trans. John Kelly (London: Alexander Strahan, 1867), p. 291.

74. Paul Gerhardt, "Thanksgiving for Gracious Sunshine," in *Spiritual Songs,* p. 300.

75. John and Charles Wesley, "Author of Life Divine," in *Hymns on the Lord's Supper* (London: H. Cock, 1751), p. 30.

76. Nathan Bangs, *A History of the Methodist Episcopal Church* (New York: T. Mason and G. Lane, 1838), pp. 134-35.

77. John Calvin, *Institutes of the Christian Religion,* 2 vols., ed. John T. McNeill, trans. Ford Lewis Battles (Philadelphia: Westminster, 1960), 3.19.9, 1:841.

78. Calvin, *Institutes,* 3.10.2, 1:720-21.

79. John Calvin, *Commentary on the Book of Psalms,* 5 vols., trans. James Anderson (Edinburgh: Calvin Translation Society, 1847), 4:155-57. See also John Calvin, *Golden Booklet of the True Christian Life* trans. Henry J. Van Andel (Grand Rapids: Baker Books, 2004), p. 86.

80. Calvin, *Psalms,* 4:157.

81. Calvin, *Golden Booklet,* p. 87.

82. Calvin, *Psalms,* 4:156.

83. Calvin, *Golden Booklet,* pp. 87-89.

84. Calvin, *Golden Booklet,* p. 89.

85. John T. McNeill, *The History and Character of Calvinism* (Oxford: Oxford University Press, 1954), p. 160.

86. John Calvin, "Catechism of the Church of Geneva," in *Calvin's Tracts, Containing Treatises on the Sacraments, Catechism of the Church of Geneva, Forms of Prayer, and Confessions of Faith,* 3 vols., trans. Henry Beveridge (Edinburgh: Calvin Translation Society, 1849), 2:89.

87. John Knox, "A Letter of Wholesome Counsel, Addressed to His Brethren in Scotland," in *The Works of John Knox,* vol. 4, ed. David Laing (Edinburgh: Johnstone and Hunter, 1855), p. 136. For Knox's use of wine in the Eucharist, see John Knox, *The First Book of Discipline,* ed. James K. Cameron (Edinburgh: St. Andrew Press, 1972), pp. 91-92. For drink as part of the Scottish minister's salary, see Knox, *Discipline,* p. 109. For the large volume of wine consumed in Edinburgh's St. Giles Cathedral under Robert Bruce, see Duncan Clark MacNicol, *Robert Bruce: Minister in the Kirk of Edinburgh* (Edinburgh: Banner of Truth Trust, 1961), p. 75.

88. Ulrich Zwingli, "Of the Clarity and Certainty of the Word of God," in *Zwingli and Bullinger*, vol. 24 of *The Library of Christian Classics*, ed. G. W. Bromiley (London: SCM, 1953), p. 75. For his warning against the "superfluity of wine," see Zwingli, "Of the Education of Youth," in *Zwingli and Bullinger*, p. 111. For his commendation of wine's use in communion, see Zwingli, "On the Lord's Supper," in *Zwingli and Bullinger*, pp. 185-238.

89. Seward bemoans the fact that no scholarly study of viticulture in medieval England has yet been done (Seward, *Monks and Wine*, p. 138). See also the helpful entry "England" in *The Oxford Companion to Wine*, ed. Jancis Robinson (Oxford: Oxford University Press, 2006).

90. See esp. Austin, *Alcohol*, p. 163. Interestingly, Mark Holt argues that the Puritans, with their rejection of church festivals and rituals, contributed to this development. See Holt, ed., *Alcohol*, p. 36.

91. John Bunyan, *The Pilgrim's Progress* (Peabody, MA: Hendrickson, 2004), p. 45.

92. Bunyan, *Pilgrim's Progress*, p. 48. Bunyan's protagonists receive more wine throughout the story: "Then said Mr. Great-Heart to Christiana and to Mercy, 'My Lord has sent each of you a bottle of wine, and also some parched corn" (p. 199). "The next they brought up was a bottle of wine, as red as blood (Deut. 32:14; Judg. 9:13; John 15:5). So Gaius said to them, 'Drink freely; this is the juice of the true vine, that makes glad the heart of God and man.' So they drank and were merry" (p. 222).

93. Bunyan, *Pilgrim's Progress*, p. 128.

94. Bunyan, *Pilgrim's Progress*, p. 127.

95. Robert Fuller, *Religion and Wine: A Cultural History of Wine Drinking in the United States* (Knoxville: University of Tennessee Press, 1996), p. 75.

96. Thomas Pinney, *A History of Wine in America: From the Beginnings to Prohibition* (Berkeley: University of California Press, 1989), p. 11. Hereafter, page references to this work appear in parentheses in the text.

97. See Fuller, *Religion and Wine*, p. 16; see esp. W. J. Rorabaugh, *The Alcoholic Republic: An American Tradition* (New York: Oxford University Press, 1979).

98. Jonathan Edwards to Esther Edwards Burr, March 28, 1753, in George S. Claghorn, ed., *Letters and Personal Writings*, vol. 16 of *The Works of Jonathan Edwards*, ed. Harry S. Stout (New Haven: Yale University Press, 1998), p. 577.

99. Thomas Jefferson to Monsieur de Neuville, December 13, 1818, in *The Writings of Thomas Jefferson*, 20 vols., ed. Andrew A. Lipscomb and Albert Ellery Bergh (Washington, DC: Thomas Jefferson Memorial Association, 1904), 15:178.

100. Thomas Jefferson to William Johnson, May 10, 1817, in *Thomas Jefferson's Garden Book*, ed. Edwin Morris Betts (Philadelphia: American Philosophical Society, 1944), p. 572.

101. Jefferson to de Neuville, in *Writings of Thomas Jefferson*, 15:178.

102. Seward, *Monks and Wine*, p. 144; see also Pinney, *Wine in America*, chap. 9.

103. Seward, *Monks and Wine*, pp. 145-50.

104. St. Francis of Assisi, "The Canticle of the Sun," available online at http://www2.webster.edu/~barrettb/canticle.htm (accessed Jan. 30, 2014).

105. Seward, *Monks and Wine*, p. 150.

106. The definition of intoxicating liquor included anything that had more than 0.5 percent of alcohol. With the Volstead Act some legal provisions were made to produce wine for religious purposes such as the Eucharist, and for medical and industrial uses. Families were

also allowed to make up to two hundred gallons annually of "fruit juices" exclusively for con-sumption in the home, effectively licensing home wine-making.

107. Fuller, *Religion and Wine*, p. 76.

108. Fuller, *Religion and Wine*, p. 82.

109. For a copy of this image, see Fuller, *Religion and Wine*, p. 86.

Chapter 3

Wine in the Lord's Supper: Christ Present in Wine

1. Jaroslav Pelikan, *The Emergence of the Catholic Tradition (100-600)*, vol. 1 of *The Christian Tradition: A History of the Development of Doctrine* (Chicago: University of Chicago Press, 1971), p. 28.

2. Joachim Jeremias, *The Eucharistic Words of Jesus* (Philadelphia: Fortress, 1977), p. 170.

3. The heresy of Gnosticism (from the Greek *gnosis*: "learned") has confronted the church throughout its existence and has remained a major threat to a Christian spirituality. The first significant theological work against Gnosticism was written in the second century by Irenaeus, entitled *Against Heresies*.

4. Early on in the tradition of the celebration of the Eucharist, the presentation of bread and wine in the Eucharist was understood to be an offering that the church brings to God as first fruits (see Deut. 26:1-11). The purpose of this offering is to acknowledge the Creator's generosity in giving the fruits of this good creation and to be grateful for it. Ireneaus, *Against Heresies*, iv. xvii.4–xviii.6. See also Dom Gregory Dix, *The Shape of the Liturgy* (New York: The Seabury Press, 1982), p. 114. Dix is a dated work on liturgy and must be read with care and dis-cernment. Thomas C. Oden, *Pastoral Theology* (San Francisco: Harper and Row, 1983), p. 121.

5. See Dix, *Liturgy*, p. 117.

6. On the frequency of the Eucharist throughout history, see Robert Taft, *Beyond East and West: Problems in Liturgical Understanding* (Washington, DC: The Pastoral Press, 1984), pp. 61-80.

7. A major point of contention became whether Christ is truly present in the elements of bread and wine. The traditional Catholic belief upholds that Christ is not only present in bread and wine but that the bread and wine in actual reality become the body and blood of Christ. This is referred to as "transubstantiation." In the Protestant tradition three major strands developed following the teachings of Martin Luther, John Calvin, and Ulrich Zwingli. Luther upheld the traditional belief of Christ's real presence in bread and wine. Calvin connects the reception of Christ to the eating of bread and wine but does not believe that Christ's body and blood are present in the bread and wine. Zwingli argued that bread and wine have a mere symbolic function, reminding us of Christ's sacrificial death. Another important point of dis-pute between Catholics and the Reformers became the question of how the celebration of the Eucharist is related to the historical death of Jesus Christ. Is it a perpetuation of Christ's sacri-fice, or is it a remembrance of this historical event? In more recent debates, the Reformation teaching, with its heavy emphasis on the gift nature of the Lord's Supper, has been challenged as it seems to eclipse the exchange dimension of the Eucharist. Are we mere recipients in the Lord's Supper, or does it include a real exchange between God and his people? For an accessible introduction to the different positions during the Reformation, see Gary Macy, *The Banquet's*

Wisdom: A Short History of the Theologies of the Lord's Supper (Akron, OH: OSL Publications, 2005), pp. 170-227. On the exchange question, see Piotr J. Malysz, "Exchange and Ecstasy: Luther's Eucharistic Theology in Light of Radical Orthodoxy's Critique of Gift and Sacrifice," *Scottish Journal of Theology* 60, no. 3 (2007): 294-308.

8. Martin Luther, "That these words of Christ, 'this is my body,' still stand firm against the fanatics," in *Luther's Works,* American Edition, 55 vols., ed. Jaroslav Pelikan and Helmut T. Lehmann (Philadelphia: Muhlenberg and Fortress; St. Louis: Concordia, 1955-1986), 37:124-25, 132. Luther refers in his argument to John 6:56: "For these who eat my flesh and drink my blood have eternal life, and I will raise them up on the last day."

9. Luther, "This is my body," p. 134. For Luther on communion wine, see T. Wengert, "Luther and Melanchthon on Consecrated Communion Wine (Eisleben 1542-43)," *Lutheran Quarterly* 15, no. 1 (2001): 24-42. For a general introduction to the early Reformers and their stance toward the body, see David Tipp, "The Image of the Body in the Formative Phases of the Protestant Reformation," in Sarah Coakley, ed., *Religion and the Body* (Cambridge, UK: Cambridge University Press, 1997), pp. 131-52.

10. John Calvin, *Institutes of the Christian Religion,* 2 vols., ed. John T. McNeill, trans. Ford Lewis Battles (Philadelphia: Westminster, 1960), 4.17.1, 2:1361.

11. See Jeremias, *Eucharistic Words,* for a careful discussion of the Passover meal as the background to the Eucharist. While some of his use of the literature is now being challenged, this work is still very important.

12. Abraham P. Bloch, *The Biblical and Historical Background of the Jewish Holy Days* (New York: Ktav Publishing House, 1978), pp. 108-9.

13. Jeremias, *Eucharistic Words,* p. 86.

14. Bloch, *Jewish Holy Days,* pp. 129, 148, 151. On the meaning of the four cups of wine, see pp. 148-49.

15. The traditional Passover celebration was not to be an occasion marked by excessive eating and drinking. The biblical sense of joy is closely tied to gratitude and is to elicit a sincere piety, a solemn awareness of our need for God (Deut. 26:5-11). See Bloch, *Jewish Holy Days,* pp. 110-11.

16. Jeremias, *Eucharistic Words,* pp. 256-58.

17. When Christ entered Jerusalem, he was greeted with lines from Psalm 118, a psalm that was recited at the end of the Passover meal, the *hallēl* (Mark 11:9; Matt. 21:9; John 12:13).

18. Craig Keener sees the Jewish Passover lamb as the primary background to this passage in John 1. See Keener, *The Gospel of John: A Commentary,* 2 vols. (Grand Rapids: Baker, 2003), 1:454.

19. Dix, *Liturgy,* p. 161.

20. For further prohibitions to consume blood, see Lev. 3:17; 7:26; 17:10-15; and Deut. 12:16, 23-25. Three times the Israelites are commanded in Lev. 17:10-15 not to consume blood because it is the center of life and therefore has the power to redeem: "For the life of the flesh is in the blood; and I have given it to you for making atonement for your lives on the altar; for, as life, it is the blood that makes atonement" (Lev. 17:11).

21. For a helpful article on the complexity of the meaning of blood in the Old Testament, see Susan Niditch, "Good Blood, Bad Blood: Multivocality, Metonymy, and Mediation in Zechariah 9," *Vetus Testamentum* 61, no. 4 (January 2011): 629-45. See also William Gilders, *Blood*

Ritual in the Hebrew Bible: Meaning and Power (Baltimore: Johns Hopkins University Press, 2004); Jacob Milgrom, *Leviticus: A Book of Ritual and Ethics* (Minneapolis: Fortress, 2004).

22. Otto Böcher, *Dämonenfurcht und Dämonenabwehr. Ein Beitrag zur Vorgeschichte der christlichen Taufe* (Stuttgart: Kohlhammer, 1972), p. 55.

23. Pliny speaks of four wine colors: white, brown, blood-red, and black. Pliny, *Natural History IV,* trans. H. Rackham, 10 vols. (Cambridge, MA: Harvard University Press, 1968), 14.11.80; see also Proverbs 23:31.

24. *The Wisdom of Ben Sira: A New Translation with Notes by Patrick W. Skehan,* trans. Patrick W. Skehan (New York: Doubleday, 1987), p. 385.

25. Pliny, *Natural History,* 14.6.58, 14.10.77, 14.21.116; see also Photina Rech, *Wine and Bread* (Chicago: Liturgy Training Publications, 2007), p. 30.

26. In warmer climates wines were stored in fired clay jars and buried in the ground while in cooler climates wine was kept in wooden barrels above ground. Pliny, *Natural History,* 14.27.132. Fired clay pots would be free of bacterial contamination, unlike modern vessels.

27. Pliny called wine "the blood of the earth" and repeatedly wrote about ancient people offering up wine to their gods. Pliny, *Natural History,* 14.6.58, 14.14.88, 14.21.117, 14.23.119.

28. See Böcher, *Dämonenfurcht,* pp. 56-57.

29. Throughout the ages it has been discussed whether it was possible to replace wine with other substances such as grape juice, beer, coffee, etc. As we shall see, a great theological loss does occur if other substances replace wine, but there are times where this substitution is necessary, such as for worshipers with addictions to alcoholic beverages.

30. See chap. 8 below on the health benefits of wine. John Calvin also emphasizes these connections (*Institutes,* 4.17.19, 2:1363).

31. Dix, *Liturgy,* p. 1. The apostle Paul uses the cognate noun *latreia* in Romans 12:1.

32. Catherine Bell, *Ritual Theory, Ritual Practice* (Oxford: Oxford University Press, 1992), p. 16.

33. See Richard Bauckham on the development of science with respect to our understanding of creation in his book *Living with Other Creatures: Green Exegesis and Theology* (Milton Keynes, UK: Paternoster, 2012), pp. 47-55.

34. For a helpful introduction to this development, see Oliver Davies, "Lost Heaven," in Oliver Davies, Paul D. Janz, and Clemens Sedmak, eds., *Transformation Theology: Church in the World* (London: T&T Clark, 2007), pp. 11-36.

35. Dietrich Bonhoeffer, *Creation and Fall: A Theological Exposition of Genesis 1-3* (Minneapolis: Fortress, 1996), p. 46. Bonhoeffer's works in general are an important corrective to this strong tendency in Protestant spirituality.

36. Bell, *Ritual Theory,* pp. 74, 91.

37. John Calvin repeatedly emphasizes that the full meaning of the Lord's Supper is incomprehensible and a "high mystery" (*Institutes,* 4.17.1-5, 2:1360-65). See also Eugene Peterson, *Christ Plays in Ten Thousand Places: A Conversation in Spiritual Theology* (Grand Rapids: Eerdmans, 2005), p. 205.

38. In this discussion I shall rely primarily on Georgia Frank's examination of the church fathers' understanding of embodiment and action in the Eucharist (Frank, "'Taste and See': The Eucharist and the Eyes of Faith in the Fourth Century," *Church History* 70, no. 4 [2001]: 619-43).

39. Cyril of Jerusalem, *Lectures on the Christian Sacraments* (New York: St. Vladimir's Seminary Press, 1951), p. 61 (4.2).

40. Cyril of Jerusalem, quoted in Frank, "Taste and See," pp. 629-30.

41. John Chrysostom, *St. John Chrysostom: Baptismal Instructions,* trans. P. W. Harkins (New York: Paulist Press, 1963), p. 60 (3.12).

42. Chrysostom, quoted in Frank, "Taste and See," p. 632.

43. I should note, however, that Cyril of Jerusalem still devalues the body in comparison to the soul when he writes that the "body is the soul's instrument, its cloak and garment" (Cyril of Jersualem, *The Works of Saint Cyril of Jerusalem,* trans. L. P. McCauley and A. A. Stephenson [Washington, DC: Catholic University of America Press, 1968], p. 131).

44. Peterson, *Christ Plays,* p. 202.

45. On alcohol abuse and addiction, see Chap. 9 below. I am in no way suggesting that people addicted to alcohol should consume wine in the Eucharist. Fortunately, many churches have recognized the importance of abstinence for recovering alcoholics and offer grape juice instead.

Chapter 4

Wine and Communal Feasting: The Joy of the Lord Is Our Strength

1. Alexander Schmemann, *For the Life of the World: Sacraments and Orthodoxy,* 2nd ed. (Crestwood, NY: St Vladmir's Seminary Press, 1988), p. 24.

2. Schmemann, *Life of the World,* pp. 53, 54.

3. Schmemann, *Life of the World,* p. 49.

4. Josef Pieper, *In Tune with the World: A Theory of Festivity* (South Bend, IN: St. Augustine's Press, 1999), p. 28.

5. Jürgen Moltmann, *Theology and Joy* (London: SCM Press, 1973), p. 33.

6. Schmemann, *Life of the World,* p. 53.

7. On the celebration of the Jewish Sabbath, see, e.g., Abraham Heschel, *The Sabbath: Its Meaning for Modern Man* (New York: Farrar, Straus, 1952), especially pp. 3-10.

8. Craig Keener, *The Gospel of John,* vol. 1 (Grand Rapids: Baker Academic, 2003), pp. 515-16.

9. Moltmann, *Theology and Joy,* p. 58. At the same time we should note that Jesus' death on the cross also reveals God's glory and painfully makes clear that our ability to glimpse God's glory comes at a great price (John 12:23-28).

10. The narrative is primarily recounted from the film itself (Gabriel Axel, *Babette's Feast,* DVD, directed by Gabriel Axel [Santa Monica, CA: MGM Home Entertainment, 2001]), though references to the novella by Karen Blixen, upon which the film is based, will be cited in quotation marks. See Karen Blixen, *Le diner de Babette* (Lausanne: La Guilde du livre, 1969).

11. Roger Scruton, "The Philosophy of Wine," in Barry C. Smith, ed., *Questions of Taste: The Philosophy of Wine* (Oxford: Signal Books, 2007), p. 15.

12. "Zu trinken ist zu beten, zu saufen ist zu sündigen."

13. Simone Weil, *Gravity and Grace* (New York: Putnam, 1952), p. 170.

14. For collections of these sayings, see Joni G. McNutt, *In Praise of Wine* (Santa Barbara: Capra Press, 1993); see also Hans-Jörg Koch, *Wein: Eine literarische Weinprobe* (Leipzig: Reclam, 2002).

15. For a helpful discussion of this, see Barry C. Smith, "The Objectivity of Tastes and Tasting," in Smith, *Questions of Taste,* pp. 41-73.

Chapter 5

Wine and Attentiveness: Tasting God, Tasting Wine

1. Pierre Poupon, quoted in Emile Peynaud, *The Taste of Wine: The Art and Science of Wine Appreciation,* trans. Michael Schuster (London: Macdonald, 1987), p. 14.

2. Jean Anthelme Brillat-Savarin, *The Physiology of Taste, or Meditations on Transcendental Gastronomy* (New York: Vintage; reprint, 2011), p. 48.

3. More recent discussions add the taste of "umami," including the taste of amino acids. Umami detects protein, sweet detects carbohydrates such as glucose and other sugars, and salt detects salt. Sour and bitter are indicative of food going bad and thus are more associated with rejection reflexes (see Mark F. Bear, Barry W. Connors, and Michael A. Paradiso, eds., *Neuroscience: Exploring the Brain* [Baltimore: Lippincott, Williams and Wilkins, 2007], p. 259). See also Carolyn Korsmeyer's helpful discussion *Making Sense of Taste* (Ithaca: Cornell University Press, 1999), pp. 75-79. She suggests that these four categories can serve as reference points to describe taste sensations.

4. Bear et al., *Neuroscience,* pp. 254-55.

5. For a more careful description, see Bear et al., *Neuroscience,* pp. 263-75.

6. Peynaud, *Taste,* p. 25.

7. Peynaud, *Taste,* p. 27.

8. See William Wordsworth, "The World Is Too Much with Us," in *William Wordsworth: The Major Works,* ed. Stephen Gill (Oxford: Oxford University Press, 1984), p. 270.

9. Constace Classen, David Howes, and Anthony Synnott, "Artificial Flavours," in Carolyn Korsmeyer, ed., *The Taste Culture Reader: Experiencing Food and Drink* (Oxford: Berg, 2005), p. 339.

10. For the development of foods and taste since the 1950s, see Robert Jütte, *A History of the Senses: From Antiquity to Cyberspace* (Cambridge: Polity, 2005), pp. 253-64.

11. Classen et al., "Artificial Flavours," pp. 340-41. For a more extended discussion, see Constance Classen, David Howes, and Anthony Synnott, "The Aroma of the Commodity: The Commercialization of Smell," in *Aroma: The Cultural History of Smell* (London: Routledge, 1997), pp. 180-205.

12. Jütte, *The Senses,* p. 262.

13. Barolo has become "glocalized" and is now grown globally.

14. Democritus, *Fragment* 11, quoted in Jütte, *The Senses,* p. 33.

15. Aristotle, *De Anima,* trans. D. W. Hamlyn (Oxford: Clarendon Press, 1968), p. 69 (3.10).

16. Aristotle, *De Anima,* p. 56 (3.3).

17. Charles Burnett, "The Superiority of Taste," *Journal of the Warburg and Courtauld Institutes* 54 (1991): 230; Jütte, *The Senses,* p. 68; C. M. Woolgar, *The Senses in Late Medieval England* (New Haven: Yale University Press, 2006), p. 23; Korsmeyer, *Taste,* pp. 19-24.

18. Aristotle, *De Anima,* p. 34 (2.9), p. 41 (2.11). Some see in Aristotle a certain ambivalence on this subject. See Jütte, *The Senses,* p. 69.

19. Thomas Aquinas, *A Commentary on Aristotle's De Anima,* trans. Robert Pasnau (New Haven: Yale University Press, 1999), p. 260.

20. Thomas Aquinas, *Summa Theologica* 1a2ae.27.1ad 3, quoted in Neil Campbell, "Aquinas' Reasons for the Aesthetic Irrelevance of Tastes and Smells," *British Journal of Aesthetics* 36, no. 2 (1996): 168.

21. What Aquinas actually means by "less cognitive" is a difficult question. Campbell argues that "[t]he key to understanding Aquinas . . . lies in recognizing the role played by the forms in the perception of beauty — particularly in the case of *claritas*. I propose that Aquinas thinks some senses are more cognitively complex than others are because, relative to other senses lower down the scale, they convey the form of the thing in a purer manner since there is less matter involved in the actual process of sensation itself. Schematically, we could say the following: the less matter the clearer the form, the clearer the form the more *claritas,* and the more *claritas* the more beauty" (Campbell, "Aquinas' Reasons," p. 171). In general, "cognitive" is a difficult concept to define and has been much misunderstood.

22. See Korsmeyer, *Taste,* pp. 26-37. Surprisingly, Roger Scruton, author of *I Drink Therefore I Am: A Philosopher's Guide to Wine,* does not consider drinking wine as an aesthetic experience and continues Aquinas's devaluation of the sense of taste in regard to aesthetics. See Roger Scruton, "The Philosophy of Wine," in Barry C. Smith, ed., *Questions of Taste: The Philosophy of Wine* (Oxford: Signal Books, 2007), pp. 1-20. Scruton's discussion is somewhat confusing. Though he refuses to call wine-tasting an aesthetic experience, his discussion of it comes very close to that. He calls it an experience of intoxication where the drinker of wine is intoxicated by the beauty of the wine, and he compares this experience to the aesthetic experience of seeing a landscape or hearing a line of poetry. Scruton, *Questions of Taste,* pp. 1-2.

23. Jütte, *The Senses,* p. 71.

24. Jütte, *The Senses,* pp. 74, 78-83; see also Woolgar, *The Senses,* pp. 111-12. On fasting practices, see Paul Freedman, ed., *Food: The History of Taste* (Berkeley: University of California Press, 2007), pp. 165-67.

25. Laura Giannetti, "Of Eels and Pears: A Sixteenth-Century Debate on Taste, Temperance, and the Pleasures of the Senses," in Wietse de Boer and Christine Göttler, eds., *Religion and the Senses in Early Modern Europe* (Leiden: Brill, 2013), p. 294.

26. Burnett, "The Superiority of Taste," pp. 234-35.

27. Peter Dronke, "Platonic-Christian Allegories in the Homilies of Hildegard of Bingen," in Haijo Jan Westra, ed., *From Athens to Chartres: Neoplatonism and Medieval Thought: Studies in Honour of Edouard Jeauneau* (Leiden: Brill, 1992), pp. 392-93.

28. For a careful discussion of this document, see Burnett, "The Superiority of Taste," pp. 231-34.

29. Burnett, "The Superiority of Taste," pp. 233-34.

30. Peynaud, *Taste of Wine,* p. 22.

31. For a visual image of this process, see Bear et al., *Neuroscience,* p. 260. For an accessible account of this complex process, see Gordon M. Shepherd, *Neurogastronomy: How the Brain Creates Flavor and Why It Matters* (New York: Columbia University Press, 2012), pp. 156-61.

32. Shepherd, *Neurogastronomy,* p. 159. While Shepherd does not single out wine-tasting in particular, his discussion is easily transferable to the realm of wine-tasting.

33. See Shepherd, *Neurogastronomy,* chap. 20. See also Bear et al., *Neuroscience,* pp. 271, 582, 758.

34. See, e.g., Richard Doty, "The Olfactory Vector Hypothesis of Neurodegenerative Disease: Is It Viable?" *Annals of Neurobiology* 63, no. 1 (2008): 7-15.

35. Classen et al., "Artifical Flavours," p. 340.

36. Marcel Proust, *Swann's Way*, in *Remembrance of Things Past*, trans. C. K. Scott Moncrieff and Terence Kilmartin, 3 vols. (New York: Random House, 1981), 1:50-51. For an interpretation of Proust's experience and literary reflections, see Shepherd, *Neurogastronomy*, pp. 174-81.

37. On the sense of smell, e.g., see Susan Ashbrook Harvey, *Scenting Salvation: Ancient Christianity and the Olfactory Imagination* (Berkeley: University of California Press, 2006); on food and eating, see Angel F. Méndez-Montoya, *The Theology of Food: Eating and the Eucharist* (Chichester, UK: Wiley-Blackwell, 2012); on taste, see Korsmeyer, *Taste*, esp. chap. 4.

38. Campbell, after carefully considering Aquinas's argument regarding the senses and aesthetic experience, argues for the inclusion of taste and touch into aesthetic experiences (Campbell, "Aquinas' Reasons," pp. 173-75). See also Korsmeyer, *Taste*, pp. 68-145; Tim Crane, "Wine as an Aesthetic Object," in Barry C. Smith, ed., *Questions of Taste: The Philosophy of Wine* (Oxford: Signal Books, 2007), pp. 141-55; Douglas Burnham and Ole Martin Skilleås, *The Aesthetics of Wine* (Oxford: Wiley-Blackwell, 2012); Cain Todd, *The Philosophy of Wine: A Case for Truth, Beauty and Intoxication* (Durham, UK: Acumen, 2010).

39. Tasting wine is a popular theme in the philosophy of wine because it touches on issues of beauty, consciousness, language, memory, and place (soil), and because the enjoyment of wine has traditionally always been associated with contemplation and the experience of the divine.

40. Peynaud, *Taste*, p. 14. Hereafter, page references to this work appear in parentheses within the text.

41. Once a region has received the American Viticultural Area (AVA) status, vintners can add that to the label if at least 85 percent of grapes used to produce the wine come from that AVA.

42. Korsmeyer, *Taste*, p. 79. Over time, physiologists have added various other categories, such as, e.g., metallic flavor and oiliness. See Korsmeyer, *Taste*, pp. 75-81.

43. Even the scientist Alex Maltman admits that geological factors might have a role in giving "typicity" to a wine, but he cautions us not to come to easy conclusions in this regard. The influence of geological factors is indirect, very complex, and extremely difficult to unravel from a scientific perspective. He suggests that it is most likely the combination of soil temperature, slope, and drainage that will have some effect on the taste of the wine (Maltman, "The Role of Vineyard Geology in Wine Typicity," *Journal of Wine Research* 19, no. 1 [2008]: 6). Vintners, on the other hand, working day in and day out with the land, feel more comfortable speaking about how the soil and geology might affect the wine, indirect and complex as this influence might be.

44. Pliny, *Natural History IV*, trans. H. Rackham, 10 vols. (Cambridge, MA: Harvard University Press, 1968), 14.58.

45. Adapted from Gerard Manley Hopkins's poem "God's Grandeur," in *God's Grandeur and Other Poems* (Mineola, NY: Dover, 1995), p. 15.

Chapter 6

The Vintner as (Practicing) Theologian: Finder or Maker?

1. Benjamin Lewin, *Wine Myths and Reality* (Dover: Vendange Press, 2010), p. 44.

2. Robert E. White, *Understanding Vineyard Soils* (Oxford: Oxford University Press, 2009), pp. 13-14.

3. White, *Vineyard Soils*, p. 17.

4. Even a writer like White, who explores the scientific dimension of soil, admits to this and calls the concept of *terroir* an "untellable story" (*Vineyard Soils*, p. 26). Benjamin Lewin is puzzled that an oenologist cannot scientifically explain his insight into viticulture and wine-making (*Wine Myths*, p. 45). For him, only what can be proven scientifically can be called real; insights of centuries of experience and tradition are "myths" if they are not substantiated by science.

5. For a more detailed description of how this happens, see White, *Vineyard Soils*, pp. 150-54.

6. White defines organic viticulture as follows: "Organic viticulture aims to produce quality wine without the use of artificial fertilizers or synthetic chemicals. To the maximum extent possible, an organic system must operate as a closed system, with external inputs used only on an 'as-needed' basis. The broad term 'organic' includes biodynamic systems, but biodynamic viticulture is recognized as having additional requirements to a simple organic system. These requirements include timing operations to coincide with phases of the moon and using special preparations . . . that are not fertilizers but are intended to stimulate the soil's biological activity and root growth. . . . Certified organic production means that grapes are grown without insecticides, herbicides, fungicides, and chemical fertilizers, other than those approved by the certifying agency, using cultural practices that minimize adverse effects on the soil and wider environment. Genetically modified plant material cannot be grown, nor can genetically modified yeast be used in fermentation" (*Vineyard Soils*, pp. 90-92). Organic viticulture, however, still permits the use of copper treatment and sulfur.

7. White, *Vineyard Soils*, p. 154.

8. For an English translation of this beautiful hymn, see http://www.hymnary.org/hymn/PGSS1867/63.

9. Begin a conversation with your local wine-shop owner and ask him or her for blog recommendations.

10. Biodynamic agriculture is based on the teachings of Rudolf Steiner (1861-1925), especially his lectures delivered in 1924, now entitled "The Agricultural Course." While many take issue with the esoteric and obscure aspects of his teaching, Steiner's emphasis on using sustainable agricultural practices profoundly shaped the organic movement worldwide, and it is now embraced by an increasing number of vintners around the world. With the rise of the scientific method, agricultural practices, like many other spheres of human life, were dramatically transformed during Steiner's lifetime. Scientists discovered how to produce synthetic nitrogen fertilizer and began using it to increase crop yield. German farmers started noticing some alarming degenerative developments in both the plant and animal world and turned to Rudolf Steiner for help. Steiner saw the earth as a living organism and understood that we live in a finely balanced ecosystem that humans need to protect and

sustain. He emphasized the importance of cultivating a healthy soil life in which plants could thrive, remain healthy, and produce a good and nutritious crop. Steiner permitted only the use of organic compost (such as humus) rather than synthetic fertilizers. What is remarkable about some of the most recent agricultural scientific research is that it focuses on some aspects that are similar to Steiner's emphases: the health of the soil and how roots can more efficiently draw water and nutrients from it. See Rudolf Steiner, *The Agricultural Course* (London: Rudolf Steiner Press, 2004). For a discussion of Steiner's thought with respect to viticulture, see Beverly Blanning, *Biodynamics in Wine* (London: The International Wine and Food Society, 2010).

11. See "Mondavi," in Jancis Robinson, ed., *The Oxford Companion to Wine* (Oxford: Oxford University Press, 2006), p. 448.

Chapter 7

Technology, Spirituality, and Wine

1. I owe these reflections to Dr. David Stearns, professional software developer, historian, sociologist of technology, and lay theologian. See also Carl Mitcham, *Thinking Through Technology: The Path between Engineering and Philosophy* (Chicago: University of Chicago Press, 1994), pp. 117-23, 157-59.

2. For a survey of the philosophy of technology, see Mitcham, *Technology*. On the sociology of technology, see Donald MacKenzie and Judy Wajcman, eds., *The Social Shaping of Technology*, 2nd ed. (Maidenhead, UK: Open University Press, 1999).

3. Mitcham, *Technology*, p. 107.

4. For another account that is more favorable toward globalization, see "The McWine Conspiracy," in Mike Veseth, *Wine Wars: The Curse of the Blue Nun, the Miracle of Two Buck Chuck, and the Revenge of the Terroirists* (Lanham, MD: Rowman and Littlefield, 2011), chap. 11.

5. Timothy Fry, ed., *The Rule of St. Benedict in Latin and English with Notes* (Collegeville, MN: Liturgical Press, 1981), 31.10, pp. 228-29.

6. Few books on the Cistercians explore their relationship to the land. The following is a notable exception: Eckhart Meffert, *Die Zisterzienser und Bernhard von Clairvaux: Ihre spirituellen Impulse und die Verchristlichung der Erde* (Stuttgart: Engel and Co, 2010).

7. Roger Scruton, *I Drink Therefore I Am: A Philosopher's Guide to Wine* (London: Continuum, 2009), p. 33.

8. Scruton, *I Drink*, pp. 35-36.

9. Social anthropologists take a more critical stance toward Burgundy and their social construction of the concept of *terroir* for marketing purposes. See, e.g., Marion Demossier, "Beyond *Terroir*: Territorial Construction, Hegemonic Discourse, and French Wine Culture," *Journal of the Royal Anthropological Institute* 17 (2011): 685-705.

10. Emile Peynaud pointed out that only about 5 percent of Bordeaux wines around the Gironde are classified wines. It is a common mistake to identify a region's production with that of its top wines. Emile Peynaud, *The Taste of Wine: The Art and Science of Wine Appreciation* (London: Macdonald, 1987), p. 89.

11. See Tyler Colman, "Who Controls Your Palate?" in *Wine Politics: How Governments, Environmentalists, Mobsters, and Critics Influence the Wines We Drink* (Berkeley: University of

California Press, 2008), pp. 117-18. Jonathan Nossiter expresses similar concerns: see Nossiter, *Liquid Memory* (New York: Farrar, Straus and Giroux, 2009), pp. 188-91. Even Paul Lukas, much more sympathetic to the global wine industry than I am, had to admit in his recent history of wine that these global wines "taste surprisingly similar these days" (Lukas, *Inventing Wine: A New History of One of the World's Most Ancient Pleasures* [New York: Norton, 2012], p. 289). In his optimistic stance toward globalization, he criticizes more suspicious voices for treating the issues surrounding globalization in moral terms (p. 288). Lukas does not seem convinced that ethical questions should be raised when it comes to questions of globalization. He does not seem to understand that matter, including wine, has moral and ethical implications. See Mitcham, *Thinking Through Technology*, pp. 132-33.

12. David Bird, *Understanding Wine Technology* (San Francisco: The Wine Appreciation Guild, 2002), p. 60.

13. See Veseth's discussion of these supermarket chains in *Wine Wars*, pp. 51-77.

14. It is rather interesting and disturbing that globalized brands try to reassert their "localness" in their marketing and advertising, giving the consumer the impression that they are buying something "local." Big corporations recognize the attraction of the local artisans and use the image for their marketing — deceptively so.

15. This critique despite the fact that globalization has also helped to develop the global palate. Mike Veseth points out that the wine choices in today's supermarkets have increased rapidly (Veseth, *Wine Wars*, pp. 27-36). But given the fact that the average consumer in the U.S. spends between eight and ten dollars for a bottle of wine, how much variety and quality does one actually get for that price?

16. Veseth, *Wine Wars*, p. 6.

17. See Colman, *Wine Politics*, pp. 118-20. For a movement in California that tries to resist this trend, see: http://www.rarewineco.com/articles/historic-vineyards-society-california/.

18. White, *Vineyard Soils*, p. 55.

19. See Veseth, *Wine Wars*, pp. 48-49.

20. See Colman, "Who Controls Your Palate?" pp. 103-23.

21. Veseth, *Wine Wars*, p. 189.

22. There are still areas where ungrafted vines are grown, such as, e.g., Chile, Cyprus, parts of Australia, and the Mosel valley in Germany.

23. Bird, *Understanding Wine Technology*, p. 9.

24. Jamie Goode and Sam Harrop, *Authentic Wine: Towards Natural and Sustainable Winemaking* (Berkeley: University of California Press, 2011), p. 177.

25. For a nuanced discussion of the general question of wine manipulation and the role of modern technology, see Jamie Goode, *The Science of Wine: From Vine to Glass* (Los Angeles: University of California Press, 2005), pp. 94-99. For a discussion of yeast cultures in particular, see Goode and Harrop, *Authentic Wine*, pp. 169-81.

26. The traditional view understands wine (i.e., grape wine) as a beverage produced via alcoholic fermentation of juice from freshly harvested grapes only.

27. There are many other artifacts and practices that could be discussed here; see Goode, *The Science of Wine*, pp. 109-14.

28. See esp. Mitcham, *Technology*, pp. 183-90.

29. Mitcham, *Technology*, p. 190.

30. The technical term for it is "osmotic transport."

31. Ted Lemon, personal correspondence with author after the interview.

32. While these reflections are taken from my interview with Ted Lemon, he has also written on the subject matter. See Goode and Harrop, *Authentic Wine,* pp. 146-48.

Chapter 8
Wine and Its Health Benefits

1. For a historical overview, see Salvatore P. Lucia, *A History of Wine as Therapy* (Philadelphia: Lippincott, 1963). In this section I shall rely on this text extensively; hereafter, page references to this work appear in parentheses in the text.

2. Hippocrates, *Ulcers* 8.1 (Potter, LCL).

3. Xenophon, *Banquet,* cited in Lucia, *Wine as Therapy,* pp. 40-41.

4. *The Dialogues of Plato,* quoted in Lucia, *Wine as Therapy,* p. 41.

5. Pliny, *Natural History IV,* 14.19.

6. Roberto Margotta, *An Illustrated History of Medicine* (Middlesex: The Hamlyn Publishing Group, 1967), p. 99.

7. See also Hugh Johnson, *The Story of Wine* (London: Mitchell Beazley, 1989), p. 62.

8. Anne Morey, personal interview with the author, June 25, 2014.

9. For a brief discussion, see Lucia, *Wine as Therapy,* pp. 72-87.

10. Andrew Crislip carefully outlines this development in *From Monastery to Hospital: Christian Monasticism and the Transformation of Health Care in Late Antiquity* (Ann Arbor: University of Michigan Press, 2005).

11. For a discussion of how the sick were and were not taken care of in Greco-Roman times, see Crislip, *From Monastery to Hospital,* pp. 42-50. There seems to have been little regard for the poor and destitute.

12. For a brief overview of early Christianity and Christians' concern for the poor, desolate, and sick, see Crislip, *From Monastery to Hospital,* pp. 50-55.

13. Crislip, *From Monastery to Hospital,* pp. 64-67.

14. Timothy Fry, ed., *The Rule of St. Benedict in Latin and English with Notes* (Collegeville, MN: Liturgical Press, 1981), chap. 36, p. 235.

15. See Crislip, *From Monastery to Hospital,* pp. 100-142.

16. Dieter Gekle, *Der Wein in der Heilkunde: Von der Antike bis zur Gegenwart* (Würzburg: Weinbruderschaft Franken e.V., 1992), p. 11.

17. For a discussion of the first two infirmaries, see Ekkehard Meffert, *Die Zisterziener und Bernhard von Clairvaux: Ihre spirituellen Impulse und die Verchristlichung der Erde Europas* (Stuttgart: Verlag Engel, 2010), pp. 222-30.

18. John Henderson, *The Renaissance Hospital* (New Haven: Yale University Press, 2006), quoted in John Varriano, *Wine: A Cultural History* (London: Reaktion Books, 2010), p. 90.

19. Varriano, *A Cultural History,* p. 89.

20. See Pam Elson, "Hospices de Beaune — the Hôtel-Dieu," burgundytoday.com, HYPERLINK http://www.burgundytoday.com/historic-places/museums/hospice-beaune.htm (accessed Oct. 29, 2014) for a short history of this astonishing hospice for the poor.

21. Another beautiful example is St. Giles's Hospital in Norwich, England. See Carole Raw-

cliffe, *Medicine for the Soul: The Life, Death and Resurrection of an English Medieval Hospital: St. Giles's, Norwich, c. 1249-1550* (Stroud, UK: Sutton Publishing, 1999).

22. Meffert, *Die Zisterziener*, p. 223; Gekle, *Wein in der Heilkunde*, p. 12.

23. Pierre C. Lile, *Histoire Médicale Du Vin* (Chaintré: Oenoplurimedia, 2002), p. 102. For a reprint, see Andrew Forbes, Daniel Henley, and David Henley, *Health and Well Being: A Medieval Guide* (Chiang Mai, Thailand: Cognoscenti Books, 2013).

24. Moses ben Maimon, *The Preservation of Youth, Essays on Health,* quoted in Lucia, *Wine as Therapy,* p. 84.

25. Lucia, *Wine as Therapy,* pp. 85-86. For a helpful introduction to Islam and wine, see Johnson, *Story of Wine,* pp. 98-108.

26. Varriano, *Wine: A Cultural History,* p. 88.

27. *Hildegard von Bingen's Physica: The Complete English Translation of Her Classic Work on Health and Healing,* trans. Priscilla Throop (Rochester, VT: Healing Arts Press, 1998), p. 6.

28. Hildegard, *Physica,* pp. 16, 19, 59, 100.

29. Hildegard, *Physica,* pp. 110, 132, 140-41, 146, 153, 155, 166. In the index of the book, the entry "wine" has by far the longest list of references and indicates that Hildegard, too, prescribed wine more than any other therapeutic agent. See also Gekle, *Wein in Der Heilkunde,* p. 12.

30. Gekle, *Wein in der Heilkunde,* p. 13; Lile, *Histoire Médicale du Vin,* pp. 41-42; Lucia, *Wine as Therapy,* pp. 101-9.

31. Lile, *Histoire Médicale Vin,* p. 41.

32. Gekle, *Wein in der Heilkunde,* p. 27.

33. The English title of the film is *Vision: From the Life of Hildegard von Bingen.*

34. It is important to note that there are no long-term, randomized, controlled trials on the risks and benefits of alcohol consumption. Much information on this subject is derived from observational studies, which are considered a lower level of evidence. It remains possible that some of the health benefits and risks of alcohol consumption represent associations that are unrelated to alcohol consumption. However, short-term trials have confirmed the beneficial effects of alcohol consumption on cardiovascular risk factors.

35. S. Renaud and M. de Lorgeril, "Wine, Alcohol, Platelets, and the French Paradox for Coronary Heart Disease," *Lancet* 339, no. 8808 (June 20, 1992): 1523-26.

36. J. H. O'Keefe et al., "Alcohol and Cardiovascular Health: The Razor-Sharp Double-Edged Sword," *Journal of the American College of Cardiology* 50, no. 11 (2007): 1009-14. In these studies one portion of alcohol was standardized as 355 milliliters of beer, 148 milliliters of wine, and 44 milliliters of distilled spirits.

37. For a summary of recent scientific research on this subject, see K. Reynolds et al., "Alcohol Consumption and Risk of Stroke: A Meta-analysis," *Journal of the American Medical Association* 289 (2003): 579-88.

38. Of the many existing studies, see, e.g., M. J. Thun et al., "Alcohol Consumption and Mortality among Middle-aged and Elderly U.S. Adults," *New England Journal of Medicine* 337 (1997): 1705-14. A study in Great Britain suggests that abstention may be a specific risk factor for all-cause mortality. See J. C. Duffy, "Alcohol Consumption and All-cause Mortality," *International Journal of Epidemiology* 24, no. 1 (1995): 100-105.

39. J. M. Gaziano et al., "Moderate Alcohol Intake, Increased Levels of High-Density Lipoprotein and Its Subfractions, and Decreased Risk of Myocardial Infarction," *New England Journal of Medicine* 329 (1993): 1829-34.

40. Yuko Miyagi, Kunihisa Miwa, and Hiroshi Inoue, "Inhibition of Human Low-Density Lipoprotein Oxidation by Flavonoids in Red Wine and Grape Juice," *American Journal of Cardiology* 80, no. 12 (1997): 1627-31.

41. L. M. Blanco-Colio et al., "Red Wine Intake Prevents Nuclear Factor-kB Activation in Peripheral Blood Mononuclear Cells of Healthy Volunteers during Postprandial Lipemia," *Circulation* 102 (2000): 1020-26.

42. See, e.g., L. Xia et al., "Resveratrol Reduces Endothelial Progenitor Cells Senescence through Augmentation of Telomerase Activity by Akt-dependent Mechanisms," *British Journal of Pharmacology* 155, no. 3 (2008): 387-94.

43. J. A. Baur et al., "Resveratrol Improves Health and Survival of Mice on a High-calorie Diet," *Nature* 444, no. 7117 (2006): 337-42. It must be noted, however, that resveratrol supplements are currently not recommended.

44. See, e.g., Curt E. Harper et al., "Genistein and Resveratrol, Alone and in Combination, Suppress Prostate Cancer in SV-40 Tag Rats," *The Prostate* 69, no. 15 (2009): 1668-82. See also K. W. Singletary and S. M. Gapstur, "Alcohol and Breast Cancer: Review of Epidemiologic Experimental Evidence and Potential Mechanisms," *Journal of the American Medical Association* 286, no. 17 (2001): 2143-51.

45. M. Stampfer et al., "Effects of Moderate Alcohol Consumption on Cognitive Function in Women," *New England Journal of Medicine* 352 (2005): 245-53.

46. See the compilation of data on current research into the health benefits of alcohol by Professor David Hanson, "Alcohol: Problems and Solutions: Health," Sociology Department of the State University of New York, Potsdam, HYPERLINK http://www2.potsdam.edu/alcohol/AlcoholAndHealth.html http://www2.potsdam.edu/alcohol/AlcoholAndHealth.html#.VBF2eBZbxg0 (accessed Oct. 29, 2014). See also O'Keefe et al., "Alcohol and Cardiovascular Health," 1009-14; Lucia, *Wine as Therapy*, pp. 188-91, 201, 206-7; and Hans Wagner, *Wein: Heilkraft der Natur* (München: Ludwig Verlag, 2000).

47. Arnold of Villanova, quoted in Lucia, *Wine as Therapy*, p. 103.

48. Louis Pasteur, quoted in Lucia, *Wine as Therapy*, p. 175.

Chapter 9

Wine and the Abuse of Alcohol:
Rescuing Wine from the Gluttons for the Contemplatives

1. Ben Sira, *The Wisdom of Ben Sira: A New Translation with Notes by Patrick W. Skehan*, trans. Patrick W. Skehan (New York: Doubleday, 1987), p. 385.

2. Peter M. Miller, ed., *Principles of Addiction: Comprehensive Addictive Behaviors and Disorders*, vol. 1 (San Diego: Academic Press, 2013). The first of this three-volume series lists and discusses each addiction.

3. Such readers suggest that the Hebrew/Greek words used in the Bible mostly refer to grape juice rather than wine, especially when the verses encourage the consumption of wine. One of the first voices in the twentieth century is R. P. Teachout, "The Use of 'Wine' in the Old Testament" (Ph.D. diss., Dallas Theological Seminary, 1979). Teachout does not seem to be aware of the French studies of his subject matter, e.g., Paul Lebeau, *Le vin nouveau du royaume: étude exégétique et patristique sur la parole eschatologique de Jésus à la Cène* (Paris: Desclée de Brouwer,

1966). Another book arguing for a biblical prohibition of the use of alcohol is Samuele Bacchiocchi, *Wine in the Bible: A Biblical Study on the Use of Alcoholic Beverages* (Berrien Springs, MI: Biblical Perspectives, 1989). Neither Teachout's nor Bacchiochi's arguments can stand the test of historical critical research, including archaeological studies on the cultural world of the Ancient Near East, Palestine in particular. See, e.g., Patrick E. McGovern, *Ancient Wine: The Search for the Origins of Viniculture* (Princeton, NJ: Princeton University Press, 2003). Recent discoveries of ancient wine cellars in Palestine reveal once again how important wine was in the Ancient Near East, including Palestine. None of the scholarly Hebrew and Greek dictionaries available in the German, Italian, French, or English languages supports such readings. For those interested in pursuing this debate, the following scholarly Hebrew and Greek theological lexica and their discussions of יין (*yyn*, Hebrew for wine) and οἶνος (*oinos*, Greek for wine) should shed considerable light on the issue: G. J. Botterweck and H. Ringgren, eds., *Theological Dictionary of the Old Testament* (Grand Rapids: Eerdmans, 1990); R. L. Harris, G. L. Archer Jr., and B. K. Waltke, *Theological Wordbook of the Old Testament*, 2 vols. (Chicago: Moody Publishers, 2003); W. Bauer, *A Greek-English Lexicon of the New Testament and Other Early Christian Literature* (Chicago: University of Chicago Press, 2001); H. G. Liddell and R. Scott, *A Greek-English Lexicon* (Oxford: Oxford University Press, 1945).

4. Martin Luther, WA 10/III (my translation).

5. In the Christian tradition, gluttony refers to the problem of overindulgence in and overconsumption of food and drink and is considered one of the seven deadly sins.

6. Bruce K. Alexander, *The Globalization of Addiction: A Study in Poverty of the Spirit* (Oxford: Oxford University Press, 2008), p. 40.

7. Substance Abuse and Mental Health Services Administration, *Results from the 2012 National Survey on Drug Use and Health: Summary of National Findings*, NSDUH Series H-46, HHS Publication No. (SMA) 13-4795 (Rockville, MD: Substance Abuse and Mental Health Services Administration, 2013).

8. The 2010 NSDUH survey includes state-by-state statistics on alcohol use, binge-drinking, and illicit drug use broken down by age. See http://oas.samhsa.gov/2k8state/Ch5.pdf (accessed Oct. 30, 2014).

9. See National Institute on Drug Abuse (NIDA), "DrugFacts: Nationwide Trends," http://www.drugabuse.gov/publications/drugfacts/nationwide-trends (accessed Oct. 30, 2014).

10. NIDA, "DrugFacts."

11. H. D. Holder, *Alcohol and the Community: A Systems Approach to Prevention* (Cambridge, UK: Cambridge University Press, 1998), p. 42.

12. U.S. Department of Health and Human Services, Substance Abuse and Mental Health Administration, *National Household Survey on Drug Abuse, 1997* (Washington, DC: DHHS 1998); J. W. Wright, ed., *The New York Times 2000 Almanac* (New York: Penguin, 1999), p. 398.

13. Health and Social Care Information Centre (HSCIC), *Statistics on Alcohol: England 2014*, available online at http://www.hscic.gov.uk/catalogue/PUB15483/alc-eng-2014-rep.pdf (accessed Nov. 4, 2014).

14. Jürgen Rehm et al., *Alcohol Consumption, Alcohol Dependence and Attributable Burden of Disease in Europe: Potential Gains from Effective Interventions for Alcohol Dependence* (Centre for Addiction and Mental Health, 2012), pp. 55-58. Available online: http://www.amphora project.net/w2box/data/AMPHORA%20Reports/CAMH_Alcohol_Report_Europe_2012.pdf (accessed Oct. 30, 2014).

15. Tian Po Sumatri Oei and Penelope Anne Hasking, "Alcohol Use Disorders," in *Prin-

ciples of Addiction: Comprehensive Addictive Behaviors and Disorders, vol. 1 (Waltham, MA: Academic Press, 2013), p. 655.

16. Oei and Hasking, "Alcohol Use Disorders," p. 647.

17. Oei and Hasking, "Alcohol Use Disorders," pp. 647-49.

18. The following discussion relies heavily on Miriam C. Fenton, Christina Aivadyan, and Deborah Hasin, "Epidemiology of Addiction," in Miller, *Principles of Addiction,* vol. 1, pp. 23-39.

19. Brenda Forster and Jeffrey Colman Salloway, eds., *The Socio-Cultural Matrix of Alcohol and Drug Use: A Sourcebook of Patterns and Factors* (Lewiston, NY: Edwin Mellen, 1990), pp. 258-59.

20. A. Verdejo-Garcia, M. J. Fernandez-Serrano, and J. Tirapu-Ustarroz, "Denial and Lack of Awareness in Substance Dependence: Insights from the Neuropsychology of Addiction," in Miller, *Principles of Addiction,* vol. 1, pp. 77-86.

21. Patricia Jones-Witters and Weldon L. Witters, *Drugs and Society: A Biological Perspective* (Monterey, CA: Wadsworth Health Sciences, 1983), p. 2, cited in Forster and Salloway, *The Socio-Cultural Matrix,* pp. 2-3. The studies collected in this volume were conducted in the United States, Israel, Australia, and the Netherlands.

22. For research that confirms this, see Forster and Salloway, eds., *The Socio-Cultural Matrix,* pp. 3, 123, 558; see also David J. Hanson, *Preventing Alcohol Abuse: Alcohol, Culture, and Control* (London: Praeger, 1995), pp. 32-36, 39, 50-51.

23. Hanson, *Preventing Alcohol Abuse,* pp. 75-78.

24. Hanson, *Preventing Alcohol Abuse,* p. 78.

25. Ernest Hemingway, *A Moveable Feast* (New York: Scribner, 1964; reprint: 2009), p. 142.

26. Forster and Salloway, eds., *The Socio-Cultural Matrix,* pp. 12-22, 316. One study specifically highlights the role and influence of the state and its political and economic organizations on alcohol use (see also pp. 498-519, 566-69).

27. Forster and Salloway, eds., *The Socio-Cultural Matrix,* p. 94.

28. Forster and Salloway, eds., *The Socio-Cultural Matrix,* pp. 265-66.

29. Alexander, *Globalization of Addiction,* pp. 57-59.

30. Alexander, *Globalization of Addiction,* pp. 60-61. The Jewish philosopher Martin Buber recognized this early in the twentieth century, and his classic book *I and Thou* explores this dynamic in some detail. See Martin Buber, *I and Thou* (New York: Scribner, 1958).

31. Many have found Gerald May's book *Addiction and Grace: Love and Spirituality in the Healing of Addictions* (San Francisco: Harper and Row, 1988) very helpful in their battle against addiction.

32. George E. Vaillant, *The Natural History of Alcoholism Revisited* (Cambridge, MA: Harvard University Press, 1995); Alexander, *Globalization of Addiction,* pp. 255-69, 294-99; Geoffrey Lyons, Frank Deane, and Peter Kelly, "Faith-Based Substance Abuse Programs," in *Interventions for Addiction: Comprehensive Addictive Behaviors and Disorders,* vol. 3, ed. Peter M. Miller (San Diego: Academic Press, 2013), pp. 147-53. It is difficult to estimate the recovery rate of such groups, since they are anonymous and follow-up periods are often rather short. Some research, however, has shown that they are most successful in conjunction with other treatments, such as hospitalization and the use of other alcohol treatment centers.

33. William Cavanaugh, *Being Consumed: Economics and Christian Desire* (Grand Rapids: Eerdmans, 2008), p. 5.

34. Cavanaugh, *Being Consumed,* p. 6.

35. Alistair McFadyen, *Bound to Sin: Abuse, Holocaust and the Christian Doctrine of Sin* (Cambridge, UK: Cambridge University Press, 2000), p. 46.

36. McFadyen explores how a Christian doctrine of sin could relate to such complex pathological dynamics as sexual abuse of children and the Holocaust (*Bound to Sin,* esp. pp. 57-130).

37. R. Plantinga, T. Thompson, and M. Lundberg, *An Introduction to Christian Theology* (Cambridge, UK: Cambridge University Press, 2010), p. 203.

38. Cavanaugh, *Being Consumed,* pp. 16-17. Cavanaugh here relies on such studies as Richard Ott, *Creating Demand* (Burr Ridge, IL: Irwin Professional Publishing, 1992); Erik Larson, *The Naked Consumer: How Our Private Lives Become Public Commodities* (New York: Henry Holt, 1992); and Michael Budde, *The Magic Kingdom of God: Christianity and Global Culture Industries* (Boulder, CO: Westview Press, 1997).

39. See, e.g., David Lewis and Darren Bridger, "Market Researchers Make Increasing Use of Brain Imaging," *Advances in Clinical Neuroscience and Rehabilitation* 5, no. 3 (2005): 36-37. Both authors work for a neuromarketing research consultancy.

40. McFadyen, *Bound to Sin,* pp. 133, 248. McFadyen suggests that we can understand these situational and pathological dynamics that shape our lives as an outworking of original sin. He writes: "It is 'original' because it is not a phenomenon of our freedom but the situational dynamics into and through which our wills are born, formed, energized and directed" (p. 248).

Chapter 10

Wine, Viticulture, and Soul Care

1. I am grateful to Dr. Loren Wilkinson for this wonderful literal translation.

2. It is noteworthy that agricultural scientists are now paying more attention to the natural and living organisms of root and soil life. They have begun to explore how roots and soils interact in order to work toward a more sustainable increase of crop production. For example, scientists are researching how they can enhance the roots' natural ability to extract nutrients from the soil and thereby reduce the use of fertilizers. See, e.g., Virginia Gewin, "An Underground Revolution," *Nature* 466 (2010): 552-53; see also Peter J. Gregory et al., "Contributions of Roots and Rootstocks to Sustainable, Intensified Crop Production," *Journal of Experimental Botany* 64, no. 5 (2013): 1209-22.

3. This is an important aspect of loving and caring for one's neighbor in Leviticus (Lev. 19:11-13).

4. When vintners speak of wine having a soul, they do not mean to imply that wine is a living being like humans. Rather, they seek to give voice to wine as an agricultural product that can evolve and mature over time, has complexity and nuance, and can bring profound delight. Jeremy Seysse does not hold any faith position and is not directly involved in the actual growing of vines; but he was still willing to reflect on the spirituality of wine.

5. Rowan Williams, *Silence and Honey Cakes: The Wisdom of the Desert* (Oxford: Lion Hudson, 2003), p. 59.

6. William Cavanaugh, *Being Consumed: Economics and Christian Desire* (Grand Rapids: Eerdmans, 2008), p. 47.

7. Cavanaugh, *Being Consumed,* pp. 35-36.

8. Cavanaugh, *Being Consumed,* pp. 45-46.

Conclusion

1. Jürgen Moltmann, *The Future of Creation* (London: SCM Press, 1979), pp. 115-19.

2. I am grateful to Richard Bauckham for making me aware of, and sharing his insights into, this beautiful reflection in *The Brothers Karamazov*.

3. Fyodor Dostoevsky, *The Brothers Karamazov* (New York: Knopf, 1992), p. 360.

4. Dostoevsky, *Brothers Karamazov*, pp. 361-62.

Bibliography

Alexander, Bruce K. *The Globalization of Addiction: A Study in Poverty of the Spirit.* Oxford: Oxford University Press, 2008.

Aquinas, Thomas. *A Commentary on Aristotle's* De anima. Translated by Robert Pasnau. New Haven: Yale University Press, 1999.

Aristotle. *De Anima.* Translated by D. W. Hamlyn. Oxford: Clarendon Press, 1968.

Augustine. *Contra Faustum.* Edited by J. Zycha. In vol. 25 of *Corpus Scriptorum Ecclesiasticorum Latinorum.* Vienna: Austrian Academy of Sciences, 1891.

————. *De bono coniugali.* Edited and translated by P. G. Walsh. Oxford: Clarendon Press, 2001.

————. *Epistolae.* Edited by A. Goldbacher. In vol. 34 of *Corpus Scriptorum Ecclesiasticorum Latinorum.* Vienna: Austrian Academy of Sciences, 1895-1898.

————. *St. Augustine's Christian Doctrine.* In vol. 2 of *The Nicene and Post-Nicene Fathers,* Series 1. Edited by Philip Schaff. 1886-1889. 14 vols. Reprint: Peabody, MA: Hendrickson, 1999.

Austin, Gregory. *Alcohol in Western Society from Antiquity to 1800: A Chronological History.* Santa Barbara, CA: ABC-CLIO, 1985.

Axel, Gabriel. *Babette's Feast.* DVD. Directed by Gabriel Axel. Santa Monica, CA: MGM Home Entertainment, 2001.

Bacchiocchi, Samuele. *Wine in the Bible: A Biblical Study on the Use of Alcoholic Beverages.* Berrien Springs, MI: Biblical Perspectives, 1989.

Bainton, Roland. *Here I Stand: A Life of Martin Luther.* New York: Abingdon, 1950.

————. *Women of the Reformation.* Minneapolis: Fortress Press, 1971.

Bangs, Nathan. *A History of the Methodist Episcopal Church.* New York: T. Mason and G. Lane, 1838.

Bassermann-Jordan, Friedrich. *Geschichte des Weinbaus.* Neustadt an der Weinstrasse, Germany: Pfalzische Verlagsanstalt, 1975.

Bauckham, Richard. *The Bible and Ecology: Rediscovering the Community of Creation.* Waco, TX: Baylor University Press, 2010.

Bibliography

————. *Living with Other Creatures: Green Exegesis and Theology.* Crownhill, UK: Paternoster, 2012.

Bauer, Joseph A., Kevin J. Pearson, and Nathan L. Price. "Resveratrol Improves Health and Survival of Mice on a High-calorie Diet." *Nature* 444, no. 7117 (2006): 337-42.

Bauer, Walter, Frederick W. Danker, William F. Arndt, and F. Wilbur Gingrich. *A Greek-English Lexicon of the New Testament and Other Early Christian Literature.* Chicago: University of Chicago Press, 2001.

Bear, Mark F., Barry W. Connors, and Michael A. Paradiso, eds. *Neuroscience: Exploring the Brain.* Baltimore: Lippincott Williams and Wilkins, 2007.

Becker, Lothar. *Rebe, Rausch und Religion: Eine kulturgeschichtliche Studie zum Wein in der Bibel.* Münster, Germany: LIT Verlag, 1999.

Bell, Catherine. *Ritual Theory, Ritual Practice.* Oxford: Oxford University Press, 1992.

Ben Sira. *The Wisdom of Ben Sira: A New Translation with Notes by Patrick W. Skehan.* Translated by Patrick W. Skehan. New York: Doubleday, 1987.

Berry, Wendell. "Christianity and the Survival of Creation." In *Sex, Economy, Freedom and Community: Eight Essays,* pp. 93-116. New York: Pantheon Books, 1993.

Bird, David. *Understanding Wine Technology.* San Francisco: The Wine Appreciation Guild, 2002.

Blanco-Colio, Luis Miguel, Mónica Valderrama, Luis Antonio Alvarez-Sala, Carmen Bustos, Mónica Ortego, Miguel Angel Hernández-Presa, Pilar Cancelas, Juan Gómez-Gerique, Jesús Millán, and Jesús Egido. "Red Wine Intake Prevents Nuclear Factor-kB Activation in Peripheral Blood Mononuclear Cells of Healthy Volunteers During Postprandial Lipemia." *Circulation* 102 (2000): 1020-26.

Blanning, Beverly. *Biodynamics in Wine.* London: The International Wine and Food Society, 2010.

Blenkinsopp, Joseph. *Creation, Un-Creation, Re-Creation: A Discursive Commentary on Genesis 1-11.* New York: T&T Clark, 2011.

Blixen, Karen. *Le dîner de Babette.* Lausanne: La Guilde du livre, 1969.

Bloch, Abraham P. *The Biblical and Historical Background of the Jewish Holy Days.* New York: Ktav Publishing House, 1978.

Böcher, Otto. *Dämonenfurcht und Dämonenabwehr. Ein Beitrag zur Vorgeschichte der christlichen Taufe.* Stuttgart: Kohlhammer, 1972.

Bonhoeffer, Dietrich. *Creation and Fall: A Theological Exposition of Genesis 1-3.* Minneapolis: Fortress Press, 1996.

————. *Life Together.* New York: Harper and Row, 1954.

Botterweck, G. J., and H. Ringgren, eds. *Theological Dictionary of the Old Testament.* Grand Rapdis: Eerdmans, 1990.

Brandt, Daniela-Maria. *Heilige Helfer für Winzer und Wein.* Würzburg: Echter Verlag, 1993.

Brillat-Savarin, Jean Anthelme. *The Physiology of Taste, or Meditations on Transcendental Gastronomy.* New York: Vintage Books, 2011.

Bromiley, G. W., ed. *Zwingli and Bullinger*. Vol. 24 of *The Library of Christian Classics*. London: SCM, 1953.

Broshi, Magen. *Bread, Wine, Walls, and Scrolls*. London: Sheffield Academic Press, 2001.

Brown, Francis, S. R. Driver, and Charles A. Briggs, eds. *A Hebrew and English Lexicon of the Old Testament*. Oxford: Clarendon Press, 1952.

Buber, Martin. *I and Thou*. New York: Charles Scribner's Sons, 1958.

Budde, Michael. *The Magic Kingdom of God: Christianity and Global Culture Industries*. Boulder, CO: Westview Press, 1997.

Bunyan, John. *The Pilgrim's Progress*. Peabody, MA: Hendrickson, 2004.

Burnett, Charles. "The Superiority of Taste." *Journal of the Warburg and Courtauld Institutes* 54 (1991): 230-38.

Burnham, Douglas, and Ole Martin Skilleås. *The Aesthetics of Wine*. Oxford: Wiley-Blackwell, 2012.

Calvin, John. "Catechism of the Church of Geneva." In *Calvin's Tracts, Containing Treatises on the Sacraments, Catechism of the Church of Geneva, Forms of Prayer, and Confessions of Faith*, 3 vols., translated by Henry Beveridge, 2:33-94. Edinburgh: Calvin Translation Society, 1849.

―――. *Commentary on the Book of Psalms*. Translated by James Anderson. 5 vols. Edinburgh: Calvin Translation Society, 1847.

―――. *Golden Booklet of the True Christian Life*. Translated by Henry J. Van Andel. Grand Rapids: Baker Books, 2004.

―――. *Institutes of the Christian Religion*. Edited by John T. McNeill. Translated by Ford Lewis Battles. 2 vols. Philadelphia: Westminster Press, 1960.

Campbell, Neil. "Aquinas' Reasons for the Aesthetic Irrelevance of Tastes and Smells." *British Journal of Aesthetics* 36, no. 2 (1996): 166-76.

Cassian, John. *The Conferences*. Edited by Boniface Ramsey. Vol. 57 of *Ancient Christian Writers*. New York: Paulist Press, 1997.

Cavanaugh, William. *Being Consumed: Economics and Christian Desire*. Grand Rapids: Eerdmans, 2008.

Chrysostom, John. *St. John Chrysostom: Baptismal Instructions*. Translated by P. W. Harkins. New York: Paulist Press, 1963.

Classen, Constance, David Howes, and Anthony Synnott. "The Aroma of the Commodity: The Commercialization of Smell." In *Aroma: The Cultural History of Smell*, pp. 180-205. London: Routledge, 1997.

―――. "Artificial Flavours." In *The Taste Culture Reader: Experiencing Food and Drink*, edited by Carolyn Korsmeyer, pp. 337-42. Oxford: Berg, 2005.

Clement of Alexandria. *Paedagogus*. Edited by M. Marcovich. Leiden: Brill, 2002.

Colman, Tyler. "Who Controls Your Palette?" In *Wine Politics: How Governments, Environmentalists, Mobsters, and Critics Influence the Wines We Drink*, pp. 103-24. Berkeley: University of California Press, 2008.

Crane, Tim. "Wine as an Aesthetic Object." In *Questions of Taste: The Philosophy of Wine*, edited by Barry C. Smith, pp. 141-56. Oxford: Signal Books, 2007.

Bibliography

Crislip, Andrew. *From Monastery to Hospital: Christian Monasticism and the Transformation of Health Care in Late Antiquity*. Ann Arbor: University of Michigan Press, 2005.

Curtis, Robert. *Ancient Food Technology*. Vol. 3. Leiden: Brill, 2001.

Cyprian of Carthage. *The Letters of St. Cyprian of Carthage III*. Edited by G. W. Clarke. Vol. 46 of *Ancient Christian Writers*. New York: Newman Press, 1986.

Cyril of Jerusalem. *Lectures on the Christian Sacraments*. New York: St. Vladimir's Seminary Press, 1951.

—————. *The Works of Saint Cyril of Jerusalem*. Translated by L. P. McCauley and A. A. Stephenson. Washington, DC: Catholic University of America Press, 1968.

Dalman, Gustav. *Arbeit und Sitte in Palästina: Brot, Öl und Wein*. Vol. 4. Hildesheim: Georg Olms Verlagsbuchhandlung, 1964.

Davies, Oliver. "Lost Heaven." In *Transformation Theology: Church in the World*, edited by Oliver Davies, Paul D. Janz, and Clemens Sedmak. London: T&T Clark, 2007.

Demossier, Marion. "Beyond *Terroir*: Territorial Construction, Hegemonic Discourse, and French Wine Culture." *Journal of the Royal Anthropological Institute* 17 (2011): 685-705.

Di Chiara, Gaetano, Valentina Bassareo, Sandro Fenu, Maria Antonietta De Luca, Liliana Spina, Cristina Cadoni, Elio Acquas, Ezio Carboni, Valentina Valentini, and Daniele Lecca. "Dopamine and Drug Addiction: The Nucleus Accumbens Shell Connection." *Neuropharmacology* 47, no. 1 (2004): 227-41.

Dion, Roger. *Histoire de la vigne et du vin en France des origins aus XIX siècle*. Paris: L'auteur, 1959.

Dioscorides. *The Greek Herbal of Dioscorides*. Translated by John Goodyer. Edited by Robert T. Gunther. New York: Hafner Publishing, 1959.

Dix, Dom Gregory. *The Shape of the Liturgy*. New York: The Seabury Press, 1982.

Dostoevsky, Fyodor. *The Brothers Karamazov*. New York: Alfred A. Knopf, 1992.

Doty, Richard. "The Olfactory Vector Hypothesis of Neurodegenerative Disease: Is It Viable?" *Annals of Neurobiology* 63, no. 1 (2008): 7-15.

Dronke, Peter. "Platonic-Christian Allegories in the Homilies of Hildegard of Bingen." In *From Athens to Chartres: Neoplatonism and Medieval Thought: Studies in Honour of Edouard Jeauneau*, edited by Haijo Jan Westra. Leiden: Brill, 1992.

Dubach, Manuel. *Trunkenheit im Alten Testament: Begrifflichkeit-Zeugniss-Wertung*. Stuttgart: Kohlhammer, 2009.

Duffy, J. C. "Alcohol Consumption and All-cause Mortality." *International Journal of Epidemiology* 24, no. 1 (1995): 100-105.

Edwards, Jonathan. Letter to Esther Edwards Burr, March 28, 1753. In *Letters and Personal Writings*. Edited by George S. Claghorn. Vol. 16 of *The Works of Jonathan Edwards*, edited by Harry S. Stout. New Haven: Yale University Press, 1998.

Elson, Pam. "Hospices de Beaune — the Hôtel-Dieu." burgundytoday.com. http://www.burgundytoday.com/historic-places/museums/hospice-beaune.htm (accessed Oct. 29, 2014).

Fenton, Miriam C., Christina Aivadyan, and Deborah Hasin. "Epidemiology of Addiction." In *Principles of Addiction: Comprehensive Addictive Behaviors and Disorders*, vol. 1, edited by Peter M. Miller. San Diego: Academic Press, 2013.

Forbes, Andrew, Daniel Henley, and David Henley. *Health and Well Being: A Medieval Guide*. Chiang Mai, Thailand: Cognoscenti Books, 2013.

Forbes, Robert. *Cosmetics and Perfumes in Antiquity*. Vol. 3 of *Studies in Ancient Technology*. Leiden: Brill, 1955.

Forster, Brenda, and Jeffrey Colman Salloway, eds. *The Socio-Cultural Matrix of Alcohol and Drug Use: A Sourcebook of Patterns and Factors*. Lewiston, NY: Edwin Mellen Press, 1990.

Francis of Assisi. "The Canticle of the Sun." http://www2.webster.edu/~barrettb/canticle .htm (accessed Jan. 30, 2014).

Frank, Georgia. "'Taste and See': The Eucharist and the Eyes of Faith in the Fourth Century." *Church History* 70, no. 4 (2001): 619-43.

Freedman, Paul, ed. *Food: The History of Taste*. Berkeley: University of California Press, 2007.

Fry, Timothy, ed. *The Rule of St. Benedict in Latin and English with Notes*. Collegeville, MN: Liturgical Press, 1981.

Fuller, Robert. *Religion and Wine: A Cultural History of Wine Drinking in the United States*. Knoxville: University of Tennessee Press, 1996.

Gaziano, J. Michael, Julie E. Buring, Jan L. Breslow, Samuel Z. Goldhaber, Berhard Rosner, Martin VanDenburgh, Walter Willett, and Charles H. Hennekens. "Moderate Alcohol Intake, Increased Levels of High-Density Lipoprotein and Its Subfractions, and Decreased Risks of Myocardial Infarction." *New England Journal of Medicine* 329 (1993): 1829-34.

Gekle, Dieter. *Der Wein in der Heilkunde: Von der Antike bis zur Gegenwart*. Würzburg: Weinbruderschaft Franken e.V., 1992.

Gerhardt, Paul. *Paul Gerhardt's Spiritual Songs*. Translated by John Kelly. London: Alexander Strahan, 1867.

Gewin, Virginia. "An Underground Revolution." *Nature* 466 (2010): 552-53.

Giannetti, Laura. "Of Eels and Pears: A Sixteenth-Century Debate on Taste, Temperance, and the Pleasures of the Senses." In *Religion and the Senses in Early Modern Europe*, edited by Wietse de Boer and Christine Göttler. Leiden: Brill, 2013.

Gilders, William. *Blood Ritual in the Hebrew Bible: Meaning and Power*. Baltimore: Johns Hopkins University Press, 2004.

Goode, Jamie. *The Science of Wine: From Vine to Glass*. Los Angeles: University of California Press, 2005.

Goode, Jamie, and Sam Harrop. *Authentic Wine: Towards Natural and Sustainable Winemaking*. Berkeley: University of California Press, 2011.

Gregory, J. Peter, Christopher J. Atkinson, A. Glyn Bengough, Mark A. Else, Felicidad Fernández-Fernández, Richard J. Harrison, and Sonja Schmidt. "Contributions of Roots and Rootstocks to Sustainable, Intensified Crop Production." *Journal of Experimental Botany* 64, no. 5 (2013): 1209-22.

Bibliography

Hamilton, Victor. *The Book of Genesis: Chapters 1–17.* New Interntional Commentary on the Old Testament. Grand Rapids: Eerdmans, 1990.

Hanson, David. "Alcohol: Problems and Solutions: Health." Sociology Department of the State University of New York, Potsdam. http://www2.potsdam.edu/alcohol/AlcoholAndHealth.html#.VH4rqIu4mRt (accessed Oct. 29, 2014).

———. *Preventing Alcohol Abuse: Alcohol, Culture, and Control.* London: Praeger, 1995.

Harper, Curt E., Leah M. Cook, Brijesh B. Patel, Jun Wang, Isam A. Eltoum, Ali Arabshahi, Tomoyuki Shirai, and Coral A. Lartiniere. "Genistein and Resveratrol, Alone and in Combination, Suppress Prostate Cancer in SV-40 Tag Rats." *The Prostate* 69, no. 15 (2009): 1668-82.

Harris, R. Laird, Gleason L. Archer, and Bruce K. Waltke, eds. *Theological Wordbook of the Old Testament.* 2 vols. Chicago: Moody Press, 1980.

Harvey, Susan Ashbrook. *Scenting Salvation: Ancient Christianity and the Olfactory Imagination.* Berkeley: University of California Press, 2006.

Health and Social Care Information Centre (HSCIC). *Statistics on Alcohol: England, 2014.* 2014. Available online at: http://www.hscic.gov.uk/catalogue/PUB15483/alc-eng-2014-rep.pdf (accessed Nov. 4, 2014).

Hemingway, Ernest. *A Moveable Feast.* New York: Scribner's, 1964/2009.

Henderson, John. *The Renaissance Hospital.* New Haven: Yale University Press, 2006.

Hengel, Martin. *Studies in Early Christology.* London: T&T Clark, 1995.

Heschel, Abraham. *The Sabbath: Its Meaning for Modern Man.* New York: Farrar, Straus, 1952.

Hildegard von Bingen. *Hildegard von Bingen's Physica: The Complete English Translation of Her Classic Work on Health and Healing.* Translated by Priscilla Throop. Rochester, VT: Healing Arts Press, 1998.

Hippocrates. Translated by Paul Potter et al. 10 vols. LCL. Cambridge, MA: Harvard University Press, 1923-2012.

Holder, H. D. *Alcohol and the Community: A Systems Approach to Prevention.* Cambridge, UK: Cambridge University Press, 1998.

Holt, Mark, ed. *Alcohol: A Social and Cultural History.* New York: Berg, 2006.

Hopkins, Gerard Manley. "God's Grandeur." In *God's Grandeur and Other Poems.* Mineola, NY: Dover, 1995.

Hyams, Edward. *Dionysus: A Social History of the Wine Vat.* London: Sidgwick and Jackson, 1965.

Irenaeus. *Against Heresies.* In vol. 1 of *The Ante-Nicene Fathers.* Edited by Alexander Roberts and James Donaldson (1885-1896). 10 vols. Reprint: Peabody, MA: Hendrickson, 1999.

Jefferson, Thomas. Thomas Jefferson to Monsieur de Neuville, December 13, 1818. In *The Writings of Thomas Jefferson,* vol. 15, edited by Andrew A. Lipscomb and Albert Ellery Bergh. 20 vols. Washington, DC: Thomas Jefferson Memorial Association, 1904.

———. Thomas Jefferson to William Johnson, May 10, 1817. In *Thomas Jefferson's Gar-*

den Book, edited by Edwin Morris Betts. Philadelphia: American Philosophical Society, 1944.

Jenni, Ernst, and Claus Westermann, eds. *Theological Lexicon of the Old Testament.* 4 vols. Peabody, MA: Hendrickson Publishers, 1997.

Jeremias, Joachim. *The Eucharistic Words of Jesus.* Philadelphia: Fortress Press, 1977.

Johnson, Hugh. *The Story of Wine.* London: Mitchell Beazley, 1989.

Jones-Witters, Patricia, and Weldon L. Witters. *Drugs and Society: A Biological Perspective.* Monterey, CA: Wadsworth Health Sciences, 1983.

Jütte, Robert. *A History of the Senses: From Antiquity to Cyberspace.* Cambridge, UK: Polity, 2005.

Keener, Craig S. *The Gospel of John: A Commentary.* 2 vols. Grand Rapids: Baker, 2003.

Knox, John. *The First Book of Discipline.* Edited by James K. Cameron. Edinburgh: St. Andrew Press, 1972.

————. "A Letter of Wholesome Counsel, Addressed to His Brethren in Scotland." In *The Works of John Knox.* Vol. 4. Edited by Kevin Reed. Edinburgh: Johnstone and Hunter, 1855.

Koch, Hans Jörg. *Wein, Eine literarische Weinprobe.* Leipzig: Reclam, 2002.

Korsmeyer, Carolyn. *Making Sense of Taste.* Ithaca, NY: Cornell University Press, 1999.

Kraus, Hans-Joachim. *Klagelieder: Threni,* vol. 20 of *Biblischer Kommentar, Altes Testament.* Neukirchen-Vluyn: Neukirchener Verlag, 1968.

Kuhn, J. "Deep Brain Stimulation of the Nucleus Accumbens: First Experiences in Severe Addiction." *Biological Psychiatry* 75, no. 9 (May 2014): 31-32.

Larson, Erik. *The Naked Consumer: How Our Private Lives Become Public Commodities.* New York: Henry Holt and Company, 1992.

Lebeau, Paul. *Le vin nouveau du royaume: étude exégétique et patristique sur la parole eschatologique de Jésus à la Cène.* Paris: Desclée de Brouwer, 1966.

Lee, Philip. *Against the Protestant Gnostics.* New York: Oxford University Press, 1987.

Lewin, Benjamin. *Wine Myths and Reality.* Dover, UK: Vendange Press, 2010.

Lewis, David, and Darren Bridger. "Market Researchers Make Increasing Use of Brain Imaging." *Advances in Clinical Neuroscience and Rehabilitation* 5, no. 3 (2005): 36-37.

Liddell, H. G., and R. Scott. *A Greek-English Lexicon.* Oxford: Oxford University Press, 1945.

Lile, Pierre C. *Histoire Médicale Du Vin.* Chaintré: Oenoplurimedia, 2002.

Lucia, Salvatore P. *A History of Wine as Therapy.* Philadelphia: J. B. Lippincott Company, 1963.

Lukas, Paul. *Inventing Wine: A New History of One of the World's Most Ancient Pleasures.* New York: W. W. Norton and Company, 2012.

Luther, Martin. Martin Luther to Katherine Luther, July 29, 1534. In *The Letters of Martin Luther.* Translated and edited by Margaret A. Currie. London: Macmillan, 1908.

————. "That these words of Christ, 'this is my body,' still stand firm against the fanatics." Vol. 37 of *Luther's Works,* American Edition, pp. 3-150. 55 vols. Edited by Jaroslav

Pelikan and Helmut T. Lehman. Philadelphia: Muhlenberg and Fortress/St. Louis: Concordia, 1955-86.

————. *Werke: Kritische Gesamtausgabe* (Weimarer Ausgabe). Vols. 1-58. Weimar, 1883ff. English translation: *Luther's Works*. Vols. 1-30 edited by Jaroslav Pelikan. St. Louis: Concordia, 1958-1967. Vols. 31-55 edited by Helmut Lehmann. Philadelphia: Muhlenberg Press and Fortress Press, 1957-1967.

Lyons, Geoffrey, Frank Deane, and Peter Kelly. "Faith-Based Substance Abuse Programs." In *Interventions for Addiction: Comprehensive Addictive Behaviors and Disorders,* vol. 3, edited by Peter M. Miller. San Diego, CA: Academic Press, 2013.

MacDonald, Nathan. *Not Bread Alone: The Uses of Food in the Old Testament.* Oxford: Oxford University Press, 2008.

MacKenzie, Donald, and Judy Wajcman, eds. *The Social Shaping of Technology.* 2nd ed. Maidenhead, UK: Open University Press, 1999.

MacNicol, Duncan Clark. *Robert Bruce: Minister in the Kirk of Edinburgh.* Edinburgh: Banner of Truth Trust, 1961.

Macy, Gary. *The Banquet's Wisdom: A Short History of the Theologies of the Lord's Supper.* Akron, OH: OSL Publications, 2005.

Maltman, Alex. "The Role of Vineyard Geology in Wine Typicity." *Journal of Wine Research* 19, no. 1 (2008): 1-17.

Malysz, Piotr J. "Exchange and Ecstasy: Luther's Eucharistic Theology in Light of Radical Orthodoxy's Critique of Gift and Sacrifice." *Scottish Journal of Theology* 60, no. 3 (2007): 294-308.

Margotta, Roberto. *An Illustrated History of Medicine.* Middlesex, UK: Hamlyn Publishing Group, 1967.

May, Gerald. *Addiction and Grace: Love and Spirituality in the Healing of Addictions.* San Francisco: Harper and Row, 1988.

McFadyen, Alistair. *Bound to Sin: Abuse, Holocaust and the Christian Doctrine of Sin.* Cambridge, UK: Cambridge University Press, 2000.

McGovern, Patrick E. *Ancient Wine: The Search for the Origins of Viniculture.* Princeton, NJ: Princeton University Press, 2003.

McNeill, John T. *The History and Character of Calvinism.* Oxford: Oxford University Press, 1954.

McNutt, Joni G. *In Praise of Wine.* Santa Barbara, CA: Capra Press, 1993.

Meffert, Ekkehard. *Die Zisterzienser und Bernhard von Clairvaux: Ihre spirituellen Impulse und die Verchristlichung der Erde Europas.* Stuttgart: Verlag Engel, 2010.

Méndez-Montoya, Angel F. *The Theology of Food: Eating and the Eucharist.* Chichester, UK: Wiley-Blackwell, 2012.

Milgrom, Jacob. *Leviticus: A Book of Ritual and Ethics.* Minneapolis: Fortress Press, 2004.

Miller, Peter M., ed. *Principles of Addiction: Comprehensive Addictive Behaviors and Disorders.* Vol. 1. San Diego: Academic Press, 2013.

Mitcham, Carl. *Thinking Through Technology: The Path between Engineering and Philosophy.* Chicago: University of Chicago Press, 1994.

Miyagi, Yuko, Kunihisa Miwa, and Hiroshi Inoue. "Inhibition of Human Low-Density Lipoprotein Oxidation by Flavonoids in Red Wine and Grape Juice." *American Journal of Cardiology* 80, no. 12 (1997): 1627-31.

Moltmann, Jürgen. *Theology and Joy*. London: SCM Press, 1973.

———. *The Future of Creation*. London: SCM Press, 1979.

National Institute on Drug Abuse. "DrugFacts: Nationwide Trends." http://www.drug abuse.gov/publications/drugfacts/nationwide-trends (accessed Oct. 30, 2014).

Niditch, Susan. "Good Blood, Bad Blood: Multivocality, Metonymy, and Mediation in Zechariah 9." *Vetus Testamentum* 61, no. 4 (January 2011): 629-45.

Nossiter, Jonathan. *Liquid Memory*. New York: Farrar, Straus and Giroux, 2009.

Oden, Thomas C. *Pastoral Theology*. San Francisco: Harper and Row, 1983.

Oei, Tian Po Sumatri, and Penelope Anne Hasking. "Alcohol Use Disorders." In Peter M. Miller, ed., *Principles of Addiction: Comprehensive Addictive Behaviors and Disorders*, vol. 1 (San Diego: Academic Press, 2013), pp. 647-56.

O'Keefe, J. H., K. A. Bybee, and C. J. Lavie. "Alcohol and Cardiovascular Health: The Razor-Sharp Double-Edged Sword." *Journal of the American College of Cardiology* 50, no. 11 (2007): 1009-14.

Organisation for Economic Cooperation and Development. "Health at a Glance 2013: OECD Indicators." OECD Publishing, 2013: http://www.oecd-ilibrary.org/social -issues-migration-health/health-at-a-glance-2013_health_glance-2013-en (accessed Oct. 30, 2014).

Ott, Richard. *Creating Demand*. Burr Ridge, IL: Irwin Professional Publishing, 1992.

Pelikan, Jaroslav. *The Emergence of the Catholic Tradition (100-600)*. Vol. 1 of *The Christian Tradition: A History of the Development of Doctrine*. Chicago: University of Chicago Press, 1971.

Peterson, Eugene. *Christ Plays in Ten Thousand Places: A Conversation in Spiritual Theology*. Grand Rapids: Eerdmans, 2005.

Peynaud, Emile. *The Taste of Wine: The Art and Science of Wine Appreciation*. Translated by Michael Schuster. London: Macdonald, 1987.

Pieper, Josef. *In Tune with the World: A Theory of Festivity*. South Bend, IN: St. Augustine's Press, 1999.

Pinney, Thomas. *A History of Wine in America: From the Beginnings to Prohibition*. Berkeley: University of California Press, 1989.

Plantinga, R., T. Thompson, and M. Lundberg. *An Introduction to Christian Theology*. Cambridge, UK: Cambridge University Press, 2010.

Proust, Marcel. *Swann's Way*. In *Remembrance of Things Past*. Vol. 1. Translated by C. K. Scott Moncrieff and Terence Kilmartin. New York: Random House, 1981.

Pu, Muzhou. *Wine and Wine Offering in the Religion of Ancient Egypt*. London: Kegan Paul International, 1995.

Quintero, G. C. "Role of Nucleus Accumbens Glutamatergic Plasticity in Drug Addiction." *Neuropsychiatric Disease and Treatment* 9 (2013): 1499-1512.

Bibliography

Rad, Gerhard von. *Genesis: A Commentary*. Translated by John H. Marks. Old Testament Library. Philadelphia: Westminster, 1972.

Rawcliffe, Carole. *Medicine for the Soul: The Life, Death and Resurrection of an English Medieval Hospital: St. Giles's, Norwich, c. 1249-1550*. Stroud, UK: Sutton Publishing, 1999.

Raymond, Irving Woodworth. *The Teaching of the Early Church on the Use of Wine and Strong Drink*. New York: Columbia University Press, 1927.

Rech, Photina. *Wine and Bread*. Chicago: Liturgy Training Publications, 2007.

Rehm, Jürgen, Kevin D. Shield, Maximilien X. Rehm, Gerrit Gmel, and Ulrich Frick. *Alcohol Consumption, Alcohol Dependence and Attributable Burden of Disease in Europe: Potential Gains from Effective Interventions for Alcohol Dependence*. Centre for Addiction and Mental Health, 2012. Available online at: http://www.amphoraproject.net/w2box/data/AMPHORA%20Reports/CAMH_Alcohol_Report_Europe_2012.pdf (accessed Oct. 30, 2014).

Renaud, S., and M. de Lorgeril. "Wine, Alcohol, Platelets, and the French Paradox for Coronary Heart Disease." *Lancet* 339, no. 8808 (June 20, 1992): 1523-26.

Renouf, V., Cécile Miot-Sertier, P. Strehaiano, and Aline Lonvaud-Funel. "The Wine Microbial Consortium: A Real Terroir Characteristic." *Journal International des Sciences de la Vigne et du Vin* 40, no 4 (2006): 209-16.

Reynolds, Kristi, Brian Lewis, John David L. Nolen, Gregory L. Kinney, Bhavani Sathya, and Jiang He. "Alcohol Consumption and Risk of Stroke: A Meta-analysis." *Journal of the American Medical Association* 289 (2003): 579-88.

Robinson, Jancis, ed. *The Oxford Companion to Wine*. Oxford: Oxford University Press, 2006.

Rorabaugh, W. J. *The Alcoholic Republic: An American Tradition*. New York: Oxford University Press, 1979.

Saunders, Benjamin T., and Patricia H. Janak. "Nucleus Accumbens Plasticity Underlies Multifaceted Behavioral Changes Associated with Addiction." *Biological Psychiatry* 75, no. 2 (January 2014): 92-93.

Schmemann, Alexander. *For the Life of the World: Sacraments and Orthodoxy*. 2nd ed. Crestwood, NY: St. Vladimir's Seminary Press, 1988.

Schreiber, Georg. *Deutsche Weingeschichte: Der Wein in Volksleben, Kult und Wirtschaft*. Köln: Rheinland-Verlag, 1980.

Scruton, Roger. *I Drink Therefore I Am: A Philosopher's Guide to Wine*. London: Continuum, 2009.

———. "The Philosophy of Wine." In *Questions of Taste: The Philosophy of Wine*, edited by Barry C. Smith. Oxford: Signal Books, 2007.

Seward, Desmond. *Monks and Wine*. New York: Crown, 1979.

Shepherd, Gordon M. *Neurogastronomy: How the Brain Creates Flavor and Why It Matters*. New York: Columbia University Press, 2012.

Singletary, K. W., and S. M. Gapstur. "Alcohol and Breast Cancer: Review of Epidemiologic Experimental Evidence and Potential Mechanisms." *Journal of the American Medical Association* 286, no. 17 (2001): 2143-51.

Sira, Ben. *The Wisdom of Ben Sira: A New Translation with Notes by Patrick W. Skehan.* Translated by Patrick W. Skehan. New York: Doubleday, 1987.

Smith, Barry C. "The Objectivity of Tastes and Tasting." In *Questions of Taste: The Philosophy of Wine,* edited by Barry C. Smith. Oxford: Oxford University Press, 2007.

Stampfer, Meir J., Jae Hee Kang, Jennifer Chen, Rebecca Cherry, and Francine Grodstein. "Effects of Moderate Alcohol Consumption on Cognitive Function in Women." *New England Journal of Medicine* 352 (2005): 245-53.

Steiner, Rudolf. *Agriculture Course.* London: Rudolf Steiner Press, 2004.

Substance Abuse and Mental Health Services Administration. *Results from the 2012 National Survey on Drug Use and Health: Summary of National Findings.* NSDUH Series H-46, HHS Publication No. (SMA) 13-4795. Rockville, MD: Substance Abuse and Mental Health Services Administration, 2013.

Taft, Robert. *Beyond East and West: Problems in Liturgical Understanding.* Washington, DC: The Pastoral Press, 1984.

Tappert, Theodore G., ed. *Luther: Letters of Spiritual Counsel.* Vancouver: Regent College, 2003.

Teachout, R. P. "The Use of 'Wine' in the Old Testament." PhD diss., Dallas Theological Seminary, 1979.

Teil, Geneviève. "No Such Thing as Terroir?: Objectivities and the Regimes of Existence of Objects." *Science, Technology and Human Values* 37, no 5 (2012): 478-505.

Thomas, Alois. *Die Darstellung Christi in der Kelter.* Düsseldorf: Schwann, 1936.

Thun, Michael J., Richard Peto, Alan D. Lopez, Jane H. Monaco, S. Jane Henley, Clark W. Heath, and Richard Doll. "Alcohol Consumption and Mortality among Middle-aged and Elderly U.S. Adults." *New England Journal of Medicine* 337 (1997): 1705-14.

Tipp, David. "The Image of the Body in the Formative Phases of the Protestant Reformation." In *Religion and the Body,* edited by Sarah Coakley. Cambridge, UK: Cambridge University Press, 1997.

Todd, Cain. *The Philosophy of Wine: A Case for Truth, Beauty and Intoxication.* Durham, UK: Acumen, 2010.

Unwin, Tim. *Wine and the Vine: An Historical Geography of Viticulture and the Wine Trade.* London: Routledge, 1991.

U.S. Department of Health and Human Services, Substance Abuse and Mental Health Administration. *National Household Survey on Drug Abuse, 1997.* Washington, DC: DHHS, 1998.

Vaillant, George E. *The Natural History of Alcoholism Revisited.* Cambridge, MA: Harvard University Press, 1995.

Varriano, John. "Regional Tastes." In *Tastes and Temptations: Food and Art in Renaissance Italy,* pp. 38-65. Berkeley: University of California Press, 2009.

———. *Wine: A Cultural History.* London: Reaktion Books, 2010.

Verdejo-Garcia, A., M. J. Fernandez-Serrano, and J. Tirapu-Ustarroz. "Denial and Lack of Awareness in Substance Dependence: Insights from the Neuropsychology of Addiction." In *Principles of Addiction: Comprehensive Addictive Behaviors and Disorders,* edited by Peter M. Miller. Vol. 1. San Diego: Academic Press, 2013.

Veseth, Mike. "The McWine Conspiracy." In *Wine Wars: The Curse of the Blue Nun, the Miracle of Two Buck Chuck, and the Revenge of the Terroirists.* Lanham, MD: Rowman and Littlefield, 2011.

Vess, Deborah. "Monastic Moonshine: Alcohol in the Middle Ages." In *Religion and Alcohol: Sobering Thoughts,* edited by C. K. Robertson. New York: Peter Lang, 2004.

Viladesau, Richard. *The Beauty of the Cross: The Passion of Christ in Theology and the Arts from the Catacombs to the Eve of the Renaissance.* Oxford: Oxford University Press, 2008.

Volpato, Stefano, Marco Pahor, Luigi Ferrucci, Eleanor M. Simonsick, Jack M. Guralnik, Stephen B. Kritchevsky, Renato Fellin, and Tamara B. Harris. "Relationship of Alcohol Intake with Inflammatory Markers and Plasminogen Activator Inhibitor-1 in Well-Functioning Older Adults." *Circulation* 109 (2004): 607-12.

Wagner, Hans. *Wein: Heilkraft der Natur.* München: Ludwig Verlag, 2000.

Walsh, Carey. *The Fruit of the Vine: Viticulture in Ancient Israel.* Winona Lake, IN: Eisenbrauns, 2000.

Waltke, Bruce. *Genesis: A Commentary.* Grand Rapids: Zondervan, 2001.

Ward, Benedicta. *The Desert Fathers: Sayings of the Early Christian Monks.* London: Penguin Books, 2003.

Weil, Simone. *Gravity and Grace.* New York: Putnam, 1952.

Wengert, T. "Luther and Melanchthon on Consecrated Communion Wine (Eisleben 1542-43)." *Lutheran Quarterly* 15, no. 1 (2001): 24-42.

Wenham, Gordon. *Genesis 1–15.* WBC series. Dallas: Word Books, 1994.

Wesley, John, and Charles Wesley. *Hymns on the Lord's Supper.* London: H. Cock, 1751.

Westermann, Claus. *Genesis 1–11: A Commentary.* Translated by John Scullion. Minneapolis: Augsburg Publishing House, 1984.

Whalen, Philip. "'A Merciless Source of Happy Memories,' Gaston Roupnel and the Folklore of Burgundian *Terroir.*" *Journal of Folklore Research* 44, no. 1 (2007): 21-40.

White, Robert. *Understanding Vineyard Soils.* Oxford: Oxford University Press, 2009.

Williams, Rowan. *Silence and Honey Cakes: The Wisdom of the Desert.* Oxford: Lion Hudson, 2003.

Woolgar, C. M. *The Senses in Late Medieval England.* New Haven: Yale University Press, 2006.

Wordsworth, William. "The world is too much with us." In *William Wordsworth: The Major Works,* edited by Stephen Gill. Oxford: Oxford University Press, 1984.

Wright, J. W., ed. *The New York Times 2000 Almanac.* New York: Penguin, 1999.

Xia, L., X. X. Wang, X. S. Hu, X. G. Guo, Y. P. Shang, H. J. Chen, C. L. Zeng, F. R. Zhang, and J. Z. Chen. "Resveratrol Reduces Endothelial Progenitor Cells Senescence through Augmentation of Telomerase Activity by Akt-dependent Mechanisms." *British Journal of Pharmacology* 155, no. 3 (2008): 387-94.

Younger, William. *Gods, Men, and Wine.* London: The Wine and Food Society Limited, 1966.

Index of Names

Adam, 17-18, 201-2
Aëtius of Amida, 171
Alexander, Bruce, 191-92, 195
Aquinas, Thomas, 41, 106-7, 247nn.20-21
Arcadian Winery, 139
Aristotle, 106, 166
Arnau de Vilanova, 173
Augustine, 39, 41, 42-43, 52
Avicenna, 171
Axel, Gabriel, 94

Barolo, 103
Basil of Alexandria, 42
Basil of Caesarea, 169
Bauckham, Richard, 3, 18, 234n.22, 235n.26
Becker, Lothar, 12
Bede, Venerable, 48
Ben Sira, 13, 41, 74
Benedict of Nursia, 44-45, 50, 123, 146, 162, 168-69
Bernard of Clairvaux, 49-50, 127
Berry, Wendell, 16
Bird, David, 147
Blixen, Karen, 94
Bloch, Abraham, 70
Boccaccio, Giovanni, 107
Bordeaux, 57, 128, 140
Brillat-Savarin, Jean Anthelme, 96, 100, 111, 113

Bunyan, John, 58
Burgundy, 45-46, 49, 90, 116-17, 129, 138, 139, 146-47, 151, 159, 161, 168, 170, 203, 206, 250n.9

California, 1, 60-61, 117, 122, 135, 137-40, 150, 158-59, 160
Calvin, John, 55-57, 63, 68-69, 242n.7
Canaan, 12-13, 19, 22, 236n.40. *See also* Palestine
Carlisle Wine Cellars, 139-40, 160-61
Cassian, John, 44
Castell-Castell, Prince Albrecht, 130-31
Cavanaugh, William, 193, 196, 212-13
Celsus, 167
Chablis, 50, 115
Christa, Sister, 130
Chrysostom, John, 37, 42, 80-81
Cîteaux, 49-50, 129
Clement of Alexandria, 41-42, 52
Clos De Vougeot, 49-50, 90-92, 94, 129
Cluny, 46, 169
Colman, Tyler, 147
Columbanus of Nantes, Saint, 48
Côte d'Or, 49, 129
Cristom Vineyards, 159
Cyprian, 39-42
Cyril of Jerusalem, 80-81, 245n.43

Davis, Joe, 139

Democritus, 105-6
Doerner, Steve, 159-60
Domaine Dujac, 139, 159, 206
Dorchester, Daniel, 62
Dostoevsky, Fyodor, 218-19

Eberbach abbey, 50, 127, 129, 155, 157
Ebrach, monastery of, 50
Edwards, Jonathan, 59
Elijah, 71
Eliot, T. S., 143
Ephrem the Syrian, Saint, 52
Eve, 17-18
Evesham Wood Vineyard, 136-37
Eyrie Vineyard, 135-36, 158-59

France, 25, 27, 38, 44, 47, 49-53, 57, 59, 60,
    89-90, 92, 140, 146-47, 149, 154, 170,
    176, 191, 205, 238n.2
Francis, Saint, 61
Franconia, 46, 48-49, 50, 103, 112-13, 115-
    16, 122, 127-28, 130, 132, 134, 153-54, 217

Galen, 166-68
Gerhardt, Paul, 54-55, 132
Germany, 25, 27, 38, 47, 48-49, 50-53, 57,
    95, 112-13, 122-24, 146, 149, 157, 191
Gevrey, 46, 50
Goethe, 96
Gregory the Great, 52

Hedwig, Sister, 127-28, 129-30, 156-57, 211
Herbert, George, 96
Hildegard von Bingen, 48, 107, 122, 123,
    125, 135, 172-73, 175-76, 211
Hippocrates, 165-66
Homer, 165
Hufsky, Father Ralf, 122-25, 154, 211

Ireland, 47, 48, 187
Irenaeus, 41, 42, 242n.3
Isaac, 19
Italy, 39, 44, 45, 47, 53, 57, 116, 167, 191

Jacob, 19-20, 21, 27, 28, 40, 86
Jefferson, Thomas, 59-60, 61
Jesus Christ: crucifixion, 76, 99, 208,
    242n.7, 245n.9; depicted in the wine-
    press, 124-25; incarnation of, 2, 67, 78,
    104; miracles of, 11, 30, 34, 85-87, 123,
    131, 218-19; and Passover/Eucharist, 35,
    70-73, 127, 242n.7; resurrection of, 66;
    teachings of, 12, 27-28, 31-32, 39, 78, 87,
    123, 168, 184, 197, 208, 220
John (the Apostle), 11, 39, 105, 124
John the Baptist, 87, 123
Johnson, Hugh, 50, 53
Joseph, 13, 26
Judah, 20, 21, 22, 27, 28, 40, 86

Kilian, Saint, 46
Kloster Eberbach. *See* Eberbach abbey
Knox, John, 57
König, Wolfram, 134, 154-55
Krammer, Edi, 131
Kreglinger, Peter, 155-56
Kreglinger-Müller, Gertrud, 132, 217
Kutschick, Bernd, 127, 155

LaFarge, Michael, 203-5
Lamech, 19
Lee, Adam, 137-38
Lemon, Ted, 138-39, 150, 161-62
Lett, David, 135, 158-59
Lett, Jason, 122, 135-36, 157, 158-59, 207-8
Littorai Wines, 138, 161
Loire River, 44
Luther, Katharina. *See* von Bora,
    Katharina
Luther, Martin, 23, 44, 53-54, 55, 56, 57,
    63, 68-69, 89, 98, 174, 181-82, 242n.7

Main River, 46, 127
Martin of Tours, 44, 53
Mary, 87
Melchizedek, 19
Meursault, 46, 50

Milton, John, 96
Moltmann, Jürgen, 84, 87
Mondavi, Robert, 140
Mondavi, Tim, 122, 140-41
Monte Cassino, 172
Morey, Anne, 168
Moses, 20-21, 22
Moses ben Maimon, 171
Müller, Herbert, 132, 217

Napa Valley, 122, 135, 138, 140, 160
Noah, 18-19, 39-40, 73, 182, 202
Nossiter, Jonathan, 146

Officer, Mike, 139-40, 160-61
Oregon, 1, 117, 122, 135-36, 157, 158-60, 207

Palestine, 12-13, 254-55n.3. *See also*
   Canaan
Paracelsus, 174
Parker, Robert, 147
Pataille, Sylvain, 204-5
Paul (apostle), 6, 12, 31, 32, 36, 39, 71, 87,
   98, 164, 168, 184-85
Pérignon, Dom, 50, 94
Perkins, William, 57-58
Peterson, Eugene, 81
Petrini, Carlo, 103
Peynaud, Emile, 101-2, 111-12
Pittacus, 13
Plato, 166-67
Pliny the Elder, 13-14, 22, 74, 116, 138, 167
Poupon, Pierre, 100
Promised Land, 20-22, 28-29, 58, 70, 75,
   94, 104. *See also* Canaan; Palestine
Proust, Marcel, 109

Raney, Russ, 136-37
Renaud, Serge, 176-77
Rheingau, 50, 59, 122, 125, 127, 129, 154,
   170, 172

Rhine River, 46, 48, 51
Rolland, Michel, 147

Salerno, 172
Schmemann, Alexander, 83-85
Scruton, Roger, 95, 146-47, 247n.22
Seward, Desmond, 60
Seysses, Jeremy, 159
Siduri Wines, 137
Socrates, 166
Solomon, 21, 29, 39-40
Sonoma Valley, 60, 135, 138-39, 160-61
Steinberg, 51, 129
Steiner, Rudolf, 249-50n.10
Stevenson, Robert Louis, 96, 162
Störrlein, Armin, 132-34

Thekla, Sister, 122, 125-27
Theophrastus, 167
Timothy, 12, 32
Titus, 185
Tuscany, 116

Uriah (the Hittite), 183

Veseth, Mike, 150, 152-53, 251n.15
Veuve Cliquot, 91
von Bora, Katharina, 53

Weil, Simone, 95
Weissensee, Bernhard, 153-54
Welch, Thomas, 62-63
Wesley, John, 55, 62
Westermann, Claus, 19
White, Robert, 129, 151, 156, 249n.4,
   249n.6
Willamette Valley, 122, 135, 159, 160

Zwingli, Ulrich, 57, 242n.7

Index of Subjects

Abstinence, 17, 25-26, 42-43, 56, 62, 173, 181, 245n.45

Addiction, 6-7, 11, 38, 81, 180-81, 185-97, 199-200, 212, 214, 244n.29, 245n.45

Advertising, 102, 213, 251n.14. *See also* Marketing

Aesthetics, 76, 87, 89-90, 93, 106-7, 109, 145, 147, 152-53, 166, 247n.22, 248n.38

Aftertaste, 101

Agriculture, 13, 59, 130, 209; in the Bible, 12, 18, 19, 31, 200, 216; biodynamic, 126, 130, 138, 150, 158, 161, 249n.6, 249n.10; organic, 126, 129-30, 136, 158, 159, 249n.6, 249n.10

Alcohol: abuse of, 6, 38, 58-59, 81, 98, 180-97, 209; and adolescents, 41, 189, 191; as an anesthetic, 47; as an antiseptic, 32, 63, 74, 76, 165, 168, 172, 173-75; and conviviality, 98, 127, 166; dependence on, 60, 187-89, 194, 199-200, 244n.29, 245n.45; fermentation of, 14, 97-98, 103-4, 140, 155; and flavor enhancement, 103-4; as a gift, 1, 15, 32, 38, 58, 59, 74, 168, 183-84; health benefits of, 164-79; high content of in some wines, 137, 138, 158, 159-60, 161, 168; and holy intoxication, 93, 97-99; and levels of intoxication, 98, 186; as a preservative, 74; rejection of, 4, 15, 38, 58, 62-63, 175, 240n.72, 241n.106, 254-55n.3; tolerance of, 188

Alcoholics Anonymous (AA), 192-93

Anthropology, 1, 108

Antioxidants, 164, 177

Anxiety, 81, 84, 182-83, 186, 191

Aroma, 96-97, 111, 114-15, 138, 139, 151, 156

Asceticism, 12, 23, 42, 43, 45, 49, 88-90, 93, 94, 107, 173

Avalon (film), 84-85, 88, 206

Babette's Feast (film), 5, 50, 88-95, 98, 99, 141, 197, 215-16

Baptism, 65, 66

Beer, 47, 53, 57, 58, 62, 111, 125, 173, 187, 191, 199, 236n.40; and craft breweries, 113

Benedictines, 46, 48-49, 50, 63, 94, 122, 124, 127-28, 139, 146, 169, 172. *See also* Rule of St. Benedict

Binge drinking, 95, 177, 186-87, 188, 189, 191, 198

Biodiversity, 140, 208

Blessing: of grapes, 134, 141; of Jacob, 19; the Johannine blessing of wine, 124; of Judah, 20, 28, 40, 86; sacrifices as solicitation of, 24; wine as a sign of God's blessing, 17, 20, 21, 30, 31, 36, 39, 47, 74-75, 82, 83, 86, 104, 168, 183-84, 220

Blood, 32, 43, 67, 69; of Christ, 34, 39-41, 52, 57, 65, 71, 72, 75-76, 82, 83, 123-24, 131, 242n.7; grape juice as a figure of, 20, 28, 40; of the Passover lamb, 70-71, 80; as a sacrifice for sin, 71, 73, 76; as a symbol of life, 73-74, 243n.20

Bouquet, 114, 116, 121. *See also* Aroma

Bread, 12, 16, 19, 22-23, 55, 56, 58, 85, 92, 105, 131; in the Eucharist, 2, 41, 48, 65-70, 78, 80-82, 83, 123, 131, 214, 242n.4, 242n.7

Brothers Karamazov, The, 218

Catholic church, 44-52, 123, 124

Celebration, 19, 29-30, 33, 47, 64, 83, 85-90, 99, 131; of the Eucharist, 4-5, 35, 39, 42, 43, 47, 48, 55, 65-69, 71-72, 75, 82, 109, 121, 122-24, 127, 220, 242n.7, 242n.10; other religious celebrations, 17, 24-25, 44, 70-71, 77, 78, 124, 132, 243n.15. *See also* Feast

Champagne, 50, 91, 93-94

Church, 66, 76-77, 125, 136, 192-93, 199-200, 205-7, 214; the early church, 4, 32, 38-43, 67, 185; history of, 4, 37-64; North American, 4, 58-64

Cistercians, 49-51, 53, 90, 94, 127, 129, 139, 146, 169, 203-4

Climate, 6, 14, 59, 96, 110, 112, 116, 125, 128-29, 151, 158, 161, 163, 205

Communion, 48, 63, 77, 190, 206. *See also* Lord's Supper; Eucharist

Consumerism, 102, 113, 136, 145, 150, 151, 153, 157, 192, 193, 196-97, 200, 202, 212-13, 216

Contemplation, 5, 97, 101, 102, 111, 118, 201, 248n.39

Conviviality, 25, 47, 55, 98, 127, 166, 179

Creation, 1-2, 3-5, 7, 12, 15-16, 17-18, 21, 24, 28-30, 32, 35-36, 37, 41-43, 47, 50, 54-55, 61, 63, 64, 67-68, 71, 75-76, 78, 82, 83-84, 93, 96-97, 102-4, 121-22, 125-26, 128, 130, 132-33, 136, 137-38, 141, 144, 146, 148, 151, 153, 156-57, 158, 162-63, 194-95, 197, 200, 201-3, 212, 214, 216, 218

Creativity, 67, 98, 144, 152, 162-63

Cross, the, 34, 51-52, 67, 72, 79, 83, 125, 127, 211, 214

Cru, 50, 239n.53. *See also* Grand Cru

Cup of Elijah, 71

Depression, 23, 179, 186, 213

Desert fathers, 43, 44-45

Drunkenness, 13, 41-43, 45, 54, 55, 56, 59, 70, 98, 182, 186-87, 190; in the Bible, 19, 31-32, 123, 182-85. *See also* Addiction; Alcohol, abuse of

Dualism, 2

Earth, 1, 15-16, 18-19, 50, 67-68, 73, 74, 116, 138-39, 145, 147, 149, 150, 152-53, 161, 162, 202, 212, 214, 249n.10; human dominion over, 126, 128, 130, 235n.26; renewal of, 28, 30, 40, 66, 93-94, 220. *See also* Land

Eastern Orthodox Church, 123

Economics, 13-14, 38, 46, 47-48, 59, 63, 134, 204, 216; free-market economics, 191-96, 200-201; and globalization, 149-153; and technology, 143, 145-48

Eighteenth Amendment, 61-62. *See also* Prohibition

Eschatology, 28-30, 35, 71-72, 122-23, 125, 220

Etruscans, 39

Eucharist, 39-42, 43, 47, 52, 54, 55, 57-58, 60-61, 65-69, 71-72, 75-76, 79-82, 83, 92, 104, 125, 134, 165; and embodiment, 77-79; production of wine for use in, 48, 127, 141; without wine, 62-63, 123. *See also* Communion; Lord's Supper

Exile, 21, 28, 94

Exodus: Christ as fulfillment of, 71-72; from Egypt, 20, 69-71, 92

Fasting, 25, 43, 107, 123. *See also* Abstinence

Feast, 5, 24-25, 79, 84-88, 90-95, 98-99, 104, 125, 131, 219-20; abuse of, 183; feast days of the church/saints, 44, 47, 124, 127; as an image of redemption, 30, 34-35, 40, 122-23; of Passover, 69-70

Fermentation, 14, 31, 50, 62-63, 75, 97-98, 103, 116, 117, 140, 151, 155-56

Fertilizers, 126, 129-30, 147, 203, 205, 249n.6, 249-50n.10

Flavors, 14, 76, 95-96, 100-104, 108, 110, 114-16, 121, 137, 138, 150, 155-56, 160; artificial flavors, 102, 111, 151, 156, 157-58; natural flavors, 111

Food, 12-14, 22, 32, 73, 104, 132, 185, 190, 206; fast food, 102; food engineering, 102, 133, 145, 147-48; food technology, 14, 126, 133, 147-48; Slow Food movement, 103, 149; spirituality of, 50, 55, 91-93, 214-15, 219

Forgiveness, 5, 24, 66, 72-73, 83, 88, 95, 99, 194, 197, 200, 201, 207, 216, 219

Franciscans, 49, 60

Genuss, 123

Globalization, 145-52, 191

Glory of God, 35, 63, 67, 86-87, 89, 93, 96, 218, 245n.9

Gluttony, 31, 41, 43, 54, 107, 123, 184-85, 255n.5

Gnostics/Gnosticism, 32, 41, 67, 82, 242n.3

Grace, 5, 18, 52, 65-66, 72, 81, 86-88, 90-94, 99, 194, 205, 207, 209

Grand Cru, 139, 146, 148. See also *Cru*

Grapes, 11-12, 14, 16, 20, 26, 60, 98, 114, 117, 122, 128, 131-36, 140-41, 167, 210; figurative references to, 27-28, 51, 74-76, 94, 127, 220; grape juice (non-alcoholic), 62-63, 68; noble grapes, 52, 76, 114, 220; varieties of, 49, 114, 159, 161. *See also* Wine

Gratitude, 5, 12, 15, 21, 24, 25, 36, 37, 55, 56-57, 68, 70, 75, 82, 83, 87-88, 93, 95, 99, 100, 110-11, 134, 137, 141, 145, 184

Health/healing: benefits of wine, 6, 32, 37, 41-43, 48, 74, 76, 164-79, 186, 197; and cancer, 178; and cardiovascular disease, 176-78; and cholesterol, 177; and resveratrol, 164, 177-78. *See also* Hospitals

Holy Spirit, 28, 52, 66, 72, 81, 197, 204, 205

Hospitality, 19, 23, 44, 48, 56-57, 170

Hospitals, 48-49, 127, 168-70, 174

Imagination, 51-52, 67, 82, 102, 106, 121, 142, 213

Incarnation, the, 2, 78

Intellect, 77-79, 106

Intoxication, 94, 186, 247n.22; holy intoxication, 93, 97-99

Islam, 171-72

Joy, 5, 11, 19, 21, 23, 25, 30, 34, 36, 37, 40-41, 43, 53-54, 56-57, 64, 70, 75, 83-89, 94, 96, 99, 100, 111, 116, 117, 121, 122-24, 127, 131, 134, 141, 153, 166, 168, 179, 180, 197, 205, 207, 209-10, 218-19

Judaism, ancient, 24

Judgment, 18, 21, 26-30, 32-33, 69-70, 74-75

Justice, 26-27, 183

Land, 2, 14-15, 16, 17-22, 29, 47-49, 53, 64, 68, 96, 124-26, 128-30, 132-34, 137, 139-41, 146, 148, 151-53, 159, 161-63, 201-2, 203, 236n.48, 248n.43. *See also* Earth

Liquor, 62, 125, 186-87, 199. *See also* Spirits, distilled

Liturgy, 70-71, 75, 77, 124, 242n.4

Lord's Supper, 2, 4, 6, 33-35, 37, 63-64, 65-82, 83, 87, 99, 109, 121, 131, 214-15, 220. *See also* Communion; Eucharist

Lutheran church, 132

Marketing, 15, 103, 152, 196, 202, 213, 251n.14
Mass, 122-23
Medicine, 6, 13-14, 23, 32, 47, 76, 164-68, 170-78, 184
Messianic age, 17, 19, 28, 30
Miracle: by Jesus at Cana, 11, 16, 30, 31, 34, 80, 85-87, 131, 218-19; by Martin of Tours, 44
Missions, Spanish, 60-61
Moderation, 6, 23, 41-43, 45, 53-54, 56, 59, 111, 164, 166, 173, 176, 179, 216. *See also* Temperance
Monasteries: Benedictine, 46, 48, 50, 146, 169-70, 172; Cistercian, 50, 127
Monasticism, 15, 42-53, 60-61; and health, 48, 168-70, 172, 174; and hospitality, 44, 48; and labor, 45, 46-47, 49, 146. *See also* Desert fathers
Mondovino (film), 146, 147
Monks. *See* monasticism
Music, 23, 25, 33, 55, 107, 135-36, 144

Nature, 6, 102, 118, 132-33, 148, 151, 158, 174, 181, 203, 207
Nazirites, 26
Neuroscience, 5, 108-10, 189, 196; and memory, 108-9; and neurological disease, 109; and the olfactory cortex, 108

Oenology, 31, 147, 153, 204

Parable(s), 32-33, 87, 107, 134, 208-9
Paradise, 124; in garden of Eden, 17; in Islam, 172; restoration of, 20, 28, 30, 93
Passover, 24-25, 35, 69-72, 78, 80, 220, 243n.15
Peasants, 45, 47-48, 53, 57, 107, 168, 219. *See also* Poor, the
Pesticides, 129-30, 145
Phylloxera, 60-61, 154

Pietists, German, 55, 58-59, 88, 92
Place, 96, 102-3, 112-13, 129, 133-34, 137, 139, 141-42, 149, 152-53, 157, 161-62, 215
Pollution, 143
Poor, the, 21, 22-23, 26-29, 44, 125, 168-70, 174, 184, 201
Prayer, 45-48, 71-72, 88-90, 97, 110, 146, 209, 214
Prohibition, 62-63, 136, 175, 181, 190
Protestants, 4, 52-58
Pruning, 26-27, 29, 199-200, 202-3, 210-14, 216
Puritans, 57-58

Redemption, 16, 26-30, 35, 58, 72, 73, 75, 83, 86, 182, 183, 194, 219
Reformation, the, 52-58, 68-69, 130, 242n.7
Remembrance, 40, 65, 70-72, 75-76, 87, 104, 108-9, 214
Rest, 84, 124, 166, 171, 173, 215
Ritual, 65, 77-79, 81-82
Roman Empire, 13-14, 38-39; collapse of, 45, 168; the Western Roman Empire, 45
Rule of St. Benedict, 44-45, 49, 50, 122, 146, 168-69

Sabbath, 25
Sacrament(s), 4, 65-66, 72, 147. *See also* Baptism; Communion; Eucharist; Lord's Supper
Sacrifice, 24, 26, 40, 66-67, 71-73, 75, 82, 83, 134; of Christ, 40, 72, 76
Salvation, 16, 35, 41, 51-52, 63, 66, 68, 69, 70, 76, 81, 83, 87-88, 104, 107, 111, 123, 219
Scripture, 1-4, 6-7, 11-12, 15-20, 28, 35, 39-40, 51, 54, 55, 66, 75, 77, 79-80, 83, 104, 136, 168, 181-82, 186, 193-94, 200, 201, 208, 209, 216, 218
Secularization, 49, 61, 64, 170
Senses, five, 5, 67, 77-79, 88, 94-95, 100,

102, 104-11, 113-14, 117-18; of smell (olfactory), 5, 76, 95, 101-4, 107-10, 110, 112-14, 117-18; of taste, 5, 67, 70, 76, 79-81, 91, 97-98, 100-117, 121, 135, 139, 149-52, 167, 172

sin(s), 18, 193-97; and alcohol abuse, 42, 57, 95, 182; forgiveness of, 24, 28, 40, 66, 71-73, 75-76, 82, 93, 99; and human freedom, 194; original sin, 257n.40; the seven deadly sins, 107

Slow Food movement, 103, 149

soil, 6, 14, 16, 19, 26, 29, 34, 64, 96, 102, 110, 112, 114-18, 126, 128-29, 138, 147, 151-52, 160, 161, 203, 204, 205, 208-10

soul care, 23, 43, 200-216

spinning cone, 158, 160-61, 162

Spirits, distilled, 60, 62, 173, 181; brandy, 103, 173, 175; gin, 181, 186; port, 175; rum, 59, 186; sherry, 91, 93, 175; tequila, 186-87; vodka, 186-87; whiskey, 59, 60, 181, 186-87. *See also* Liquor

Spirituality: Christian spirituality, 1-7, 37, 39, 62, 64, 69, 77, 79, 82, 84-85, 87, 99, 133, 144, 148, 162, 181, 218; and creation, 1-2, 4, 12, 61, 67, 71, 82, 125, 148

Suffering, 5, 30, 32, 88, 125, 127, 184, 191, 198, 209; of Christ, 40, 51-52, 66, 125, 127, 208-9

Supermarkets, 126, 132, 147, 149, 213

Sustainability: agricultural sustainability, 145, 157, 249n.10, 257n.1; environmental sustainability, 134, 153; of joy, 87; and technology, 157-62

Tannins, 103, 117, 157

Technology, 6, 85, 143-44, 213; and food, 14, 126, 127, 131-33, 137, 138, 141-42, 144-48, 151-52, 153-58, 160-63; and sustainability, 157-62

Temperance, 13, 14, 42, 43, 62, 64, 175, 181, 185. *See also* Moderation

Terroir, 15, 103, 112, 114, 116, 122, 129, 137,

138, 139, 141-42, 146, 150, 152, 159, 203, 234n.21, 249n.4, 250n.9

Transubstantiation, 242n.7

Vigneron, 15, 159

Vine(s), 11-14, 16, 17, 19-21, 26, 28-29, 35, 44-46, 48-51, 53, 58-61, 64, 71, 72, 75, 76, 110, 112, 114-16, 121-31, 133-34, 136-41, 143, 146-48, 151-55, 157, 159-60, 163, 200-201, 203-5, 208-12, 214, 217, 220; the vine as a metaphor for Israel, 26-27, 201, 208; the vine as a metaphor for Jesus, 12, 27-28, 33, 40, 50, 76, 199, 202, 205-6, 209

Vineyard(s), 1-2, 6, 12-15, 19-20, 22, 27-31, 33-34, 38-39, 46-51, 53, 58-59, 64, 73, 104, 107, 110, 113-14, 123-26, 128-33, 135-38, 140-41, 145, 147, 151-57, 160-62, 170, 182, 200, 203-5, 207-11, 217-18; the vineyard as an image of the church, 200-202, 205, 209-10

Viniculture, 11, 14, 39, 46

Vintners, 1-2, 5-6, 12, 14-15, 19, 29, 44, 50, 60-61, 64, 68, 96, 103, 110, 112-18, 121-24, 127-39, 141-42, 143-48, 150-63, 168, 199-200, 203-13, 215, 217-18; the vintner as an image of God, 26-27, 107, 200-203, 209-10

Vitamins, 164

Viticulture, 7, 11-12, 14, 15, 16, 17, 18-19, 22, 26, 28, 31, 32-35, 38-39, 44, 45-48, 49, 50, 51, 52-53, 60-62, 63-64, 122, 125, 127, 128, 130-31, 135, 140, 154, 158, 200-202, 204, 216, 249n.6

Vocation, 6, 8, 19, 26, 50, 59, 103, 117-18, 121-22, 128, 130, 144, 162-63, 204, 206-7, 219

Westminster Catechism, 83

Wine: Amontillado, 91; Barbaresco, 103, 112; blogs about, 137; Cabernet Sauvignon, 112, 117, 140; Chardonnay, 50, 112, 115, 151, 160; Chenin Noir, 44;

Chianti Classico, 116; Chianti Rufina, 116; dessert wines, 112, 113-14, 154; and the international market, 15, 103, 136-37, 140-42, 145-53; labeling of, 112-13; mass production of, 126, 145-48, 151-52; Merlot, 112; Nebbiolo, 103; New World, 116, 122, 132, 134-41, 151, 157-63; Old World, 122-28, 132, 153-57, 163; Pinot Grigio, 151; Pinot Gris, 115; pinot noir, 51, 116-17, 129, 135, 137, 138, 139, 159; premium wines, 147; Rieslaner, 113-14, 153-54; Riesling, 51, 112, 113-14, 124, 129, 155; Sangioevese, 116; Sauterne, 113; Silvaner, 50, 114, 115-16; wine-tasting, 95, 97, 101, 108-12, 116-18, 150, 152-53; wine tourism, 140; and writers, 50, 115, 136-37, 147; Zinfandel, 139, 160-61

Winepress, 22; depictions of Christ in, 4, 27, 51-52, 82, 99, 125, 127, 220; as an image of divine judgment, 27, 40, 74-75
Women: and alcoholism, 187-88; in Paul's letters, 185; as sources of temptation, 39, 41, 43, 54, 181; and wine as medical treatment, 171, 173, 178
Worship, 144, 185, 214; and the Eucharist, 65-66, 68, 79-82; in the Old Testament, 24, 26, 71; and ritual, 77

Yeast, 14, 68, 97-98, 131, 140, 155-56, 197, 237n.61; cultivated strains, 151, 156; genetically modified strains, 156, 249n.6; removal of to prevent fermentation, 62-63

Index of Scripture References

OLD TESTAMENT

Genesis

1	126, 128
1:12	68
1:26	18
1:26-28	128
1:28	18
1:29	68
1:29-30	202
2	17-18, 128
2:5	18, 202
2:7	18, 202
2:9	17, 55
2:15	18, 202
3:18-19	19
3:23	18
4	18
5:29	19
6	18
6:8	18
8:17	18
8:22	18
9:1	19
9:1-5	18
9:4	73
9:9-10	18
9:10	73
9:12	18
9:15-17	18
9:20	19, 73
9:20-26	182
14:18	19
19	182
19:30-38	182
21:8	25, 236n.54
27:25	19
27:28	19
27:37	19
29:21-22	25
40	13
40:20	25
49	20, 28, 40
49:8-12	86
49:10-12	20, 21, 40
49:11	74
49:11-12	28
49:22	26

Exodus

12:3-6	69
12:7-13	70
12:8	70
12:14	70
12:26-27	70
12:42	71

16:13	92
23:11	22
29:40	24

Leviticus

10:9	26
17:11	73
19:10	23
23:13	24

Numbers

6:1-4	26
6:3-4	26
6:20	26
13:21-27	20, 22, 75
13:23	94, 104
13:24	20
15:5	24
15:7	24
15:10	24
18:12	24
18:27	24
20:5	20
28:14	24

Deuteronomy

6:11	21
7:12-13	21

7:13	21	**1 Chronicles**		**Song of Songs**	
8:7-10	22	12:40	25	1:2	21
8:8	20, 21			1:4	21
11:18-21	81	**Psalms**		4:10	21
12:23	73	4:7	23	5:1	21
14:22-23	24	16:11	88	7:2	21
15:14	24	34:8	105	7:9	21, 96
20:6	23	80:7-9	201	8:2	21
22:9	23	80:8	26		
23:24	23	80:8-9	208	**Isaiah**	
24:21	23	80:14	26	1:22	22
26:1-11	68	104	15-16	2:4	29
28:39	22	104:14-15	23	3:13-15	27
32:14	74	104:15	16, 19, 21, 55-56,	3:14-15	201
33:28	21		75, 88, 99	5:1-7	27
		113–118	71	5:11-12	183
Judges		119	105	5:22	183
9	134	128	23	11	28-29
9:13	21, 134			18:4-6	27
13:1	26	**Proverbs**		24:7-11	30
13:4	26	3:10	29, 184	25	30
13:7	26	9:2	23	25:6	30
13:14	26	9:5	23, 105	25:6-8	219
		20:1	183-84	25:8	30
1 Samuel		23	184	27:2-3	202
1:11	26	23:20-21	23	27:2-6	27
1:14	182	23:23	184	27:5	202
1:15-16	209	23:31-35	184	28:1-3	183
1:16	182	24:13-14	105	28:7-8	183
16	23	31:4-5	23, 184	36:16-18	21
		31:4-9	26	49:26	74
2 Samuel		31:6	184	51:3	17
3:20	25	31:6-7	19, 23, 168	56:12	183
11	183	31:7	23	62:4	58
16:2	23	31:8-9	184	63	27
				63:1-6	27
1 Kings		**Ecclesiastes**		63:2-6	74-75
4:25	21, 29	2:24	23	63:3	51
		3:13	104	65:17-25	30
2 Kings		8:15	23		
18:28-33	21	9:7	104	**Jeremiah**	
		10:17-19	23	2:21	26-27
		10:19	23	6:9	27

8:13	27	9:13	30	21:28-31	33
16:7	19	9:14-15	29	21:33-41	33
31:5	29-30			22:1-14	33, 86
31:12	30	**Micah**		24:45-51	184
		4:4	19, 21, 29	25	66
Lamentations				25:36	169
1:15	27, 74-75	**Habakkuk**		25:40	169
		2:15	183	26:17-29	35, 69
Ezekiel				26:26-28	73
3:1-3	105	**Zephaniah**		26:29	35, 123, 220
15:1-6	27	1:13	22		
17:1-10	27			**Mark**	
19:10	27	**Zechariah**		2:16	104
28:13	17	3:10	21, 29	2:22	31
36:35	17	8:12	21, 29	7:20-22	31
44:21	25-26	9:15	74	12:1-9	27
		10:7	23	12:1-12	33
Hosea				14:12-25	35
2:18-22	86			14:12-26	69
2:18-23	30			14:24	75
4:11	183	**INTERTESTAMENTAL**		14:25	35, 7
4:18	183	**LITERATURE**			
7:5	183			**Luke**	
9:2	22	**Sirach**		1:46-47	87
10:2	27	31-33	23	2:9-10	86
14:1	27	31:26-27	41	5:37-38	31
14:7	27, 202	39:26	74	5:39	31
				7:34	31, 184
Joel				10:25-37	32
1:5	183	**NEW TESTAMENT**		12:45	184
1:7	27			15:28-31	87
2:3	17	**Matthew**		15:32	87
2:18-19	29	9:17	31	20:9-19	33
2:21-24	29	11:19	31, 184	21:18	35, 220
2:23-24	30	13:3-9	208	21:34	31, 184
3:3	183	13:20-21	209	22:7-23	35
3:13	27, 74-75	15:11	31-32	22:14-20	69
3:18	30	15:17	31-32	24	78-79
		15:18	31-32	25:29-37	168
Amos		15:19-20	31		
2:8	183	16:5	197	**John**	
4:1	183	20:1-6	33	1:1-4	201
5:11	22	20:1-16	107	1:14	87

1:14-18	86	21	78	**1 Thessalonians**	
1:29	71			5:6-11	185
2	11, 30	**Acts**		5:16	87
2:1-11	33, 34-35	13:2	77		
2:1-12	85			**1 Timothy**	
2:10	11, 86, 98, 124	**Romans**		3:3	31
2:11	86	13:13	31, 185	4:1-4	32
3:29-30	87	14:19-21	185	4:1-5	12
6:56	34			4:3-4	32
12:24-26	208	**1 Corinthians**		4:4	12
13:1-4	69	5:7	35, 71	4:4-5	36
15	11-12, 124, 202	5:11	32, 185	5:23	12, 32, 168
15:1	199	6:10	32, 185		
15:1-3	200	11:21	185	**Titus**	
15:1-6	33	11:23-25	65	2:3	185
15:1-17	33	11:25	71		
15:2	210	13:12	220	**Revelation**	
15:4-10	72			2:7	17
15:5	27-28	**Galatians**		6:6	31
15:8-11	210	3:27-29	207	10:9-10	105
15:9	210	5:19-21	31, 185	14:19-20	27, 75
15:10	34	5:21	32	14:20	74
15:11	34, 87			18:13	31, 39
15:12-13	34	**Ephesians**		19:6-7	86
15:15	210	1:10	16	19:15	27
15:15-16	210	5:18	98	21:1-4	220
15:16	87	5:18-20	185	21:4	219
15:20-21	87				
15:24	87	**Philippians**			
17:13	87	3:1	87		
17:20-25	207	4:4	87